Speeches and Trials
of the
Militant Suffragettes

Emmeline Pankhurst being arrested, 1914.

Speeches and Trials
of the
Militant Suffragettes

The Women's Social and Political Union,
1903–1918

Edited by

Cheryl R. Jorgensen-Earp

Madison • Teaneck
Fairleigh Dickinson University Press
London: Associated University Presses

Associated University Presses
440 Forsgate Drive
Cranbury, NJ 08512

Associated University Presses
16 Barter Street
London WC1A 2AH, England

Associated University Presses
P.O. Box 338, Port Credit
Mississauga, Ontario
Canada L5G 4L8

The paper used in this publication meets the requirements
of the American National Standard for Permanence of Paper
for Printed Library Materials Z39.48-1984.

Library of Congress Cataloging-in-Publication Data

Speeches and trials of the militant suffragettes : the Women's Social
    and Political Union, 1903–1918 / edited by Cheryl R. Jorgensen-Earp.
        p.   cm.
    Includes bibliographical references and index.
    ISBN 0-8386-3788-4 (alk. paper)
    1. Suffragists—Great Britain—History—Sources. 2. Women—
Suffrage—Great Britain—History—Sources. 3. Women's Social and
Political Union (Great Britain)—History—Sources. I. Jorgensen—
Earp, Cheryl R., 1952–
JN979.S67   1999
324.6'23'094109041—dc21   98-42465
                                                                 CIP

PRINTED IN THE UNITED STATES OF AMERICA

For Rab and Doc

Contents

Acknowledgments

MANY THANKS ARE IN ORDER TO THOSE WHO HAVE MADE THIS VOLUME of WSPU speeches and trial transcripts possible. I must begin with my "home" library, the Knight-Capron Library at Lynchburg College. Once again, the patient and knowledgeable research librarians at Knight-Capron have proven the excellence of small libraries. My thanks also to the Fishburn Library at Hollins College. I first came across the Verbatim Report of Mrs. Pankhurst's Speech at Hartford, Connecticut in the History of Women microfilm collection located at Fishburn. The speech is reproduced in this volume with the kind permission of the General Research Division, The New York Public Library, Astor, Lenox and Tilden Foundations. Unless otherwise indicated, speeches and trial transcripts in this collection are taken from the pages of *Votes For Women* and *The Suffragette,* available on microfilm from The British Library. I would like to thank the Museum of London for permission to reproduce suffragette photographs and to thank Anna Payne for her assistance in photograph selection. Photographic reproduction costs were covered by a research grant through Lynchburg College.

I am especially grateful to Gail Cameron, Assistant Curator of Later London History and Collections at the Museum of London. Gail was wonderfully helpful during the time I spent with the Suffragette Fellowship Collection housed at the Museum of London. I am also very grateful to David Doughan of the Fawcett Library who took my hastily arranged visit in good stride. For years I have seen his enthusiasm and vast knowledge cited in acknowledgments by suffrage scholars, and he certainly deserves the accolades.

As always, my love and heartfelt thanks go to Darwin and Ethan who continue to tolerate boxes of papers, stacks of books, and endless discourse on these fascinating women. My love and gratitude also go to my mother, Neva, and sister, Marcia, who respond to my studies of suffragette rhetoric with the enthusiasm only families can muster.

Speeches and Trials
of the
Militant Suffragettes

Part I
Introduction

Lapse of time dignifies and magnifies events; or perhaps more truly, it shows them in their due proportions, and just as in these days, eighty years afterwards, the militancy of men is deemed epoch-making, so in the year 1990, when the Votes for Women battle is long since fought and won, the Women's militancy of 1913 will be recognised as the wonderful revolution that it is.[1]

Christabel Pankhurst, 1913

WHEN CHRISTABEL PANKHURST WROTE THESE WORDS IN A 1913 ARTICLE, she was not simply indulging in a stray bit of prophecy. Pankhurst was one of the leaders of the Women's Social and Political Union (WSPU), a militant branch of the British women's suffrage movement, and a prime strategist in the Union's turn to arson, bombing, and general property destruction in the cause of women's suffrage. Violent militancy was undertaken partly as a response to the repressive measures instituted by the government against the movement in its nonviolent militancy phase; yet, the move to violence against property sparked still more repression against the Union. Pankhurst looked ahead to the day when posterity would judge the suffragettes' actions objectively and without the passion that occurred on both sides in the struggle over this monumental reform. Of course, she also felt that justification of the Union's actions would come from those future women who benefited from the franchise.

Christabel Pankhurst did, however, prove prophetic in her estimation of the growing interest in understanding the suffragettes. Interest in the militants cannot be explained by the size of the WSPU, for it was considerably smaller than the constitutional suffrage societies. Suffragette Mary Richardson felt that the twenty thousand membership estimate given by the press in 1914 was inflated and believed that there were only one thousand members actually taking part in militant action.[2] I believe that interest in the WSPU, often overshadowing the work of the constitutionalists and nonviolent militants, comes largely from the perceived incongruity of middle- to upper-class Edwardian women taking part in such militant actions as "firing" letterboxes and railway stations, bombing Lloyd-George's summer home, and slashing artwork in museums. Many of the early studies (1930s–1970s) focused on this incongruity as either a source of humor[3] or an occasion for vitriol.[4] There have, of course, also been intriguing biographies and autobiographies of the suffragettes[5] and excellent studies of the history of British suffrage.[6] Recently, however, various strands of scholarship (studies of violence and terrorism, feminist theory and women's studies, and studies of dissent and social movements, among others) have sparked a need to examine with fresh eyes the eleven years of the Union's active struggle for the vote.

The act of militancy itself is today receiving focus, and several authors have examined the personal impetus for taking part in such an act and the justificatory discourse surrounding it.[7] In a challenge to the conclusions of previous studies, Sandra Holton argues that "the militant was more than a victim of her own temper or psychology, more than a vehicle for forces beyond herself, or for processes in which she had become locked."[8] Just as it is incorrect to view militancy as a psychological aberration, it is improper to speak of militancy as a single, monolithic strategy. Militancy for the WSPU consisted of escalating actions in response to a series of rhetorical exigencies. As each traditional (and even untraditional) path of reform was blocked, the WSPU countered by constructing a new persuasive response, often forging their way through uncharted territory. During her 1912 trial for conspiracy, Emmeline Pankhurst gave confirmation of the responsive nature of escalating militancy when she said, "I want you to realise that no step we have taken forward has been taken until after some act of repression on the part of our enemy, the Government."[9] Despite its obvious self-justificatory purpose, this statement acknowledges the strategic, responsive nature of each escalating act of militancy. To illuminate the rhetorical nature of this pattern of response and counterresponse, I have chosen to organize this collection of speeches and trial transcripts around the five primary exigencies that prompted changes in Union strategy. Briefly, the Union strategies taken to meet these exigencies consisted of: 1) nominal militancy and arrest to end the press blackout of suffrage news; 2) stone throwing and simple assault to force early arrest, thus avoiding police and crowd violence; 3) hunger strike to obtain status as political prisoners; 4) reformist terrorism (violent militancy against private property) to force government action on suffrage bills; and 5) cessation of suffrage activity to support government policy during World War I.

As is clear from this list, much of the Union strategy took the form of nonverbal rhetoric. The discursive rhetoric that accompanied Union acts provided the explanation and justification for militancy at the same time that it provided arguments in support of women's suffrage. So intricately are the verbal and nonverbal rhetoric of the WSPU linked that they cannot be considered apart from each other. With this linkage of verbal and nonverbal discourse in mind, the introductions to each section of this collection will provide a summary of Union activity and point to major verbal arguments and images in the pages to follow. Of course, the Liberal government was not without its resources in dealing with the WSPU, and space will be given in these introductions to such countermeasures as police attacks on suffrage deputations, forcible feeding to end hunger strikes, and the 1913 "Cat and Mouse Act."

Because I am a rhetorician, I tend to emphasize argument and protest strategy in this volume. However, it is not my intent simply to provide these materials for use by others in my discipline. Historians, political scientists, and women's studies scholars, to name a few, will focus on very different aspects of these speeches and trial transcripts. My intention is to make the raw material readily available for further research by others. By interweaving a basic chronological history of the WSPU and including notes on the more obscure references made by speakers, I hope to make these speeches and trial transcripts accessible to researchers new to this area as well as to established scholars. We are very far from writing the final word on the WSPU militants, but there could be no better place to continue our studies than with the words of the suffragettes themselves.

Part II
Breaking Silence

Issues of speech and silence surrounded the Women's Social and Political Union from the time of its founding on October 10, 1903. On that date, Emmeline Pankhurst invited a group of women to her Manchester home in order to form a new political organization. The new Union would be open only to women and was not affiliated with any political party. As the widow of Dr. Richard Pankhurst, who had worked with John Stuart Mill to include women in the Reform Bill of 1867, Emmeline Pankhurst had long been vocally active in a variety of causes. Now, she planned to concentrate her considerable abilities as a voice for the enfranchisement of women, a cause that had existed in waning strength since the failure to achieve the ballot in 1867. Pankhurst possessed a natural charisma, a dignified calm, and a rich, low voice that, according to her contemporaries, "could move men to tears."[1] In a recent analysis, Sandra Holton described Emmeline Pankhurst as "the foremost practitioner of, and apologist for, suffrage militancy. She was renowned in her day for her eloquence in public speaking, for her ability to communicate the authenticity of her convictions."[2]

The foremost issue facing the new organization was not the speaking ability of its members but the silence that had been imposed on the issue of suffrage. Most recently, the Boer War in South Africa had been used as a reason for women to put their own political concerns aside while "our lads" were fighting. The close of this divisive war in 1902 offered a renewed hope for suffragists that the movement for the female franchise could be lifted out of the thirty year "period of 'doldrums,'" during which suffrage efforts had continued, but in a "muted and diffuse" manner.[3] From the beginning it was the position of the WSPU that words would not be enough to attain the franchise, but must be accompanied by action. Whereas women suffragists of the past had accepted reassurance of support by politicians who then took no action on their behalf, the WSPU adopted the motto "Deeds not Words."[4]

In 1905, the leaders of the WSPU came up in a visceral way against the problem of being silenced. Several WSPU leaders traveled from Manchester to London in 1905 in preparation for the opening of Parliament on February

19

13. Sylvia Pankhurst accompanied her mother to London to lobby the members of Parliament. For Sylvia, this would inaugurate a long career in political work, particularly on the behalf of the poor. Her artistic talent was indispensable to the Union, and she would later lead the suffrage campaign in the East End of London. The Pankhursts concentrated their efforts on Mr. Bamford Slack, who had drawn a place on the ballot. This simply meant that he would have the opportunity to present the suffrage bill as a Private Member's Bill on May 12, 1905.[5] This suffrage bill was very simple, expanding all references to the masculine gender in previous suffrage bills to include women. The suffrage bill would be introduced as the second bill of the day. It would follow the Roadway Lighting Bill, a bill requiring that lights be placed on the back of a cart in traffic.[6]

Suffrage supporters from the WSPU and Lancashire textile workers, among others, filled the lobbies of Parliament on May 12. Well aware that a Private Member's Bill like the suffrage bill required a full two hours' debate, they watched in increasing frustration as talk on the Roadway Lighting Bill was strung out. In what appeared to be a grand joke shared by the members of Parliament, the mock "debate" on Roadway Lighting continued amid howls of laughter and applause. Thus, the suffrage bill was "talked out."[7] Angry at the obvious contempt granted to a serious bill, Emmeline Pankhurst and a small group of women held a spontaneous demonstration at the entrance to Parliament. Mrs. Wolstenholme-Elmy, whose gray ringlet curls and petite stature belied her fame as a determined suffragist and reformer, started to speak. Police forced the women to move along to the Broad Sanctuary, where a brief protest meeting was held. The police contented themselves with taking down the names of the participants.[8] Thus the WSPU experienced firsthand the methods by which Parliament had long silenced debate on women's issues and countered that silencing with what is generally considered as their first peaceful militant act.

Firmer action would be needed to overcome the silence imposed by newspapers on reporting news about the suffrage cause. Just as Parliament greeted bills concerning women and children with raucous laughter and rude jokes, the press responded to the suffrage movement with what amounted to a press blackout. The need to overcome this blackout formed the first major rhetorical exigency leading to an increase in WSPU militant tactics. The new tactic would be inaugurated at a preelection meeting held at the Free Trade Hall in Manchester on October 13, 1905. Sir Edward Grey was speaking in support of Winston Churchill's candidacy. The meeting was attended by Christabel Pankhurst, the oldest of Emmeline Pankhurst's daughters and considered the foremost Union strategist. Christabel was accompanied to the meeting by Annie Kenney, a former Lancashire factory worker who would prove to be a loyal and brave Union member throughout the campaign. In the middle of the meeting Annie Kenney rose and asked "Will the

Liberal Government give votes to women?" as Christabel displayed a "Votes For Women" banner. Sir Edward Grey refused to answer, even after the question was submitted in writing. When the women once again interrupted the meeting, they were roughly removed from the meeting and restrained as they tried to speak in the street. Christabel pursed her lips in a dry simulation of spitting at a police officer. As Pankhurst intended, both women were arrested. Christabel Pankhurst was given one week's imprisonment, and Annie Kenney was given three days. These brief sentences were considered a small price to pay, because news of this first WSPU imprisonment broke the long press blackout on suffrage news.[9]

The strategic significance of this act, one that Jane Marcus describes as "on both the real and symbolic levels the bold breaking out of the straitjacket of the female role," should not be underestimated. Nor should we underestimate the courage needed for middle-class Englishwomen to violate the expectations of their gender and class. As Marcus puts it, "How difficult it was to break down women's learned silence, the culture's equation of her virtue with politeness."[10] Far from isolating the Union as a group of extremists, news of the first imprisonment attracted many Manchester women to the suffrage ranks. Flora Drummond, nicknamed "The General," a stocky, humorous woman with the tenacity of a bulldog, joined the movement at this time. After the Union moved its primary base of operation to London in January 1906, Emmeline Pankhurst was joined in the leadership by Emmeline Pethick-Lawrence, who became treasurer of the Union. Emmeline and Frederick Pethick-Lawrence would devote their considerable talents and financial resources to the cause. The Pethick-Lawrences started the newspaper *Votes For Women* in October 1907, and it quickly became a major propaganda tool of the Union.[11] It was also early in the Union's life in London that the *Daily Mail* reportedly coined the term "suffragette" to distinguish the new militant woman from her constitutional suffragist sister.[12] The term's diminutive ending was probably intended as an insult, but the WSPU embraced the nickname, apparently appreciating its lively sound and the instant recognition the word would impart.

A few months after the 1905 Free Trade Hall meeting that resulted in the first suffragette arrests, the Balfour Conservative government was replaced by a solid Liberal government with Sir Henry Campbell-Bannerman as Prime Minister.[13] On May 19, 1906, Campbell-Bannerman consented to receive a deputation of the combined suffrage societies. He listened to their speeches and then replied with a long speech of his own. The Prime Minister made clear his personal support and his recognition of the national benefit to be gained by women's suffrage. Yet, in the face of opposition from his cabinet, he could make no pledge. This statement unintentionally verified what his audience already knew: that one of the most influential opponents to suffrage was the Chancellor of the Exchequer, Mr. Herbert Henry As-

quith.[14] The women were not content with Campbell-Bannerman's suggestion that they "go on converting the country." Annie Kenney stood on her
seat and stated, "Sir, we are not satisfied. The agitation will go on." The
WSPU dramatized this intent that very afternoon with their first large open-
air meeting to a crowd of seven thousand at Trafalgar Square.[15]

Militancy at this early stage of the movement generally consisted of heckling speakers, making speeches in dramatic locations (such as the Lobby of
Commons), and attempting to deliver resolutions to the House of Commons. Men's deputations had often been sent to Commons to publicize a
grievance and to deliver a particular viewpoint directly to the politicians in
power. Peaceful, small deputations were usually greeted politely and attended to by the politicians (whether or not minds were changed about the
issue in question). The women of the WSPU found themselves met with
very different treatment when they attempted the same political strategy.
The deputation on February 13, 1907, may be viewed as typical. When
Parliament convened on this day, the Union called a Women's Parliament
for the same day at Caxton Hall. A resolution was drafted expressing anger
at the omission of women's suffrage in the King's Speech, the speech given
by the monarch (although composed by the party in power) at the beginning
of the Parliamentary session to outline expected legislation. Well aware that
the suffragettes were threatened with a revival of the Tumultuous Petitions
Act that would prohibit groups of more than thirteen within the one-mile
radius of Parliament, a small deputation carried the resolution to the House
of Commons. Equally small groups of supporters (also careful to meet any
legal requirements for size) followed at varying distances. Unlike the average
men's deputations, the WSPU deputation was met by mounted and foot
police who blocked their way. As the resolution bearers (and each group of
supporters) attempted to continue forward, they were arrested, later to be
charged with "obstructing the police." These were mass arrests that occurred
at deputations: 57 women and 2 men were arrested on February 13; several
weeks later, 130 women were sent to prison after being arrested at a similar
deputation.[16] It was further early proof that women as political activists
could expect different treatment than men, and that they faced greater obstacles in having their voices heard.

All the obstacles to effective action did not come from outside the Union
at this early stage, and the autumn months of 1907 saw major changes take
place in the WSPU. Under the constitution of the Union, drafted when the
founders came to London in 1906, there were to be quarterly meetings of
the Executive Committee as well as an annual meeting of the members.
As the annual conference of delegates approached this autumn, there were
complaints that the Emergency Committee, under the sway of Mrs. Pankhurst and her daughters, rather than the Executive Committee, was running
the show. Several members wanted a more democratic organization where

the membership would have some say in policy and strategy. One of the primary members leading this desire for change was Teresa Billington-Grieg, a former close friend of Christabel Pankhurst. Their personal falling-out and Billington-Grieg's realization that she would be unlikely to attain a leadership position may have been major factors in the "mutiny." Mrs. Pankhurst was ardently opposed to allowing the politically untrained membership to help determine policy. She feared that the new Union would be mired in the same politeness and hesitancy to take extreme action that marked earlier suffrage efforts. Hers was a vision of inspired, daring leadership and unified, unquestioning followers.[17]

At the conference Mrs. Pankhurst claimed her position as founder of the Union. Any member of the Union who did not accept her leadership could, she said, leave the Union and form an organization based on democratic ideals. Mrs. Despard, a striking figure noted for years of social action and an experienced suffragist who had joined the WSPU at the same time as Emmeline Pethick-Lawrence, could not accept such terms. In the first of a number of "splits" in the Union, Mrs. Despard withdrew and with her followers formed the Women's Freedom League (WFL).[18] Interestingly, in letters circulated to WFL members, Teresa Billington-Grieg and Mrs. How Martyn would later make the same charges of autocracy against Mrs. Despard. The WFL would continue the suffrage fight with what some called "constitutional militancy," acts such as tax resistance and resistance to the census. Although overshadowed by the showier WSPU action, the League exercised classic civil disobedience and maintained its suffrage work even through the years of World War I.[19]

Not all of this initial period was marred by external and internal opposition, and early bills, though unsuccessful, garnered enough support to make victory seem closer to hand than it really was. Two of these bills are worth noting, for they show the ongoing efforts at a constitutional solution. In 1907, W. H. Dickinson, a Liberal member, introduced a Woman Suffrage Bill to which the Prime Minister pledged his support. This bill was similar to the one introduced by Bamford Slack in its expansion of masculine gender terms to include women. Women, too, could not be disqualified from voting by marriage. Objections were immediately raised that this bill continued the property qualification for voting and was, therefore, unfair to working women. Attempts to show that large numbers of working women *did* meet the property requirement were ignored, and the bill was allowed to be "talked out" on March 8, 1907.[20] In 1908, a bill identical to the Dickinson Bill was introduced by Liberal M. P. Mr. Henry Yorke Stanger. The debate of the bill was the twenty-third on the issue since 1867, and produced the memorable inanity by Liberal anti-suffragist, Sir John Rees, "Petticoat is a good thing, and government is a good thing, but it does not follow that petticoat government is a good thing." The Stanger Bill passed its second reading on February 28, 1908, by a margin of 271 to 92.[21]

The first speech in this collection, "The Importance of the Vote," was a major address made by Emmeline Pankhurst at one of the regular Monday afternoon "At Homes" held in the Portman Rooms situated in Baker Street, London. Soon, these meetings drew such crowds that they had to be moved to Queen's Hall. This particular address, given by Mrs. Pankhurst on March 24, 1908, was considered of sufficient importance that it was published and sold in pamphlet form during the subsequent years of the movement.[22] The section of the speech wherein Pankhurst details the legal position of women in Edwardian society is a good reminder of the need for reform to those of us reading these speeches at such a separation of time. Most of the reforms sought by the WSPU and other women's groups were not included even in the Liberals' ambitious plans for change. This speech clearly makes the expediency argument common to the suffrage movement. Expediency claimed that women have a unique viewpoint and could benefit the community as a whole by bringing that view to bear on political issues. Notice how Pankhurst concentrates this more general argument in a very specific argument over the Deceased Wife's Sister Act and the lack of corresponding legislation to benefit women.

Pankhurst mentions at some length the problem of "sweated labour," the women's employment issue of greatest concern and a mainstay issue of the suffragists. "Sweating," work generally done at home or in crowded, unsanitary shops for excessive hours and at starvation wages, was considered one of the great evils by late-Victorian and Edwardian reformers. It embraced a wide variety of work from making matchboxes and toothbrushes to sewing baby clothes and men's shirts.[23] What made the labor so oppressive was the staggeringly low pay. A capper of safety pins would have to complete 14,400 pins to earn three shillings. A cocoa packer would fill 21,792 little square packets, fold down the tops, and put labels on them to earn seven shillings. A shirtmaker, working by machine, might complete nearly five dozen shirts in a week (except for sewing the buttons and making button holes). For this work she would earn five shillings, eight pence and out of that she would have to purchase the shirt cotton, buy needles, and perhaps even rent the machine.[24] Pankhurst shows in this speech the lack of help for the sweated woman in the Liberal government plans for reform. She shows how even reform bills favored by specific Members of Parliament could increase the number of sweated women.

One interesting aspect of this speech is the way Pankhurst uses conservative discourse in support of radical change. Pankhurst does not directly reject the "Cult of True Womanhood," that Victorian social template of a world where the public sphere of business and politics was controlled by men and the private sphere of home was under the gentle influence of women.

Through the conservative images she uses, Pankhurst implies that the vote will be a support to the Perfect Lady (the "Angel of the House"), the belle-ideal of the Separate Spheres ideology). She further implies that the vote will help to solve problems wrought by the Fallen Woman (the prostitute) and the Redundant Woman (the spinster), the two negative incarnations of woman who formed a counterpoint to the Perfect Lady. In a speech designed to find acceptance by even the most conservative audiences, Pankhurst positions voting as an integral part of a neotraditional view of women.[25]

The second part of this section is given over to the trial at the Bow Street Police Station during the fall of 1908. The preceding spring the women's suffrage movement had sustained a vital, if indirect, blow. The Prime Minister, Campbell-Bannerman, had been in declining health. On March 27 he had an audience with Asquith during which he complimented Asquith on his loyalty and ability. One week later, Campbell-Bannerman resigned, leaving Asquith to form the new Liberal government. Thus, the greatest friend of the women's cause in the Cabinet was replaced at the head of the government by one of its primary foes.[26] When Emmeline Pankhurst returned to London following work in a by-election in Newcastle in September 1908, she wrote to the new Prime Minister. In her letter, Emmeline Pankhurst asked the Prime Minister to insure that, when Parliament sat again in October, time would be accorded to the Stanger Bill. Asquith refused. The WSPU then organized a mass meeting in Trafalgar Square where, on October 11, 1908, Emmeline and Christabel Pankhurst and Flora Drummond spoke to a large crowd from the plinth of the Nelson monument. Pictures of this meeting clearly show large banners and a sign reading, "Votes For Women! Come to the House of Commons on October 13th at 7:30 p.m." However, in handbills circulated among the crowd, the term used was *"rush the House of Commons."* A warrant was quickly issued for the three speakers to appear at Bow Street Police Court at 3:30 p.m. on Monday, October 12.[27]

To understand this summons by the Bow Street magistrate, it is important to realize that suffrage was only one point of unrest in the autumn of 1908. Unemployment was very high; marches of the unemployed and hunger marches were becoming common. There was a not unreasonable rumor that the Union had appealed to the unemployed to join them. By charging the suffrage leaders with "conduct likely to provoke a breach of the peace" and removing them from participation, the government hoped that the October 13 demonstration would dissolve from lack of guidance.[28]

The Union sensed that this was a possibility, too. Accordingly, the leaders ignored the summons and appeared at the regular Monday night "At Home" in Queen's Hall. Although officers appeared at the meeting, the massed presence of Pankhurst devotees made public arrest unwise. The summons was postponed until the next morning. Again the leaders delayed, hiding in a private apartment at the top of Clements Inn after leaving an announcement at WSPU headquarters that they would surrender at 6 o'clock that evening. At the appointed time, the three women appeared at the WSPU office and surrendered to Inspector Jarvis.[29]

These developments left Emmeline Pethick-Lawrence to appear alone at Caxton Hall on Tuesday evening with the dramatic news of the leaders' arrest. A resolution was passed urging that Parliament grant facilities for the Stanger Bill to be considered. Eleven women volunteered to take the resolution to the House; they were followed by the Union forces in groups. The police, foot and mounted, filled Parliament Square. Mrs. Pethick-Lawrence was later to tender her opinion that the police had orders to exhaust rather than arrest the suffragettes. If true, they failed in their orders; for twenty-four women and twelve men were arrested and, refusing to be bound over to keep the peace for twelve months, were sentenced to three weeks imprisonment.[30]

The Bow Street trial of Emmeline Pankhurst, Christabel Pankhurst, and Flora Drummond is notable for several reasons. It was a triumph for Christabel Pankhurst, who had obtained her LL.B. degree and used her knowledge of law to help in conducting the defense. Here, she makes the most of her cross-examination of David Lloyd-George, Chancellor of the Exchequer, and the Home Secretary, Mr. Herbert Gladstone.[31] Both men had been successfully subpoenaed by the WSPU to give evidence: Lloyd-George because he was present at the Trafalger Square meeting and had received a copy of the handbill in question, and Gladstone because he was a spectator at the June 30 confrontation between Union members and police at Westminster.[32] Note in particular Christabel's adroit handling of the presence of Lloyd-George's daughter at Trafalgar Square and her references to his past political stance in the "Welsh graveyard" case. In this event, which took place in the 1880s, Lloyd-George had upheld the Burials Act of 1880. This act gave Nonconformists the right to burial in parish churchyards conducted under their own denominational service. In opposition to this act, a Llanfrothen parish stipulated that the new addition to its graveyard would only allow burials conducted under Anglican rites. When the family of a Methodist quarryman, Robert Roberts, sought to bury him beside his Anglican daughter, the funeral party was denied entry to the graveyard. Lloyd-George encouraged the family to break into the graveyard and conduct their service. In the court case that followed, Lloyd-George was ultimately victorious.[33] Christabel also confronted Herbert Gladstone with the past: the immediate past of his own words on *"force majeure"* and the more distant past of his father's words before him.[34] When the Stanger Bill had passed its second reading by such a clear margin, the WSPU had sought the support of the government for the bill and had received in reply these words from Home Secretary Gladstone, during the second reading debate:

Comes the time when political dynamics are far more important than political argument ∴ . . . Men have learned this lesson and know the necessity for demonstrating the greatness of their movement and for establishing that *force majeure* which actuates and arms a Government for effective work.[35]

With these words, Gladstone clearly appeared to counsel the very actions on the basis of which the suffragettes would later be charged in Police Court. At the very least, his words could be construed as taunting the women's movement for lacking adequate physical action for their cause. Christabel also makes reference to William Gladstone's remark of 1884: "if no instructions had ever been addressed in political crises to the people of this country except to remember to hate violence, love order, and exercise patience, the liberties of this country would never have been attained."[36] Again, such implied counsel for radical action to male franchise reformers pointed up the hypocrisy of the current government in trying female reformers for taking milder action in pursuit of the same goal.

Clearly, Christabel's dramatic nature combined happily with the dramatic situation. Dramatist Max Beerbohm attended the trial and wrote of the "lively arabesques" of Christabel's hand gestures as "she stood there, with her head inclined merrily to one side, trilling her questions . . . like . . . a little singing bird born in captivity."[37] This performance expanded Christabel's visibility and made her "a personality" in London political society.

Two other aspects of the trial are of particular interest. First, there is a good humor in this trial, especially in the defense witnesses, which will be ground away by subsequent years of frustration and perceived Government betrayal. The tone and language used here are substantially different from post-1912 speeches and trials (allowing, of course, for the increased seriousness of later charges). Of equal importance to rhetoricians is the key defense issue of definition centering around the term "rush." At the close of the trial, the Bow Street Magistrate, Henry Curtis Bennett, ordered Emmeline Pankhurst and Flora Drummond bound over in their own recognizances of £100 and required to find two £50 sureties for twelve months. Christabel Pankhurst was bound over in recognizance of £50 and required to find two sureties of £25 each for twelve months. Magistrates could impose "binding over" as an alternative to imprisonment, and such orders required the person to keep the peace for a specified period of time. In a process resembling bail, sureties were then required from the person's friends for the same period. As was becoming common practice, the three women refused to be bound over. The magistrate's sentence that Emmeline Pankhurst and Flora Drummond serve three months and Christabel Pankhurst ten weeks in the second division then took effect. Unlike the first division of prison, where political prisoners were generally sent, the second division did not allow prisoners to wear their own clothing and restricted privileges to a greater extent. Although a criminal division, the second division, unlike the third division, acknowledged that the prisoners had a previously good character.[38]

Due to her ill health, Flora Drummond was soon released for hospital treatment. When Christabel's sentence expired on December 8, Emmeline Pankhurst was also released.[39] The report of the trial is presented as it appeared in the October 22 and October 29, 1908, issues of *Votes For Women*.

The final speech in this section is Christabel Pankhurst's speech at Queen's Hall on December 22, 1908. Aimed less at the general populace and more toward the suffrage faithful, this address ("The Political Outlook") strongly attacks the Liberal government at the same time that it exhorts suffrage workers to greater action. In this relatively early speech we can see many of the elements that would later become important in justifying the turn to violent militancy after 1912. Pankhurst needed to show that women could be successful in taking political action and used membership numbers and finances as proof of the Union's strength. She portrayed the suffrage activists as a gallant band that stood against injustice even when they faced tremendous odds. Pankhurst also contrasted the treatment accorded female deputations to that granted to men. Yet, despite the double standard, where men's heckling of speakers was considered part of English tradition and women's heckling was severely repressed, Pankhurst stood against any interference with free speech and asserted her willingness to deal with hecklers herself.

Finally, Pankhurst astutely anticipated the Lords' Crisis that would come to a head in 1909 and 1910. I will briefly mention the details of this crisis because it figures in several upcoming speeches. Following the Liberals coming to power, it had soon become clear that their opposition would not come from the weakened Conservatives in Commons but from the House of Lords. In rapid succession, the Lords attacked the Liberals' Education Bill, the Plural Voting Bill—which would have prevented double voting by certain property owners—and a Licensing Bill which would have lessened the number of public houses. The lack of subtlety in the Lords' methods made it clear that a showdown was in the offing.[40] That moment came with Lloyd-George's "People's Budget" of 1909. Deficits were large and Lloyd-George sought revenues for, among other items, the Army, the Navy, and the Old Age Pension Fund.[41] Lloyd-George turned to the rich to provide the extra funds with a five pence "super tax" on incomes of £5,000, with a capital tax on the value of undeveloped land and minerals, and with increased death duties. Taxes were increased on spirits and tobacco and, for the first time, there were taxes on automobiles and gasoline.[42] The attack on landed wealth sent tempers flaring in the House of Lords. Spurred by the sardonic speeches of Lloyd-George, the Lords defied the Constitutional tradition against vetoing a budget and voted 300 to 75 to reject.[43] Asquith immediately called an election under the Liberal slogan "the peers versus the people."[44] To the surprise of most, in the ensuing election the Liberals diminished and the Conservatives grew to the point of near parity. No longer were the Liberals independent. Now they were forced to rely upon the eighty-two Irish Nationalists under John Redmond in order to stay in office.[45] The Lords must have quickly realized the ramifications of their earlier budget veto. Now, if the People's Budget was to survive passage through Commons again, it could only be with Irish support. And the Irish votes could only be attained with a guarantee that an Irish Home Rule Bill would follow.[46] On April 28, the Lords passed the budget.[47] The next step for the government was to limit the powers of the Lords and to that purpose the Parliament Bill had been introduced on April 14, 1910.[48] Under the Parliament Bill, the Lords would lose their power where money bills were concerned and, although they could delay legislation for two years, Commons could pass a measure without their approval by sending it up in three successive sessions.[49] Complicated machinations were necessary, but the Parliament Bill was passed by seventeen votes in 1911. Of course, all of this lay in the future. In this speech Pankhurst simply accused the Liberal government of hiding behind the House of Lords, counting on the Lords to reject a women's suffrage bill in their stead. It was an accusation of duplicity and political cowardice against the Liberal government, charges that the suffragettes would make repeatedly throughout the suffrage campaign.

1

The Importance of the Vote

Emmeline Pankhurst's Speech in the Portman Rooms, London.
March 24, 1908

IT SEEMS TO ME A VERY STRANGE THING THAT LARGE NUMBERS OF WOMEN should have met together to-night to consider whether the vote is of importance, while all day long, across the water, in the Peckham Bye-election,[1] men whether they realise the importance of the vote or not, have been exercising it, and in exercising it settling for women as well as for themselves great questions of public importance.

What, then, is this vote that we are hearing so much about just now, so much more than people have heard in discussion at least, for a great many years? I think we may give the vote a threefold description. We may describe the vote as, first of all, a symbol, secondly, a safeguard, and thirdly, an instrument. It is a symbol of freedom, a symbol of citizenship, a symbol of liberty. It is a safeguard of all those liberties which it symbolises. And in these later days it has come to be regarded more than anything else as an instrument, something with which you can get a great many more things than our forefathers who fought for the vote ever realised as possible to get with it. It seems to me that such a thing is worth fighting for, and women to-day are fighting very strenuously in order to get it.

Wherever masses of people are gathered together there must be government. Government without the vote is more or less a form of tyranny. Government with the vote is more or less representative according to the extent to which the vote is given. In this country they tell us we have representative government. So far as women are concerned, while you have representative government for men, you have despotic government for women. So it is in order that the government of the country may be made really representative, may represent not only all classes of the community, but both sexes of the community, that this struggle for the vote is going on on the part of women.

To-day, women are working very hard for it. And there is no doubt whatever that very, very soon the fight will be over, and victory will be won.

31

Even a Liberal Government will be forced to give votes to women. Gentlemen with Liberal principles have talked about those principles for a very long time, but it is only just lately that women have realised that so far as they are concerned, it began in talk and ended in talk, and that there was absolutely no intention of performance. To-day, we have taken off the mask, and we have made these gentlemen realise that, whether they like it or not, they will have to yield. People ask us, "Why force it on just now? Why give all this trouble to the Liberals, with their great and splendid programme of reform?" Well, we say, after all, they are just the people to whom we ought to give trouble, and who, if they are sincere, ought to be very glad that we are giving them trouble, and forcing them to put their great principles into practice.

To-night, it is not for me to talk to you very much about the agitation. I have to talk to you about what the vote will do for women, and what being deprived of the vote has caused women to suffer. And so I mean to devote most of the time at my disposal to this side of the question. What I am going to say to you to-night is not new. It is what we have been saying at every street corner, at every bye-election during the last eighteen months. It is perfectly well known to many members of my audience, but they will not mind if I repeat for the benefit of those who are here for the first time to-night, those arguments and illustrations with which many of us are so very familiar.

In the first place it is important that women should have the vote in order that in the government of the country the women's point of view should be put forward. It is important for women that in any legislation that affects women equally with men, those who make the laws should be responsible to women in order that they may be forced to consult women and learn women's views when they are contemplating the making or the altering of laws. Very little has been done by legislation for women for many years— for obvious reasons. More and more of the time of Members of Parliament is occupied by the claims which are made on behalf of the people who are organised in various ways in order to promote the interests of their industrial organisations or their political or social organisations. So the Member of Parliament, if he does dimly realise that women have needs, has no time to attend to them, no time to give to the consideration of those needs. His time is fully taken up by attending to the needs of the people who have sent him to Parliament. While a great deal has been done, and a great deal more has been talked about for the benefit of the workers who have votes, yet so far as women are concerned, legislation relating to them has been practically at a standstill. Yet it is not because women have no need, or because their need is not very urgent. There are many laws on the Statute-book to-day which are admittedly out of date, and call for reformation; laws which inflict very grave injustices on women. I want to call the attention of women who are here to-night to a few Acts on the Statute-book which press very hardly and very injuriously on women.

Men politicians are in the habit of talking to women as if there were no laws that affect women. "The fact is," they say, "the home is the place for women. Their interests are the rearing and training of children. These are the things that interest women. Politics have nothing to do with these things, and therefore politics do not concern women." Yet the laws decide how women are to live in marriage, how their children are to be trained and educated, and what the future of their children is to be. All that is decided by Act of Parliament. Let us take a few of these laws, and see what there is to say about them from the women's point of view.

First of all, let us take the marriage laws. They are made by men for women. Let us consider whether they are equal, whether they are just, whether they are wise. What security of maintenance has the married woman? Many a married woman having given up her economic independence in order to marry, how is she compensated for that loss? What security does she get in that marriage for which she gave up economic independence? Take the case of a woman who has been earning a good income. She is told that she ought to give up her employment when she becomes a wife and mother. What does she get in return? All that a married man is obliged by law to do for his wife is to provide for her shelter of some kind, food of some kind, and clothing of some kind. It is left to his good pleasure to decide what the shelter shall be, what the food shall be, what the clothing shall be. It is left to him to decide what money shall be spent on the home, and how it shall be spent; the wife has no voice legally in deciding any of these things. She has no legal claim upon any definite portion of his income. If he is a good man, a conscientious man, he does the right thing. If he is not, if he chooses almost to starve his wife, she has no remedy. What he thinks sufficient is what she has to be content with.

I quite agree, in all these illustrations, that the majority of men are considerably better than the law compels them to be, so the majority of women do not suffer as much as they might suffer if men were all as bad as they might be, but since there are some bad men some unjust men, don't you agree with me that the law ought to be altered so that those men could be dealt with?

Take what happens to the woman if her husband dies and leaves her a widow, sometimes with little children. If a man is so insensible to his duties as a husband and father when he makes his will, as to leave all his property away from his wife and children, the law allows him to do it. That will is a valid one. So you see that the married woman's position is not a very secure one. It depends entirely on her getting a good ticket in the lottery. If she has a good husband, well and good: if she has a bad one, she has to suffer, and she has no remedy. That is her position as a wife, and it is far from satisfactory.

Now let us look at her position if she has been very unfortunate in marriage, so unfortunate as to get a bad husband, an immoral husband, a vicious husband, a husband unfit to be the father of little children. We turn to the Divorce Court. How is she to get rid of such a man? If a man has got married to a bad wife, and he wants to get rid of her, he has but to prove against her one act of infidelity. But if a woman who is married to a vicious husband wants to get rid of him, not one act nor a thousand acts of infidelity entitle her to a divorce; she must prove either bigamy, desertion, or gross cruelty, in addition to immorality before she can get rid of that man.

Let us consider her position as a mother. We have repeated this so often at our meetings that I think the echo of what we have said must have reached many. By English law no married woman exists as the mother of the child she brings into the world. In the eyes of the law she is not the parent of her child. The child, according to our marriage laws, has only one parent, who can decide the future of the child, who can decide where it shall live, how it shall live, how much shall be spent upon it, how it shall be educated, and what religion it shall profess. That parent is the father.

These are examples of some of the laws that men have made, laws that concern women. I ask you, if women had had the vote, should we have had such laws? If women had had the vote, as men have the vote, we should have had equal laws. We should have had equal laws for divorce, and the law should recognise that they have two parents.

I have spoken to you about the position of the married woman, who does not exist legally as a parent, the parent of her own child. In marriage, children have one parent. Out of marriage children have also one parent. That parent is the mother—the unfortunate mother. She alone is responsible for the future of her child: she alone is punished if her child is neglected and suffers from neglect. But let me give you one illustration. I was in Herefordshire during the bye-election. While I was there, an unmarried mother was brought before the bench of magistrates charged with having neglected her illegitimate child. She was a domestic servant, and had put the child out to nurse. The magistrates—there were colonels and landowners on that bench—did not ask what wages the mother got; they did not ask who the father was or whether he contributed to the support of the child. They sent that woman to prison for three months for having neglected her child. I ask you women here to-night, if women had had some share in the making of laws, don't you think they would have found a way of making all fathers of such children equally responsible with the mothers for the welfare of those children?

Let us take the law of inheritance. Often in this agitation for the vote, we have been told by advanced members of the Liberal Party that to give

votes to women on the same terms as those on which men now have the
vote, would be to strengthen the influence of property, and to help to
continue the existing laws of property.

When you look at the laws of inheritance in this country, it makes you
smile to hear that argument. Men have taken very good care that women
do not inherit until all male heirs are exhausted. So I do not think these
democratic gentlemen are quite sincere in the fears they express lest the
influence of property should be very much strengthened if women got the
Parliamentary franchise. I do not think it is time yet for women to consider
whether the law that the eldest son shall inherit the estate is a just law. I
think we should put it in this way: if it is to be the eldest child, let it be the
eldest child, whether that child is a man or a woman. I am perfectly certain
that if women had had the vote when that law was made, that that is how it
would have been settled, if they had decided to have a law of primogeniture.

Well, one could go on giving you many more of these examples. I want
now to deal with one objection which may be in the minds of some people
here. They say, you are talking about laws made a long time ago. Laws
would not now be made like that. If a new law were made, it would of
course be equal between the sexes. But as a matter of fact, it seems almost
impossible for men, when making new laws that will affect both sexes, to
recognise that there is any woman's side at all. Let us take an illustration
from the last session of Parliament. For many years we have been accustomed
to see pass through the House of Commons and go up to the House of
Lords that hardy evergreen, the Deceased Wife's Sister Bill. I used—it is
many years since I began reading the debates on that measure—I used to
read the speeches carefully through to see if I could find one speech from a
man which showed any kind of realisation of the women's side of that Bill.
You read eloquent appeals to make it possible for a man who had lost his
wife to give to the children the best kind of step-mother that they could
have. Who could make a better step-mother, it was asked, than the sister of
their deceased mother? By natural ties, by old associations, by her knowledge
of the children, she was better fitted than anybody else to take the mother's
place. But you never heard of a man who thought there might be another
side to the picture. So you have on the Statute-book a piece of legislation
which gives relief to the widower who would like to provide a kind step-
mother for his children, but does not give relief to the widow who would
like to give a kind step-father to her children. I do not think it ever entered
into the minds of these legislators that there might be a widow who would
like to fulfil the behest of the Old Testament that the living brother should
take up his deceased brother's burden and do his duty to his brother's family.
So you see, even in this twentieth century, you have got the same spirit.

The man voter and the man legislator see the man's needs first, and do
not see the woman's needs. And so it will be until women get the vote. It

is well to remember that, in view of what we have been told of what is the value of women's influence. Woman's influence is only effective when men want to do the thing that her influence is supporting.

Now let us look a little to the future. If it ever was important for women to have the vote, it is ten times more important to-day, because you cannot take up a newspaper, you cannot go to a conference, you cannot even go to church, without hearing a great deal of talk about social reform and a demand for social legislation. Of course, it is obvious that that kind of legislation—and the Liberal Government tell us that if they remain in office long enough we are going to have a great deal of it—is of vital importance to women. If we have the right kind of social legislation it will be a very good thing for women and children. If we have the wrong kind of social legislation, we may have the worst kind of tyranny that women have ever known since the world began.

We are hearing about legislation to decide what kind of homes people are to live in. That surely is a question for women. Surely every woman, when she seriously thinks about it, will wonder how men by themselves can have the audacity to think that they can say what homes ought to be without consulting women. Then take education. Since 1870 men have been trying to find out how to educate children. I think that they have not yet realised that if they are ever to find out how to educate children, they will have to take women into their confidence, and try to learn from women some of those lessons that the long experience of ages has taught to them. One cannot wonder that whole sessions of Parliament should be wasted on Education Bills. For, you see, it is only just lately that men have begun to consider education, or to try to learn what the word means. So as we are going to have a great deal more time devoted to education, I think it will be a great economy of time if we get the vote, if only that we may have an opportunity of deciding how girls are to be trained, even in those domestic duties which gentlemen are so fond of reminding us we ought to attend to.

I suppose you all read your newspapers this morning. You saw that a great statesman[2] was pouring out words of wisdom on a subject which one may think might well be regarded as women's business, and which they might at all events have some share in deciding. How it makes one smile to hear a statesman comparing whisky and milk, and discussing whether babies should have natural mother's milk, or humanised milk, or sterilised milk, or what is a sufficient quantity of milk. All these things Cabinet Ministers have discovered that they are quite competent to decide without us. And when a few women ventured to make a small protest and suggested that perhaps it would be best to give to women, the mothers of the race, an opportunity of expressing themselves on the subject, they were characterised as disgraceful, and turned out of the meeting for daring to raise their voices in protest.

Well, we cannot wonder that they are deciding what sort of milk the babies are to have, for it is only a few months ago that they decided how babies should be brought into the world, and who should officiate on the occasion. The Midwives Act, owing to the extreme difficulty and slowness with which, during twelve years of ceaseless agitation, it was carried through Parliament, has made of the women who agitated for it convinced suffragists, since, if they had had votes the measure could have been passed in a couple of years. Even when carried, it was at the expense of many concessions, which, had the women promoting the Bill possessed the franchise, they would certainly have been able to avoid. To this day the midwives have no direct representation on the Central Board which administers the Act. Still, in spite of legislation like that, we find politicians, responsible members of the Government, saying that women ought to have nothing to do with politics, and that they ought not to ask for the vote.

What limits are there to be to this? The same gentleman who thinks himself quite competent to say how babies ought to be fed tells us that he is going to interfere not only with babies, but with their mothers as well. He is going to decide by Act of Parliament whether married women are to be allowed to earn an economic independence, or are to be prevented from doing so. He thinks married women who are earning their living are going to submit to a virtual repeal of the Married Women's Property Act,[3] and to leave it to their husbands to decide whether they shall have any money to spend as they please. To deprive married women of the right to go out to work, to decide this for them without consulting women voters whether they are to earn wages or not, is an act of tyranny to which, I believe, women, patient and long-suffering as they are, will not submit. I hope that even the Liberal women will revolt when it comes to that. But I am not over hopeful about them, because, unfortunately for poor married women who know what it is to need to earn a living, those who decide what the policy of the Liberal women shall be are women who have never had to earn a living, and do not know what it is to have little children dependent upon them and liable to be starved if their mothers are prevented from going out to work. But fortunately the women who are going to be interfered with are not the kind of women who will submit to be interfered with quietly. Women who belong to the aristocracy of industry, women such as the cotton workers in the Lancashire mills, are not likely to be driven into the ranks of the sweated without protest.

What is the reason for the proposal? We are told it is to set these women free, to let them stay at home. I do not see that Mr. John Burns proposes to compensate women for the loss of their earnings. I do not see that he proposes to compel husbands to give to their wives a definite portion of their income for house-keeping purposes. All he proposes is that women, who are earning from ten shillings to thirty shillings a week shall be prevented from earning that income for themselves. He does not propose if the husband is sick or weakly and unable to earn enough to keep the home, to supplement that income by a grant from the State. All he proposes to do is to take away from the married woman the right to earn an income for herself. This, he says, will stop infantile mortality and put an end to race degeneracy. Could you have a greater example of ignorance of the real facts of the situation? I come from Lancashire. I was born in Lancashire. I think I know more about Lancashire than Mr. John Burns. I can tell you this, that infantile mortality and physical degeneration are not found in the homes of the well-paid factory operatives, but they are found in the home of the slum-dweller, the home of the casual labourer, where the mother does not go out to work, but where there is never sufficient income to provide proper food for the child after it is born. That is where babies die—in those horrible slum districts, where families have to be maintained on incomes of from sixteen shillings to eighteen shillings per week, and where you have rents from five shillings to eight shillings per week to pay. What woman can feed her children on an income like that, even if her husband brings the whole of it home?

I know the cotton workers of Lancashire. Not long ago, we were in the Rosendale Valley, Mr. Harcourt's[4] constituency. In that constituency more women earn wages than men. You find daughters earning more money than their fathers. You find wives earning more money than their husbands. They do piece work, and they often earn better wages than the men. I was talking one day to one—a married woman worker whom I met in the train. She was going home from the mill. She had a child three or four years of age, well dressed, very blithe, and looking well fed. I asked her if she worked in the mill. She said, "Yes." I asked her what wages she earned. She said, "Thirty shillings a week." She told me she had other children. "Who looks after the children while you are at work?" "I have a housekeeper," she answered. I said to her, "You are not going to be allowed to work much longer. Mr. John Burns is going to make you stay at home and look after the children." And she said, "I don't know what we shall do then. I suppose we shall have to clem." I don't know whether you all know our Lancashire word "clem." When we say clem, we mean starve. In thousands of homes in Lancashire, if we get Mr. John Burns' proposal carried into law, little children, now well clothed and well fed and well cared for, will have clemmed before many months are over. These women say a shilling that they earn themselves is worth two shillings of their husbands' money, for it is their own. They know far better than their husbands how much money is needed for food, how much is needed to be spent on the home. I do not think there is a woman in Lancashire who does not realise that it is better to earn an income of her own than to be dependent on her husband. They realise it better than women of the upper classes who provide nurses and governesses for their children. I put it to you whether the woman of the working class, so long as she sees that her children are well fed and are well enough cared for, has not as much right as her well-off sister to provide a nurse for her children. We should like to say this to Mr. John Burns, that when women get the vote, they will take very much better care of babies than men have been able to do.

There may be many women in this room to-night who do not know much about the industrial women from practical experience. I want to say something about them. Here in London last year there was the Sweated Industries Exhibition. That Exhibition went to Manchester. It went to Birmingham. The papers were full of it. After it was held there were conferences in the Guildhall, conferences in the large centres of population, and resolutions were carried demanding legislation to deal with the sweating evil. Nothing has come of it all. If any of you women are doubtful about the value of the vote to women, that example ought to be enough. Look at the Government's proposals. What do you get in the forefront of their programme? You get an eight hours' day for miners. But you get nothing for the sweated women. Why is the miner being attended to rather than the sweated worker? The miner is being attended to because he, the miner, has got a vote. You see what the vote will do. You see what political power will do. If women had had the vote there would have been proposals to help the sweated woman worker in the Government programme of this session. I think that women, realising the horrible degradation of these workers, the degradation not only to themselves, but to all of us, caused by that evil of sweating, ought to be eager to get political freedom, in order that something may be done to get for the sweated woman labourer some kind of pay that would enable her to live at least a moral and a decent life.

Now let me say something on another point. Among those here are some professional women. You know what a long and a weary struggle it has been for women to get into the professions, some of which are now open to women. But you all know that the position of women in those professions is not what it ought to be, and is certainly not what it will be when women get the franchise. How difficult it is for women to get posts after they have qualified for them. I know this from practical experience on a public body. Every time we had applications from women for posts open to them, we had applications also from men. Usually the standing of the women was very much higher than that of the men. And yet the women did not get those appointments. The men got them. That would all be altered if we got political equality. It is the political key that is needed to unlock the door.

Again, in all grades of education, certainly in elementary education, women are better qualified for the work than the men. You get a better type of woman. Yet for work equal to that of men, she cannot get equal pay. If women teachers had the Parliamentary vote, those men who go to the House of Commons to represent the interests of teachers would have to represent the interests of women teachers as well as the interests of the men. I think that the gentleman who made the teachers the stepping-stone to office, and who talks at bye-elections about manhood suffrage would have taken up the interests of the women who have paid his wages if he felt that he was responsible to women voters.

Almost everywhere the well-paid posts are given to men. Take the College of Arts. Women art students do quite as well as the men students. And yet after their training is over, women never get any of the posts. All the professorships, all the well-paid posts in the colleges and Universities are given to men. I knew the Head of one of the training colleges in one of our great cities. She said to me: "It makes me feel quite sad to see bright young girls expecting to get their living, and finding after their training is over that they can get nothing to do." The Parliamentary vote will settle that. There is no department of life that you can think of in which the possession of the Parliamentary vote will not make things easier for women than they are to-day.

Then there is the administrative side of public life. We want the vote not merely to get laws made. I think the possession of the Parliamentary vote is very important on the administrative side of politics. I have every reason to think that, because I have just come out of prison. We may congratulate ourselves that the Militant Suffragists, of whom I am one, have at least succeeded in forcing the Government to appoint the first woman inspector of prisons. Of course, it is a very small thing, but it means a very great deal. It means the beginning of prison reform, reform in prison discipline and prison treatment that have been needed for a very long time. Well, when we get the vote, it won't take many years talking about things to get one woman inspector appointed. The immediate result of our getting the vote will be the appointment of many more women inspectors of factories. When I last made inquiries there was only one woman inspector of factories in all Ireland. Yet in Belfast alone, more women and girls are working in factories than men and boys. The need there for inspection is enormous in those linen and jute factories. It is perfectly obvious that when you have women and girls working in factories, if they are to be properly inspected, you must have women inspectors. We shall get them as soon as we are able to get women's interests properly attended to, which we shall only be able to do when we are in possession of the vote.

There is the same thing with regard to education. Women inspectors of schools are greatly needed. Moreover, there is not a single woman Poor Law inspector, nor a woman inspector of workhouses and workhouse hospitals. And yet it is to the workhouses and the workhouse hospitals that we send old people, sick people, and little children. We need to get women relieving officers appointed. I cannot get away from Mr. John Burns. You would think that a working man by origin, and the son of working people, might have been able to realise that it would have been a good thing to have women as relieving officers. And yet when Mr. John Burns, shortly after his appointment, was asked whether he would sanction the appointment of a woman relieving officer in a large Union in the North of England, he said it was not illegal, but it was a practice not to be encouraged. We shall get that position for women. We shall get it made possible for women to manage the business which men have always conceded is the business of women, the care of the sick, the care of the aged, the care of little children.

Well, I could go on giving you many, many more of these illustrations. In fact, the more one thinks about the importance of the vote for women, the more one realises how vital it is. We are finding out new reasons for the vote, new needs for the vote every day in carrying on our agitation.

I hope that there may be a few men and women here who will go away determined at least to give this question more consideration than they have in the past. They will see that we women who are doing so much to get the vote, want it because we realise how much good we can do with it when we have got it. We do not want it in order to boast of how much we have got. We do not want it because we want to imitate men or to be like men. We want it because without it we cannot do that work which it is necessary and right and proper that every man and woman should be ready and willing to undertake in the interests of the community of which they form a part. It has always been the business of women to care for these things, to think of these home questions. I assure you that no woman who enters into this agitation need feel that she has got to give up a single one of her woman's duties in the home. She learns to feel that she is attaching a larger meaning to those duties which have been woman's duties since the race began, and will be till the race has ceased to be. After all, home is a very very big thing indeed. It is not just your own little home, with its four walls, and your own little private and personal interests that are looked after there. The home is the home of everybody of the nation. No nation can have a proper home unless women as well as men give their best to its building up and to making it what a home ought to be, a place where every single child born into it shall have a fair chance of growing up to be a fit, and a happy, and a useful member of the community.

2

The Prisoners at Bow Street.

Trial Transcript
*Mr. Lloyd George and Mr. Herbert Gladstone
in the Witness Box.*

THE ADJOURNED HEARING OF THE CHARGE AGAINST MRS. PANKHURST, Miss Christabel Pankhurst, and Mrs. Drummond was taken at Bow-street on Wednesday morning.

On Mr. Curtis Bennett, the magistrate, taking his seat, Mr. Muskett said the case for the prosecution was concluded last week.

The magistrate, addressing the defendants, said: I would just make one suggestion. It may be for the benefit of two gentlemen who are here, that before you make any remarks their evidence should be taken, because they have, I know, important engagements elsewhere.

Miss Pankhurst: I desire first to submit that, as a matter of law, you ought not to bind us over at all, having regard to the form of the summonses and the nature of the evidence that has been adduced by the prosecution in support of them

The Magistrate: Won't you submit that afterwards?

Miss Pankhurst: I think with your permission it might be well to submit it now.

The Magistrate: I am only suggesting that you should call these two gentlemen first.

Miss Pankhurst: Do I understand that if I take their evidence now it will be open for me to raise this later?

The Magistrate: Certainly.

Mr. Lloyd George.

Mr. Lloyd-George then went into the witness-box.

Miss Pankhurst: You are Mr. Lloyd-George?——Yes.

Privy-Councillor and Chancellor of the Exchequer?——Yes.

Were you present at the meeting addressed by Mrs. Pankhurst, Mrs. Drummond, and myself in Trafalgar-square on October 11?——I think I was there for about ten minutes. I believe I heard Mrs. Pankhurst—partly.

Did you see a copy of the bills which were being distributed to members of the audience?——Yes. A young lady gave it to me the moment I arrived— it invited me to rush the House of Commons.

How did you interpret the invitation conveyed to you as a member of the audience? What did you think we wanted you to do?——I really should not like to place an interpretation upon the document. I don't think it is quite my function.

Well, I am speaking to you as a member of the general public.——I heard what Mrs. Pankhurst said, and I thought she placed the interpretation you desired to be put upon the document.

I want to deal with the matter in this way. First of all to get the meaning conveyed by the bill, quite apart from anything you may have heard said; and then we must throw some light upon the meaning of the bill by examining the words which were spoken on the platform. Let us take the bill itself. Imagine you were not at the meeting at all, but were walking up the Strand, and someone gave you a copy of this bill and you read it—"Help the Suffragettes to rush the House of Commons." And suppose you forgot you were a member of the Government and regarded yourself just as an ordinary person like myself—quite unofficial. You get this bill. What would you think you were called upon to do?——Really, I should not like to be called upon to undertake so difficult a task as to interpret that document.

Now, this word "rush," which seems to be at the bottom of it all. What does it mean?——I understood the invitation from Mrs. Pankhurst was to force an entrance to the House of Commons.

No, no. I want you to keep your mind centred on the bill. Let us forget what Mrs. Pankhurst said. What did the bill say?——I really forget what the bill said.

I can refresh your memory. The bill said, "Help the Suffragettes to rush the House of Commons."——Yes; that's it.

I want you to define the word "rush"?——I cannot undertake to do that.

You can't offer any definition of the word "rush"?——No, I cannot.

Well, I will suggest some to you. I find that in Chambers' English Dictionary one of the meanings of the word is "an eager demand." Now what do you think of that?——I can't enter into competition with Chambers' Dictionary. I am prepared to accept it.

"Urgent pressure of business." That is another meaning. Ogilvie gives the same meaning—"eager demand." Now, if you were asked to help the Suffragettes to make an eager demand to the House of Commons that they should give votes to women, would you feel we were calling upon you to do an illegal act?——That is not for me to say.

The Magistrate: The witness is perfectly right. That is for me to say on the evidence. I have not interfered so far.

Miss Pankhurst: Here is another sense in which the word "rush" is used, and I think it will be of some interest to you. We use it in this connection—to rush bills through Parliament.

Witness: Yes, I think I have some experience of that.

Miss Pankhurst: "On the rush," we are told in another dictionary, means in a hurry. There is nothing unlawful in being in a hurry.

The Magistrate: I have already said you must address those remarks to me afterwards.

Miss Pankhurst: Did you understand we asked you to go in a hurry to the House of Commons to make this eager demand for enfranchisement? Was that the meaning which the bill conveyed to you?——I cannot express any opinion as to that. I can only give evidence as to what I really saw.

You can't tell me what you, as a member of the public, understood?

The Magistrate: Miss Pankhurst, you must take my ruling, please.

Miss Pankhurst (to witness): Can you tell me at all what were the words you heard Mrs. Pankhurst use in Trafalgar-square?——I really could not. If you insist upon my giving my vague recollection I shall do so.

I should like to have it.——My vague recollection is that Mrs. Pankhurst insisted upon the right of women to have access to the House of Commons, and she said if that was refused they meant to force an entrance, and she invited the crowd to assist her. I am only giving a vague impression of the words that were used.

Did you hear this: "On Tuesday evening, at Caxton Hall, we shall ask those who support the women to come to Parliament-square. There will be a deputation of women, who have no rights in the House of Commons such as men have. The Government does not know its own mind, it changes so; but we know we want the vote and mean to have it"?——Yes; I was there when Mrs. Pankhurst said that.

She was the only speaker you heard?——Yes.

Now, what impression did you form from the demeanour of the crowd in Trafalgar-square as to whether they were likely to respond to this invitation to rush the House of Commons?——I thought they were a very unlikely crowd to respond.

You didn't think they would come?——Not from the demeanour of the crowd—certainly not.

You thought that although we issued the invitation it would not be accepted?——Not by that particular crowd.

Did you think on other grounds that there would be a large public response to this invitation?——That I should not like to say.

Did you hear the speaker threaten any violence to you or to any member of the Government?——Oh, no.

She didn't invite others to attack you in any way?——Oh, no.

She didn't urge the people to come armed?——Oh, no; I never heard anything of that sort.

There was no suggestion that public or private property should be in any way damaged?——Oh, I do not suggest anything of that sort.

You heard nothing of that kind?——No.

What did you anticipate that the consequence would be to you yourself personally if the public responded to the invitation to rush the House of Commons?——Well, I didn't think it was very formidable.

You didn't think you would be hurt?——(The witness smiled and shook his head.)

Or that any of your colleagues would be hurt?——Oh, there was no suggestion of any personal violence to anybody.

No suggestion of violence at all. Then you are able to tell me that the speeches were not inflammatory. They were not likely to incite to violence?——I should not like to express an opinion as to what the result would be of inviting a crowd of people to force an entrance to the House of Commons. I should not have thought it possible to do that without some violence.

You didn't hear any violence advocated?——Except to force an entrance to the House of Commons.

You didn't hear the word "force"?——I have only a very vague impression as to the words used. If Mrs. Pankhurst says she didn't use the word force I would not contradict her.

There were no words so likely to incite to violence as the advice you gave at Swansea, that women should be ruthlessly flung out of your meeting?

Mr. Muskett: That is quite irrelevant.

The Magistrate: That was a private meeting, and not of the same character.

Miss Pankhurst: A public meeting.

The Magistrate: Well, it is private in a sense.

Miss Pankhurst: They are private nowadays. That is quite true. (To witness): You didn't hear any speeches made by myself or by Mrs. Drummond?

The Magistrate: The witness has already said he only heard Mrs. Pankhurst.

The Witness: I only heard Mrs. Pankhurst for about ten minutes or a quarter of an hour.

Am I right in assuming that you read the official organ of our society?—— Well, I only read, I think, one copy that was kindly sent me by Mrs. Pethick Lawrence.

You didn't read the copy in which Mrs. Pankhurst issued a manifesto dealing with the plans for the 13th——No; I don't think it was included in that.

Listening to the speeches in Trafalgar-square, what did you gather as to the object we had in view in planning a rush to the House of Commons?——I was not quite clear.

You were not quite clear as to the object?——No, except to force an entrance to the House of Commons; that is all I heard.

Did you gather for what reason this rush had been planned?

The Magistrate: You are not entitled to cross-examine your own witness. I am loth to stop you. I should have stopped counsel before this.

Miss Pankhurst: I rather anticipated this difficulty, and I looked up "Taylor on Evidence," and I saw words which I thought gave me a good deal of latitude. (To witness): Were you in the neighbourhood of the House of Commons on the evening of the 13th?——I was in the House of Commons.

Before you reached the House of Commons you were necessarily in the street, and you saw something of what took place?——Yes, I saw a little bit.

You were not alone, I think?——No, I had my little girl with me.

How old is she?——She is six.

Did you think it safe to bring her out?——Certainly. She was very amused.

You thought it was quite safe for a child of those tender years to be amongst the crowd?——I was not amongst the crowd.

You thought that, in spite of the contemplated rush, you were safe to have her inside and outside the House of Commons?——Yes, considering the police arrangements.

Were the streets crowded?——Not by the House. You see I only brought her from Downing-street to the House, and I think that was clear.

Were you in the crowd itself?——No; it was quite clear.

Did you see any women you supposed to be members of our Union?——I don't think I did.

Did you see any women arrested?——I was not anywhere near that.

Had you any opportunity of noticing the attitude of the crowd?——I don't think there was much of a crowd by the House of Commons. I think it was on the Embankment; so I heard.

Had you any opportunity of seeing any arrests or what was going on in the crowded part?——No, I did not see the crowd at all.

Were you yourself attacked or assaulted in any way?——Oh! dear me, no.

Did you apprehend any attack or assault?——No.

Can you tell me, according to your own knowledge, what harm has resulted from the events of the 13th?——I don't think I can tell you that.

You can't tell me?——No.

Do you know of any serious injury having taken place?——I should not like to express any opinion. It is hardly my function in the witness-box.

The prosecution asserts that a serious breach of the peace took place. Do you concur with that statement?

The Magistrate: The Chancellor of the Exchequer would have nothing to do with that.

Miss Pankhurst: I believe you are a lawyer?——Well, I hope I am.

Don't you think the offence alleged against us would be more properly described as unlawful assembly?——There again, I was not put in the witness-box to express an opinion of that sort.

The Magistrate: That has nothing to do with Mr. Lloyd George.

Miss Pankhurst: Of course, I am subject to your guidance, your worship. (To witness): You have seen the form of summons issued against us?——No.

You don't know with what we are charged?——No, I don't really.

The Magistrate: Have you any other question?

Miss Pankhurst: Well, I think it is desirable he should know. But I am subject to your guidance.

Witness: I have nothing to do with it.

Miss Pankhurst: You know we are asked to show cause why we should not be bound over for having incited people to commit an unlawful act?—— I take it from you, Miss Pankhurst, but I don't know.

Miss Pankhurst: Yet the result of the summons being in this form is that we are denied the right of trial by jury.

The Magistrate: The witness has nothing to do with that. That is the law of the land.

Miss Pankhurst: Does it occur to you that the authorities, in choosing this form of procedure against us, deliberately wished to deprive us of the right to trial by jury?

The Magistrate: That, again, is not a question for the witness.

Miss Pankhurst: May I put the question if you think it a very serious thing——this proposal to rush the House of Commons?

Witness: Oh, yes. I should have thought you would have thought that too, Miss Pankhurst.

Still, it is in the nature of a political offence?——Well, I should not like to say anything about that. In fact, I am simply here as a witness to give evidence of what I saw. I really cannot go into the political aspect of the matter.

You are aware that we argue that, as we are deprived of a share in the election of Parliamentary representatives we are entitled to go in person to the House of Commons?——That was a point put by Mrs. Pankhurst.

Do you agree with that point of view?——I should not like to express an opinion.

The Magistrate: It is not for the witness to express an opinion.

Miss Pankhurst: I should like to put this question, Do you think that coercion is the right way of dealing with political disturbers?

The Magistrate: That, again, is not for the witness.

Miss Pankhurst: You refuse to answer?

Witness: I don't refuse to answer, but I must obey the decision of the Bench that I cannot express an opinion about things in the witness-box.

Miss Pankhurst: Am I to understand that an answer must not be given to that?

The Magistrate: No.

Miss Pankhurst: Not even if the witness would like to do so?

The Magistrate: No.

Miss Pankhurst: Well, is it likely to be a successful way of dealing with political disturbances?

The Magistrate: That, again, is not admissible.

Miss Pankhurst: But for these restrictions, your worship . . . ! (To witness): Can you tell me whether any interference with public order took place in connection with previous movements for franchise reform?——I should have thought that was an historical fact.

Have you yourself taken part in any such movement? Does your mind go back to 1884?

The Magistrate: That is cross-examination. Your witness cannot go into that.

Miss Pankhurst: In a sense, he is my witness.

The Magistrate: In every sense at present.

Mr. Lloyd George's Encouragement.

Miss Pankhurst: Have we not received encouragement from you, or, if not from you, from your colleagues, to take action of this kind?

Witness: I should be very much surprised to hear that.

You would be surprised to hear that?——Very.

You deny that we have been encouraged by Liberal statesmen to take action of this kind?——I simply express astonishment at the statement.

Miss Pankhurst: Have you ever heard these words spoken by us at Trafalgar-square or by any Liberal statesman? "I am sorry to say that if no instructions had ever been addressed in political crises to the people of this country, except to remember to hate violence and love order and exercise patience, the liberties of this country would never have been attained"— have you heard these words before?——I cannot call them to mind.

Miss Pankhurst: These were the words of William Ewart Gladstone.—— I accept your statement.

Miss Pankhurst: Is not that encouragement to such action as we have taken?——You ask me a question of opinion again. I am not competent to express an opinion in the witness-box.

Were you present in the House of Commons when Mr. Herbert Gladstone gave advice to the women of this movement, while addressing the House on women's suffrage?——No.

Miss Pankhurst: You were not present.——When was it?

In this present Parliament.——I don't remember.

You don't know, then, that he encouraged us to action of this kind?

The Magistrate: He says he doesn't remember.

Witness: I don't think I heard him on the subject. I was probably attending to the duties of my department.

Miss Pankhurst: Is it not a fact that you yourself have set an example of revolt?

The Magistrate: You need not answer that question.

Miss Pankhurst: Well, your worship, my point of view was—

The Magistrate: You must not attack your own witness.

Miss Pankhurst: My point of view was that, when it comes to the moment when you make your decision, you will inquire a little into the motive.

The Magistrate: Yes, but you must not attack your own witness.

Mr. Lloyd George: I certainly never incited a crowd to violence.

Miss Pankhurst: Not in the Welsh graveyard case?——No.

You did not tell them to break down the wall and disinter a body?——I gave advice which was found by the Court of Appeal to be sound legal advice.

Miss Pankhurst: We think we are giving sound legal advice too. Are you aware that in planning the action of the 13th we were carrying out literally the advice given by Liberal statesmen?——Oh, I could not tell you.

You don't know that John Bright[1] advised the people to take a precisely similar course?——No.

Are you aware that Mr. Chamberlain[2] in 1884 threatened precisely the same action?——I did not know.

You don't know that he threatened to march 100,000 men on London?

The Magistrate: He has answered the question—he never heard of it.

Miss Pankhurst: Do you know what action was taken against him by the Liberal Government?—Was he prosecuted?

Witness: Miss Pankhurst, I have already said that I do not remember the incident you refer to.

You might remember Mr. Chamberlain being in the dock?——I don't know.

You don't know what action the House of Commons took? Your mind is a blank upon the subject?——Since you put it to me, I don't believe Mr. Chamberlain ever threatened to use violence and break the law.

I must refer you to the pages of Hansard.[3]——Certainly.

Do you know what advice another eminent statesman gave? Do you know that Lord Randolph Churchill[4] urged the men of Ulster to fight, and said they would be right? He advised them to use the arbitrament of force?——Yes.

Did he ever stand in the dock? Was he prosecuted? Yet are you not of opinion that he incited to violence more than we have done?——Well, I think I have already told you, Miss Pankhurst, I cannot express opinions here in the witness-box.

Mrs. Pankhurst again quoted from "Taylor on Evidence," as to the discretion of the magistrate in allowing questions to be put to a witness who obviously appeared to be hostile or interested for the other party.

The Magistrate: I have seen neither one nor the other.

Miss Pankhurst: Or unwilling to give evidence.

The Magistrate: I think the witness is giving his evidence most fairly.

Miss Pankhurst: I think I need not trouble him with any further questions.

Questions by Mrs. Pankhurst.

Mrs. Pankhurst: I should like to ask Mr. Lloyd George one further question about his being present with his little girl. You remember you told my daughter that you anticipated no danger for your little girl, and that you were rather amused?

Mr. Lloyd George: I said the little girl was amused.

You took her out to be amused by the sight of the crowd?——She wanted to see the crowd, and I took her out.

Don't you think that from that fact we might gather that probably if it had been less possible for your little girl to go out to be amused that the people with whom you are associated would have taken the thing a great deal more seriously? That the very self-restraint which allowed your little daughter to go out and be amused——I am not sure as to the question you are putting, but I think you are asking me for an opinion again. I am here to give evidence as to facts.

I want to ask you a question about what you heard me say on Sunday. Did I ask the crowd to help the women get into the House of Commons because it was the people's House of Commons; women formed part of the people, and they had as much right to be represented there as men?——Yes, that seemed to be the argument.

Then perhaps you remember I said that since women were not in the position of men, and could not send representatives to press their claim on the Government, they had a constitutional right to go there themselves?—— Now that you remind me, I remember you saying that.

And that they were unlawfully shut out from the House of Commons?——Yes, that was the argument.

Mrs. Pankhurst: Now, I put it to you; Mr. Lloyd George, to show cause why we should not be bound over.

Mr. Lloyd George: Well, you have asked me to come here and go into the witness-box to say what I have seen, that is all.

The Magistrate: Yes, that is the only thing a witness can do.

Mrs. Pankhurst: I want to ask you whether we can ask Mr. Lloyd George some questions—

The Magistrate: You have asked him a great many.

Mrs. Pankhurst (to the Magistrate): Questions which would show you cause why we should not be bound over?

The Magistrate: No, that is for me.

Mrs. Pankhurst: My point is that the evidence he would give would assist you.

The Magistrate: Well, the evidence he has given will assist me.

Mrs. Pankhurst: But we want him to give more. I want to ask him some further questions about what he and other Liberal statesmen have advised people to do.

The Magistrate: We have had a great deal of that from your daughter. Do you wish to have it again?

Mrs. Pankhurst: I want to ask you whether, in your opinion, the whole of this agitation which women are carrying on, very much against the grain, would not be immediately stopped if women got their constitutional rights conceded to them?——I should think that is very likely.

I want to ask you whether, in your opinion, the women who are in the dock here to-day are women who are ordinary law-breakers, or who would have occasion to come into this Court for any other than political reasons?——No, of course not.

Questions by Mrs. Drummond.

Mrs. Drummond: When you received the bill in Trafalgar-square, did you say anything to the lady who gave it to you?——No; I took it from her.

Did you not consider it would rather be your duty to draw attention to the bill to the lady who gave it to you?——It is not my business. Certainly not.

Mrs. Drummond: Well, I am asking you as a responsible member of the public.——Well, the Commissioner of Police would be the person to attend to that.

Mrs. Drummond: Did you draw the attention of the police to the bill?——No.

Mrs. Drummond: I should like to ask Mr. Lloyd George this question. Many times he has refused to answer me. When do you intend to put a stop to these things by giving us the vote?

The Magistrate: That is not a question.

Mrs. Drummond: Perhaps he cannot answer me; but there is one thing, he cannot run away. You refuse to answer?

The Magistrate: You cannot ask it.

Mrs. Drummond: You and your Colleagues are more to blame for this agitation.

The Magistrate: You must not make a statement.

Mrs. Drummond: You see, we ladies don't get a chance.

Mr. Lloyd George (smiling): Indeed, you do.

Mr. Muskett did not cross-examine the Chancellor of the Exchequer.

Miss Brackenbury and Mr. Horace Smith.

Mr. Curtis Bennett at this point wished Miss Pankhurst to call Mr. Herbert Gladstone, but Miss Pankhurst asked leave to call one other witness first. The magistrate demurred, and Miss Pankhurst said: "I have only one question to put to this lady."

The Magistrate: Very well, then, *one* question.

Miss Marie Brackenbury, in reply to Miss Pankhurst, said she had suffered six weeks' imprisonment in connection with the votes for women agitation.

Miss Pankhurst: Did Mr. Horace Smith tell you that in sentencing you to that term he was doing what he was told?

"You must not put that question," said the magistrate; but the witness had already replied, "He did."

Mrs. Pankhurst: The witness has said "Yes" upon oath.

Mr. Gladstone's Evidence.

Mr. Herbert Gladstone, the Home Secretary, was next called, and questioned by Miss Pankhurst.

By virtue of your office as Home Secretary, have you not immediate control over the Metropolitan police?——No, not exactly immediate control.

Then who has immediate control?——The Commissioner.

And he is responsible to you?——To me.

You also appoint the police-magistrates in the metropolis, and the regulation of the business of their courts is entirely in your hands?

The Magistrate: You must not go into questions of State, you know. That is clearly laid down.

Miss Pankhurst: You are, therefore, ultimately responsible for the proceedings which have been taken against us?——The responsible department.

Did you not, as a matter of fact, instruct the Commissioner of Police to take the present proceedings?

Mr. Muskett: I object to that.

The Magistrate: That question cannot be answered.

Miss Pankhurst: Are the Government as a whole responsible for these proceedings?

Mr. Muskett: I object to that.

The Magistrate: That, again, you cannot put.

Miss Pankhurst: Did you instruct Mr. Horace Smith to decide against Miss Brackenbury and give her six weeks?

The Magistrate: You cannot put that question either.

Miss Pankhurst: It is a pity that the public interest should suffer on that account. To Witness: Did you ever give any instructions to Mr. Horace Smith?

Mr. Muskett: I object to this. It is contempt of Court to continue putting these questions.

Miss Pankhurst: The public will answer them. To Witness: What do you suggest is the meaning of what Mr. Horace Smith has said?

The Magistrate: The same ruling applies. This witness is here to answer any question you have got to ask him about what he saw when he was in Parliament-street on the day in question.

Miss Pankhurst: Is this question permissible? Did you see a copy of the bill issued by us inviting the public to the House of Commons?——I have seen it.

The Magistrate: If it was shown to you in your official capacity it is not admissible.

Witness: I am under your ruling, sir.

Miss Pankhurst: Was it given to you as an ordinary member of the public in the street?——No, certainly not.

Can you define the word "rush"? What impression has it made on your mind?——I can hardly give any definition of it, but a rush implies force.

Do you deny that it implies speed rather than force?——Speed generally involves force.

Miss Pankhurst: Suppose I am standing near the door of the House, and I run up the steps—I have rushed the House of Commons?——Yes, but I should say you must exert a considerable amount of force to do that.

Energy, perhaps, but I should not offer any force to anybody or anything?——I hope not.

I suggest that it is possible to rush the House without attacking anybody or hurting anybody?——If you ask me that, I don't think it is possible.

Miss Pankhurst: Not according to present regulations, perhaps. There are so many people in one's way. We did not know what amount of force would be directed against us.

Mr. Muskett: Put questions, please.

Miss Pankhurst: I think it is important we should ascertain how this is understood.

The Magistrate: He has told you he thought it meant force. You must take the answer.

Miss Pankhurst: Were you anticipating you would be in bodily danger as a consequence of the issue of this bill?——I didn't think of it at all. I didn't think whether the possibility existed or not.

You are like us. You are above those considerations. You were not in fear?——No, not at all.

Did you think public property was in danger as a consequence of this bill having been issued?——Do you mean on the 13th?

Yes, as a consequence of this bill.——I thought it was quite possible.

You thought the public would be violent?——I thought there would be danger from the crowds.

Then you were agreeably disappointed on the morning of the 14th, when you found no harm had been done?——No, I was not. The police measures were sufficient to stop any serious accident or danger.

You were in the street on the 13th?——Yes.

Did you see the public make any attack on anybody? Do you think that, but for the action of the police, they would have assaulted you?——I was in the street for a very short time.

During the time did you form the impression that, but for the protection of the police, your life would have been in danger?——Not my life. Certainly the situation required very strong and careful action by the police.

You were in the street on the 13th. Did you see the public make any attack on anybody?——I was only in the street for a short while. Certainly the situation required very strong and careful action by the police.

Miss Pankhurst: Do you assert that the crowd showed a hostile spirit?—— I was only in one or two places.

But you can speak for that portion of the crowd that you did see?——I saw a certain crowd at six o'clock when I went out.

Was their demeanour violent or hostile? Did you feel that but for the line of police protecting you they would have rushed upon you and attacked you?——The police were not protecting me.

Had it not been for the presence of the police, do you think you would have been attacked by the crowd?——I don't know what object the crowd would have in attacking me. I didn't consider it.

You didn't feel in fear?——I felt no personal fear.

Did any other person seem in danger of attack?——The police gave them very little chance.

What made you think them a dangerous or hostile crowd?——Of course, I am quite accustomed to seeing these crowds, and I know what has happened before.

What has happened?——Disorderly scenes.

You mean in connection with our demonstrations?——It is not for me to connect disorder with your demonstrations. I am referring to crowds which have assembled during the last two years.

What harm have they done?——Very little, as it happened.

What harm have they attempted to do?——That is not for me to answer.

Have they attempted to do more than secure an interview with the Prime minister?

The Magistrate: That is not a question for him to answer.

We will get back to the 13th. Do you think anyone was obstructed in their passage to the House?——I cannot speak for other people.

You saw no attempt to waylay members or Ministers?

The Magistrate: He hasn't said he did. You must not cross-examine your own witness.

Miss Pankhurst: Well, but for the presence of the police do you think you would have been attacked by the crowd?——I do not know what object the crowd would have had in attacking me.

Did you see the crowd do any harm whatever?——I did not.

Now you saw a portion of the crowd. Did you see them attack property?——No, certainly not.

Did you see them attack any person?——Not where I was.

Did you see them do any harm whatsoever?——No, I did not.

What were these people doing?——There was a great crowd.

But a great crowd assembles when the King goes to open Parliament.——Presumably they were waiting to rush the House of Commons.

Did you see any women whom you identified as Suffragists?——I didn't see many women.

Did you see any women wearing our colours, purple, white, and green?——I did not notice any.

Did you see any arrests?——I saw no arrests.

Did you see anyone injured?——No.

Did you hear of anyone being injured?——I have seen it stated that certain police-constables were injured.

You did not hear that ten people were received in hospital, but discharged?——I know nothing about that.

Will you tell me what harm has resulted from what took place?——All I can say is that there were thirty-seven arrests and over forty complaints of losses of purses and watches.

Comparing that with the net result of a Lord Mayor's Show crowd, or any sort of procession, really less harm resulted?——I could not say that.

I suppose I may not ask how many policemen were on duty?

The Magistrate: I don't suppose the Home Secretary knows that.

Miss Pankhurst: I suppose I may not ask these questions either. This would have been more suitable to the other witness (Mr. Lloyd George). What has been the cost to the country?

The Magistrate: We cannot go into these questions.

Will you tell me why we were not charged with unlawful assembly?——
I cannot tell you.

You know the consequence to be that we are deprived of trial by jury?——
You tell me. I am not acquainted with the particular part of the law you are
referring to.

If I say that the reason is that the Government are afraid to send us to a
jury . . . (Continuing) What have you to say with regard to our contention
that the offence with which we are charged is a political offence?

The Magistrate: You must not put that question.

How do you define political offence?——I wish you would give me a
good definition. I am often asked that question in the House of Commons.

Well, with the Magistrate's permission, I will. A political offence is one
committed in connection with political disturbances and with a political
motive.——I don't think that a sufficient explanation.

If I am at liberty after this day's proceedings are over, I shall have pleasure
in sending you a fuller account. Do you recollect that when a deputation of
women went to the House of Commons, instead of being allowed to enter
they were arrested?——I have not immediate knowledge of that. I have a
general recollection.

Do you remember that when a deputation went to the House of Commons to see the Prime Minister instead of being allowed to enter they
were arrested?

The Magistrate: That does not arise on the issue.

Miss Pankhurst: It throws a little light on it.

The Magistrate: Please do obey, otherwise I shall have to stop it altogether. I have given you much more license than I should give counsel.

Miss Pankhurst: In the action we took on the 13th, is it within your
knowledge that in taking that action we were acting on advice given by
yourself?——I wish you would take my advice.

We are trying to take it. What did you mean when you said men had
used *force majeure* in demanding the vote?——If you hand me the speech I
daresay I can tell you.

I have a copy of the speech.

The Magistrate: How is this material as to what Mr. Gladstone saw. You
are cross-examining your own witness, Miss Pankhurst, and you must not
do that.

Miss Pankhurst: May I not ask any explanation whatever as to the counsel
given to us?

The Magistrate: No, you may not.

Miss Pankhurst: We never have any other opportunity. May I ask whether
he made certain statements. Did you say it was impossible not to sympathise
with the eagerness and passion which have actuated so many women on this
subject?——Yes.

Did you say you were entirely in favour of the principle of woman's suffrage?——Yes.

Did you say men had had to struggle for centuries for their political rights?——Yes.

Did you say men had had to fight from the time of Cromwell, and for the last 130 years the warfare had been perpetual?——Yes.

Did you say that on this question experience showed that predominance of argument alone—and you believed that had been attained—was not enough to win the political day. Did you say that?——Yes.

Predominance of argument alone will not win the political day. Did you say that we are in the stage of what is called "academic discussion," which serves for ventilation of pious opinions, and is accompanied, you admit, by no effective action of the part of the Government or of political parties, or of voters throughout the country?——Yes.

Did you say that members of the House of Commons reflect the opinion of the country, not only in regard to the number of people outside, but in regard to the intensity of the feeling in support of a movement, and that the Government must necessarily be a reflex of the party which brought it into being?——Yes.

Did you say this? "There comes a time when political dynamics are far more important than political arguments." You said that?——Yes.

And that "Men had learned this lesson"?——Yes.

And that they know the necessity for demonstrating that *force majeure* which actuated and arms a Government for effective work?——Yes. I think it a most excellent speech. (Laughter.)

I agree with you. Did you say that that was the task before the supporters of this great movement?——Yes.

Did you speak of people assembling in tens of thousands in the 'thirties, 'sixties, and 'eighties, and do you know that we have done it on Woodhouse Moor and in Hyde Park?——Yes.

Miss Pankhurst: Why don't you give us the vote then? (Laughter.) Are you aware of the words your distinguished father spoke on the matter?—— I heard the quotation.

Do you assent to the proposition he laid down?——Yes.

Then you cannot condemn our methods any more?——That is hardly a matter for my opinion.

Miss Pankhurst: It is a very interesting question, though. I think I need not trouble you further.

Questions by Mrs. Pankhurst.

Mrs. Pankhurst: I want to ask Mr. Gladstone if he is aware that the consequence of our being ordered to be bound over is that we cannot consent and we shall go to prison?

The Magistrate: That is a matter of law, not for the witness.

Mrs. Pankhurst: If that happens to us, if we go to prison, I hope Mr. Gladstone will see that we go as political prisoners.

The Magistrate: That you must not ask.

Mrs. Pankhurst: But may I ask Mr. Gladstone this—if he is aware that in the City-square in Leeds on last Friday night 10,000 people, at six hours' notice, assembled, and carried, with two dissentients, a resolution calling upon the Government to pass Mr. Stanger's Bill during this session?

Mr. Muskett: That is not a question for Mr. Gladstone.

Mrs. Pankhurst: Well, Mr. Gladstone has answered some other political questions, sir.

(Continuing) I should like to ask Mr. Gladstone whether he recognises this morning that this is a political agitation?——I suppose it is a political agitation to get the franchise for women.

Do you think we should be likely to break the criminal law if we had the same means of representation as men?——I am sure your motive is excellent. It is a hypothetical question which I cannot answer.

Mrs. Pankhurst: I will ask Mr. Gladstone whether in his opinion he thinks we should be treated as ordinary criminals—searched, stripped, and put into the cells, as though we were drunkards or pickpockets?

The Magistrate: You must not put that question.

This concluded Mr. Gladstone's evidence, and as he and Mr. Lloyd-George were about to leave the court Miss Pankhurst said: May we tender our warm thanks to these two gentlemen who have done us the favour of coming forward as witnesses?

Miss Pankhurst proceeded to quote numerous authorities in support of her contention that the charge should have been one of unlawful assembly, and that the magistrate had no power to bind the defendants over.

Mr. Curtis Bennett said he would give his decision later.

A Succession of Witnesses.

Further evidence was then called.

Colonel Percy H. H. Massy stated that he was in Victoria-street on the evening of October 13, and in his opinion the crowd was perfectly orderly. He saw nobody attacked or injured.

Lady Constance Lytton said she considered the crowd was remarkably well-behaved and respectable.

Miss Annie Moor stated that she had been more roughly treated at society weddings than she was in this crowd. She was in the crowd on the occasion of Mr. Winston Churchill's marriage, and was much more jostled than on the evening of the 13th.

Mr. Henry Wood Nevinson and Dr. Louisa Garrett Anderson both agree that the crowds sympathised with the suffragists, and that there was no disorder.

In cross-examination, Dr. Anderson, after some hesitation, said she approved of the Bill containing the invitation to "rush" the House.

Mrs. May, replying to Mr. Muskett, said she worked as actively as possible for the cause, but she did not speak or organise.

Spiritual Forces.

Miss Sylvia Pankhurst said the suffragists' instructions were to meet physical force with spiritual force.

After the luncheon adjournment several witnesses testified that there was never any intention to make use of violence, and that the demeanour of the crowds which collected was perfectly orderly. It was also frequently stated that the people appeared to sympathise with the women more than they had done upon any previous occasion.

Miss Evelyn Sharp, the well-known writer, said she regarded the bill as an invitation to go to the House of Commons, and not to turn back if possible. Witness herself "doubled," and got past the biggest policeman she ever saw. She was, however, afterwards caught by an inspector, and sent back. It was like a rush at hockey.

Albert Rettick said he looked upon the bill as an invitation to the public to support the women in going to the House, and possibly to see fair play.

Miss Florence Elizabeth Macaulay gave historical instances of women going to the House of Commons for the purpose of presenting petitions.

Miss Pankhurst: It appears that we were within our constitutional rights in going to the House?

Witness: I have been a student of history for many years, and I think you were only reviving an ancient custom.

Mrs. Celia M. McKenzie thought the commonsense of Mr. Asquith would have caused him to receive a deputation of 13 quiet ladies.

Sidney Dillon Shallard, a journalist, said the police made a desert of about a quarter of a mile round the House of Commons.

Miss Pankhurst: They made a desert, and called it peace.

At a quarter-past seven the magistrate asked how many more witnesses there were for the defence.

Miss Pankhurst: About 50. We are sorry to take up the time of the Court, but we are fighting for our liberty.

The hearing was then adjourned until Saturday, the defendants being released on the same bail as before.

Upon the three ladies being brought into Court, on Saturday, October 24, the Magistrate said: I have carefully considered what steps should be taken by me to prevent the conduct of this case being so continued as to become a serious obstacle in the administration of justice at this Court. I may at once state that simple repetition of the same class of evidence given by the last twenty-four witnesses will not affect my judgment, and therefore I must refuse to hear a continuation of that class of evidence. If you wish me to hear any particular person or persons on even the same lines of evidence as that already given I will consent now to hear them, but not more that two or three of such witnesses. If the defendants have evidence of a different nature which they wish me to hear I am quite willing to do so, provided it is limited to what is absolutely relevant to the matter before me, and is admissible in point of law. As this may take you a little by surprise I give you half an hour to consider what further evidence you may desire me to hear.

Miss Pankhurst: Would you kindly give us some definition of what evidence you think admissible?

The magistrate repeated that he was not going to take the same class of evidence as that of the witnesses he had already heard. He was willing to hear witnesses who could speak to a different state of facts, if their evidence was relevant.

Mrs. Pankhurst: Would you say what evidence you consider relevant?

The Magistrate: I cannot say more than I have done.

James Murray, M.P.

The case was then put back for a while. Upon resuming, Miss Pankhurst said the first witness they wished to call was Mr. James Murray, M.P. for East Aberdeen. That gentleman went into the witness-box, and was asked by Miss Pankhurst whether he was present at the Suffragists' meeting in Trafalgar-square on the 11th inst.

Witness: I was going in the National Gallery, and saw a congregation of well-dressed people in the square. I think your mother was speaking but I could not hear anything: What struck me was that the crowd listening to her was composed of exactly the type of men and women who go to Church on Sunday in Scotland.

Miss Pankhurst: Then they must have been very respectable. Did you get a copy of the bill?——No.

I dare say you saw it in the papers?——I saw a statement in the paper.

How did you understand the word "rush"?——I didn't take the matter seriously at all.

The Magistrate: That really is for me, Miss Pankhurst, as I have told you.

Miss Pankhurst: Did you resolve to act on the invitation?——I could not very well, you see, because I was inside the citadel.

The Magistrate: He has the right of entry.

Miss Pankhurst: Were you near Westminster on the 13th——I was in the House, and sitting down to dinner when I got a telegram sent from the neighbourhood of Bow-street from your mother, asking me to come across here.

The Magistrate: This cannot be relevant.

Witness: In coming here I drove in a hansom up Parliament-street. The whole place was like a besieged city, except that we had police-officers instead of soldiers. A little beyond Doyer House the crowd was held back by a cordon, but I had not the slightest difficulty in getting through in a hansom. Afterwards I returned to the House by the Strand and the Embankment, and had very little difficulty in getting back.

Miss Pankhurst: Was it a disorderly crowd?——No; I should think you could say an ordinary London crowd.

Mrs. Pankhurst: Did you come to the conclusion that the persons who had called the meeting desired to incite the crowd to disorder or damage?——No. I thought if it was for any purpose at all it was simply to advertise the cause.

Mrs. Pankhurst: You know something of the women who are conducting this agitation?

Witness: Yes; and I have the highest admiration for them for their earnestness of purpose, ability, and general management of the whole scheme. I don't say I approve of everything they do, but most of it I approve of.

You know they have tried every other political method?——Yes; and if they had been men instead of women they would not have been in the dock now, judging by the past.

Mrs. Pankhurst: Do you agree with Mr. Lloyd George when he said that if the Government would give us what we were asking for this agitation would cease——I have no doubt it would. I go further than Mr. Lloyd George, and say you are entitled to it.

Dr. Miller McGuire

Dr. Miller McGuire stated that he was at the Trafalgar-square meeting, and heard nothing that anyone could object to. He spent most of the 13th looking at the "performance." There was nothing remotely approaching disorder of any kind.

Miss Agnes Murphy, of Hampstead, said the crowd in Victoria-street was the most orderly she had ever seen. She attributed this to the goodwill of the people towards the women, who had been ill-treated and grossly misrepresented in the Press.

The Magistrate: Those are three witnesses on exactly the same lines as the others.

Miss Pankhurst: We shall be delighted to follow other lines, with your permission.

The Magistrate: If you have any witnesses or different lines I will hear them.

Miss Pankhurst: I can call witnesses of different lines, but I don't know that the lines will be admissible. We can call witnesses to show that in taking this course we are taking the only possible course.

The Magistrate: That will not do.

Miss Pankhurst: We can call witnesses to show that we have been incited to this kind of action by our political opponents, the members of the Government.

The Magistrate: No; that you must not.

Miss Pankhurst: We can call witnesses to testify to our good character.

The Magistrate: That has not been raised in issue.

Miss Pankhurst: Then, if you will permit us to call no further evidence, I will proceed to address the Court.

The luncheon adjournment was then taken, and afterwards Miss Pankhurst stated that some fresh witnesses were forthcoming. One lady had travelled 50 miles to give evidence.

The Magistrate: Is it on the same lines?

Miss Pankhurst: I think that will appear when she is in the box.

The Magistrate: No; I will not hear it.

Miss Pankhurst: I have now to ask you to state a special case.

The Magistrate: Not at present.

Miss Pankhurst then applied for an adjournment, in order that she and her companions might be in a position to do themselves full justice when they addressed the Court.

The Magistrate: You have had a long time to take this matter into consideration. I think you must either address me now or not at all.

Miss Pankhurst: I can only do it under protest, and I want to point out that you are rushing this case through the Court. (Laughter.) You are not setting us at all a good example. I want again to insist upon our right to call further witnesses.

The Magistrate: I have decided that point once and for all. Are you going to address me or not?

The three prisoners then delivered their speeches from the dock. These speeches, which roused great feeling in the Court, are reported verbatim [on the following pages].

The Speeches From the Dock
By Christabel Pankhurst, LL.B., Mrs. Pankhurst, and Mrs. Drummond.

Christabel Pankhurst.

In the first place, I want to point out that the proceedings that have been taken against us have been taken out of malice and for vexation. I think I shall have little difficulty in proving this, because of the attitude which the authorities have taken against us from the beginning of the agitation, which has been in progress for the past three years. But before I come to this point, I want to draw your attention, and the attention of the general public—(the Magistrate: Never mind the general public)—*your* attention, sir, to the very serious scandal which has been unearthed in the course of these proceedings. We have had it sworn to in the witness-box that one of the justices, Mr. Horace Smith, has allowed himself to be coerced by the Government, and has settled in conjunction with them whether a certain lady, charged in connection with this agitation, was guilty, before the evidence was heard, and Mr. Horace Smith and the Government had, moreover, decided before-hand what term of imprisonment should be inflicted upon that lady.

Now, this policy of the Government of weighting the scales against us is not of interest only to us, but is of interest to the whole community. In the course of British history we have seen many struggles for the purification of our judicial system. It is within your knowledge, sir, that in days gone by the judges have had many a fight against the King, in order to maintain their independence and to vindicate the purity of their office. It has been left to the twentieth century—it has it has been left to these so-called demo-cratic days—to see our judicial system corrupted for party ends. I am glad that we have been able to perform the public duty and service of doing something to attack this evil while it is in the bud. I am quite sure that if we had not been privileged to unearth this very serious scandal, that the process of corruption would have gone on until a fair trial was absolutely impossible in the case of those charged with political offences. And if injus-tice creeps in in political cases, it would not be long before the same corrup-tion was prevalent in every law court in the land, and in the case of every person brought up under some charge, no matter of what kind.

I think too much attention cannot be paid to the disgraceful action of the Government; the Home Secretary and his colleagues have disgraced and degraded themselves. They have been false to their duty, they have tried to destroy the liberties which it has taken so long to build up. It is worth while standing in this dock if we have been able to do no more than do something to check a state of affairs which is going to reduce this country below the level of any other civilised country if it is not stopped and stamped out now. The Liberal Government have outdone the monarchs of old times in their attempt to corrupt the fountain of British justice; and both they and the magistrate who has allowed himself to be made a tool, who has so far forgotten his duty to us, his duty to the public, his duty to his profession, deserve to be hounded out of civilised society. I know that this action the Government have taken in corrupting the justices will not be forgotten, and will be remembered against them when next they face the verdict of popular opinion.

A Malicious Prosecution.

I shall now proceed with my argument that these proceedings have been taken against us out of malice and in order to lame, in an illegitimate way, a political enemy. Take the form of the summons.[5] We are not openly charged with the offence of illegal assembly. If we have in any way broken the law, we have broken it in that way. The only charge that could possibly be preferred against us is that of illegal assembly. Now, why have the authorities, why have the Government feared to take this course? The reason is that they want to keep us in the police-court. They believe, rightly or wrongly, that by this means they will succeed in prejudicing the public against us. We know perfectly well that up till recently the general public shunned the police-court as a disgraceful place. The fact of having been proceeded against in a police-court was in the eyes of the ordinary man or woman a stain upon the character which could hardly be wiped out in later days. Well, I think that by our presence here we have done something to relieve the police-court of that unenviable reputation. We have done something to raise its status in the public eye, and we have also done something to throw light upon the obsolete procedure, and the unsuitable procedure which obtains in courts like this. But even if the procedure which we find here is suitable for committing "drunks," I am sure every reasonable person will agree that it is no place for the political offender. But political offenders are brought here in order that something may be done to smirch their character, and to prejudice them in the public eye.

Another reason why the authorities have feared to charge us with unlawful assembly is that they dare not see this case come before a jury. They know perfectly well that if this case was heard before a jury of our countrymen we should be acquitted, just as John Burns was acquitted years ago for taking action far more serious, far more dangerous to the public peace than anything that we have done.[6] Yes, I say they are afraid of sending us before a jury, and I am quite sure that this will be obvious to the public, and that the Government will suffer by the underhand, the unworthy, and the disgraceful subterfuge by which they have removed this case to what we can only call a Star Chamber[7] of the twentieth century. Yes, this is a Star Chamber, and it is in order to huddle us into prison without a fair trial that these proceedings have been taken in their present form. I daresay it was not anticipated by the prosecution that this case was ever to be defended. I am quite sure it has come to them as a surprise; they are accustomed to see us disposed of and sent to Holloway Gaol very much as the animals are dealt with in the Chicago stockyards. Prisoners are brought up here and disposed of at the rate of one a minute, or, perhaps, three in two minutes! That sort of thing has been the rule; we are accustomed to that. But those days are gone for ever. We are going to make this time a fight for our liberty. We owe it to ourselves, we owe it to our country that we should not let the disgraceful proceedings of this court go on any longer. Yes, we are deprived of trial by jury. We are also deprived of the right of appeal against the magistrate's decision. Very very carefully has this procedure been thought out; very, very cunningly has it been thought out to hedge us in on every side, and to deprive us of our rights in the matter!

We Will Not be Bound Over.

Then, we are also rendered liable to six months' imprisonment, and yet we are denied the privileges in making our defence that people liable to three months' imprisonment alone enjoy. We shall be told in the House of Commons no doubt—we have been told the same thing before now—that we are only bound over, we need not go to prison, if we go to prison we have only ourselves to thank. Well, if Mr. Herbert Gladstone were in the dock that would be perfectly true. He would be very willing, as a Member of Parliament was only yesterday, to be bound over, to express his repentance, to say he will not repeat the conduct that he has pursued up to now. But we are not prepared to betray our cause; we are not prepared to put ourselves in a false position. If the case is decided against us, if we are called upon to be bound over, it must be remembered that that amounts to imprisoning us, and that therefore the authorities cannot possibly escape their responsibility for sending us to prison by saying that we could be at liberty if we liked.

To sum up what I have just said, Magna Carta has been practically torn up by the present Government. We are liable to a term of so long as six months' imprisonment, and we have had no fair trial. We protest against that with all the force at our disposal. We think it is a disgrace; we think it is a scandal; we think the way in which we have been proceeded against disgraces the Government, and when we add to that the fact that they have attempted—and possibly still attempt—to corrupt justice, and decide the sentences upon us before we come up for trial, when we take these two facts in conjunction, I think you will agree with us that it is not we who ought to be in the dock to-day, but the people who are responsible for such a monstrous state of affairs.

I want now to deal with the reasons for issuing this bill. We do not deny at all that we issued this bill; none of us three here wish to deny responsibility. We did issue the bill; we did cause it to be circulated; we did put upon it the words "Come and help the Suffragettes to rush the House of Commons." For these words we do not apologise; for our action we do not apologise. We had good reason for taking it, and what is more, at the first opportunity—on the first occasion when we think it desirable—we shall do it again!

Why We Issued the Bill.

Now, it is very well known that we take this action in order to press forward a claim, which, according to the British Constitution we are well entitled to make. After all, we are seeking only to enforce the observance of the law of the land. The law of the land is that taxation and representation must go together. The law of the land is that who obeys laws must have a share in making them. Therefore, when we claim the Parliamentary vote, we are asking the Government to abandon the illegal practice of denying representation to those who have a perfect right to enjoy it. For 40 years women have claimed that the law should be obeyed; for 40 years Governments have been called upon to cease from unconstitutional action, and to carry out the law of the land—to obey Magna Carta. Our agitation's peacefully conducted, our petitions, our public meetings have been disregarded. Now we have in power a Liberal Government professing to believe in that principle, I say, but refusing to carry it into practice. We have appealed to them, we have called upon them for justice, we have demanded of them that they do what we ask them—without the smallest success. We have a Prime Minister who will not even receive a deputation. Time after time have we wended our way to the House of Commons with a view to asking him to see us. Sometimes—generally—we have not called upon the general public to be with us at all, we have not asked them to come in their thousands to give us their support, we have gone alone; but that has made absolutely no difference to the case. We might go 3, we might go 6, we might go 13, we might go 60,000 strong, but the result is the same. We are sometimes escorted to the House of Commons, but we are arrested if we insist upon our right to enter. Well, what has happened? We have been arrested, and we have been imprisoned without trial—for I will not dignify these proceedings in the police-court with the name of trial—we have been imprisoned without trial. Sometimes the police have arrested us on our emerging from the Caxton Hall, sometimes they have escorted us to the door of the House of Commons, and there we have been arrested. The result has always been the same. We have been deprived of our constitutional right to see the Prime Minister, and we have been arrested for attempting to do so.

A Constitutional Right.

Now, I want here to insist upon the action which we have taken in these proceedings. We have a perfectly constitutional right to go ourselves in person to lay our grievances before the House of Commons, and as one witness—an expert student of history—pointed out to you, we are but pursuing a legitimate course which in the old days women pursued without the smallest interference by the authorities. Now, the principal point we had in view in issuing the handbill for the 13th of October was to call upon the House of Commons to carry into law a Bill, the second reading of which has already been carried. We have met with many refusals already to carry that Bill, and therefore we thought it necessary to make some demonstration of popular support. The Prime Minister has challenged us to do it. We gathered together in Hyde Park on June 21 an immense, a vast audience, but that meeting in Hyde Park was absolutely ignored. It remained for us then to summon our friends to meet us nearer the House of Commons itself. We did this on June 30. No proceedings were taken against us. No harm was done then, as no harm was done on October 13. We were allowed to do without opposition in June what we are punished for doing—or, at least, prosecuted for doing—on October 13. Well, this handbill we felt to be necessary in order to put the final pressure upon the Government, with a view to getting the measure carried this Session. The time now remaining is short; a firm stand we felt must be taken. The time of the House is being occupied by matters far less important than that which we have on hand. Juvenile smoking, the Education Bill—which nobody is eager upon—the Licensing Bill, which the Government hardly expect to carry. With these matters the time of the House is being wasted, while a far greater measure awaits their consideration. We felt we must bring pressure to bear upon the Government with a view to getting the Bill carried, but before we took the action of which the prosecution complain, we desired to make our position clear, and we therefore wrote to the Prime Minister as follows:

> I am instructed by the Committee of the National Women's Social and Political Union to write you as to the Intentions of His Majesty's Government with regard to the measure introduced by Mr. Stanger, M.P., which passed second reading by a large majority.
>
> At many very large demonstrations, held all over the country, resolutions have been carried with practical unanimity, calling upon the Government to adopt this Bill, and pass it into law this year. At a succession of by-elections the voters have shown unmistakably their desire that the Government should deal with the question without further delay.
>
> We shall esteem it a favour if you will inform us whether it is the intention of the Government to carry the Women's Enfranchisement Bill during the Autumn Session of Parliament.

To that letter we had an unfavourable reply, and it was in consequence of the unfavourable nature of that reply that the arrangements for October 13 were proceeded with. In consequence of the unsatisfactory attitude of the Government, our plans went forward, and I would remind you that in making these arrangements we were but acting literally upon the advice given by John Bright in 1867. I do not know how it was that John Bright escaped being prosecuted by the Government of his day for inciting the public to the commission of an unlawful act, for he called upon the people of London, called upon the men who wanted votes, if they hoped to succeed, to gather in their thousands in the space which extends from Trafalgar-square to the Houses of Parliament. I cannot imagine why, if this Government think it necessary to proceed against us, that an earlier Government should not have done the same thing. I can only suppose that the Government of that day had more sense of proportion, more sense of their own duty, were less panic-stricken, and more courteous, and more disposed to do their duty to the public, because in view of such words as John Bright used (with the possibility that the action he counselled would be taken), they resolved to give the men of this country their political rights, and the Reform Bill of 1867 was carried into law. In passing, I would suggest that to take such a course as that in regard to our movement would be more creditable to the Government than the course of instituting legal proceedings against us.

The Word "Rush."

Now, I want to deal with the meaning of the word "rush." You have stated, sir, that the meaning of this word is a matter of law, but you have been good enough to allow us to ask a large number of witnesses the meaning of the word "rush," and all these witnesses have told us that, according to the British interpretation of the word "rush," no violence was counselled. Now, the word "rush" appears to be very much the rage just now. Nobody can get away from its use. We find that at a meeting of the League for the Preservation of Swiss Scenery Mr. Richard Whiteing, discussing the question of Swiss railways, said they ought not to be too hard on railways. Under certain atmospheric conditions a railway was the most beautiful thing in the world. He made other remarks about railways, and then he proceeded to suggest that a general rush to the Italian Alps might induce the Swiss to listen to reason. Well, I do not think that anyone here would suggest that Mr. Whiteing meant to offer any violence to the Swiss in his use of the word "rush." He meant to imply that a speedy advance should be made to the Italian Alps. Then we have Mr. McKinnon Wood counselling the electors to rush the County Council, and get a lady elected to that body. I want to submit that "rush" as a transitive verb cannot mean "attack," "assail," "make a raid upon," or anything of that kind. The "Century Dictionary," which is the largest and most authoritative completed dictionary of the English language, gives numerous instances, all of which imply "hurry" or "hasten," it may be to unduly hurry—although, of course, we have waited so long that undue haste is not to be wondered at. "To unduly hurry" or "hasten," but never "to assail." Now, I have in my hand a little leaflet, which someone has been good enough to send to me. It is used in America, and it is put upon parcels which are expected to reach their destination in good time; when a parcel is wanted to be sent by an express train, they put this label, "Rush by first train leaving." Well, as our witnesses have one and all testified, the interpretation they placed upon the word "rush" was that they should make haste. We have heard various meanings attributed to the word "rush" by dictionaries. "Rush" equals "an eager demand"; "urgent pressure" (as of business); a "rusher" is "a go-ahead person"—so says Chambers' English Dictionary. "Rush" means "an eager demand"—this we find in Ogilvie's Imperial Dictionary. "Rush" means "to go forward over-hastily"; for example, a number of Bills are rushed through Parliament—or a case is rushed through a law court. Then we have "on the rush," meaning "in a hurry." "In modern colloquial language," says Farmer and Henley's Dictionary of Slang, "rush" enters largely. As a substantive, it means "extreme urgency of affairs," "an eager demand"; as a verb, it means "to hurry," "to force," or "to advance a matter with undue haste." "On the rush," or "with a rush," means "with spirit," "energetically." "On the rush" means "on the run," "hard at it." One witness told us that, in her opinion, the word "rush," used as we have used it, might be compared with the word "dash," as we have it used in the expression, "a dash for the Pole." Everybody knows that you cannot get to the Pole in a hurry, but you can try to get there in a hurry, and that is what "a dash to the Pole" means. Everybody knows that with a timid Government like the present one in power, having at its service the entire Metropolitan Police force, if one woman says she is going to rush the House of Commons, there will be an immense number of police to prevent her from doing it. Nobody, then, having regard to the facts I have mentioned, thought the women would rush the House of Commons, but that they would be there—it may be there with their supporters—to show their indignation against the Government, and I am glad to say that they were there. It may mean six months' imprisonment, but I think it is worth it.

Now, if we had used the expression "*storm* the House of Commons," I could understand that a little fear would creep into the heart of Mr. Herbert Gladstone, because we know he is a rather timid person. It was all very well for him to say in the witness-box that he knows no fear, but the facts are against him. I know perfectly well that when we are in any physical danger, as we sometimes are at meetings, owing to the kind and considerate remarks of Cabinet Ministers, no such elaborate police precautions are taken for our protection as are taken for the House of Commons in general, and Cabinet Ministers in particular, when there is thought to be any demonstration contemplated.

An Illegal Act?

Now, the next question I want to raise is this: Is it, as a matter of fact, an illegal thing to rush the House of Commons? The only woman who has

done it has gone scot free. Mrs. Travers Symons rushed the House of Commons. She got in by strategy. She eluded the police, she got in, and she
rushed the House of Commons. Nobody seems to mind her having done it
at all; no proceedings have been taken against her. There she is! We who
have not rushed the House of Commons are in the dock! Is her action
illegal? She did it as the consequence of words that we had written and
spoken—she is the only person who has actually succeeded in carrying out
the mandate we are considered to have given to the public. She is the only
person who has rushed the House of Commons, and yet she is not supposed
to have broken the law of the land. Still, if she who has done it, is not to
be punished, it is an extraordinary thing that we, who have not done it, are
liable to imprisonment at the present moment.

We can take another instance of someone who not only "rushed" the
House of Commons, but stormed the House of Commons, and sent the
members of the House of Commons flying in all directions. We have the
case of Cromwell. I am not aware that he was ever made the subject of legal
proceedings. It may be that by seeking to enter the House of Commons we
have infringed the Speaker's regulations, but we have certainly not infringed
the law of the land. We are told in our summons that it is not only illegal,
but it is both wrongful and illegal. Well, you may say it is wrongful according
to some moral law. We do not. It is rightful according to every law. But we
want to know how it can be said that it is an illegal act. We are anxious to
know by what statute it is illegal to go to the House of Commons, walk up
the steps, and make our way to the strangers' entrance? We should like to
know whether that is an illegal thing to do, and, if it is not illegal to go at
a slow pace, we should like to whether it is illegal to go at a quick pace,
because that is what the word "rush" means. To "rush the House of Commons" is to go with all possible speed inside the House of Commons, and
I hope that we shall be told what statute we have contravened by doing it
ourselves, or sending anybody to do it, or inviting others to do it.

Now, the prosecution have drawn attention to the speeches made in
Trafalgar-square on October 11. We do not in any way object to their doing
this. I do not think what we have said there is strictly relevant, but I am
glad they have raised this point, because it is all in our favour. We have
called a number of witnesses, who have told us that they heard the speeches
on that occasion, that they heard us interpreting the bill, because the
speeches made there were made in interpretation of the famous bill. They
have heard our speeches, and have one and all said that there was nothing
inflammatory in those speeches, that there was no incitement to violence
whatever. I am quite content to abide by the story of the other side in regard
to this matter. The witnesses called by the prosecution all say that we used
the following words, and I am sure no rational person can find in these
words anything which incites to violence, and if the meaning of the word

"rush" is to be drawn from these speeches, then it will be a monstrous miscarriage of justice if we are sentenced to imprisonment. Here are the words spoken by Mrs. Pankhurst:

On Tuesday evening, at Caxton Hall, we shall ask those who support women to come to Parliament Square. There will be a deputation of women who have no right in the House of Commons to a seat there, such as men have. The Government does not know its own mind, it changes so. But we do know that we want the vote, and mean to have it.

Then we have my own remarks:

I wish you all to be there on the evening of the 13th, and I hope that that will be the end of this movement. On June 30 we succeeded in driving Mr. Asquith underground. He is afraid of us, and so are the Government. Years ago John Bright told the people that it was only by lining the streets from Charing Cross to Westminster that they could impress the Government. Well, we are only taking a leaf out of his book. We want you to help the women to rush their way into the House of Commons. You won't get locked up, because you have the vote. If you are afraid, we will take the lead, and you will follow us. We are not afraid of imprisonment. We know we shall win because we are in the right.

There are the very dreadful words uttered on the platform that day; but what is even more important, because it comes direct from the pen of Mrs. Pankhurst, and ought to be listened to and taken into account far more than anything that we are reported to have said, are these words, written by Mrs. Pankhurst as an order to our members and to the general public:

On the 13th, in Parliament Square, there will be many thousands of people to see fair play between the women and the Government. Let us keep their support and co-operation by showing them, as we have done before, with what quiet courage, self-restraint, and determination women are fighting against tyranny and oppression on the part of a Government which has been called the strongest of modern times. It is by the exercise of courage and self-restraint and persistent effort that we shall win in this unequal contest.

Now, returning to the question of the Trafalgar-square meeting, we have been able to get evidence from a Cabinet Minister, and he tells us that he heard nothing of an inflammatory nature in Trafalgar-square. He did not hear us counsel people to do violence, he did not hear us counsel the people to do harm, he did not hear us say that we ourselves should do anything violent; in fact, if the matter were to rest upon words that he has spoken, it would certainly appear to everybody that we have said nothing to the public which could be taken as inciting them to do anything violent or illegal. We are quite prepared to take our stand upon what Mr. Lloyd George said of the words we spoke in Trafalgar-square.

The Events of the 13th.

Now, let us come to the events of the 13th of October. The prosecution suggested—it was in some way raised by them—that Mrs. Pethick Lawrence, the chairman of the Caxton Hall meeting, had counselled violence to the women who were going forth into the streets to seek an interview with the Prime Minister. Well, we were able to call a great deal of evidence to show that that was an absolute fabrication. Mrs. Pethick Lawrence did not counsel the use of force; she urged the women to meet physical force with spiritual force; to show determination, and to make their way forward so far as they could, and not to be deterred lightly from entering the House; but as for the use of force directed against the police, directed against property, directed against Members of Parliament or Cabinet Ministers, she deprecated the use of such force, and discountenanced it. So that we have been able to clear ourselves of any suggestion that wild or inflammatory language was spoken in the Caxton Hall on the 13th.

An Orderly Crowd.

Now, as to what happened outside on the 13th. We have heard over and over again that this was the most orderly crowd that has ever been known within the memory of living people to assemble in the streets of London. Mr. Lloyd George thought so little of its dangers that he actually brought with him his young daughter of six years. It is all very well for him to say that he relied upon the police arrangements. It is obvious to any intelligent person that 6,000 police are no match for 60,000 people if they really desired to force a way through the police lines. If there had been a violent spirit in that crowd, the police would have been as nothing, they would not have been able to restrain the crowd, and Mr. Lloyd George and his daughter, and even the police line would have been brushed aside, had the people been incited by us to do any violence. As a matter of fact, they knew what we wanted them to do, and they did it, and the fact that this child was brought into the crowd by her father shows that there was no apprehension in anybody's mind of any harm being done. But it is not because of anything serious that occurred on that night, or was expected to occur, that we are here; we are here in order that we may be kept out of the way for some months, and may cease from troubling the Government for as long a period as they can find it in them, or for which the public will allow them, to deprive us of our liberty.

We have had Mr. Herbert Gladstone telling us that he was not afraid on that night. Well, if there had been any danger, he would have been afraid. It was because he knew perfectly well that that public had no hostile intention, and that we had not hostile intention, that he ventured to come into the streets. If there had been a riot, if there had been a violent mob, he would have kept very carefully in the House of Commons, and it is perfectly absurd to argue that he thought the crowd was a disorderly one.

While we can show from our evidence that this was an orderly crowd, what have we got on the other side? We have two police officers. That has been the only evidence that has been brought against us. I think it is a monstrous thing if the evidence of two police officers, however reliable, however worthy they may be, is to be believed against the host of witnesses that we have already called, and the large number of witnesses that we could have called to say the same thing. It seems to me that there is no justice in this court if the word of the police is to be believed against the public. I want to call your attention to the fact that the prosecution have been unable to bring forward any impartial person to say that the events of the 13th were a danger to the public streets. This state of affairs must end. It is in the public interest that it should. It is not right that police evidence should be the only evidence upon which we are to be judged. It seems to me that the prosecution, the witnesses, the authorities, the magistrates, are all on one side, they are all in the same box, and the prisoner charged with an offence is absolutely helpless whatever facts he may bring forward. Those facts are set aside. It is indeed a waste of time to bring forward evidence in a police-court. Over the doors of this court ought to be the motto: "Abandon hope all ye who enter here." We do not care for ourselves, because imprisonment is nothing to us; but when we think of the thousands of helpless creatures who come into this monstrous place, and know perfectly well that they are found guilty before they have a chance of defending themselves, it is almost too terrible to think of the horrible injustice that is done day after day in these courts. Nobody to help them, nobody to plead for them. But I am thankful to think that we have been able, by submitting ourselves to the absurd proceedings that are conducted here, to ventilate this fearful wrong.

Well, I say that the crowd was orderly, and nobody could compare it with other crowds. The Eucharistic Procession drew together a far more disorderly crowd than that which we assembled, and yet, who has been proceeded against for that? Nobody has. Somebody ought to be in the dock, because they brought together a crowd which might possibly have led to riot and bloodshed. As for the Protestants who threatened that if they did not get their own way there would be bloodshed, no proceedings have been taken against them. Why are they not bound over? How anybody can say that we are treated with fair play I do not know. These things will be written up against the Government in the time to come.

Take the crowd which assembled for the C.I.V.'s and the crowd which assembled on Mafeking night[8]—we all know, and our witnesses have said, that there was a disorderly crowd, yet nobody was proceeded against. Why, even at the Churchill wedding[9] the crowd was far more violent than that of the 13th. The crowds that try to get in and hear a popular preacher are more disorderly than the crowd which came to support us on the 13th. Of the Jubilee[10] procession the same thing has been said. The crowds at Lord Mayors' Shows, too, are more disorderly, while at a meeting in Trafalgar-square some years ago blood shed was narrowly averted, and yet the man who was responsible for it was acquitted by his countrymen.

Now, the prosecution have said that owing to the crowd brought together by us on the 13th 40 watches and purses were stolen. Are we to take the responsibility for that? Are we to be responsible for the stealing of 40 watches and purses? Why, I daresay, 60 watches are stolen when the King goes to open Parliament!

There is not a single arrest which is traceable to the issue of our bill. Are we to understand that, once arrested, you are deemed guilty before you are tried? We know that in the higher courts the assumption is that a prisoner is innocent before he is proved to be guilty, but in this Court the assumption is that the prisoner is guilty before he is tried, and it is only in ninety-nine cases out of a hundred that he has a chance of getting off. People would have been there whether there had been a bill or not. Members of our Union would have been there whether there had been a crowd or not. The arrests have nothing to do with our action on the 13th, and therefore we deny absolutely the statement that because we issued that bill arrests were made. We are not responsible for pickpockets, they may be arrested whether we have a bill or not; we are not responsible for "drunks," and we are not responsible for the unemployed; we are responsible for ourselves, and as for the deputation, they were arrested not because we had issued a bill, but because they wanted to see the Prime Minister.

It is very interesting to notice what very elaborate police arrangements were made on the 12th. It just shows that members of the Government are afraid of their own shadow. I am glad they are reduced to this state of panic, because we shall get justice out of them. At present they are in fear lest they be a little inconvenienced, lest they be unable to get home and back again because of the crowds round the House of Commons.

Following the Advice of Statesmen.

Now I come to another point—that in taking the course we are taking we have been encouraged by statesmen, and especially by Liberal statesmen.

The whole of our liberties have been won by action such as ours, only of a far more violent kind. We have not broken the law, though we have offended certain persons who seem to think they can do injustice and escape with impunity. They seem to think they can have their cake and eat it. Well, we are prepared to show them that they cannot.

Therefore, we repudiate the charge that we are law-breakers. Still, we are prepared to say that even if we were law-breakers, we should be justified in being so. Magna Carta itself was won by a threat of a breach of the peace. Hampden, whom we all honour now, was a law-breaker. Charles I., because he did not rule in a manner acceptable to his subjects—just as Mr. Asquith is not ruling today in a manner acceptable to us—was beheaded. Revolution after revolution has marked the progress of our country. The Reform Bills were got by disorder. We are told that, prior to 1832, the Mansion House, the Custom House, the Bishop's Palace, the Excise Office, three prisons, four toll-houses, and 42 private dwellings and warehouses were burnt. There was a general rebellion, but as a consequence the Reform Bill of 1832 was won. Then we have the Reform Bill of 1867. That was won in consequence of the breaking down of the Hyde Park railings. In 1884 we had the Aston Park riots. They made it impossible for the legislators or any section of them to withstand the enfranchisement of the agricultural labourers.

I think I have already quoted the example set us by John Bright. Although he got off scot-free, we are now liable to a long term of imprisonment. Then there were the Fenian outrages, the killing of a policeman in Manchester, and the blowing up of Clerkenwell Gaol.

Mr. Gladstone himself said:

The whole question of the Irish Church was dead; nobody cared for it, nobody paid attention to it in England. Circumstances occurred which drew the attention of people to the Irish Church. When it came to this that a great gaol in the heart of the metropolis was broken open under circumstances which drew the attention of English people to the state of Ireland, and when a Manchester policeman was murdered in the exercise of his duty, at once the whole country became alive to Irish questions, and the questions of the Irish Church revived.

And in a subsequent explanation he said:

When at an election you say that a question is out of the range of practical politics you mean it is not a question likely to be dealt with in the Parliament you are now choosing. That is the meaning of it. It was said, and truly said, that in the year 1867 there happened certain crimes in England—that is to say, a policeman was murdered in circumstances of riot and great excitement at Manchester; the wall of Clerkenwell Prison was blown down in a very alarming manner—in consequence of which, it was said, I changed my mind about the Irish Church.

To explain how the matters referred to had had the effect of drawing the attention of the people of this country to the Irish question, he says that agitation of this kind is like the ringing of the church bell; it reminds those who were forgetting to go to church, that it is time they were up and doing, to perform their religious duty.

Then there was Chamberlain threatening to march one hundred thousand men on London. Now, what difference is there between his action and ours, except that his action was far more likely to lead to law-breaking than any action we have taken. He proposed to bring a mob to storm the House of Commons. Was he prosecuted? No! The Gladstone of those days was a less absurd and hesitating and cowardly and peaceful person than the Gladstone of this time and the colleagues of the present Gladstone, and therefore Mr. Gladstone took the statesmanlike action of pressing forward the Reform Bill instead of taking proceedings against Mr. Chamberlain. And so Mr. Chamberlain was not legally proceeded against, and when a vote of censure was moved in the House of Commons, even that was defeated. On that occasion Mr. Gladstone said that if no instructions had been issued to the people of this country in political crises save only to remember to hate violence and love order and exercise patience, the liberties of this country would never have been attained.

Then there was Lord Randolph Churchill, who spoke words which were literally disgraceful for a public man addressing those who were voters. He counselled the voters—and, mind you, those who have votes have not the excuse for violence that those who have not got votes have—he counselled the voters to resort to the supreme arbitrament of force. He said, "Ulster will fight, and Ulster will be right," and as a consequence of what he said, dangerous riots, increasing in fury until they almost amounted to warfare, occurred in the streets, firearms were freely used by the police and by the combatants. Houses were sacked, and men and women were killed. So savage, repeated, and prolonged were the disturbances, breaking out again and again in spite of all efforts to suppress them, that they became in the end the subject of a Parliamentary Commission. But the author of these riots was not made the victim of prosecution. He was not placed in the dock; he was not proceeded against. What a monstrous thing it is that we who have led to no trouble, who have not caused the loss of a single life, who have not caused damage to property, who have not done any harm at all, we should be imprisoned, or threatened with imprisonment, while a man who spoke those words, who counselled action which resulted in the death of his fellow countrymen, should be allowed to escape without even a vote of censure! If the Government had been as vindictive as the present one, penal servitude for life would have been the fate of Lord Randolph Churchill because of his encouragement to murderous attacks. He certainly was deserving of some punishment. But we, who have broken no law, or urged others to do so, we are threatened with this long term of imprisonment.

Then there was John Burns, who was far, far more violent; who was absolutely unrestrained in his language, which was utterly irresponsible— this man was brought up at the Old Bailey, and acquitted. If we were at the Old Bailey, I feel sure we should be acquitted; that is why we are not allowed to go there. He said in his speech that he was a rebel, because he was an outlaw. Well, that fact will support us in all that we have done. If we go to far greater lengths than we have done yet, we shall only be following in the footsteps of a man who is now a member of the Government.

We have been told by Mr. Haldane[11] that we were entitled to fight the Government, but were fighting them with pin-pricks. Why not use weapons? We do not want to use weapons, even though we are taunted in this way with our restraint. They know that if we have a fault, it is that we are too gentle—not formidable enough. How, then, can anybody contest my statement that we have been incited to real violence, which we have not yet committed.

Mr. Herbert Gladstone himself, though in the witness-box he denied that he counselled our action, yet in a speech which I read to him, told us that the victory of argument alone is not enough. As we cannot hope to win by the force of argument alone, it is necessary to overcome the savage resistance of the Government to our claim for citizenship by other means. He says: "Go on. Fight like the men did." And then, when we show our power and get the people to help us, he comes forward in a manner which would be disgraceful even in the old days of coercion, in a manner which would be thought disgraceful if it was practised in Russia.

Then there is Mr. Lloyd George, who, if any man has done so, has set us an example. His whole career has been a series of revolt. Even as a child he counselled the breaking of school regulations. Then he incited the Welsh Councils to disobey the law. He has authorised the illegal and lawless action of the Passive Resisters, and even to us he has given counsel that we should break the law. He has said that if we do not get the vote—mark those words—we should be justified in adopting the methods which men had to adopt, namely, in pulling down the Hyde Park railings.

Then, as a sign of the way in which men politicians deal with men's interests, we have Lord Morley[12] saying: "We are in India in the presence of a living movement, and a movement for what? For objects which we ourselves have taught them to think are desirable objects, and unless we can somehow reconcile order with satisfaction of those ideas and aspirations, the fault will not be theirs; it will be ours; it will mark the breakdown of British statesmanship."

Apply those words to our case. Remember that we are demanding of Liberal statesmen that which for us is the greatest boon and the most essential right. Remember that we are asking for votes, that we are demanding the franchise, and if the present Government cannot reconcile order with our demand for the vote without delay, it will mark the breakdown of their statesmanship. Yes, their statesmanship has broken down already. They are disgraced. It is only in this Court that they have the smallest hope of getting bolstered up. It is only by keeping us from the judgment of our countrymen that they can expect to be supported in the action that they are taking.

We Make No Apology.

Whatever be the result of the proceedings to-day, we know that by public opinion we shall be acquitted, and I do not want you, sir, to suppose that in all I have said I have wished to make any apology. Far from it. We are here to-day to say that if you call upon us to be bound over we shall go to prison, because our honour forbids us to do anything else, and if we go to prison, when we come out, we shall be ready to issue another bill calling upon the public to compel the House of Commons and compel the Government to do us justice.

Mrs. Pankhurst's Speech

Sir, I want to endorse what my daughter has said, that in my opinion we are proceeded against in this Court by malice on the part of the Government. I want to protest as strongly as she has done. I want to put before you that the very nature of your duties in this Court—although I wish to say nothing disrespectful to you—make you perhaps unfitted to deal with a question which is a political question, as a body of jurymen could do. We are not women who would come into this Court as ordinary law-breakers, and we feel that it is a great indignity—as have felt all the other women who have come into this Court—that for political offenses we should come into the ordinary police-court. We do not object to that if from that degradation we shall ultimately succeed in winning political reform for the women of this country.

Mrs. Drummond here is a woman of very great public spirit; she is an admirable wife and mother; she has very great business ability, and she has maintained herself, although a married woman, for many years, and has acquired for herself the admiration and respect of all the people with whom she has had business relations. I do not think I need speak about my daughter. Her abilities and earnestness of purpose are very well known to you. They are young women. I am not, sir. You and I are older, and have had very great and very wide experience of life under different conditions. Before you decide what is to be done with us, I should like you to hear from me a statement of what has brought me into this dock this morning.

Why I am in this Dock.

I was brought up by a father who taught me that it was the duty of his children, boys and girls alike, to realise that they had a duty towards their country; they had to be good citizens. I married a man, whose wife I was but also his comrade in all his public life. He was, as you know, a distinguished member of your own profession, but he felt it his duty, in addition, to do political work, to interest himself in the welfare of his fellow countrymen and countrywomen. Throughout the whole of my marriage I was associated with him in his public work. In addition to that, as soon as my children were of an age to permit me to leave them, I took to public duties. I was for many years a Guardian of the Poor. For many years I was a member of the School Board, and when that was abolished I was elected onto the Education Committee. My experience in doing that work brought me in contact with many of my own sex, who in my opinion found themselves in deplorable positions because of the state of the English law as it affects women. You in this Court must have had experience of women who would never have come here if married women were afforded by law that claim for maintenance by their husbands which I think in justice should be given to them when they give up their economic independence and are unable to earn a subsistence for themselves. You know how inadequate are the marriage laws to women. You must know, sir, as I have found out in my experience of public life, how abominable, atrocious, and unjust are the divorce laws as they affect women. You know very well that the married woman has no legal right of guardianship of her children. Then, too, the illegitimacy laws; you know that a woman sometimes commits the dreadful crime of infanticide, while her partner, the man who should share her punishment, gets off scot-free. I am afraid that great suffering is inflicted upon women because of these laws, and because of the impossibility that women have of getting legal redress. Because of these things I have tried, with other women, to get some reform of these laws. Women have petitioned members of Parliament, have tried for many, many years to persuade them to do something to alter these laws, to make them more equal, for they believe, as I do that in the interests of men quite as much as of women it would be a good thing if laws were more equal between both sexes. I believe it would be better for men. I have a son myself, and I sometimes dread to think that my young son may be influenced in his behaviour to the other sex by the encouragement which the law of the land gives to men when they are tempted to take to an immoral life. I have seen, too, that men are encouraged by law to take advantage of the helplessness of women. Many women have thought as I have, and for many, many years women have tried by that influence we have so often been reminded of, to alter these laws, but we have found for many years that that influence counts for nothing. When we went to the House of Commons we used to be told, when we were persistent, that Members of Parliament were not responsible to women, they were responsible only to voters, and that their time was too fully occupied to reform those laws, although they agreed that they needed reforming.

I Have Tried Constitutional Methods.

Ever since my girlhood, a period of about 30 years, I have belonged to organisations to secure for women that political power which I have felt was essential to bringing about those reforms which women need. I have tried constitutional methods. I have been womanly. When you spoke to some of my colleagues the day before yesterday about their being unwomanly, I felt that bitterness which I know every one of them felt in their hearts. We have tried to be womanly, we have tried to use feminine influence, and we have seen that it is of no use. Men who have been impatient have invariably got reforms for their impatience. And they have not our excuse for being impatient.

You had before you in this court yesterday a man who has a vote, a man who had been addressing other men with votes, and he advised action which we would never dream of advising. But I want to say here and now, as a woman who has worked in the way you advised, that I wonder whether this womanly way is not a weakness that has been taken advantage of. I believe that Mr. Will Thorne was right when he said that no action would have been taken against him, if his name had not been mentioned in this court, because it is a very remarkable thing that the authorities are only proceeding against him when goaded to it by the observations which women made here.

Now, while I share in the feeling of indignation which has been expressed to you by my daughter, I have lived longer in the world than she has. Perhaps I can look round the whole question better than she can, but I want to say here, deliberately, to you, that we are here to-day because we are driven here. We have taken this action, because as women—and I want to you to understand it is as women we have taken this action—it is because we realise that the condition of our sex is so deplorable that it is our duty even to break the law in order to call attention to the reasons why we do so.

I do not want to say anything which may seem disrespectful to you, or in any way give you offence, but I do want to say that I wish, sir, that you could put yourself into the place of women for a moment before you decide upon this case. My daughter referred to the way in which women are hud-dled into and out of these police-courts without a fair trial. I want you to realise what a poor hunted creature, without the advantages we have had, must feel.

I have been in prison. I was in Holloway Gaol for five weeks. I was in various parts of the prison. I was in the hospital, and in the ordinary part of the prison, and I tell you, sir, with as much sense of responsibility as if I had taken the oath, that there were women there who have broken no law, who are there because they have been able to make no adequate statement.

You know that women have tried to do something to come to the aid of their own sex. Women are brought up for certain crimes, crimes which men do not understand—I am thinking especially of infanticide—they are brought before a man judge, before a jury of men, who are called upon to decide whether some poor, hunted woman is guilty of murder or not. I put it to you, sir, when we see in the papers, as we often do, a case similar to that of Daisy Lord, for whom a great petition was got up in this country, I want you to realise how we women feel, because we are women, because we are not men, we need some legitimate influence to bear upon our law-makers.

Now, we have tried every way. We have presented larger petitions than were ever presented for any other reform, we have succeeded in holding greater public meetings than men have ever had for any reform, in spite of the difficulty which women have in throwing off their natural diffidence, that desire to escape publicity which we have inherited from generations of our foremothers; we have broken through that. We have faced hostile mobs at street corners, because we were told that we could not have that representation for our taxes which men have won unless we converted the whole of the country to our side. Because we have done this, we have been misrepresented, we have been ridiculed, we have had contempt poured upon us. The ignorant mob at the street corner has been incited to offer us violence, which we have faced unarmed and unprotected by the safeguards which Cabinet Ministers have. We know that we need the protection of the vote even more than men have needed it.

I am here to take upon myself now, sir, as I wish the prosecution had put upon me, the full responsibility for this agitation in its present phase. I want to address you as a woman who has performed the duties of a woman, and, in addition, has performed the duties which ordinary men have had to perform, by earning a living for her children, and educating them. In addition to that, I have been a public officer. I enjoyed for 10 years an official post under the Registrar, and I performed those duties to the satisfaction of the head of the department. After my duty of taking the census was over, I was one of the few Registrars who qualified for a special bonus, and was specially praised for the way in which the work was conducted. Well, sir, I stand before you, having resigned that office when I was told that I must either do that or give up working for this movement. I want to make you realise that it is a point of honour that if you decide—as I hope you will not decide—to bind us over, that we shall not sign any undertaking, as the Member of Parliament did who was before you yesterday. Perhaps his reason for signing that undertaking may have been that the Prime Minister had given some assurance to the people he claimed to represent that something should be done for them. We have no such assurance. Mr. Birrell[13] told the women who questioned him the other day that he could not say that anything would be done to give an assurance to the women that their claims should be conceded. So, sir, if you decide against us to-day, to prison we must go, because we feel that we should be going back to the hopeless condition this movement was in three years ago if we consented to be bound over to keep the peace which we have never broken, and so, sir, if you decide to bind us over, whether it is for three or six months, we shall submit to the treatment, the degrading treatment, that we have submitted to before.

Although the Government admitted that we are political offenders, and therefore, ought to be treated as political offenders are invariably treated, we shall be treated as pickpockets and drunkards; we shall be searched. I want you, if you can, as a man, to realise what it means to women like us. We are driven to do this, we are determined to go on with this agitation, because we feel in honour bound. Just as it was the duty of your forefathers, it is our duty to make this world a better place for women than it is to-day.

I was in the hospital at Holloway, and when I was there I heard from one of the beds near me the moans of a woman who was in the pangs of child-birth. I should like you to realise how women feel at helpless little infants breathing their first breath in the atmosphere of a prison. We believe that if we get the vote we will find some more humane way of dealing with women than that. It turned out that that woman was a remand prisoner. She was not guilty, because she was finally acquitted.

We believe that if we get the vote it will mean better conditions for our unfortunate sisters. We know what the condition of the woman worker is. Her condition is very bad. Many women pass through this Court who I believe would not come before you if they were able to live morally and honestly. The average earnings of the women who earn their living in this country are only 7s. 7d. a week. There are women who have been driven to live an immoral life because they cannot earn enough to live decently.

We believe your work would be lightened if we got the vote. Some of us have worked, as I have told you, for many years to help our own sex, and we have been driven to the conclusion that only through legislation can any improvement be effected, and that that legislation can never be effected until we have the same power as men have to bring pressure to bear upon our representatives and upon Governments to give us the necessary legislation.

Now, sir, I do want to say this, that we have not wished to waste your time in any way; we have wished to make you realise that there is another side of the case than that put before you by the prosecution. We want you to use your power—I do not know what value there is in the legal claims that have been put before you as to your power to decide this case—but we want you, sir, if you will, to send us to trial in some place more suitable for the trial of political offenders than an ordinary police court. I do not know what you will do; I do not know what your powers are; but I do think, speaking as a woman to a man, I do say deliberately to you—I think your experience has been a large one—I come here not as an ordinary law-breaker. I should never be here if I had the same kind of laws that the very meanest and commonest of men have—the same power that the wife-beater has, the same power that the drunkard has. I should never be here if I had that power, and I speak for all the women who have come before you and the other magistrates.

This is the only way we can get that power which every citizen should have of deciding how the taxes she contributes to should be spent, and how the laws she has to obey should be made, and until we get that power we shall be here—we are here to-day, and we shall come here over and over again. You must realise how futile it is to settle this question by binding us over to keep the peace. You have tried it; it has failed. Others have tried to do it, and have failed. If you had power to send us to prison, not for six months, but for six years, for 16 years, or for the whole of our lives, the Government must not think that they can stop this agitation. It will go on.

I want to draw your attention to the self-restraint which was shown by our followers on the night of the 13th, after we had been arrested. It only shows that our influence over them is very great, because I think that if they had yielded to their natural impulses, there might have been a breach of the peace on the evening of the 13th. They were very indignant, but our words have always been, "be patient, exercise self-restraint, show our so-called superiors that the criticism of women being hysterical is not true; use no violence, offer yourselves to the violence of others." We are going to win. Our women have taken that advice; if we are in prison they will continue to take that advice.

Well, sir, that is all I have to say to you. We are here not because we are law-breakers; we are here in our efforts to become lawmakers.

Mrs. Drummond.

I want to point out to you why I came into this Court. I think, if you wished to find out, you will not find that I have ever been in this Court as an ordinary law-breaker; in fact, I am proud to say that I never entered a Police-court until I came here to fight for my political liberty.

I am charged with issuing a bill. I wish to say here, and now, that I do not want to apologise for circulating that bill. I want to say that we did circulate it, because we had lost all faith in the Government, and because we trusted the people. We knew that if we could get the people to the House of Commons there would be a better chance of getting what we have been asking for so many years. Mrs. Pankhurst has pointed out to you how women have tried to get the vote in a quiet way, and have been no nearer gaining it.

Superintendent Wells has told you that I am an active organiser of this Union, and I rather think that is the reason why I have been included in these proceedings. The Government find that this organisation is becoming so powerful, and so determined, and that women are coming in every way, coming forward to us, giving all their lives to gain this point. The Government can see for themselves that this agitation is extending all over the country.

Now, I want to say why I am an organiser in this Union, and why I am in this position to-day. It is because I want my sex to be recognised as a person in the eyes of the law. To-day, if I had appeared to you as a mother asking for exemption from vaccination of my child, I should have been told by you and your colleagues that I was not a person in the eyes of the law, and that you could not deal with me. Now, I stand before you on another charge, and in that position you will deal with me. I want my political rights, and I am not sorry at all that I caused that bill to be published, because I made up my mind that nothing else would gain that for which we have been fighting.

It has also been brought to your notice that I spoke in Trafalgar-square. I want to tell you that our two leaders, Mrs. Pankhurst and Miss Christabel Pankhurst, restrained us. They said: "No, you must not be impatient; you must be prepared to try some peaceful means." Now, I say to you that in our speeches we have done what we could to instill into the minds of the people the fact that we did not want them to practice violence. If the people who were round the House of Commons had believed that we had invited them to violence, not even 6,000 policemen would have prevented these people from getting into the House of Commons.

Now, you say we have broken the peace. I should really like you to tell us what is meant by breaking the peace. Mrs. Pankhurst left the Caxton Hall with twelve other women; she was arrested and imprisoned for six weeks. Later on, under the same circumstances, that same number of women left the Caxton Hall, and they were not arrested. Now, in the first place, they broke the peace; in the second place, they did not. We women are fairly at sea as to what is a breach of the peace.

Do you realise what I, as a wife and mother, am wanting? I want women to be looked upon as human beings in the eyes of the law. I do not want the little boy in the street—and I put it down to the status of women legally—to say: "Votes for women, votes for dogs!" I want you to realize, you men, that we want to look after our own interests, and we want justice to be done to our sex.

It is not that we go out into the streets to break the law. I should say that you know that you would never see us before you in any other circumstances.

I do not know what you intend to do to us, but whatever you intend to do, whatever sentence you intend to give us, we look only upon the sentence, we shall take no notice whatever of the binding over to keep the peace. I want to say to you that the agitation will go on—and I can speak on good authority—that it will go on stronger than it has ever done before, because the action which the Government have taken has fired the bosoms of women, who are determined to take up the flag that we women have had to lay down to-day.

I have been twice to prison, and I am prepared to go as many times as necessary; and I say again, we women are prepared to do it for this agitation. I am glad to say, also, that we have left everything in working order, and that the agitation will go on, and we shall find it stronger than it was when we left it. I should like to assure you that whatever you do, it will not stop the agitation that is going on at the present time.

At the close of the speeches, Mr. Muskett, in reply to the magistrate, said Mrs. Drummond had been convicted twice, and the other two defendants had each been dealt with once.

The Magistrate's Decision.

Mr. Curtis Bennett said there could be no doubt that it was for that court, and that court alone, to deal with the offence for which the defendants were in the first place summoned. The case of Wise v. Dunning, argued in the King's Bench Division on November 19 and 20, 1901, absolutely decided the point, to his mind, as to whether these proceedings were right or wrong. As to the facts, the defendants admitted that they were responsible for the distribution of this handbill, and although they were warned of the danger and difficulty which might arise in consequence of it, they persisted in going on. He had heard the very able speeches of the defendants, but he did not wish to make any further observations upon them, because it was not for him to discuss political matters. He was simply there for the purpose of endeavouring to carry out the law in order to preserve the peace and well-being of the metropolis, and there could be no question that that handbill, which was circulated, was by its contents liable to cause something to occur which might and probably would end in a breach of the peace. The Chief Commissioner of Police was bound to keep Parliament-square and the vicinity free and open, and he felt that it would be impossible to do that if crowds assembled together in order to help and see the women rush the House of Commons.

Between 5,000 and 6,000 police were required to keep order in consequence of this circular. Ten persons were taken to hospitals, seven policemen were placed on the sick-list, thirty-seven persons were charged at that court the following morning, and it was reported that no fewer than thirty watches were stolen. Could it for one instant be said that that circular asking the public to rush the House of Commons was not liable to create breaches of the peace? Therefore, as to the law there could be no question. To call a number of people to assemble together for that avowed object must bring the persons who called that meeting within the limits of this section, namely, they were doing something which was calculated to bring about a breach of the peace. Each of the two elder defendants would be bound over in their own recognisances of £100, and they must find two sureties in £50 each to keep the peace for twelve months; in default, three months' imprisonment. In the case of the younger defendant, her own recognisances would be £50, with two sureties of £25 each, the alternative being ten weeks' imprisonment.

Miss Pankhurst: I ask you to state a case on a point of law, namely, the construction of the leaflet.

The Magistrate: I shall not state a case.

Miss Pankhurst: I ask you to suspend judgment until after the return of a writ of certiorari.

The magistrate refused.

3

The Political Outlook.

Speech Delivered by Christabel Pankhurst.
Queen's Hall, December 22, 1908

FRIENDS, I CANNOT HELP THINKING TONIGHT OF THE MANY HUNDREDS of meetings that have been held in this country in defence of the principle of women's enfranchisement. How many times have noble women poured forth their very soul in an appeal for political justice? How many times has such an appeal been made, and made to ears that were deaf and unheeding? It is well for us all to remember that we are engaged in no new movement. There were those who came before us, pioneers of 40 and 50 years ago, who began the agitation for woman suffrage. They worked well, they worked devotedly, and yet, after all those years of work, women have not yet got the Parliamentary vote.

Well, I am afraid the reason of this is that the rulers of our country are not to be moved by appeal or by persuasion. The ordinary person, I believe, is, but among those who get into high places, those who have power over others, something seems often to go wrong with their nature, and frankly, they don't understand the kind of enlightened appeal upon which Suffragists used to place their sole reliance. You know, friends, there is an old saying, and a very true one, and that is, "God helps those who help themselves." Now, the Suffragists of old times made a mistake, which experience—theirs and our own—has taught us to avoid. They relied too much upon the justice of their cause, and not enough upon their own strong right arm. They thought justice could go forward without help from those who wanted it. My friends, that can never be, and never has been. An idea only has life and power in so far as it is backed up by deeds. Now, that is the whole secret of success, the whole secret of getting reform. It is because we have realised that the policy of persuasion, and of argument, and of talk has failed that we have undertaken the new militant campaign, which I believe, and I think you believe, is so very nearly at a successful end. When men begin an agitation like ours, they are, of course, open to all kinds of criticism and attack, but I do not think that the very dangerous and difficult form of attack is brought to bear against them that is brought to bear against us. Men are never told that they are hysterical, and that they do not know what they are doing. They may be told they are violent, they may be told their action is reprehensible, but people are usually willing to admit that at least there is method in their madness, and that, as there is a limit to human endurance, if men are very much oppressed, they have a right to revolt against oppression. We in this woman's movement, on the other hand, have been accused of not having thought things out, and of simply running along in a headstrong fashion without knowing where we are going or why we do go.

I want you to understand, however, that our militant campaign has been thought out with the utmost care. Whatever else we may be, we are neither heedless, rash, nor unthinking and we realise that the recognition of this fact is beginning to become more general, because when they stop abusing us for being foolish and unwise, they begin to charge us with doing all this in cold blood, and not being spontaneous enough.

No, my friends, we did not undertake this campaign in any light or heedless spirit. We knew what we had got to face; we knew we had to face danger, sheer physical danger. We knew well that in what we did we ran the risk of imprisonment. Now, that is a very serious thing. Imprisonment is what you reserve for those who are preying upon society, those who are enemies of the body politic; imprisonment is the worst thing you have to offer them, and yet we knew full well that we, who were trying, at any rate, to do our duty to other people, must realise that for us this fate was in store. We knew that we should have to meet the bitter attack of the party politician—and I think there is no form of attack which is more venomous, which is more unscrupulous—and as we were women, we had to face another thing, we had to face censure as being unwomanly, as being unladylike (you know, that is worse than being unwomanly), as being, well, unconventional, and ridiculous, and all the rest of it. Now, you know, to some women that is the worst thing of all, and to all men that is the worst thing of all too.

Well, I have summed up the price that had to be paid by those who adventured the perilous course of militant methods, and it astounds me to find that there should be any left (and there are not very many) who presume to condemn the people who have principles, and are trying to vindicate those principles, even though it means that the penalties fall upon themselves. It is, indeed, extraordinary how much blindness there is even in these enlightened days; people never seem to be able to read the signs of the times, they never seem able to understand what is going on under their very eyes, and yet we live in a great Christian country. We live amongst people whose minds are always turning back towards One who paid in greater measure than we have done the price of purchasing the regeneration of others. It seems to me you, none of you, understand the story of which you hear over and over again in the churches. Why, you are brought up from your cradles to understand this thing, and when, on a smaller and humbler scale, the whole thing is acted out under your very eyes, you don't seem to see at all what it means—at least, you don't see for a good long time.

Well, I assure you that if there were not a great thing at stake, we should all of us prefer to follow a course of life which would not expose us to the difficulties of which I tell you. But think what is at stake! Human liberty! The most priceless thing there is, the only thing that is worth fighting for, the only thing that is worth paying for. We are fighting for that. We are fighting for the emancipation of women; the emancipation of men was begun a long time ago, and men are now working out their salvation, although they will never see it in full measure until the women, whose brothers and whose partners they are, see their emancipation too. We are working for the bread of women, we are working that women may not go hungry, we are working for what is even more important—we are working for the dignity of women. How can they say other questions are more important? How can they say it? They cannot really think it. Why, it is the most important question; it is the most vital question of the present day! The freedom of men and the freedom of women, the liberty of human beings—what can transcend that? When worldly affairs are concerned, what is our Government for? Government is not a game, it is not something remote from human affairs; it is something that concerns us all. Therefore, the first duty of statesmen ought to be to attend to the claims of those who are still without the elementary rights of citizenship.

Now, I am going to speak to those women here who want the vote, but don't agree with our methods. I ask them, why do you hold aloof, why do you not believe in the methods and why if you believe in them don't you practise them? Because you know neither from you nor from Cabinet Ministers do we want sympathy. No, what we want is action. We would rather have you marching along with us side by side than we would have your cheers or your support or your praise. We do not look for that, we should miss it; we do not want you to come and say that we have done well; we want you to come and do with us! Why, then, do you not throw yourselves into this agitation, why are not you ready for prison? You should not see prison through other people's eyes, you should go there yourselves if you think that we have done well to go there. You know the old methods of working for the vote are futile, and not only futile, but humiliating, unworthy of you. I say any woman here who is content to appeal for the vote instead of demanding and fighting for it is dishonouring herself! That she may have a right to do, but she has no right to dishonour her sex, and I say you drag our women's banner in the very mud, that political roughs may trample upon it and defile it, when you are content with the old proved failures of methods of getting votes for women. Is the price too great? Cannot you make the necessary sacrifice? I can tell you that we who are prepared for it take a great joy in it. Why, sometimes when you say that we are brave and self-sacrificing, and all the rest of it, we feel that we ought to reject your compliments because we are so much happier than you. Because we don't feel we are giving up anything, because we are not giving up anything. We are getting everything. Why, the women in this Union are the happiest people in the world! We have the love of our comrades, we have the respect of our enemies, we have the support of the people, we have something to live for, and we are going to do something worth doing. We are sorry for the people who go through their lives achieving nothing, leaving the world no richer than they have found it. Those people are poor, indeed; those people we pity. As for us, we have the glorious pride of being made the instrument of those great forces that are working towards progress and liberty.

But suppose it were not so; suppose there were nothing but sorrow and sacrifice and pain and renunciation in our movement, have not women always been ready to undergo these things? We are told it is the very law of our being. [A voice: "No!"] Well, we have been told so. We do know this, that women are prepared to sacrifice themselves. Sometimes they sacrifice themselves rightly, and sometimes wrongly. When I think of the futile sacrifice which is being made every day we live by countless women, I think how well it would be if all that devotion, all that readiness to give could be directed towards great ends. Now, we in this movement are sometimes told that we are selfish, that we are unwomanly, and that we are expecting women to be different from what people have hoped they would be. Some people say: "You want women to be as bad as men, as selfish as men," but I don't think devotion to others should be or is a sex characteristic. Still the fact remains that women are always ready to give themselves in order that others may benefit. We in this movement say a woman does gloriously who will make every possible sacrifice if what she is working towards is worth while. But we know well that is not because you are afraid, you women, that you do not join forces with us, for that is a thing one may be sure of where women are concerned. No, the old idea that women must cling to duty is, I think, at the root of the difficulty. You say: "Yes, we ought to have the vote, and the only way of getting the vote is by adopting these militant methods, but is it right that we should do so, is it right that we should break law, defy convention, and give trouble to other people? No, we cannot think it is right, and it were better to go forever without votes than to do wrong." But, my friends, I want to point out to you that those who wish the end wish the means. If you want the vote you must do what is necessary to get the vote. If there are no other means of getting that vote than those that are militant, then the militant means must be adopted. But it is not upon this line of argument that we depend. No, we depend upon our belief that so far from being a necessary evil, revolt is a great and a glorious thing

in itself when injustice has to be broken down. Therefore, we do not apologise for our methods. We say emphatically that they are right in themselves.
The women who are in the wrong to-day are the women who are submitting
to injustice.

Now, the rightness of revolt, the rightness of our militant methods does
not depend upon success. You may resist injustice and fail, or seem to fail,
and still you have done right. When you are confronted by oppression,
when you are confronted by the forces of evil, then you must go and do
battle against them. Unless you believe that might is right you must agree
with what I say. Now, we none of us really think that might is right. There
is not one here who has not read of the brave deeds of people who were
few in number and weak in strength, who went forward against countless
numbers greatly their superior in force. I think even when we were at school
and read Macaulay's Lays our hearts used to thrill at the idea of "fighting
against fearful odds"; we all of us feel proud of those members of the human
race who have stood perhaps alone against overwhelming strength and overwhelming numbers. So often the gallant stands that men and women have
made against superior force have seemed to be in vain. We read of their
being crushed under foot and every trace of them being trampled away, but,
somehow, I think there is, in the heart of every one of us a conviction that
somehow and somewhere that heroism is recorded, that heroism is counted,
and that we to-day are the richer for it, and that the forces of good have
been strengthened by the action of these heroes who have seemed to fail,
but in reality have triumphed. And I want you to believe that even if we
had no hope of success, even if we thought that our militant campaign were
destined to failure, we should go on with it. We should go on with it while
life was ours, we *are* going on with it; so long as we live we are never going
to renounce this struggle. But we are going to win, for victory is not always
with the big battalions. We are going to win because we have got right on
our side. No, you must not forget that "thrice is he armed that hath his
quarrel just, and he but naked though locked up in steel whose conscience
with injustice is corrupted." Well, my friends, there is great truth in those
words, and I think you will admit that our quarrel is just. Why, even the
enemy has to admit that. We could never win if we were not in the right,
but because we are in the right we are going to win.

Now, if I had been talking about a men's agitation, a men's revolt, there
is not one in this hall who would not have said, "Yes, you are right, you are
right. But," you will say, "it is different with women." You say, "Women
are weak, they can't fight." But have not we just made up our minds that
weakness—apparent weakness—is often the real strength? Though we are
women, we can win. Do not say that a curse has been laid upon us because
we are women, that the fact of being women deprives us of the power of
getting votes, and of the right to fight for justice, even if we do not win.

No, my friends; we women have as good a right as the men, and our sex is no excuse for submission, for sloth, and for yielding to injustice. The woman who shelters herself behind her sex, and says, "I need not come out to fight because I am a woman, and I ought not to," that woman either has not a woman's spirit, or has not the right woman's spirit. That is not the kind of woman that we want to see in our country and that is not the kind of woman who will bring into the world the men that we want to see.

But when driven to the last argumentative pitch, some of our women friends will say, "Yes, it is all very well, but, you know, there is the Liberal Government. They are so strong, and we women, you know—well, how *can* we"—and they think, helplessly, "it cannot be done." Now, when I was in prison I was reading "The Seven Lamps of Architecture," and it begins with a very interesting passage dealing with this question. Ruskin thinks that failure in art, and even more in politics, comes from the fact that those who want to do something, instead of looking to their end, and steering directly towards it, enter too much into the consideration of what is possible. Now, says Ruskin, how can any of you know what is possible? Who can tell their own strength, who knows the strength of the enemy, who knows all the attending circumstances, who can possibly tell what can be managed and what cannot? We know what we ought to strive for, and I believe that nothing is impossible to the human will and the human spirit, because, you see, after all, we, every one of us, believe that it partakes of the divine, and in so far as it does that, it can bend outside circumstances. Well, we in this Union have already learnt the truth of that. We know perfectly well that the only limit to our power is our own determination. If we are determined, if we banish all thought of sloth, if we go straight forward, looking neither to the left nor to the right, we can perform miracles. Human beings have done it. Why, when you think of air-ships, wireless telegraphy, and things of that kind, when you think of how Nature has been bent to human purposes and human needs, how are we to suppose that women banded together with a knowledge of what they want, and a knowledge of how to get it, would fail to make the Liberal Government give in! Therefore, I say to women: Take courage, never mind whether Mr. Asquith is an obstinate man or not, never mind whether the men are going to back you up or not; just do your duty, just you go straight forward, and if the Government don't give in at the first attempt, then try, try again! That is what we have been doing for some years now, and we are going to have what we think will be a final try next Session.

We have every reason to be hopeful, because we have had so much success already. Look at our Union! Just see how it is growing in numbers; see the enthusiasm of the women, see the officers of our Union, see what keen politicians they are—not a few people following blindly a few who understand, but everyone understanding for herself, and ranging herself under the banner of the commanding officers of the Union. We are like an orchestra—each one playing her own part, and producing—we think at any rate—a very harmonious result. You see, this is all the result of the militant methods. Look, also, at our finances! They are in an exceedingly satisfactory condition, and we hope they are going to be in an even more satisfactory condition as time goes on, because the Liberal leaders, as you know, are very materially-minded; they do not care for argument, or anything of that kind—all that they want to know is, What are the resources of these women? Can we tire them out, or can they tire us out? Is this a bubble that will burst when its season has run, or will they go on for ever? Then, I say, look at the attitude of the public—see how it has changed! We are supposed to have alienated the people. But neither we nor the Liberal Government can see any evidence of that.

Well, I have been telling you why we adopt our methods; I have been trying to explain to you the frame of mind in which we are, and the reasons why we have taken to these methods, and what the methods are. If you read the leading articles in some of our newspapers, you would think our methods were Russian methods, or even worse. You really would suppose that we were the most dangerous set of people and the most violent set of people, that have ever been seen. The fact is, however, that we are singularly mild—indeed, we are just as mild as we can be, consistently with doing our duty. We do not want to go an inch further than the Liberal Government drive us, because we do not want to waste our forces; we do not want to overstep the mark by a hair's breadth, and we have never done so. We go to by-elections, and work against the Government. Surely that is not very unconstitutional or very violent! I see the Welsh members are threatening to do that. I see the Welsh party say that they will go against the Government if they don't get what they want. If they can do it, why can't we? Our protests at public meetings have been very effective, but they involve no danger to life or limb—unless our own. Mr. Lloyd George—[loud and prolonged hisses]—well, you see, it all shows how foolish Mr. Lloyd George and these other people who want to be popular are to go against Votes for Women. As I say, these protests don't involve any danger to the physical safety of our Cabinet Ministers, yet they produce a marked impression. Ministers are simply terrified. They hide from us behind locked doors. They go in secret nowadays! They dare not run the risk of meeting women even in a railway train. Have you read the *Daily News* today, and seen the account of Mr. Lloyd George's attempt, not only to keep women out of his meeting, but to escape them? Well, if it were the Czar of Russia going amongst his subjects, it might be natural. Why this fear? Why not trust the people? They are dreadfully afraid of women in these days—and then you say women cannot pursue militant methods with success! The proof of the pudding is in the eating, and I know this—they are more afraid of one Suffragette than they are of 5,000 men!

Then we go on deputations to the House of Commons. What is there wrong in that? Men are constantly having deputations, and I have never heard of a men's deputation going to prison yet—but we have to go to prison! I wonder how it is that you do not see that, instead of our being violent, violence is used against us! We have not caused Mr. Asquith to languish for a single day in gaol—it is he who has vicariously attacked and imprisoned us. We are very sorry to have to give all this trouble; we would rather militant methods should cease, and they would cease if we were to have the vote. Now, how simple it all is! Can't you understand that the Government have brought these troubles down upon their own heads? We are not responsible for it—they are responsible. Do not waste your sympathy upon them, my friends. It is all their own fault. If they would give us the vote, they would have no more trouble from us.

Now, what is the present position? I want to deal with that as a conclusion to my speech to-night. The third session of the present Government has now come to an end. I do not think they can be feeling very happy to-night. This Session has witnessed a great decline in their prestige and in their influence. They are weakened and discredited. While I was in prison, I had, towards the end of my sentence, the opportunity of reading the newspaper, and I read of the inglorious figure the present Government cut in connection with the education question. What an insight all that education business gave you of the true character of this Government! I do not care which side you take in the matter, and it is not the business of anyone at this meeting to express an opinion on the rights and wrongs of the education question— we are for Votes for Women—but you can see that in that measure the Government had not care at all for their own professed principles, no care at all for the pledges they have given to their supporters, all they wanted to do was to please everybody and to have an easy time themselves.

They got to loggerheads during this year with the House of Lords, they are always getting to loggerheads with the House of Lords, and they are always announcing that this time the great campaign is going to begin. What would you say to us if we were like that? You would not respect us. You would think we were absurd, inconstant, bragging people, all talk and no action. No, we take care to be very different, but the Government have shown an attitude of contemptible weakness towards the House of Lords, which, whilst it is a matter of regret on some grounds, is a great encourage- ment to us. We shall make them give in, but, my friends, what a farce it is to have the present Government talking about the House of Lords and their desire to overcome its unconstitutional action!

Mr. Lloyd George said last night that the Liberal party were going to fight, among other things, for free institutions. We only wish we could take him at his word, and that we could make him prove his words to be true. Are they for free institutions, or are they against them? They have been proved to be against them. Why, on this very question in which they profess to be so deeply interested, they have shown themselves unwilling to move either hand or foot; and when it is a question of making the House of Commons itself a free institution, representative not only of half the people, but of the whole of the people, the women as well as the men—why, they are more reactionary, they are more obstinate in their opposition to justice than any other Government, of whatever complexion, could possibly be.

In addition to all this they have refused to carry our Bill, and that I think in days to come will seem to be the one outstanding feature of this Session. When the Education Bill, that hotch-potch of conflicting principles, is long forgotten, it will be remembered that a Bill for Woman Suffrage passed its second reading by a large majority, and that rather than let that Bill come to law women were imprisoned as common criminals in one of our gaols.

Yet, my friends, they have had time to pass another Bill. In a panic they have carried through a private member's measure, a measure of coercion— that's what it is, pure and simple—and because they were so anxious to put an end to action on our part, (which they could have ended in a better manner by giving us the vote), they have reduced the right of public meeting in this country to a farce. Before I say more of that, I want to tell you that if at the General Election this Bill had been in force, a great many of Mr. Asquith's supporters would have been in gaol on polling-day. We are entitled to protest at public meetings, because we are voteless, if for no other reason, but let me remind you of the fact—I speak of Manchester, where I was at the General Election—no Conservative candidate could get a hearing. Meetings were smashed, furniture was destroyed, scenes of extraordinary violence were witnessed at election meetings, and all this was done by the men whose votes have placed Mr. Asquith where he is, and have given him the power to carry this measure in order to deal with us. Now I say, better that a thousand meetings should be destroyed than that we should have this kind of interference by the police with assemblies of citizens met together to discuss public affairs. As a public speaker, I say I want none of their Bill. If I can't get a hearing by the force of my own will, by my own knowledge of how to deal with an audience, by the strength of the cause I wish to promote, then I will wait and hold a meeting some other time. Yes, we are prepared to hold our own at any meeting, and I do not see why the men politicians cannot do what we can. Do you think this Bill is going to make any difference to us? It may make it very difficult for Liberals to do as they did in Ipswich the other day, get roughs at a shilling a head to come to our meetings and make a disturbance, they will have to be ready to pay down at least £5 in future, but this Bill will not deter women from demanding the vote. We are not so poor in spirit, nor so deficient in courage that a month in prison is going to prevent us from claiming justice.

But, friends, when you look at the record of this Government, you who are Liberals, what do you feel? Are you proud of them, or do you feel deeply ashamed of them? I am sorry for you that you have such leaders. [A voice: "So are we!"] I tell you, they are not leaders, they are false to your principles, and it seems to me they are like some pirate gang who have boarded the good old ship of Liberalism and are steering her on the rocks.

Now, what of next Session? Whilst I was in prison I read Mr. Asquith's "epoch-making speech," his "great utterance" upon the future policy of his party, upon his action for next Session. He certainly made one thing very evident, that those who shout the loudest will get the first attention. He does not study in a statesmanlike way the condition of the people, and consider which are the most pressing questions to be dealt with. No, he is looking all round, he is saying, "Who is going to worry me the most, because who worries me the most must get what he, or she, wants," and he turns—he looks at Sir Alfred Thomas, he looks at Dr. Clifford, and he looks at this, that, and the other leader, and I do not suppose—I am sure—he does not forget to keep an eye on what the Suffragettes are doing. Then he weighs it all up, and those who are the most obnoxious and active will get a place in the King's Speech.

Then he told us of another thing. A very remarkable Budget is to be introduced. Yes, ladies, they are going to take our money and play their own political games with it. If there had been women there, he would hardly have had the courage to say it—but even as it was I wonder that he could get up and say that women taxpayers were to have their pockets picked—because that is what it means when they do not give them the vote. Women are going to have their pockets picked so that Mr. Lloyd-George may see what he can do to revive the sinking fortunes of the Liberal Government. And yet it is said that the predominating political issue is the question of the House of Lords. Well, they may say so, but they do not seem to think so. We know what *we* think the predominating issue—Votes for Women.

We handle this question of the vote in a very different fashion from that in which the Government handle the question of the House of Lords. It is all very well to say they are going to do something—but when?—what? Well, I think before they get to the House of Lords they will have plenty of time to give votes to women. They have made us an offer with scorn at the Albert Hall. [Prolonged cheers.] That was one of the brightest days of our sentence in Holloway. It was absolutely necessary that you should do that. It was right, it was statesmanlike, it was wise. Mr. Lloyd George told us that he was going to convert the country, but we have spared him the trouble of doing that; we have done it ourselves. It is not for him to convert the country, it is for him to *do* something, and for his colleagues to *do* something, and the chief reason why you did well in going to that meeting and making your protest was this: You made it unmistakable that we would have nothing to do with that offer; you rejected it in the most dramatic and effective way possible. For what was the offer? The same thing that we had from Mr. Asquith months ago. I suppose they thought that of the two political cooks, Mr. Lloyd George is more skillful at dishing up. We rejected the spread that Mr. Asquith laid before us; we said it wasn't fit to eat, so Mr. Lloyd George said, "Oh, I will pour a nice sauce over it; they will take it then." But no, we did not, and we shall not.

We are told that a Reform Bill is to be introduced—it was only to be for men at first, but a private member can move an amendment, and if it is carried, then the Liberal Government will send the whole thing up to the House of Lords. Now, that does not satisfy us, because we do not know when the Reform Bill is going to be introduced, for one thing. Before they go out of office, they say. But, my friends, once bitten, twice shy. The last Government was going to introduce a Redistribution Bill, and carry it before they went out of office. Now, it was our intention to try to get an instruction moved which would have led to the provision for woman suffrage in that Bill, and we were working very hard for that. The times we have moved resolutions—and got them carried—in favour of such an amendment to the Redistribution Bill! Then, as you know, the ground was cut from under our feet, because Mr. Balfour resigned office. I think the same thing is certain to happen in the present case. This Government is on its death-bed. What would you say of some hardened old sinner, who, when he was asked to repent at the eleventh hour, were to say, "Well, two or three years hence I will think about it"? You would say that was wrong, and it is wrong for a discredited Government to tell women who are crying for enfranchisement, who mean to have the vote at the next General Election, that they must wait until the last Session of Parliament, that they must wait for the Reform Bill. The Reform Bill may never be introduced. It will certainly not be carried, because it is not meant to be carried. It is a war-cry for the Liberal Party at the next General Election, and woman suffrage may or may not be part of the Government war-cry, but we shall never be a war-cry, if we can help it, for any party.

We want to vote at the next General Election. If they had wanted to go to the country on this question they ought to have done it in 1906, but now they cannot do it. It is too late for that, they must carry our Bill now. This Reform Bill, if it ever comes to life, will be too complicated to get through the House of Lords, and if it does not get through, I am afraid that, in order to facilitate its passage through the narrow legislative door, the women will be left behind as they have been before. We stand for a separate, a distinct measure for Woman Suffrage, just a Bill to say that if women show the same qualifications as men voters, they shall be voters too.

We know what we want. It is not as though we were uncertain as to that; we know what we want, they have only now got to give it to us. Then, they say, as a last excuse, "We know the House of Lords won't pass it." But they must not be too sure of that. The House of Lords often disappoints this Government! They were not crocodile tears that Mr. Asquith shed at the Reform Club, they were real tears that stood in his eyes when he said he did not know why they had passed the Trades Disputes Bill. The Government has never got over it from that day to this, they did so hope the House of Lords would save them from that, and they hope, too, that the House of Lords will reject a Woman Suffrage Bill. If we compel them to pass it through the House of Commons, they hope the Lords will come to their rescue. But I, for one, do not believe the Lords will do anything of the kind. Probably the Lords will carry our Bill. I speak with all possible seriousness when I say that. But if they don't, very well then, we must try to change their minds. I am sure we shall manage better in dealing with the House of Lords than the Government can do. It seems to me that the Government think we are such good fighters that they want to get us mixed up with their Reform Bill, so that we may do the fighting and they may take the credit. But no, no, no! We won't have such feeble allies as this Government. In any possible future conflict which may arise between us and the Upper House we can fight better without them. They would hinder us, they would prevent us from winning. We will not have anything to do with them as allies against the House of Lords.

Now, friends, I do want you all to take this question very, very seriously. One has a good deal of time for meditation in prison. We used to read the papers, and then think of what we had read, and I noticed this one thing—it is very extraordinary just to see how the world is moving on, how the conditions are changing. I noticed that in the two months in which we were in prison airships came out of the region of theoretical and problematical things into being something quite practical—they are to be as useful to us as motor-cars, or even more so. Now, a thing like that—and there are sure to be other things in the air—a thing like that means that the world is going to be far different in future from what it is to-day, and it means, above all, that our own national conditions are going to be changed. It means that we in this country will have to rise to new occasions, and will have to base our place among the nations on a different foundation. We shall have to readjust ourselves. Other countries are wealthy, other countries have greater territory than ours, and other countries have even greater natural resources; if we are to hold our own in the world in future we men and women of Great Britain, we have got to be well equipped. Ours must be an Empire of mind and intelligence and spirit, or we shall be left behind—other countries will hold the place that we hold to-day.

Now, I think we are all enough of patriots to want our country to stand high. We are the heirs of a great past; what are we going to hand on to posterity, what are we going to hand on to the Great Britain of the days to come? Well, I do not think things are well with our nation at the present time; I do not think the physical condition, or the mental or the spiritual condition of the mass of our people is what it ought to be, and therefore it is as patriots that we are here to-night; we want to take our share in saving our country. Will you deny us that—shall we be denied that? I do not think so; I think all men of generous and pure mind and heart will be with us in this fight. This is not a party question, it is a question for the nation. This is not a question of the moment, it is a question for all time. I call on the men who are here to-night to join forces with us, help us to overcome the Government which at the present moment is the greatest obstacle in the path of human progress. If men's eyes are still shut to these truths, yet nevertheless the women are awake, and the women have the power; they have the absolute power to gain the reform which they want; they have the power and the capacity to seize this indispensable weapon of reform, which in their own interests, and in the interests of the country that is dear to them, they ought to have, and which they speedily will have.

Part III
Hunger Strike

THE SECOND MAJOR ESCALATION IN MILITANT STRATEGY BEGAN AS AN isolated symbolic act. On June 30, 1908, following the exclusion of a deputation of women from Parliament and the arrest of twenty-nine women in the resulting protest, Mary Leigh and Edith New each threw a stone at the Downing Street residence of the Prime Minister. This was a purely symbolic act and appears to have been spontaneous on the part of the two women. In fact, both women fully expected a reprimand from headquarters for initiating a new militant act on their own authority. Far from taking the women to task, Emmeline Pankhurst personally went to visit Leigh and New in custody and expressed her wholehearted approval of the act.[1]

Despite its symbolic beginning, stone throwing was quickly adopted by WSPU members as a practical response to meet a second exigency often encountered during suffrage protests. Before they would arrest suffrage speakers or members of suffrage deputations, the police would subject the women to a period of "buffeting." Buffeting was a term used at the time to describe a delay of arrest during which time the suffragette would be pummeled and manhandled by police and angry male crowds. Injuries to Union members were inevitable, and it was clearly the hope of the government and police that the threat of such injury would dissuade suffrage activism. Then, too, the practice of buffeting allowed the police to inflict maximum physical punishment while simultaneously claiming that they arrested the suffragettes only when absolutely necessary. Quickly, Union members discovered that if they threw a stone (even if it did not reach its target) or committed simple assault (dry "spitting" or slapping a policeman), they would be arrested in short order and not subjected to as much physical damage. This initial step into illegal action caused such mental anguish for many of the suffragettes that they swaddled the stones in heavy paper and even took the precaution of tying long strings from stone to wrist, thus avoiding injury to bystanders.[2] Despite their scruples, Union members came to agree with Sylvia Pankhurst's assertion, "Since we must go to prison to obtain the vote, let it be the windows of the Government, not the bodies of women, which shall be broken."[3]

The first instance of officially sanctioned window-breaking occurred on June 29, 1909, when thirteen women broke government office windows. This window breaking was staged to coincide with a deputation that tested the limits of English legal rights. Emmeline Pankhurst had resolved to test the right to petition the King, a right written into the Bill of Rights in 1689 as a condition to the accession of William and Mary.[4] Pankhurst wrote to the Prime Minister to inform him that, as he now held the power previously resting in the monarch, a deputation would await to petition him at Parliament at 8:00 in the evening on June 29. Asquith's reply was a written refusal to receive the deputation. The Union continued its plans and advertised that the deputation would go forward.[5] On June 26, Wallace Dunlop, an artist wielding a stamp with violet printer's ink, managed to print upon the wall of St. Stephen's Hall at the House of Commons, the following:

> Women's Deputation
> June 29th
> Bill of Rights
> It is the right of the subjects to petition the King—
> and all commitments and prosecutions for such
> petitioning are illegal.

Dunlop was arrested, charged with "willful damage," and—as she refused to pay a fine—was sent on July 2 to prison for one month.[6] All of this was fairly standard. The new twist came when Dunlop took action to meet a third exigency faced by the WSPU. Dunlop had been refused the status of a political prisoner. That is, she was sentenced to the second division of prison, the division of prison that (along with the third division) was reserved for criminal rather than political offenders. This issue of criminal versus political status was not a minor complaint of the Union, for it had great symbolic as well as practical impact. By denying the suffragette prisoners political status, the government characterized the militants as common felons rather than political reformers. This was not the treatment commonly afforded to male reformers who had broken the law in order to achieve a political reform. Of course, there was also a practical impact on the prisoners, because first division prisoners had certain privileges, such as the rights to wear their own clothing and to receive letters and books from the outside. As with their attempts to retain suffragette trials in the police courts, the government obviously hoped that second division status would further humiliate and dissuade Union activists. Overcoming this criminal stigma had become so important that Emmeline Pankhurst had recently declared that Union members would not abide by prison regulations unless they were given their bona fides as political rather than criminal prisoners.[7]

Acting on her own authority, Wallace Dunlop adopted a hunger strike until such time as she should be given first division status. Prison officials seem to have been flummoxed by this first hunger strike. They fixed tempting dishes and brought them to Dunlop's cell, only to have her throw them out of her cell window. Reportedly, when asked one day, "What would you like to eat?" she replied, "My determination." Following a ninety-one hour fast, Dunlop was released.[8] The women who were convicted of stone throwing were quick to follow suit, and after several days they too were released. Hunger strikes thus became a permanent part of Union strategy; and, as Emmeline Pethick-Lawrence put it, "Never again were suffragettes to suffer the insult of being treated as criminals without making this protest of the hunger-strike."[9]

The government did not delay long in its retaliation. Rather than avoid the problem of the hunger strike by granting the suffragettes first division status, the government behaved as though the Union members were hunger striking to obtain a release from prison. In September 1909, Herbert Gladstone, the Home Secretary, introduced a program of forcible feeding of hunger striking suffragettes. A few words should be inserted here about the nature of forcible feeding. Feeding by tube was well-known in hospitals (and lunatic asylums). It consisted of passing a tube through the mouth or nose to the stomach and pouring in a "nourishing liquid," often Valentine's meat juice and lime juice-cordial.[10] It was an uncomfortable and disagreeable process when the patient was cooperative. For the suffragettes, who were anything but cooperative, it was torture. The description given by suffragette Ethel Moorhead of her forcible feeding experience appears to have been typical:

> I was held down on the operating table, my body was held as if in a vice, and without any examination of heart or pulse, a tube was forced down my nose. I coughed it up into my mouth, as I opened my eyes to spit out the tube a steel gag was forced into my mouth, and the tube was then shoved down my throat. It seemed to be far too big, it wrinkled up and had to be shoved down repeatedly. I felt I was suffocating and dying during the operation and afterwards laid with teeth chattering and body trembling.[11]

If Moorhead's was an average forcible feeding, there were more harrowing accounts where the feeding tube reached the lungs rather than the stomach, and one instance when a tube was forced up a nostril that the prisoner had forewarned authorities had always been blocked. Only the great quantity of blood that resulted caused the forcing of the tube to stop.[12]

In true "blame the victim" fashion, the suffragettes were advised to cooperate and were told that the pain involved was largely their own fault. For Mary Richardson, it was not the pain but the "moral humiliation" that was hard to take and that made cooperation impossible. Richardson claimed at the time, "To remain passive under it would give one the feeling of sin; the sin of concurrence. One's whole nature is revolted: resistance is therefore inevitable."[13] In Richardson's words and in the visual representations of forcible feeding that were produced by the Union, the analogy to rape is clear and has been remarked upon by several recent scholars.[14] As Lisa Tickner put it, "It is not hard to understand how the instrumental invasion of their bodies by force, in a process accompanied by great pain and personal indignity, was felt as a kind of rape by the women who suffered it (though the word is not used directly)."[15] The comparison to rape would have been inescapable for those women whose forcible feeding was attempted through the rectum or the vagina.[16] Even for those who may not have made the sexual violation analogy, forcible feeding was—as Dr. Forbes Ross described it—"an act of brutality beyond common endurance." Concern over the women's health led 116 surgeons and physicians to protest forcible feeding in writing to the Prime Minister.[17]

Although the general public knew about the hunger strikes and forcible feeding, it took Lady Constance Lytton to give a human face to the anonymous many who carried out Union policy and suffered the results. Lytton was the third child of the first Earl of Lytton, Viceroy of India, and the granddaughter of the novelist Bulwer-Lytton. Her childhood was spent in India and, by 1909, she lived quietly in the country with her widowed mother. A woman in her thirties at this time, she was interested in folk songs and folk dances and their potential to "socially regenerate" the working classes.[18] "Lady Con" was a handsome if retiring woman, frail from birth with a weak heart. If not for her belief in the good that women's suffrage would bring to the lives of the poor, she probably would have remained contentedly with her mother in the country, involved in whatever "good works" her health would permit.

In 1908, Lady Constance met Emmeline Pethick-Lawrence and heard stories from the suffragettes newly released from prison. Some of the prison images they recounted never left her and on January 28, 1909, Lady Constance became a member of the WSPU.[19] She was first arrested on February 24, 1909, along with Emmeline Pethick-Lawrence and others in a deputation sent to the Commons protesting the omission of the women's suffrage issue from the King's Speech. She was sent to prison with the rest, but was not allowed to join her colleagues in the common cells. Instead, she served most of her time in the prison hospital, a decision that prison officials claimed was based on her health. Lady Constance and others suspected it to be based more on her social rank.[20]

On October 8, 1909, Lady Constance was arrested at Newcastle for throwing a stone at Sir Walter Runciman's car. Sir Walter was acting as host to Lloyd-George, who was in Newcastle to make a speech. The stone was wrapped in paper and was aimed low for the safety of those in the car. The paper read, "To Lloyd George—Rebellion against tyranny is obedience to God—Deeds not words."[21] Lady Constance was sentenced, as were ten other women, to one month's imprisonment in the second division. Because this arrest came after the success of the Dunlop strategy, the women went on an immediate hunger strike. Although other women in the hunger striking contingent were then forcibly fed, Lady Constance was not only *not* forcibly fed but was released from prison. Again, authorities cited her weak heart, and not her titled family, as the reason.[22]

Lady Constance was determined to share in the forcible feeding ordeal or at least to ascertain if her exemption was due to class considerations. She affected a disguise as a seamstress and rejoined the WSPU under the pseudonym Miss Jane Warton. The disguise was excellent; it is difficult to recognize photographs of her as being the same woman. She cut her hair to collar length and combed it, center-parted, down straight. Her dress sleeves were too short; her coat, long and green; and her hat, tweed. She wore a pair of pince-nez spectacles and was even careful to remove any initials from her underclothes. As she put it, she was "determined to put ugliness to the test."[23]

On January 14, 1910, "Jane Warton" addressed a crowd outside Walton Gaol in Liverpool and led a demonstration toward the prison. She was immediately arrested and sentenced to fourteen days hard labor. As before, she entered into a hunger strike. This time, however, the doctor who examined her proclaimed her heart to be "perfectly ripping."[24] Where Lady Constance Lytton was too delicate to even remain in prison, "Miss Jane Warton" was forcibly fed eight times. As the days passed, prison officials became suspicious about her identity, presumably because she was not a professional actress and under stress her accent and manner of speech were likely to give her away. She was released on Sunday, January 23. Unfortunately, the damage had been done, and this brave and gentle woman never recovered her health. In 1912, she had a severe heart attack. Although paralyzed on the right side, she spent two years recording her experiences in a book, *Prisons and Prisoners,* painstakingly written with her left hand. Lady Constance died on May 22, 1923.[25]

The address at the Queen's Hall presented first in this section, made a week after her release from Walton Gaol, presented both the political theory behind hunger striking and Lady Constance's experiences and reflections while in prison. This speech expanded the debate on forcible feeding and added a new issue for class-conscious Edwardian Britain. Particularly notable in this speech are Lytton's appeals to metaphors of sight and blindness, variations on the archetypal metaphor of light and darkness.[26] She begins with the inability of the average person to "see" the important nature of women's place in society. Lytton then moves to the inability of officials to see through her disguise as Jane Warton. It is during this part of her speech that she recounts her prison experience and gives a harrowing, graphic account of forcible feeding. Lytton's honesty is impressive both in her recounting of the psychological impact of forcible feeding and in her admission that the experience caused her to hate her tormentors. Finally she describes two prison images—symbolic of Calvary and the Madonna and Child—and the new vision and strength they gave her. Included, following the speech, are two letters that appeared in the *Times* of London. The first letter by Edward Troup, an official of the Home Secretary's office, shows the official face the government hoped to put on Lytton's experience. The second letter by Lord Lytton, Lady Constance's brother, is a coldly angry but detailed refutation of the government version of events. These two letters illustrate only some of the public furor that followed the revelations in Lady Constance's speech.

4

A Speech by Lady Constance Lytton.

Delivered at the Queen's Hall, January 31, 1910.

I AM GRATEFUL FOR YOUR KINDNESS, AND I APPRECIATE IT AS FULLY AND as deeply as any human being can, but let me remind the strangers here that though what I have done is something rather different perhaps to what other women have done, because the circumstances concerning me were different, and because there was something to lay hold rather freshly of the imagination of outsiders; yet they must remember this fact, that thirty-five other women have been treated as I have been treated, and of these women I have suffered almost the least. Before I tell you my story I want to impress that fact on the strangers and the outsiders. I am one of thirty-five to whom this has been done, and of this number there are two women in the prison from which I come, who are now being treated like that; two women who, as I did, are watching the waning of the light, and knowing that when the light fades it is only a question of minutes before this torture—one can call it by no other name—is inflicted on their helpless bodies at the bottom of a prison cell, where there will be no witnesses and no appeal.

Since I have been released I have had many letters not only from strangers, but from personal friends, who try to show sympathy, but who say in a curious, blind, and ignorant fashion: "But, after all, what is it all about? Why do it? It is all unnecessary." Therefore I want to give as briefly as I can a little sketch of my experiences during the last year. When first I joined this movement my life was literally transformed by contact with the four great leaders, who in these brief years have framed and created a movement which, I think, even in the history of the whole world will ever be considered as remarkable.

When I first came across those great forces I stood as an absolute outsider, an impartial critic. Let me tell a little incident which occurred in the country town where I was. One day I came on a great crowd forming a ring round a sheep being taken to the slaughter house. It looked old and misshapen. I suddenly saw a vision of what it should have been, on its native mountain side, when all its forces were rightly developed, and there was a hideous

107

contrast between that vision and the creature in the crowd. It seemed to be an ungainly thing. Presently it was caught again, and one man gave it a great cuff on the head. At that I felt exasperated. I said, "If you have got this creature in your power, don't you know your own business? If you were holding it properly it would be still. You think that insult is the proper thing at this moment?" Over and over again I have thought of that incident, of how women have been thought unwomanly, unnatural, held in contempt, a thing outside the pale, and laughed at and then insulted, because of conditions which they had not produced, but which were the result of mistakes and injustice of civilisation. When one joins this cause one must expect derisive misunderstanding, and misinterpretation of all one's motives. A friend told me recently that her brother, who had an important post in South Africa, condemned the movement when first he heard of her joining it. Presently, he came back from South Africa, and said he was a complete convert to Woman Suffrage. His reason was that as he moved among the aboriginal tribes he found that the status of the tribe was exactly gauged by the status of the women in that tribe. Where they were honoured and respected it was the same with the tribe, and where it was otherwise the tribe was dishonoured. I think that is a very good instance of what happens in all countries, civilised as well as uncivilised. Only the very day before I went into Liverpool prison as Jane Warton, I met at one of my meetings a factory inspector. She seemed what you could describe as a "red tape" official, an unimaginative, official woman. Yet she said this: "If only one of these well-to-do, happy women could sit in the police-court, as I have to do, there would be no need to argue with them about the position of women in this country at the present moment." She told me she was in a police-court the other day when three prisoners were brought before the magistrate, a man and two women. The man and a woman were arrested for being together in the public street at night, the other woman for mounting guard. The facts were clear—the man had bribed the woman and had paid her money—and yet this was the verdict: The two women were sent to prison and the man was allowed to go free. People talk of sex war. Is not that sex war? It is sex peace we want.

Women's Weapons.

People say, what does this hunger-strike mean? Surely it is all folly. If it is not hysteria, at least it is unreasonable. They will not realise that we are like an army, that we are deputed to fight for a cause, and for other people, and in any struggle or any fight, weapons must be used. The weapons for which we ask are simple, a fair hearing, but that is refused us in Parliament, refused us by the Government, refused us in the magistrates' courts, refused us in the law courts. Then we must have other weapons. What do other people choose when they are driven to the last extremity? What do men choose? They have recourse to violence. But what the women of this movement have specially stood out for is that they will not kill, they will not harm while they have other weapons left them. These women have chosen the weapon of self-hurt to make their protest, and this hunger-strike brings great pressure upon the Government. It involves grave hurt and tremendous sacrifice, but this is on the part of the women only, and does not physically injure their enemies. Can that be called violence and hooliganism? But it is no good taking a weapon and being ready to drop it at the very first provocation, so when the Government retaliated with their unfair methods, with their abominable torture and tyranny of feeding by force, did you expect the women to drop their weapons? No, of course not. I had been in this movement many months, and although I absolutely approved of the method of getting in our messages by means of stones which did nothing but convey our meaning to the Ministers and to the world, still I felt I could not throw a stone myself. However, as I have told you here before when I saw the first of these women released—a mere girl—from Birmingham Gaol, I took another view. I went to Newcastle for a protest, meaning to share what these women endured. I went in my own name, and, as you know, I was released after a very short hunger-strike, a heart specialist being called in, who examined me for something like a quarter of an hour. I made a tremendous protest. I said that in that same prison where I was, there was a woman, a first offender, who had done much less violence than I had, and she was fed by force without having her heart tested at all. "Whatever you think of the subject," I said "whatever you think of the militant movement, surely you can see that justice is done between one human being and another!" I tried all I could, when I came out, and I got others whom I know to fight that question with truth and exposure, and what did they give us back?

Lies, and nothing but lies!

Well, I thought, you choose your weapons, I will fight with the same weapon, and you shall take my life, and do with it what you will! So I disguised myself; I changed my personality, and I went and made my protest outside that very gaol where these hideous, abominable things were being done. It was easier than I thought. I merely cut my hair. I bought clothes of a different type to my own, I removed the initials from my underclothes, I put on glasses, and that was more than sufficient. I had one rather unhappy moment. They had taken my belongings, brooches, handkerchief, etc. I saw in the first bundle a reel of cotton with "Lytton" on it, and a handkerchief from which I had omitted to remove the initials. I thought the game was up, but they were so little suspicious that I simply placed my hand upon these two things and put them into the fire. The prison world is so used to Suffragettes doing strange things that they were not at all surprised.

I was always on the alert for being discovered, but the first day of the hunger-strike went by, the second day went by, and the third day went by, and it was quite obvious from the way they treated me they did not suspect my identity. It was the first time I had been to prison without my name, and I can assure you it made a great deal of difference. Perhaps it is only human. I do not complain of position influencing people like wardresses or policemen, but when it comes to law and the Home Office, surely one can expect something more like justice? On the fourth day of my hunger-strike the doctor came to my cell and said he must feed me at once. I was so desirous of gaining my object—I knew that if I was only fed once it would be a test—that I did not look upon it with horror—I welcomed it. To my surprise and to my great relief they did not examine my heart, which I had managed for two days, but which by the fourth day of starvation was becoming difficult.

At last they came. It is like describing a hospital scene—and much worse. The doctor and four wardresses came into my cell. I decided to save all my resistance for the actual feeding, and when they pointed to my bed on the floor I lay down, and the doctor did not even feel my pulse. Two wardresses held my hands, one my head. Much as I had heard about this thing, it was infinitely more horrible and more painful than I had expected. The doctor put the steel gag in somewhere on my gums and forced open my mouth till it was yawning wide. As he proceeded to force into my mouth and down the throat a large rubber tube, I felt as though I were being killed; absolute suffocation is the feeling. You feel as though it would never stop. You cannot breathe, and yet you choke. It irritates the throat, it irritates the mucous membrane as it goes down, every second seems an hour, and you think they will never finish pushing it down. After a while the sensation is relieved, then the food is poured down, and then again you choke, and your whole body resists and writhes under the treatment; you are held down, and the process goes on, and, finally, when the vomiting becomes excessive the tube is removed. I forgot what I was in there for, I forgot women, I forgot everything except my own sufferings, and I was completely overcome by them.

What was even worse to me than the thing itself was the positive terror with which I anticipated its renewal. Very soon I thought to try and appeal to that man as a doctor to perform the operation in a better way, but whatever one said or suggested was treated with most absolute contempt.

There was one even worse thing, and that was the moral poisoning, if one may call it that, of one's whole mind. I always closed my eyes. I tried not to see the beings who came to do this thing. I felt it was all too hideous, and I did not wish it imprinted on my eyes. Nevertheless I got to hate those men and women, I got to hate infinitely more the powers that stood behind them, I got to hate the blindness, the prejudice, in those who turn away and won't look or listen to what is being done under their very eyes. I tried to think of the splendid heroes and heroines since the world began, of all the martyrs, all the magnificent women in this movement, and I felt a tremendous gratitude to them, an admiration which overpowered me. But it was no use to me—it did not help me and it did not strengthen me.

I must go back a little, and tell you that when the chaplain visited me he seemed to have said to himself, "This is a Suffragette; one must mend her ideas of women." So he began speaking in this style: "I can tell you one thing, any woman you see in this prison, you may take it from me, is as bad as bad can be. Everything has been done to help her, but she is absolutely hopeless." These remarks came back to me later, and I thought, "Here is this man, the only man in this prison who could strike a different note, who could help the wretched souls, and that is his summing up of all the unhappy people under him—'as bad as bad can be.'"

Two Pictures.

Then one evening, as I lay on the bed on the floor of my cell, I looked up. There were three panes of clear glass, and on them as the light fell there came shadows of the moulding that looked like three crosses. It brought to my mind the familiar scene of Calvary with its three crosses, and I thought: What did they stand for? One for the Lord Christ who died for sinners, and one for the sinner who was kind, and one for the sinner who had not yet learnt to be kind, and behind those crosses I saw those hateful faces, the self-righteous, all those hateful institutions of superior goodness and moral blindness of officialdom, of all the injustice done, not only in prison, but in the world outside, and I thought surely it was for these that Christ died and is dying still and will have to die until they begin to see. When I thought that my blind hatred should be standing between these people and their better selves, I felt the hatred and the hell-like surroundings go from me. I was grateful to those panes, and the next day I put the table and the chair together and roused myself to wash the three windows cleaner, and as I looked through the glass, I saw, in the waning evening light, suffused by a pink glow, a scene which was to me more beautiful than the most beautiful picture I had ever seen. Outside was a little exercise yard, into which I had never been. Wandering round and round in the evening light, quite alone, was a slight figure of a woman, and as she turned the corner I saw that in her arms, under her shawl, she had another little prisoner, a baby, and she was happy and talking and singing to it; she seemed the very symbol of what we are fighting for, fighting to restore what has been lost—and I looked at that woman, who seemed so helpless, and I thought of the parson's words, "Bad as bad can be." And I felt as strong as Samson! A strength which no stories of heroic people had been able to give to me came to me.

After each time the hideous process of forcible feeding was repeated it meant a ghastly kind of washing up. Two or three times I was so completely unmanned that I was not able to do it myself, and an ordinary prisoner came in to do it. She was a new hand, and the wardresses said contemptuously in her presence, "Just look at that; look at the way she is doing it." But the woman's face never changed, there was no resentment and no anger. I ventured to say, "At any rate, she is doing the work I ought to do myself, and I am very grateful to her." and from that woman there came to me an immense strength, and I felt I could fight on and live on to the end. As I was taken out to be weighed I passed a little girl, she was not more than a child. She may for aught I know have been taken straight off the streets, but she had at that moment the face of an angel, and she looked down on me with a smile which you can never see out of prison. She gave me that angel's smile, and it positively touched my very soul. When I went out of the prison, I felt my resentment and anger were gone. In a way my physical courage was no better than before, but at least I could go on. I knew that I should last out.

Then you come out of prison, and you hear people say: "You have gone in as a practical joke to do the Home Secretary," or "You went in for a piece of hooliganism," and so on. What are these people made of? Is that what we want? No. We want that from those helpless officials who are only blindly doing what they are told to do, there should be removed these hideous orders from high quarters, that it should become impossible for orders of that kind to be carried out on women who can in no sense be compared with ordinary criminals. It must not be left to the magistrates and the law, but in public opinion it must be made impossible.

Even now there are many people to-day who kindly extend their personal sympathy to me. What are those people? Everyone counts immensely. Do not, at any point where you touch this movement, think you are of no account. Do your part and leave the rest. We want your sympathy, and are glad of it. We want your money, and I will tell you a story about that. One woman, a poor working woman, wrote to the Union, and enclosed a postal order for half-a-crown, and she said: "Will you take this and use it in any way Constance Lytton would like best." Another said: "I should have liked to send you flowers, but I thought you would like the money better." With this I mean to start a fund simply for educating this blind world, for trying to take the scales from the eyes of those who do not yet understand. We want your help for that, and we want your money for that, but we want, even more than that, that you should stand by us. Let me tell you one more personal anecdote. When the doctor first came into my cell I said: "Will you shake me by the hand?" And what I had been going to say to him if he had granted me my request was, "I want to shake hands with you for you have taken service on the wrong side. Those who back the Government in this matter are on the wrong side, and when they discover it they will have a very black moment, so let us shake hands over it now." Well the doctor, being a prison official, could probably do nothing else; he did not shake hands. But do not let it come to you—that black moment when you will find you have taken service on the wrong side. This is the most glorious fight that has ever been. Become a member of our Union. It is so easy to do that. Before you leave this hall, say: "I will stand by you whatever the world says, whatever public opinion says, I am for you now, before another minute goes by."

5

The Times of London
February 10, 1910

Prison Treatment of Woman Suffragists

THE HOME SECRETARY HAS CAUSED THE FOLLOWING LETTER TO BE AD-dressed to a correspondent who called his attention to a leaflet which has been recently circulated with reference to the imprisonment of Lady Constance Lytton at Liverpool:

Home Office, Whitehall, Feb. 9, 1910

Sir,

    With reference to your letter of the 28th ult., I am directed by the Secretary of State to say that the statement that Lady Constance Lytton was released from Liverpool Prison only when her identity was discovered is untrue. The release of "Jane Warton" was recommended by the medical officer and authorised by the Secretary of State upon purely medical grounds before her identity with Lady Constance Lytton was suspected by any official either at the Home Office or at the prison.

    As regards the allegation that the treatment of "Jane Warton" differed from that of Lady Constance Lytton, I am to inform you that Lady Constance Lytton was released from Newcastle Prison in October last because the medical authorities at that prison considered that, owing to the condition of her heart, the violent resistance which she was expected to offer to the necessary artificial feeding would be attended with risk. Their diagnosis of the case has recently been fully confirmed by the opinion of her own medical attendant.

    Upon her reception at Liverpool Prison under the name of "Jane Warton" on the 15th ult., she refused to allow her heart to be examined. From her demeanor and conversation there was no reason to anticipate that she would resist being fed, and the examination of her heart which she allowed the doctor to make before he fed her did not indicate that the operation would involve risk to her health. She was accordingly artificially fed for a few days like any other prisoner who persists in refusing to take food. On the 22nd ult. the medical officer, finding that the injury to her health which was being caused by her persistent refusal to take food could not be prevented by artificial feeding, recommended her discharge on

114

the ground of her state of health, and she was released in accordance with the usual practice in such cases.

The suggestion that any differences in her treatment at the two prisons was due to considerations of social position is entirely without foundation, and the Secretary of State is satisfied, after careful enquiry, that there is no justification whatever for the charges made by Lady Constance Lytton against the officers employed at Liverpool Prison.—I am, Sir, your obedient servant,

Edward Troup

6

The Times of London
March 30, 1910

Lady Constance Lytton and the Home Office

To the editor of *the times:*

Sir,

On February 10 a letter was sent to the Press by Sir Edward Troup, relative to a statement made by my sister Lady Constance Lytton regarding her treatment in Liverpool Prison, in which he declared on behalf of the Home Secretary that there was no foundation for any of the charges which she had made. I am anxious to explain why this official imputation of untruthfulness has hitherto remained unanswered.

Lady Constance was seriously ill at the time as the result of her prison experiences, and unable to defend herself. I therefore undertook the task of vindicating her veracity. Before making any public statement on her behalf, I was anxious to find out what steps had been taken by the Home Office to investigate the matters referred to in her statement, and I hoped by a friendly intervention to secure a full and impartial enquiry into all the circumstances of her treatment by the prison officials.

I have had several communications with the Home Office on the subject, and owing to the retirement of Mr. Gladstone and the appointment of a new Home Secretary they have necessarily been protracted over a considerable period. My attitude throughout has been entirely conciliatory, and the only claim which I have made was that in the interests of justice charges of this nature should be submitted to a full and impartial enquiry, which would, of course, involve a separate examination of both the parties concerned. This claim has been refused by the Home Office on the grounds that the prison officials have been closely interrogated, and that as they deny entirely every one of the charges made, "no useful purpose would be served" by granting my request.

In the absence of such an enquiry as I asked for the matter must be left to the opinion of unbiased minds. I desire, however, to say that nothing which I have been able to learn has in any way shaken my belief in the substantial accuracy of my sister's account. The idea that her charges can be disposed of by the bare denial of the persons against whom they are made is not likely to commend itself

116

to anyone outside the Home Office, and no amount of denial can get over the following facts:

1. Lady Constance Lytton, when imprisoned in Newcastle, after refusing to answer the medical questions put to her and adopting the hunger-strike, received a careful and thorough medical examination, which disclosed symptoms of "serious heart disease," and on these grounds she was released as unfit to submit to forcible feeding.

2. Three months later "Jane Warton," when imprisoned at Liverpool, also refused to answer medical questions or to take prison food. On this occasion she was entered in the prison books as having refused medical examination, and was forcibly fed eight times. Such medical examination as took place during the forcible feeding failed, according to the medical officer's report, to disclose any symptoms of heart disease, and she was eventually released on the grounds of loss of weight and general physical weakness.

These facts are incontrovertible, and though the Home Office is quite satisfied that in both cases the prison officials performed their duty in the most exemplary fashion, your readers will form their own opinions of the justice of a Government Department which brings accusations of untruthfulness against an individual whilst refusing the only means by which the truth can be established.

I am, your obedient servant,

Lytton

Senior WSPU at Caxton Hall Meeting, 1908.

Part IV
Black Friday

THE YEAR 1910 BEGAN AS ONE OF TRUCE BETWEEN THE GOVERNMENT and suffrage forces, although it ended in unprecedented violence directed at the WSPU. As mentioned previously, following the November 30, 1909, House of Lords' veto of the Liberal government's "war on poverty budget,"[1] Asquith called a general election in January 1910. The Liberal government was seeking a public mandate against the House of Lords' right of absolute veto.

In this election, Emmeline Pankhurst continued the election policy followed previously by the Union; that is, she urged opposition to Liberal candidates, although the Liberal party was considered the party most favorably disposed toward woman suffrage. Pankhurst's view was that the party in power should actively work to bring about women's suffrage and that simple claims of support unaccompanied by action were mere hypocrisy. Much has been made of this policy by historians in the past, usually with implications that the WSPU leadership was acting irrationally. Roger Fulford described the election policy variously as "the convulsion of the drowning man who puts all his strength into an attempt to drag down with him the friend who has come to his aid," and as Emmeline Pankhurst "firing her howitzers at her own side."[2] Of course, as Fulford admits, this election policy was not original with Pankhurst, but was the policy followed by Parnell and the Irish Party in the 1880s. Despite the obvious drawbacks of this election policy, it is difficult to view as a superior policy the thirty years of solid campaigning by women for those who mouthed their support for suffrage and then refused to act on its behalf. In any case, the WSPU campaigned hard in 1910 against Liberal candidates. For a variety of reasons, the Liberal party lost one hundred seats and remained in power only with the aid of Irish Nationalist and Labour seats. With the Liberals and Conservatives practically even (and meeting in conference to hammer out the House of Lords question) and with the death of King Edward VII in May, the atmosphere was that of serious compromise. Because rumors were flying through the suffrage ranks that a compromise bill on suffrage might make it through

Parliament, the WSPU and Women's Freedom League called a truce on militant activity.[3]

A parliamentary committee, soon to be called the Conciliation Committee, was formed from suffragists across party lines. It consisted of twenty-five Liberals, seventeen Conservatives, six Irish Nationalists, and six Labourites. Chairing the committee was Lord Lytton, the brother of Lady Constance Lytton (See *Times* letter in the previous section), and serving as Honorary Secretary was H. N. Brailsford, whose wife had served time in prison for suffrage activities. It was the job of these men to design a bill that would have some chance in the newly formulated Parliament.[4] It is for that reason that the final bill had such a strongly Conservative slant. The bill would give the Parliamentary vote to all women householders (that is, women owning a house, part of a house, or even a room) and to women occupying business premises who paid £10 or more a year in rent. Marriage could not disqualify women, although men and women could not use the same property as qualification.[5] This bill was certainly not ideal to all suffragists, because it did not enfranchise unpropertied women who had a particular stake in social reform. However, with the possibility of success after years of struggle, even a half-a-loaf measure was ardently embraced.

The Conciliation Bill was introduced on June 14, 1910. To keep enthusiasm for the bill high, the WSPU staged a remarkable demonstration four days later. A procession so long that it took an hour and a half to pass each point along the way was held in the streets of London.[6] Women marched in well-organized groupings: the 617 women who had been in prison, a group of 800 "learned ladies," contingents of women athletes, writers, actresses, and on and on. Along the way, they were cheered by crowds of enthusiastic spectators, and the sense of imminent victory was palpable.[7] Then came the blow: Lloyd-George and Winston Churchill (replacing Herbert Gladstone as Home Secretary in 1910), who had both previously expressed sympathy for suffrage, spoke strongly against the bill. They claimed their opposition was based on the lack of democracy in the bill, on the fact that it did not enfranchise poor women, and on the assertion that it would be impossible to amend.[8]

Despite the attack on the bill, the voting on the second reading was 299 in favor and 189 opposed[9]—a greater majority than any other bill that session.[10] Asquith was able to convince even some supporters of the bill that, due to its Constitutional importance, the bill should go to a Committee of the Whole House rather than a Grand Committee. A Committee of the Whole House was simply the House sitting under a different name, and the government had control over granting Parliamentary time for such a committee. This move put the bill securely in Asquith's power, and he refused to give any more time for the bill that session, basing his refusal on its unamendable nature. The Conciliation Committee could only hope to recast the bill and try again in the autumn session.[11] During the proceedings on the bill, Asquith made comments that were rather remarkable in light of the recent vote, the current truce, and the massive June 18 demonstration:

> . . . the cause which cannot win its way to public acceptance by persuasion, argument, organization and by the peaceful methods of agitation is a cause which has already in advance pronounced upon itself its own sentence of death.[12]

Such a pronouncement could only make those working for suffrage feel that any efforts, constitutional or militant, would be equally distorted by an obdurate government.

The repressive steps that the government and the new Home Secretary were willing to take against the suffragettes became clear in November 1910. In her detailed study of the day that became known as "Black Friday" in suffrage circles, Caroline Morrell claims that all minority movements need their definitive moment of repression. Black Friday was the equivalent for the suffrage cause to the Bloody Sundays of Northern Ireland and the Russian Revolution. Such events crystalize a moment in time when the government reveals the iron fist inside the statesman's glove.[13] The resulting frustration and anger of movement members then serve as goads to deeper dedication and stronger action.

On Friday, November 18, 1910, Asquith announced that the negotiations between Liberals and Conservatives in Parliament had given way. He further announced a General Election on the House of Lords question and made clear that there would be no time that session for anything but immediate government concerns. This would spell the end for the Conciliation Bill.[14] The WSPU had anticipated this announcement and had gathered in Caxton Hall while the Prime Minister was still speaking. Emmeline Pankhurst was accompanied to Parliament by Dr. Elizabeth Garrett Anderson, the sister of constitutional suffragist Millicent Fawcett and the first woman to qualify as a doctor and the first female Lord Mayor in Britain. Also composing the deputation of twelve was Mrs. Hertha Ayrton (a scientist who later developed an invention against poison gas effects in World War I), Dr. Louisa Garrett Anderson, and the elderly Mrs. Saul Solomon, widow of the former Governor General of the Cape Colony. This initial deputation reached the Parliament with difficulty; age and eminence could not prevent Mrs. Solomon from being grabbed by the breasts and flung down.[15] Yet, these were minor difficulties when compared to the treatment accorded to the some 450 women who followed. Moving in small legal groups, they carried clever banners reading, "Where There's a Bill There's a Way," and "Women's Will Beats Asquith's Won't." These banners were ripped from their hands and shredded by the police.[16] It became quickly apparent that these were not the usual Westminster police but police brought in from the East End—men accustomed to dealing with prostitutes and rowdy drunks. It is hard to know if their orders from the Home Office were to intimidate the women physically into retreat, but arrest was delayed for six hours while the usual "buffeting" was replaced with actual beating.[17] Emmeline Pankhurst described the police action, thusly:

> Then they laid hands on the women and literally threw them from one man to another. Some of the police used their fists, striking the women in their faces, their breasts, their shoulders. One woman I saw thrown down with violence three or four times in rapid succession, until at last she lay only half conscious against the curb, and in a serious condition was carried away by kindly strangers.[18]

Most of the pictures taken of Black Friday were suppressed, but the few available show women being lifted bodily into the air or lying on the ground. One picture in particular shows what was generalized as "Acts of Indecency" at the time. There is a photograph of six laughing men holding a petite suffragette while they pulled her dress up over her head.[19] Generally, the act of indecency was the seizing of women in the breast or genital area. A memorandum prepared by the Secretary of the Conciliation Committee and Dr. Jessie Murray reported that the most common violence was the "twisting round, pinching, screwing, nipping or wringing the breast. This was most often done in the most public way so as to inflict the utmost humiliation."[20] Although the desire to humiliate and cause physical pain may have been a motivation, there is a more sinister element to assaults directed at a woman's breast. At the time, it was common belief that injury to a woman's breast was the primary cause of breast cancer, a belief that would have been shared by both the policeman and the woman being assaulted. Certainly, though, it is hard today to look at photographs of men entertaining themselves by pulling a woman's skirts over her head or to read about men grabbing the breasts of women who are members of a deputation without making the connection to gang rape.

The day ended with the arrest of 115 women and 4 men. Home Secretary Winston Churchill ordered their release the next morning, ostensibly as preelection clemency, more likely so that the reports of police violence would not be aired in a public trial. The Conciliation Committee sought a public inquiry, but were refused this by the Home Office.[21] It is only through the Brailsford and Murray Memorandum that testimony about specific violent acts was available, and most of this material was suppressed and distorted by the press. For example, here is testimony by Mary Francis Earl of her Black Friday experience. She had barely recovered from a policeman's fist striking her nose and causing it to bleed when another policeman bent back her thumbs:

> He also twisted my wrist which was black and blue the next day and is painful still. He flung me to the ground and proceeded to kick me as I lay as he had previously said he would do.[22]

This very personal and unilateral violence was turned by the press into assaults on policemen who were simply doing their job. According to *The Times*, "several of the police had their helmets knocked off, one was disabled by a kick on the ankle, and one had his hand cut" and *The Standard* maintained that "the police had to use considerable force to protect themselves from injury." In all cases the mainstream press portrayed the women as the ones being violent and refusing "to be happy until they were arrested."[23]

Four deaths were attributed by the suffragettes to Black Friday, although the direct causal connection has never been proven. Emmeline Pankhurst's sister Mary Clarke came to London from Brighton to join the deputation. Family members and friends were concerned for her health, and she promised to break a window rather than allow herself to be hurt in the deputation. Nevertheless, she reportedly sustained injuries that troubled her throughout her one month's imprisonment. A few days following her release from prison, she quietly excused herself from the dinner table on Christmas Day. When Emmeline Pankhurst went to check on Mrs. Clarke, she found that her sister had suffered a cerebral hemorrhage.[24] The second Black Friday death was that of the elderly Henria Williams. Her testimony in the Brailsford and Murray Memorandum could best be described as motherly, in that she spoke of the policemen who injured her almost as if they were big children who, because of their "strong large hands . . . cannot possibly know how tightly they are holding and how terribly at times they are hurting." She was grasped and squeezed just over her heart until she was breathless. Just over a month later, on January 1, 1911, she died suddenly of a heart attack.[25] Both Clarke and Williams were fragile women in poor health, and their deaths could just as easily have been coincidental. Two other deaths happened much later, but perhaps could be more accurately traced to Black Friday. Cecilia Wolseley-Haig died in December 1911 after suffering for a year from injuries sustained during the deputation. Nurse Ellen Pitfield also received a wound on Black Friday that never healed. Cancer developed at the site of the injury, and she died in August 1912.[26] Whether or not these deaths were actually a result of Black Friday, they served as symbols of the very real violence the suffragettes suffered that day. Later in the movement when the suffragettes turned to a policy of violence against property, Black Friday would serve as proof that women's violence was defensive in nature.[27]

On the Tuesday following Black Friday, an event happened that is mentioned by Christabel Pankhurst in this next section of speeches. On November 22, following a Caxton Hall meeting, Mrs. Pankhurst led the way to an unprepared Downing Street. Asquith appeared and was "well hooted" and "well shaken" by suffragettes before the police helped him escape in a taxicab. Mr. Birrell, a Cabinet Member, injured his leg by leaping into another taxicab to escape the women. A number of windows were smashed that day and evening in houses belonging to Mr. Winston Churchill and John Burns, among others. One hundred and sixty suffragettes were arrested that week; all but the seventy-five accused of window smashing and assault were discharged the next morning.[28]

It was at this point that the Declaration of War written by Christabel Pankhurst appeared in the November 25 *Votes For Women*. This declaration outlined Union response to Asquith's statement in the House of Commons. It is followed here by speeches made by Emmeline and Christabel Pankhurst at Queen's Hall about the events of the previous weeks. Emmeline Pankhurst addressed the violence against legal deputations. However, she put a positive face on events by thanking the gallant band of male supporters, predicting that soon it would not just be a handful of men demanding justice for women but "thousands upon thousands." This speech lends credence to Holton's claim that Pankhurst never lost her "appeal to an essentially chivalrous conception of male-female relations. Although Mrs. Pankhurst spoke often of the wrongs of women and children at the hands of men, she also continued to rely on men's capacity to rise above their lower natures when confronted with the 'sorrowful wrath' of women."[29]

7

We Revert to a State of War.

Statement by Christabel Pankhurst, November 25, 1910

> The Government will, if they are still in power, give facilities in
> the next Parliament for effectively proceeding with a Bill which is
> so framed as to admit of free amendment.
> *—Prime Minister's statement in the House of Commons,*
> *Tuesday, Nov. 22.*

AT LAST WE HAVE THE GOVERNMENT'S EAGERLY AWAITED STATEMENT ON woman suffrage. The recent declarations made by individual Cabinet Ministers had aroused some expectation that the Government would promise to give full facilities for a Woman Suffrage Bill next year. The Women's Social and Political Union had determined beforehand to accept no declaration from the Government which did not comply with certain conditions. The more important of these were as follows:—The pledge must be to give full facilities for a Woman Suffrage Bill next session. The Bill in question must be no more extended in its scope than the Conciliation Bill introduced by Mr. Shackleton or the Women's Enfranchisement Bill introduced two years ago by Mr. Stanger, a pledge to give facilities to a Bill on a so-called democratic basis being worthless, because such a Bill would have no chance of passing through either House of Parliament.

The statement made by the Prime Minister on Tuesday fulfils neither of these vital conditions and has accordingly been indignantly rejected by the Women's Social and Political Union. In the first place the pledge does not guarantee the enfranchisement of women *next session*. The promise for next *Parliament* is utterly worthless. There is no precise moment when we could call for its fulfilment. Session after session the Prime Minister could reply to our demand for instant enfranchisement that he had undertaken to let the Suffrage Bill be carried not in any particular session but in the existing Parliament. After thus postponing the satisfaction of any demand for a year or two, he could, and his past record teaches us that he would, suddenly cause the life of that Parliament to be brought to an end. With a new Parliament the same farce would begin again. The trick is too obvious to deceive anyone for a single moment.

The Government strongly desire a cessation of the militant movement. Therefore their plan is that during the next Parliament we shall, session after session, be led on in quiet and peaceful courses by hope deferred—hope which it is their intention finally to disappoint. Into so open a trap not the most guileless would fall; and the women of the present day possess a ripe political intelligence and knowledge. It would indeed be strange if they had learned nothing from the history of the past half century, packed full as it is with instances of treachery and duplicity displayed by politicians in their dealing with the Woman Suffrage Movement. Especially does our experience during the present Parliament prevent us from cherishing any illusion as to the true nature of the Prime Minister's latest "pledge." Let us recall the facts! Before the last General Election Mr. Asquith declared at the Albert Hall that "the question of Woman Suffrage is clearly one on which the new House of Commons ought to be given an opportunity of expressing its view," and on a subsequent occasion he said that the House ought to have an opportunity of effectively dealing with this whole question. The undertaking so expressed Mr. Asquith has deliberately broken, and by terminating the existence of the present Parliament he has now made its fulfilment impossible. It will be seen that the Government's new promise is virtually the same as the promise which they gave before the last General Election, and (unless women can prevent this second breach of faith) they will have as little compunction in breaking their new promise in the next Parliament as they had in breaking the old promise in this Parliament.

Again, the Government's "pledge" does not comply with the second condition above referred to—that is to say, it does not apply exclusively to a moderate and practicable Bill.

To this second grave defect in the Government's statement the Conciliation Committee have already drawn attention in the following words: "Mr. Asquith's promise applies not to our Bill specifically but generally to a Bill so framed as to admit of free amendment. The Conciliation Committee had already undertaken to make its Bill conform to this condition by giving it a general title, but Mr. Asquith's promise would apply to any Suffrage Bill, even to an Adult Suffrage Bill. It would be open to any private Member, without consulting other Suffrage Parties or the Women's Societies, to introduce a Bill which would not receive wide support."

This in itself is a sufficient reason for regarding the Government's pledge as worthless.

At the moment when the Prime Minister was making his statement in the House of Commons a great deputation of women representing the Women's Social and Political Union was assembled in Caxton Hall.

When the news came of the Prime Minister's hostile declaration there was but one thing to be done, and they did it. They went instantly to Downing Street to see the Prime Minister and to protest against his refusal to give an undertaking that the question of women's enfranchisement shall be honestly and finally dealt with in the coming year. The brave, prompt, and determined act of the deputation told the world more clearly than mere words could have done that women are not to be deceived by any illusory promise, and that they are determined to have justice, and to have it now. In a word, the Government having uttered false political coin, the women of this Union nailed that false coin to the counter.

The Prime Minister's statement, constituting as it does a message of defiance to us, means that we revert to a state of war. At the beginning of the present Parliament we declared a truce, which, if the Government had acted in the same spirit of reasonableness and conciliation that we have displayed, would have ended in peace; but the Prime Minister, by his recent statement, so injurious to our right as citizens and so insulting to our intelligence, has put an end to all hope of a peaceful settlement of the issue between us. "Negotiations are over. War is declared."

Christabel Pankhurst

8

Fighting Speeches At Queen's Hall.

By Emmeline and Christabel Pankhurst

Mrs. Pankhurst.

AFTER DESCRIBING THE EVENTS OF LAST WEEK, MRS. PANKHURST SAID: Can you wonder that women resented that insult by doing what other politicians in this country have done from time immemorial by damaging Government property? On the night before, I saw one woman bruised from head to foot, bruises she had got as a member of a peaceful deputation. I can only say, as the leader of that deputation and as one of the older women on that deputation, that I thank those women who resented the treatment they had received by acting in the way the women now in prison have done.

Speaking of the police arrangements in Parliament Square, Mrs. Pankhurst said: I say without fear of contradiction from the Home Secretary that he had permeated that crowd with policemen in plain clothes, to hustle law-abiding and peaceful women who were going in an orderly way to the House of Commons. Imitating French police methods they sent agents provocateurs to incite the more disorderly members of the public to attack the women.

I know all of you want to know what is happening to those women in prison. I went to Holloway this morning to pay a prisoner's fine. It may seem an extraordinary thing for me to do, but the prisoner is Mrs. Hawkins, the wife of the man who is now in Bradford infirmary suffering from a doubly fractured leg because he dared to ask Mr. Winston Churchill a question about Woman Suffrage. When Mrs. Hawkins, who is the wife of a working-man, decided to come up from Leicester as a delegate, her husband undertook to look after the home and the children for her while she was away, but, as you know, he did what he could to keep the cause going while she was in prison, and he suffered in consequence. It seems to me that the new "privileges" are rather more apparent to the ear than they are in fact. I understand that there is dissatisfaction amongst the women there, and that many protests are being made. We shall hear more about that later on, but

I mention it in order that you may be prepared to discount anything you may hear or see in the Press stated on behalf of the Home Secretary as to the comfortable conditions in which women Suffragists are now kept in prison.

We cannot meet on this occasion without some thought of the future. What are we outside going to do to support those women who have made this great sacrifice for us, and who are now in prison? We are going to do our best to keep the Liberal out. We want volunteers, we want women to come into the fighting line and take the place of those speakers and workers—and those in the forefront of the battle are always the best speakers and workers. I do not think that those of you who have simply supported us passively up to now quite realise how much we women in this movement get for ourselves. I do not think you realise the sense of joy and freedom that we get, even when we are being battered about by the police. We know that we are fighting for the freedom of womanhood. It is not until you make up your mind to give yourself that you really find yourself. So we ask you to take part in this election and do your best to make it a decisive one. We want those women who have already worked to make up their minds to work still harder.

Reference has been made to the way in which the Press have reported our deputation. Well, there is only one way of bringing to the public a true knowledge of what occurred, and that is by selling our own paper, and we want volunteers for doing that work. If you do not wish to stand in the street selling the paper, there is another way in which you can extend its circulation. A lady told me the other day when I was up in the North of England that every week she went from house to house, selling copies of *Votes For Women,* and there were dozens of houses at which, week after week, the paper was bought. That seems to me a very good way of enlarging the circulation of our paper, and I recommend it to those women who do not feel that they are able to stand out in the street, but would like to do something to help forward this movement.

I want to say a word about the men who have come into this fight. We women have known what the little gallant band of men have been doing for a very long time past, and we have been more grateful to them than I think perhaps they have realised. There have been times when we have felt very inclined to be bitter about the men of this country. We have asked, we older women, where were the men we had thought would rouse themselves when they saw women being treated like that? We thought when the first deputation took place that men would never stand that; but we found that men would stand a good deal where women were concerned, and some of us began to lose faith and grow very bitter, and I want as a woman to thank our men friends for having sweetened our hearts about men, for having done something to take the stigma off their sex where this movement is concerned. I believe that just as each one of those men probably did not understand at first, yet when they did understand felt it was their duty to come out and show people how they felt in the matter, so more and more men who did not at first understand will come forward, and in the end there will be not a mere handful of men, but there will be thousands upon thousands of men who will insist that bare justice shall be done to women, who are as much entitled to make the conditions of their lives as they are themselves.

This afternoon, although seventy of our dear women are in prison, although we have difficulty in getting our cause before the public on account of the attitude of the Press, we are full of hope and full of courage; yes, and I may say we are also full of joy in the new chivalry which is growing up amongst men, and we are full of joy because of the growing courage of women. Men have kept from us many things. There is one thing which they have kept from us, and that has been the joy of battle. They tell us women cannot fight. They tell us that warfare and strife are things that women must be kept out of because coming into it would destroy all that is best in them, all that is noblest in womanhood, and we have found out that they were influenced not altogether by a desire for our welfare or our well-being. We know—every woman who took part in that Battle of Downing Street on Tuesday will agree—that there is something very strengthening in this strife, something very ennobling, and I believe it is good for the race that women should feel the joy of battle as well as men. I believe that it is good for the race that we women are having to fight for our freedom. I believe that we shall have a nobler and a finer race than we ever had when courage was a monopoly of men and submission was the monopoly of women.

Miss Christabel Pankhurst.

Miss Christabel Pankhurst, after giving a vivid description of the men's protest at Mr. Churchill's Bradford meeting, said:—

My friends, I think the supporters of Woman Suffrage had the best of it on that occasion. It is true they were thrown out, but the cause was not thrown out! One of our men friends is now lying in the Bradford Infirmary with a broken knee and a fractured leg. I wonder what they will say now about Mr. Birrell's knee! I think we shall not hear much more of that, in view of the much more serious injury which has been wantonly and brutally inflicted upon a man who was doing nothing but defending the cause of the wronged and oppressed.

It is a monstrous thing that Liberals should so deal with people who come to their meetings in defence of a great cause. We turn to the Liberal Press, and what do we find? Articles and accounts glorying in the interruptions made by Liberals at Unionist meetings. There you have deliberate incitement to supporters of the Liberal Party to wreck the meetings of their political opponents, although the Liberals who take this action have the vote, and therefore a voice at the ballot box, and have no need whatever, except for wilful mischief and perversity, to go to Unionist meetings at all. You find in the Liberal Press long accounts of "pertinent remarks" made by Liberal partisans at Unionist meetings, but not one word of condemnation. Yet when women who go to Liberal meetings to ask a simple political question are treated with brutality, and their safety of life and limb is endangered because Liberals are not prepared to carry their own principles into practice.

The Referendum.

I want to draw your attention to some observations which Cabinet Ministers have been making at these meetings. They have been discussing the Referendum. Mr. Asquith strongly opposes it. Mr. Lloyd George says it is not a method of administering justice, but an expensive method of denying justice. Then we turn to Mr. Churchill and we find that he also does not want it. "But," he says, "I think there are some questions for which the Referendum might be an appropriate solution. I think that the question of female Suffrage is one which might be dealt with in this way." Is this the Government's plan? To use this "expensive method of denying justice" for the purpose of defeating and delaying the women's claim to the vote? Listen further, to what Mr. Churchill has to say: "I think this question is one which might well be a subject of direct appeal to the whole mass of the electorate. It is a question which is a moral and social question at once. It is a great question which appeals evenly and equally to the whole of his Majesty's subjects in the United Kingdom. It is a great national and social question, and it is a question on which every man in his cottage or in his house or in his palace should form a perfectly clear and direct and immediate opinion. But believe me," he says, "the general adoption of a system of Referendum would not be a satisfactory method of conducting the Government of the British Empire." My friends, we will not hear of the Referendum where our question is concerned. You did not refer the subject of men's suffrage to the vote of the women of the country, and we are not going to abide by the vote of the men of the country. If they took a Referendum to-morrow, and it proved that the men were against this reform, do you think that would make any difference to us? No, we should go on with our militant campaign more vigorously than ever, and what is more, we should still make the Government the responsible party, and we should still direct our attack upon them. They may try the Referendum; they may try sham pledges, but they will not get the better of us, because they are fighting with crooked weapons and we are fighting with straight ones; we are fighting in a just cause and they are fighting in an unjust cause; we have courage, and they have none.

We are quite confident of "frustrating their knavish tricks"—that is the expression which best describes their policy. We are confident in our own power to win, and we have with us to-day men who are prepared to fight with us. Yes, my friends, they have got men as well as women to reckon with, and I think they are getting rather afraid. The Government are at last beginning to take the movement seriously, and it is just as well for all concerned that they are. Too long have they hid their heads in the sand like ostriches, thinking that if they did so the movement would die out. Instead of dying out, it is becoming more widespread and militant.

The Liberal Women.

The Liberal women have condemned our action. We do not think that very loyal. We think women should stand by women to-day. The Liberal women will not refuse the vote which is won by our exertion and sacrifice; therefore we say silence would be more becoming if they had no word of praise of gratitude for the hundreds of women who have done so much for this cause! But we can forgive them their criticism of our Union more readily than we can forgive them the weak and wrongful action of condoning the Prime Minister's treachery. That, we think is deplorable. Either these women have not the political insight to understand a sham pledge when they see one or else they are willfully endangering the women's cause in the interests of the Liberal Party. Which is it? They can take their choice. If I were they I should rather say, "We did not understand. We thought this pledge was worth something, but now that it has been explained to us we see that it is not worth anything, and we give Mr. Asquith the choice of losing our support or giving us the vote." If they put this alternative to him now they can retrieve the great mistake that they have made. If they are going to tell us that they prefer party to principle—the interests of the Liberal Party to the interests of womanhood—we shall know what to think. We need not say more than that, except that we cannot be too much surprised, when we remember that women have been trained through generations to accept an inferior position, and have been taught disloyalty to other women. That is the one lesson that men have taught us: that woman's enemy is woman. What we prefer to do is to glory in the splendid spirit of our great deputation. In their courage and unselfishness one can see a vision of what all women will be when they have fair and just conditions under which to live. This is the true type of womanhood; these are the women we shall have in thousands and millions in our country when women are free.

The Conciliation Committee.

Now a word as to our very loyal and true friends of the Conciliation Committee. We thank them with much gratitude for all the splendid work that they have done in the House of Commons. Nobody feels more strongly than we do what splendid service the members of the Conciliation Committee have rendered to the women's cause. We hope that they will continue their efforts, and that they will be able to bring the Government to a sense of what is right and fit in this matter. We hope that counsels of conciliation may prevail next year, and that women will have their enfranchisement given to them, and if that should come about, as I believe it will if we all play our part, then the Conciliation Committee will deserve a very great share of the gratitude and the praise. The Conciliation Committee have been giving us good advice. They have been giving us a scolding. Well, we have been scolded and advised so often during the past five years that we are pretty well hardened to both things. Now, we give great attention and great weight to the advice and counsel of the Conciliation Committee, just as we do to the advice and counsel of all friends of this movement. But when we find ourselves at variance with the Conciliation Committee we are bound to prefer our own opinion and our own judgment. One thing we lay down here definitely and finally: this is a woman's movement, led by women, and we are not prepared to surrender the leadership of this movement to men, however well-meaning, however earnest, and however devoted.

Part V
The Argument of the Broken Pane

THE CLOSE OF THE YEAR 1911 WOULD MARK THE FINAL ESCALATION OF WSPU militancy, this time to the level of reformist terrorism. Despite the dramatic end that the year would bring, the Coronation year opened calmly. This peace was largely due to a statement by Asquith that, if the Liberal government was still in power, facilities would be granted to a suffrage bill permitting free amendment. A new election did return the Liberals but, as in the previous election, only with the help of Irish Nationalists and Labour. The Conciliation Committee formed again and devised a new bill that was more amendable and that did away with the £10 occupation clause.[1] In the late spring and summer of 1911, the prospect seemed encouraging for the new Conciliation Bill. An uneasy truce held between government and suffragettes was broken only by a classic act of civil disobedience. Suffragist women staged a boycott of the census (April 2, 1911) by filling out the forms to only reflect male relatives (as the only governmentally recognized persons in the household) or by spending census night at hidden parties where census takers could not find them.[2]

The Conciliation Bill was debated May 5 and carried by the impressive majority of 255 to 88. Lloyd-George told the Commons that, although there would not be an opportunity in the 1911 session, the Conciliation Bill would be granted a second reading in 1912. Should the bill then carry, it would receive a week to run through the final stages.[3] Asquith gave his assurances in a letter to Lord Lytton that such would be the case.

On June 17, 1911, five days before the coronation of King George V, the combined suffrage forces held another vast procession of women through London. The contingent of former suffrage prisoners now numbered one thousand and, dressed in white and carrying a banner reading "From Prison to Citizenship," they marched with an air of victory.[4] This day, with its feeling of celebration, was a peak experience for the suffrage movement. Emmeline Pethick-Lawrence made this later assessment:

> On June 17th, 1911 [the day of the great procession and the Albert Hall Meeting], we stood upon the mountain top in the sun. From that day forward we descended step by step through the clouds into a darkened world.[5]

Emmeline Pankhurst left confidently in October for an extensive speaking tour of the United States. Yet, practically in a repeat of 1910, the hope that was blooming in early summer was killed by treacherous November frosts. Prime Minister Asquith announced his intention to introduce a Manhood Suffrage Bill in the next session of Parliament. Lloyd-George happily declared that the Conciliation Bill was "torpedoed" but that this new Reform Bill could be amended to include women. The WSPU well knew that such an amendment, with the Prime Minister opposed to women's suffrage and without the support of the Liberal government, would never take place.[6]

It is at this point that the WSPU made the tactical decision that would come to define their organization. Escalation of militancy had earlier broken the press boycott and put the issue of women's suffrage on the government agenda. Anger over Black Friday, forcible feeding, and continuous repression of Union political rights now combined with frustration over repeated government duplicity and made restrained militancy appear inadequate. On November 16, 1911, Emmeline Pethick-Lawrence addressed an Albert Hall meeting, promising a deputation of protest if the government continued with its plans. The deputation came to pass on November 21, 1911, when Pethick-Lawrence led a deputation of protest from Caxton Hall to Parliament Square. Another group of suffragettes met at 7 P.M. at 156 Charing Cross Road and, armed with bags of stones and small hammers, set off to break windows at government offices and business residences. Along with damages at the Home Office, Treasury, and National Liberal Federation, windows were broken at the Guards' Club, the *Daily Mail* and *Daily News,* Swan and Edgar's, Lyon's, and a variety of small businesses, such as a bakery and tailor shop.[7] Until this time, officially planned and sanctioned violence had been directed at property belonging to and/or symbolic of the government. By attacking private property, the WSPU entered into a classic terrorism strategy where a third party is attacked in order to force a crisis to which the government must respond. Unlike revolutionary terrorism, reformist terrorism is generally confined to attacks on property, a restraint that was closely followed by the WSPU, even when militancy escalated to arson and bombing. As the Union put it "not even a cat or a canary must be harmed."[8]

Although there would soon be acts of arson initiated by individuals, officially sanctioned violence against property was initially confined to window breaking. Yet, the sense of having taken a monumental step is clear in the first two speeches included in this section. The first is Emmeline Pethick-Lawrence's address at Albert Hall on November 16, 1911, that preceded the step into violence against property. The second speech was given on February 16, 1912, by Emmeline Pankhurst who had returned from America and spoke at a dinner honoring released prisoners. The most famous line of this speech (and one often quoted in connection with Pankhurst) was her description of stone throwing as "that time-honoured official political argument." Important in these speeches is the portrayal of the militant campaign for suffrage as a "just war." Although military images had always peppered the speeches of constitutional and militant suffragists alike, Union speakers now incorporated into their rhetoric a justification of violence that very closely follows just-war doctrine. Just as the Christian Church devised the concept of the just war (*justum bellum*) to justify the use of necessary violence, this group of very moral reformers fell quite naturally into the same form of justification. Primary to this justification is the claim that the WSPU had just cause in entering into violence because their violence was in self-defense and in defense of the women and children of England. From this point on, the Union hones its portrayal of the Liberal government as a duplicitous and violent opponent against whom only an answering violence will serve to protect the lives and health of reformers such as the suffragettes. The Union also carefully shows how the laws of England did very real violence to the women and children of England and how Union violence was only undertaken to obtain the power to protect the innocent. Portraying the new level of militancy as part of a just war was a necessary step to having the public understand the rationale behind reformist terrorism, especially because the public's own property would now be attacked. As Pankhurst says in "The Argument of the Broken Pane":

> Directly you talk of a revolution or a civil war, then you understand the breaking of glass; then you understand every kind of weapon, and the use of every weapon in our warfare.

It was assumed that with understanding would come support, and the public would join in pressuring the government to support the female franchise.[9]

9

Albert Hall, November 16, 1911.

"Liberty never yet failed those who are determined to have it."

THE HALL WAS CROWDED IN EVERY PART WHEN MRS. LAWRENCE, MISS Pankhurst, Miss Goldstein, and Miss Annie Kenney mounted the platform. A beautiful bouquet from Mrs. Saul Solomon was presented, in the colours of the Union, with a "fiery cross" in scarlet flowers. Mrs. Lawrence then read a cablegram from Mrs. Pankhurst, who was that day in Minneapolis. She sent this message:

"I share your indignation at the Government's insult to women and am ready to renew the fight. Shall return with practical help from America."

Then followed a special message from Mrs. Saul Solomon, who had been unable to sit or to walk or to write or to do anything without pain since "Black Friday." She wrote to say that she had found a doctor who had made her able to walk, and she was coming, if necessary, on Tuesday. She sent undivided sympathy and devotion, welcoming "every eager woman who at this tremendous crisis, having heard the divine trumpet call to action, feels constrained to follow you on Tuesday in our victorious deputation to the Government." Then followed the chairman's speech.

Mrs. Pethick Lawrence.

After a long period of truce with the Government, we meet to-night, a united army on the eve of battle; not because we have chosen to fight, not because we desire militancy, but because the Government has broken its terms of peace. The announcement of the intention of the Government to bring a Manhood Suffrage Bill is a declaration of war upon the womanhood of the country. To refuse to take up this challenge would be to turn our back upon public honour and public duty. We are going to put through this fight for women's emancipation, cost what it may.

This meeting was, as you know, originally called together as a demonstration in support of the Conciliation Bill, which was first and foremost an

139

attempt to save the face of the Government and yet to secure women the vote. For many years women had demanded Votes for Women as a Government measure. This the Government had refused, and as a consequence of this refusal there arose a militant agitation which grew ever stronger. Things had come to a serious pass. Seven hundred women had been imprisoned. There was the scandal of the Hunger Strike; there was the barbarity of Forcible Feeding (Shame!); the conscience and the feeling of the country were shocked at this new kind of civil war, and men of both parties called— Halt! Let us see, they said, if we cannot devise some scheme which will take this question outside the realm of party politics. And so they met together, and as a result of a Parliamentary Committee, drawn from all sides of the House, the Conciliation Bill was drawn up. It did not fulfil our demand that the Government should bring in a Bill. It was also a concession with regard to the exact terms of our demand. Why was that concession made? In order to conciliate the so-called democratic section of the Government, led and represented by Mr. Lloyd George.

The Wreckers.

Ladies and gentlemen, as soon as the consent of all the Suffrage societies, militant and non-militant, had been won for this non-party measure, certain members of the Government set themselves to wreck it. You remember in 1910 Mr. Lloyd George used all his eloquence in order to defeat the second reading of the Bill, and called upon his followers in the house to vote against it. When, in spite of all that he said and urged, a great and overwhelming majority was secured, then the Government refused to give time to carry the Bill through its further stages. In 1911 the Government openly and publicly boycotted the second reading, and a yet larger majority was obtained, and again they refused time for the Bill to go through its further stages. But a pledge for full facilities in 1912 was wrung from the Prime Minister. That pledge was given in a most explicit form with the promise that it was to be fulfilled not only in the letter but in the spirit, and no sooner was that pledge given than at once Mr. Lloyd George proceeded in the attempt to make it of no effect. He immediately announced that he should bring in widening amendments, calculated to destroy the non-party character of that Bill. But again Mr. Lloyd George found himself foiled by the strength of this movement, which time after time he has attempted to injure in vain, and as an outcome of that defeat we had the other day the announcement that the Government were going to bring in next Session a Manhood Suffrage Bill.

Well, ladies and gentlemen, now Mr. Lloyd George has attained what he tried in vain to attain by his announcement of widening amendments. He has irrevocably destroyed the non-party character of the Conciliation Bill, and he has divided the Liberal and the Conservative supporters of Woman Suffrage into two camps. He has for all practical purposes made Woman Suffrage a party question, but the Government have refused to make Woman Suffrage a party measure, since they have refused to embody it in the Reform Bill. Now it is between these two stools—Woman Suffrage as a party question, but Woman Suffrage not as a party measure—that the Government intend that Woman Suffrage shall fail.

Women, are we going to be baulked at this stage of the fruit of our labour and our sacrifice? (Cries of "No!") No, I agree with you, a thousand times, No. Conciliation is dead, slain not by our hand. But that which brought conciliation to life is not dead. What was it brought conciliation? Militancy. (Cheers.) Militancy is not dead; militancy will not be dead till hundreds and thousands of women living to-day are dead, or until victory is assured. Now the Government have nothing to fear from women except militancy, nothing at all. There is no way in which women can bring home to them the enormity of this suggestion except by militancy. The Government would pay any price to stop militancy short of giving women citizenship. It was to stop militancy that the pledge was given last year for 1912. They wanted to get the Coronation over without unpleasantness. They did not want our representatives from the Dominions overseas, who came to the Imperial Conference, to see an exhibition like "Black Friday." They wanted to get salaries for all their members of Parliament in peace, and they bought peace with that pledge, which Mr. Asquith has now for all practical purposes torn up. It is because they want to stop militancy that they are going to receive a deputation at last. After all these years, after all these attempts, we are politely invited to lay our case before Mr. Asquith and Mr. Lloyd George to-morrow.

I will tell you what will stop militancy, and I will tell them. Nothing short of the withdrawal of this insulting Manhood Suffrage Bill and the substitution for it of a Government Bill to give equal franchise rights to men and to women. I do not anticipate any such pronouncement to-morrow from Mr. Asquith and Mr. Lloyd-George; I wish I did. I think we have got to do more fighting first. The militant movement is as strong as it ever was—(A Voice: "Stronger!")—but I think we have got to prove it. Mr. Chamberlain, you remember, threatened that if the Franchise Bill of 1884 did not pass, he would march a hundred thousand men into Parliament Square. He never fulfilled his intention, because it was not necessary—the Bill did pass. But I believe that we shall have to fulfil our intention of marching to Parliament Square next Tuesday evening one thousand women strong. I want to know who is coming with those hundreds of women. Is there any woman in this audience who can refuse to come? I ask you, are you willing that every youth of twenty-one, every shopboy, every undergraduate—yes, and even the roysterer and the wastrel, and the man who lives on the earnings of women—that every one of these shall have a vote, and shall be your rulers and your masters, simply because they are males? I ask the women here, are you willing that the neck of womanhood shall be placed underneath the heel of sex? Well, I will tell you what I feel about it. Speaking for myself, I would rather die than submit to this humiliation. If you feel like that, can you—any one of you—stay behind and let other women go forward to fight for your honour? Perhaps, though, you don't look at it like that. Perhaps you have not that feeling of pride, or whatever you call it—that feeling which is in some of us. Perhaps you feel more deeply the call of others more unhappy than yourself. Well, then, I say to you, for the sake of the girl-mother, for the sake of the widow and the sweated woman, for the sake of the girl who is thrust upon the street because of economic conditions, for the sake of the outraged children of whom we hear so much at the present day, for the sake of these women and children, if not for the sake of your own self-respect, will you stay behind, will you refuse to go forward and cut the fetters that bind you and them?

Don't you sometimes hear an even higher, deeper call than these? Does it not seem to you a great thing that you should answer the call of that Spirit which gave you being, and gave you your body, and say: "Here is my body, here am I to do Thy Will, to be used in the fulfilment of Thy great purposes and destiny"? by all these claims, by your sense of honour, by the cry of the needy, by the call of destiny upon your own soul, I say to every woman here: Come with us, be amongst us, take your place in the ranks when we go forward to make our protest next Tuesday.

A Call to Arms.

Speaking politically, everything depends upon the strength of this first blow in this new campaign. Don't you remember how we reduced the Government to helplessness over the Census Protest—(laughter)—so that they could neither use repression against offenders nor vindicate their law? Now it would be possible to bring that state of things about on Tuesday. It would be possible to make this protest in such numbers that repressive measures would be impossible, and you know when you have a Government which is founded upon tyranny it can only rest upon repression, and if you destroy the possibility of repression you make the Government impossible. After all, did not Garibaldi with a thousand volunteers set a whole nation free? Just so, a thousand women combining now and striking together could set the womanhood of the nation free! You remember Garibaldi's motto— "Liberty never yet failed those who are determined to have it." Yes, that is true, but liberty as an ideal only of opposition, of vested interests, of inertia, and of prejudice. But liberty linked with human will and with resolute action will never fail those who are determined to have it.

We, ladies and gentlemen, the women of this country, are determined to have liberty. Let us, then, go forward and prove ourselves worthy of it. Let us be proud to win it. Now I have very much pleasure, and I feel it is a very serious thing, too, to do—I am very conscious of the gravity of the action—I move the following resolution:—

"That this meeting expresses its profound indignation at the announcement by the Prime Minister of the Government's intention to introduce a Manhood Suffrage Bill in 1912, and demands
> "That the Government abandon the Manhood Suffrage Bill, and intro-
> duce in its stead a measure giving precisely equal franchise
> rights to men and women.
> "That the measure be carried through next session, in order that the
> protection of the Parliament Act shall be secured.
> "That the Government stake their existence upon the Bill as a whole,
> and undertake to stand or fall as much by the provisions for Votes for
> Women as by the provisions for Votes for Men.
"And this meeting further pledges itself if such assurances be not given, to take such action as the urgency of the situation demands."

10

The Argument of the Broken Pane.

By Mrs. Pankhurst.

Part of a Speech Delivered at the Dinner at the Connaught Rooms in Honour of the Released Prisoners.

I RISE TO PROPOSE THE HEALTH OF OUR GUESTS, THOSE BRAVE PEOPLE who have recently come to us from Holloway prison. It is difficult for me to find the right words to express our gratitude, but I say to them to-night, from the bottom of my heart, that what they did last November has done more during the last three months to bring this question to where it is than perhaps all the patient work done by women since the movement for the emancipation of women began. It is perhaps one of the strangest things of our civilisation that it should be necessary to say that; to think that women in the twentieth century are in a world where they are forced to say that an appeal to justice, that an appeal to reason, that evidence of their fitness for citizenship, should be of less value than the breaking of panes of glass. And yet there is no doubt that it is true.

We honour these women because having learnt that the argument of the broken pane of glass is the most valuable argument in modern politics, they nerved themselves to use that argument; and they used it with such effect that we are to-day waiting eagerly the issue of dissensions in the very heart and seat of Government itself. The fact that we have a Cabinet crisis is due to Mrs. Pethick-Lawrence and her deputation of November 21. And those of us who feel the truth of what I am saying are going to thank these women who are with us to-night, by imitating, at the earliest opportunity, their excellent example. "Deeds, not words," is the motto of this movement, and we are going to prove our love and gratitude to our comrades by continuing the use of the stone as an argument in the further protests that we have to make.

We cannot say too often that the success of the next protest depends upon its size. I have been reading only to-day the history of Europe during the memorable year of 1848, and in reading the history of revolt and the struggle for political freedom that went on in this country and in every country of Europe I am impressed with the success that attended numbers and determination wherever that struggle went on. Wherever the struggle failed it was due to two causes—lack of courage and determination and lack of numbers. We have the courage and the determination in this movement. No one doubts that. What we lack is in actual fighting members. We have plenty of sympathy, we have a great deal of support, but we want the actual fighting army to be bigger than it ever has been before.

The Time is Now.

Nearly two years ago a professional friend of mine said to me, "I know the day is coming when we shall every one of us be compelled to cast every other consideration aside, and come along all together, an irresistible, mighty band of women." When my friend said that to me I could not say to her then, "The time is now!" I realised that we had not yet created the political situation when we might with certainty say, "Now is the time for every woman to strike." But I do believe now, largely due to what the last deputation did, that we may with something like political certainty say the time is now ripe. Well, then, if we have come to the tide in our fortunes, when if we take it we shall win, and if we neglect to take it our victory may be postponed, have not the leaders in this movement—those women you have chosen to follow, whose judgment you accept—have we not the duty laid upon us of saying to women, "Come if you can? *Come, if it is humanly possible for you to come!*" We go as far as that. We cannot go into the conscience of every woman. We cannot weigh her reasons for and against coming with us. That is the responsibility put upon each of us, but I can say, and my colleagues can say with me, that we believe the call now is so great that nothing but the most vital necessity should prevent women, who honour their womanhood, from coming to take part in this protest.

Suppose that if instead of an announcement of a Manhood Suffrage Bill the Prime Minister had said, "Women have struggled for fifty years of Constitutional means to win their political freedom. For six years they have participated in a passionate revolt against their political outlawry. We are engaged in legislation which calls pre-eminently for the cooperation and the experience of women, and so since we dislike the present franchise anomalies, and we do not like to give women the vote on a basis of representation of which we disapprove, we will have a Reform Bill for women, uncharacterised by these anomalies; and, since we believe in the fullest measure of democracy, we will give the vote to those people who need it most, without restriction—the women of the country; and we will postpone dealing with the grievances of men until we have time, since their grievances are not so pressing, every class of men having won a certain amount of representation."

What would the men of this country do in such a case—not so hard a case as ours? What would they do? There is not a man in this meeting, or outside this meeting, who would not say to the Prime Minister, "If you are going to do this for women, if you are going to give the fullest measure of enfranchisement to women, then you will have to give it to men at the same time."

That being so, there cannot be a man here to-night who does not agree with the appeal that I am making to women; and there cannot be a husband here tonight who dare stand in the way of his wife, if she feels it her duty to postpone for a time her duties to her family and to him, and do her duty to womanhood. I say this because I know it is the domestic call which stands in the way of many women.

Wanted Good Citizens.

You know what has always been said about women married to men who cared very much for public causes. When the husband has said, "I wish to volunteer for danger service in defence of my country," or "I want to fight this reform out, although I may run great business or professional risks in doing it"; if the woman said, "Oh, think of the children, think of their future; what is to become of me and the children?"—we know what is said of women like that. They say these women block the man's way, they make him a worse citizen: and every man who has sacrificed even his family is honoured when he does it in a public cause. And yet, what is said of women? Quite the contrary. If the woman wants to stand for a great human cause, and if she leaves a child or a husband sometimes for a week or two, they say, "Look at this woman. How unfaithful of her duty: how careless of her duty as a woman she is."

Now we are going to alter all that. If it is a good thing for a man to sacrifice for the public good, then it is a good thing for a woman to sacrifice for the public good; and just as the woman to-day is honoured if she consents to suffer in order that her husband may do his public duty, so in the future the husband will be honoured who agrees to his wife making her sacrifice for the public good.

I have said this because I want to make women feel as men have always felt, that great human causes and great human needs transcend all our private duties. In saying this, I repeat that each of us must always be a law to ourselves in making a final decision, but I emphasize the fact to-night as I have never, as you know, done before, that now, in my opinion, is the time. We should put this public call above every private consideration except of the most urgent and important kind. I believe from the bottom of my heart that if we are determined enough, if we are courageous enough, the enemy will be glad to bring this struggle of ours to a speedy close.

One word about the form of our argument. The women we delight to honour to-night are women who threw stones. Don't let us forget that. Don't let us forget that they were active fighters in this cause. Last night, in the Savoy Theatre, I was very glad that my daughter in her speech compared our movement with the Chinese revolution. I think a comparison like that really gives you the right point of view about this movement of ours. Even those who have been taking part in it have not always seen it in its right perspective. Directly you talk of a revolution or a civil war, then you understand the breaking of glass; then you understand every kind of weapon, and the use of every weapon in our warfare. If any criticism is to be allowed on women who are fighting for their liberty, it is perhaps that we have not used weapons sufficiently, shall I say, persuasive. We don't want to use any weapons that are unnecessarily strong. If the argument of the stone, that time-honoured official political argument, is sufficient, then we will never use any stronger argument. I believe myself it is. And that is the weapon and the argument that we are going to use next time. And so I say to every volunteer on our demonstration:—"Be prepared to use that argument." I am taking charge of the demonstration, and that is the argument I am going to use. I am not going to use it for any sentimental reason, I am going to use it because it is the simplest and the easiest and the most readily understood. Why should women go into Parliament Square and be battered about and be insulted, and, most important of all, produce less effect than when they use stones? We tried it long enough. We submitted for years patiently to insult and to assault. Women had their health injured. Women lost their lives. We should not have minded that if that had succeeded, but that did not succeed, and we have made more progress with less hurt to ourselves by breaking glass than ever we made when we allowed them to break our bodies. We have so peculiar a sense of proportion in these sentimental days.

After all, is not a woman's life, is not her health, are not her limbs more valuable than panes of glass? There is no doubt about that, but most important of all, does not the breaking of glass produce more effect upon the Government? If you are fighting a battle, that should dictate your choice of weapons. Well then, we are going to try this time if mere stones will do it. I do not think it will be necessary for us to arm ourselves like the Chinese women have done, but there are women who are prepared to do that, if it should be necessary. In this Union we don't lose our heads. We only go as far as we are obliged to go in order to win, and we are going on the next protest demonstration in full faith that this plan of campaign, initiated by our friends whom we honour to-night, will on this next occasion prove effective.

Part VI
The 1912 Conspiracy Trial

THE EVENTS THAT CULMINATED IN CHRISTABEL PANKHURST'S SELF-EXILE in Paris and the conspiracy trial of the other Union leaders were initiated in November 1911, but reached a culminating point in March 1912. The Union planned and announced a demonstration for March 4; they planned and did *not* announce one for March 1. On March 1, Emmeline Pankhurst, accompanied by Mabel Tuke, took a taxi to 10 Downing Street; and, at half past five, they threw four stones through the window panes. They were promptly arrested. During the next hour, at fifteen-minute intervals, Union members smashed plate glass windows all over London. First came attacks in Haymarket and Picadilly; fifteen minutes later Regent Street was attacked; fifteen more minutes and Oxford Circus/Bond Street came under assault; and, finally, many of the windows along the Strand were destroyed.[1] Ironically, the very day this siege was taking place, a Cabinet Minister, C. E. H. Hobhouse, would say to an antisuffrage meeting in Bristol:

> In the case of the suffrage demand there has not been the kind of popular senti-
> mental uprising which accounted for Nottingham Castle in 1832 or the Hyde
> Park railings in 1867. There has not been a great ebullition of popular feeling.[2]

Although it seems unlikely that Hobhouse really wished to challenge women to burn down a castle as male suffragists had done, the provocative words were a poorly timed goad to the Union. Sylvia Pankhurst described the effect of Hobhouse's words as being "like a match to a fuse."[3] The Union could point with some justification to these words (as well as those of other government officials) as proof that the greatest incitement to violence came from the government itself.

As the Union intended, after the experience of March 1, the government and police were worried about the announced demonstration on March 4. Emmeline Pankhurst invited women to assemble in Parliament Square in the evening. Police arrived in force, shops in the immediate vicinity were barricaded; yet no fearful demonstration took place. This was a classic piece of misdirection by the WSPU that proved both their ability to trick the government into overreaction and the fear that the government had of the Union's power to conduct violent action. The actual demonstration had happened that morning in Knightsbridge. More than one hundred women marched single file down the street, then smashed almost every pane of glass along the way. In all, over two hundred women were arrested for their actions during the two days in March.[4] Charges were brought against Emmeline Pankhurst and Mabel Tuke for their participation in the stone throwing on March 1. On this charge, Pankhurst was sentenced to two months imprisonment. With the actual participants in the demonstrations arrested, tried, and imprisoned, the government made plans to round up the remaining Union leadership. Emmeline Pankhurst later summarized government thinking, as follows:

> The similarity of the stones used; the gathering of so many women in one building, prepared for arrest; the waiting at the Gardenia Restaurant; the apparent dispersal; the simultaneous destruction in many localities of plate glass, and the bailing of prisoners by a person connected with the headquarters mentioned, certainly showed a carefully worked out plan. Only a public trial of the defendants could establish whether or not the plan was a conspiracy.[5]

Charges of conspiracy to commit offenses against the law were brought against the Union leadership. Emmeline Pankhurst and Mabel Tuke learned of the new charges against them while still in prison. On March 5 the police appeared suddenly at Clement's Inn with warrants for the arrest of Emmeline and Frederick Pethick-Lawrence and Christabel Pankhurst. Christabel was not there when the police arrived. Word was quickly sent to her through an emissary, and she escaped to France. For the next two years, until the start of World War I, Christabel Pankhurst would head WSPU strategy from a secret location in Paris.[6]

The transcript of the Conspiracy Trial of Emmeline Pankhurst and the Pethick-Lawrences appears as the centerpiece of this volume of suffragette rhetoric. The trial was truly the centerpiece of the militant movement. It raised issues central to the role of the Union in the suffrage movement: did the Union, in planning for public protest, cross a line into "conspiracy"; were Union leaders or opposition rhetoric responsible for inspiring militant actions; and was the suffrage movement, the WSPU in particular, unfairly singled out for government attack? The trial opened May 15, 1912, at the Old Bailey with charges actually brought against Emmeline Pankhurst and the Pethick-Lawrences. Mabel Tuke had been acquitted of conspiracy charges after the preliminary hearing before a magistrate at Bow Street police court ascertained her WSPU work to be merely secretarial.[7]

This transcript of the trial begins with prosecution evidence brought on Wednesday afternoon, May 15, 1912. On Wednesday morning crowds of those who hoped to obtain a good seat for such a high profile case had gathered early. According to *Votes For Women,* "colour was given to the scene outside by the white dresses and sunshades of the women who were selling copies of *Votes For Women.*" Upon the start of the trial, the defendants pleaded not guilty to the 54-count indictment, and the jury was sworn. One interesting event occurred during the swearing in of prospective juryman T. E. Gatehouse. When Gatehouse was handed the Testament in preparation to being sworn, he rose and stated that he knew Dr. Ethel Smyth, the prominent composer and WSPU member who was present to testify for the defense. Gatehouse had led the performance of the overture to Dr. Smyth's opera, "The Wreckers"; and he, therefore, questioned his suitability as a juryman. Gatehouse was easily replaced by a juror-in-waiting, but the incident points up the prestige of some of the women who were taking part in suffragette militancy.[8]

The trial is printed here as it appeared in *Votes For Women,* with some aspects of the trial presented in summary and some in verbatim form. In the interest of space, I have confined myself primarily to the defense case and only included vital excerpts of the evidence presented. Because the summation of the judge was so heavily weighted toward the prosecution, it is presented here as a good condensation of the prosecution case. Government charges of "conspiring to incite certain persons to commit malicious damage to property"[9] brought against the defendants were countered by defense claims "that the conspiracy and incitement in the case were not that of the defendants, but of the Government, which had deliberately deceived and thwarted the women's movement."[10] The reader should note the way that the defense, both in evidence and cross-examination, focuses on the healthy finances of the Union, the increased attendance at Union meetings, and the superior quality of the women involved as proof of the potential success of militant methods. Violence against property is characterized as caused by the incitement of cabinet ministers, the repression taken against earlier nonviolent militancy, and the need to make the concerns of women salient to the male elector.

In his address to the jury, Frederick Pethick-Lawrence uses a series of analogies to make the case that a third-party strategy of violence to private property was the only avenue open to the suffragettes. He carefully portrays the Union members as peace-loving women driven to protect the race from the evils of sweating, white slavery (a term referring to the procuring of girls and young women into brothels or overseas prostitution), and infant mortality. His first analogy is to a person dealing with a tradesman and the ability of that person to take his or her trade elsewhere if the tradesman is dishonest. This, Pethick-Lawrence claims, is what a elector can do with his votes should the government prove inept or dishonest. It is a constitutional avenue of response unavailable to voteless women, and this reality necessitated women taking extra-legal action. Pethick-Lawrence's second analogy is a little jewel that does the best job of explaining the need for violence to the property of a third party. It is an involving little melodrama where a child in need (symbolic of the legislatively neglected women and children of England) is rescued by the hero only with the help of neighbors who are awakened to the child's plight by having their windows broken. The hero only breaks the windows after spending forty minutes (equivalent to the forty years of constitutional suffragist efforts) trying to talk his way into the house to save the child. The neighbors appear unconcerned about the injury to their private property as they force open the door (of legislation) to rescue the child. Pethick-Lawrence's third analogy is considerably weaker because it does not clearly justify a third-party strategy. In this analogy, the reference is to the recently sunk *Titanic* and features a hypothetical sleeping wireless operator who must be awakened to the ship's plight by the breaking of "a few windows."

In her address to the jury, Emmeline Pankhurst presented a vision of women in the WSPU not as criminals but as political activists. She defined the militant as not necessarily violent but as willing to suffer for the cause of political reform. Many of her references were to the past political lessons of male reformers and the efficacy of violence in extending political rights for men during the campaigns for the Reform Bills of 1832, 1867, and 1884. As in previous speeches, Pankhurst made use of her own considerable ethos and her experience as a member of the Board of Poor Law Guardians to discuss details of the lives of poor women and children. Pankhurst described how, as women sought to change the laws and help these unfortunates, their efforts were met first with laughter by the Parliament and then by repression. Pankhurst's primary point was that, far from the suffragettes conspiring against the government, it was the government who was guilty of conspiring against the suffragettes.

Their best arguments did not avail the suffrage leaders, and the trial ended in a guilty verdict. Following the verdict, Emmeline Pethick-Lawrence appealed to the judge for a fair sentence and a proper assigning to the first division. She used examples of the sentences and division assignments of men convicted of crimes against women and children as a point of comparison. Despite the jury's call for "clemency and leniency" for the defendants because of their "undoubtedly pure motives," the judge imposed a sentence of nine months imprisonment and, once again, ordered the defendants to second division status. In his autobiography, Frederick Pethick-Lawrence provided the final touch when he revealed that the judge's two daughters, who had attended most of the trial, soon joined the WSPU.[11]

11

Opening Day of the Trial
[May 15, 1912]

[W<small>EDNESDAY</small> <small>MORNING WAS GIVEN OVER TO THE OPENING SPEECH BY</small> the Attorney General, Sir Rufus Isaacs. The Attorney General described the history of the WSPU, its financial accounts, and the editorship of *Votes For Women*. According to the Attorney General, "The paper plays a very important part in the conspiracy." He then described briefly "secret codes" used by the Union: "The word 'Fox' in the code stands for 'Are you prepared for arrest?' The word 'Foxes,' 'How many are prepared for arrest?' The word 'Goose,' 'Don't get arrested.' Then the word 'Duck,' 'Don't get arrested unless success depends upon it.'" In summary, the Attorney General's speech divided the case into two periods (November 1911 and March 1912) during which the same type of events and incitement took place. Sir Rufus pointed to circulars sent to WSPU members urging protest, the inflammatory speeches made by WSPU leaders, and the bailing out of WSPU members arrested for window breaking. As summarized in *Votes For Women,* the Attorney General focused upon the demonstration of March 4, "In the afternoon there was a meeting at the Pavilion Theatre, at which Mrs. Lawrence and Miss Christabel Pankhurst spoke, expressing their readiness for imprisonment. After the meeting many of those present were followed to the Gardenia Restaurant, which was taken for that day. Admission was by ticket; they received their weapons there, and then distributed themselves in the streets. At a moment evidently pre-arranged, they broke their selected windows . . . The Attorney-General concluded with the words, 'You will not be surprised when you hear that drastic action was taken by the authorities, that the defendants were arrested, that papers were seized at the office, and that they stand here on their trial before you to-day.'"[1]]

Wednesday Afternoon.

Court No. 1 at the Old Bailey was again crowded on Wednesday afternoon, May 15, when the trial of the leaders of the Women's Social and Political Union for conspiracy was resumed before Mr. Justice Coleridge.

153

The name of Miss Christabel Pankhurst was bracketed with those of Mrs. Pankhurst and Mr. and Mrs. Pethick Lawrence for trial, and the Clerk of Arraigns called upon her to surrender, but there was no reply. Mrs. Pankhurst entered the dock first, followed by Mrs. Pethick Lawrence, who carried a shower bouquet of carnations and roses. Mr. Pethick Lawrence was the last to enter the court. . . .

The Attorney-General (Sir Rufus Isaacs, K.C.) led for the prosecution, and with him were Mr. A. H. Bodkin, Mr. S. A. T. Rowlatt, and Mr. Graham Campbell. Mr. Tim Healy, K.C., Mr. R. D. Muir, and Mr. Blanco White appeared for Mrs. Pethick Lawrence. Mr. Pethick Lawrence and Mrs. Pankhurst conducted their own defence.

The Purchase of Hammers.

Richard Melhuish was called after the luncheon interval, and, answering Mr. Bodkin, said he was a merchant carrying on business at 50, Fetter Lane. On February 22 or 23 he distinctly remembered a lady coming into his shop . . .

The Attorney-General said all they were seeking to prove now was the fact that these hammers were subsequently discovered on persons committing offences.

Mr. Bodkin: What did the lady order?——A pattern hammer and some more like it.

Had you some in stock?——A large number.

Did you show her some samples?——Yes; a hammer with a claw.

How many did she order?——She asked how many we had of that particular pattern. We had three dozen, and she said she would take them.

Witness said he had one hammer left of the kind selected. It bore his name stamped on it.

Did you pack them?——Yes: I did so myself. The lady was so anxious to get them away and so imperious in her manner that I did it myself. When she had gone I noticed that one had been left out.

Did she pay for the full number?——Yes.

Has she ever been back to claim the odd hammer?——No; but I think I saw her in April when I was on holiday in the South of France and in Italy.

You had not the hammer with you in the South of France, had you?—— Oh, no. (Laughter.)

How much did the lady pay?——A little less than 1s. a hammer. She got a reduction. I don't remember the exact amount. I can produce the bill if necessary.

Did she take them away?——Yes; I was anxious to send them, but she carried them away herself.

Witness identified other hammers shown to him as those which he had supplied; they bore his name.

Mr. Pethick Lawrence put a number of questions in cross-examination, eliciting that Mr. Melhuish had fifty assistants in his employ. He did not manufacture the hammers, but bought them from the makers, and ordered several gross at a time. Witness could not recollect, nor could his assistants, selling any other hammers of this pattern to anyone else; they had been in stock as the remnant of a big order. There were several dozens in stock, and he was not aware of any having been sold to anyone else.

Mr. Pethick Lawrence: Can you rely upon your recollection?——Yes; I may make mistakes, but I don't make many.

You have just said you sold three dozen hammers to the lady?——Yes.

And you said at Bow Street that it was two dozen?——I thought it was three dozen.

That indicates that your recollection is not to be relied upon very closely?——I thought it was three dozen. What I said at Bow Street was the correct number.

Do you suggest that you know what all your employees are selling every day?——I am on the premises all day.

Do you suggest you know that your employees never sold hammers of that kind to anyone else?——I know we never sold any hammers of that kind for a long time.

These hammers may have been sold from your shop to other people?—— It is possible.

And the fact that these hammers (produced) bear your name does not necessarily mean that they were those bought by this lady?——The lady was anxious to have this particular kind with claws. They were cheap hammers; the usual claw hammer is more expensive.

Are you certain that no such hammers as these were disposed of except to this lady?——I am not certain. How could I be?

Mr. Pethick Lawrence: That is sufficient.

Mr. Bodkin: You have been questioned about your recollection. Will you ever forget this lady?——No. (Laughter.)

P.C. Surman, 124B, deposed that he had attended the Women's Social and Political Union meeting held in the Albert Hall on November 16 . . .

Public Sympathy.

Mrs. Pankhurst: Did you notice the character of the meeting in the Albert Hall?——Yes madam.

Was it a large meeting?——Yes, madam. There were 9,000 persons present.

Did you find out that every seat was paid for?——I understood that.

What sort of people were they in the meeting?——In the body of the hall and in the galleries and balconies there were very well-to-do ladies and gentlemen, and the top gallery was filled with middle-class people.

You know there was only one dissentient from the resolution?——Yes, madam.

Did it receive a good response?——Yes, madam. A good response.

Did you gather that large number of people were in sympathy with what was said and done?——Yes, madam: they were very much in sympathy—very enthusiastic.

And you considered the meeting representative of what is called public opinion?——Yes, madam.

Mr. Bodkin: Do you mean that it was your opinion of public opinion? (Laughter.)

The Judge: That is rather a shame . . .

The place of the witness was taken by Mr. Hart, manager of the St. Clement's Press. Replying to Mr. Bodkin, he stated that his firm had printed *Votes For Women* by contract with Mr. Pethick Lawrence. Mr. Pethick Lawrence paid for it by cheque. About 30,000 copies were printed weekly and were delivered at the offices of the Women's Social and Political Union, at 4, Clement's Inn. Witness said that he did not know Mrs. Pethick Lawrence. Beneath the title of the paper was printed the information that it was edited by "Frederick and Emmeline Pethick Lawrence." Witness recollected that on March 4 last a proof-reader called his attention to a certain article, and witness read the proof . . ".

Mr. Bodkin then read the following letter, which the witness had written after reading a proof of the article referred to:

> Dear Mr. Pethick Lawrence,—I have just seen a proof of the handbill which is being set-up for the Women's Social and Political Union. It seems to me that this is an incitement to extreme measures, which we cannot agree either to print or publish at such a time as the present.
>
> It is also necessary for me to point out that it will be impossible for us to print any similar matter which may be considered of a seditious or libellous character in the newspaper, *Votes For Women.*—Yours faithfully.

The witness stated that the issue of *Votes For Women* of March 8 this year did not contain the article in question. The heading of it, "A Challenge," appeared, and the signature, "Christabel Pankhurst." He also pointed out blanks on other pages of the same number, denoting passages which his firm objected to print. In December, 1911, he printed 20,000 copies of an article, and in March, 1912, the circular was re-set. He saw the proof, however, and objected to print it. He received the order for that circular from *Votes For Women*.

Mr. Healy: *Votes For Women* are not in the dock. (Laughter.)

Witness said that on seeing the proof he instructed an assistant to tele-phone to the office of *Votes For Women*, stating that they could not print the article.

Mr. Bodkin: Did you see the assistant at the telephone and hear him?

Mr. Healy objected.

Mr. Bodkin suggested that the witness could hear what the conversation was.

Mr. Healy: Can you hear what somebody at the other end of the wire said.

Mr. Bodkin: Yes.

Mr. Healy: This is a new invention, my lord. (Laughter.)

The witness said he heard his assistant say he declined to print the circular.

Mr. Bodkin: Did you hear an answering voice?——No.

Witness added that in consequence of having informed them he did not print the circular . . .

Mr. Bodkin then read the whole of the article headed with the quotation from Mr. Lloyd George's speech at Bath.

"Black Friday."

The Judge interposed to ask what was Black Friday.

Mr. Bodkin replied that it was the occasion of one of the largest of the Suffrage riots, when many women were charged with assaulting and ob-structing the police . . .

Answering Mr. Pethick Lawrence, witness explained that when he said things were ordered by *Votes For Women* he did not mean the newspaper of that name but the Women's Social and Political Union, whose stationery was headed "Votes For Women." Some of the accounts were paid by cheques signed by Mr. Pethick Lawrence. He was not prepared to say they all bore Mr. Pethick Lawrence's signature. He explained in answer to further ques-tions that after copy was set up a proof was sent. The proof was corrected and in many cases the matter was substantially altered. In some cases the matter was still further altered on a revised proof, so that only a final proof could be said to represent the considered opinions of the writer.

The leaflet headed "Broken Windows" was first published as an article in *Votes For Women* of December 1, and subsequently as a leaflet in December.

Mr. Pethick Lawrence: Why did you refuse to re-publish the same article in March?——In consequence of what had happened one of my directors came to see me, and after a consultation we decided not to print it.

Did no one else come to see you on the matter?——No; only the direc-tor . . .

Who was Assaulted?

Mrs. Pankhurst: It seems to me something was said by the learned counsel for the prosecution which is calculated to prejudice your lordship and the jury very much. You, Mr. Bodkin, sir, said in answer to the learned Judge's inquiry, "What is Black Friday?" that it was the occasion of the riot in which women were charged with assaulting the police. This witness published a report of those cases, and he would be able to testify that hardly any of the women were charged with assaulting the police.

The Judge: We will drop Black Friday. I don't know anything about it.

Mr. Lloyd George's View.

Mr. Healy: Did you refuse to print this:

> Broken Windows.
>
> I lay down this proposition—democracy has never been a menace to property. When power was withheld from the democracy, when they had no voice in the Government, when they were oppressed, and when they had no means of securing redress except by violence—then property has many times been swept away.
>
> *Mr. Lloyd George at Bath, November 24.*

Witness: Yes.

Mr. Healy: That is all I have to ask.

Mr. Bodkin, in further examination, elicited from the witness that the following appeared in the issue of December 1:

> The Next Protest.
>
> Names of volunteers for active service continue to come in; they include those of many who took part in the demonstration of Tuesday, November 21, while others are of women who have not yet taken militant action. The following are typical letters:
>
> "As I was discharged at Bow Street last Thursday, I am ready for the next. Please enter my name upon the militant list, for I have not 'learnt better,' as Mr. Muskett advised me!"

* * *

> "You may count on me till the crack of doom! If it is a mere question of the more the merrier I don't think I could stay away. In the future, when we have reached our goal, I can imagine what a mean cur I should feel at having watched other people doing the dirty work without having raised a finger to help."
>
> Names should be sent to Miss Christabel Pankhurst, 4, Clement's Inn, W.C.

In reading the sentence, "When we have reached our goal," Mr. Bodkin read, "When we have reached our gaol," the witicism producing a smile.

Mr. Healy solemnly asked witness: Can you say which is the correct pronunciation, goal or jail?

The Judge: It depends on the spelling.

Mr. Bodkin: His lordship is quite correct.

The Court adjourned at this stage for the day.

12

Evidence for the Prosecution
[May 16, 1912]

The Union's Extensive Premises.

Banking Transactions.

WHEN THE PROCEEDINGS WERE RESUMED ON THURSDAY, MR. THOMAS Short Graham, manager of the Temple Bar branch of Barclay's Bank, who attended on subpoena, stated that there had been an account at his bank in the name of the Women's Social and Political Union for many years past. The cheques were required by a written instruction to be signed by two out of four persons—Mr. F. W. Pethick Lawrence, Mrs. Pethick Lawrence, Mrs. Mabel Tuke, and Miss Christabel Pankhurst. One of the two signatures had necessarily to be either that of Mr. Pethick Lawrence or Mrs. Pethick Lawrence, and the other signature might be one of the other two.

The Attorney-General: So that Mrs. Tuke and Miss Christabel Pankhurst could not sign cheques alone?——No . . .

Mr. Pethick Lawrence: You have given evidence of several cheques having been drawn on the Women's Social and Political Union general account for hall-keepers and halls during the period from July, 1911, to February, 1912. Can you state generally whether during the previous two years there had been also a considerable number of cheques drawn to hall-keepers or to halls in London and in the country?——Speaking from memory, I should say it is probable that that is so.

The Attorney-General: I should be quite prepared to admit it.

The Growth of the Funds.

Mrs. Pankhurst: Does Barclay's Bank also act as bankers for any of the local unions?——No; we have no accounts with any of them.

Then all the money that passes through your hands is exclusively the money that comes into the funds of the National Union?——Yes.

You would describe this account, would you not, as an active account?——Oh, very.

Money coming in and going out?——Constantly.

Large sums and small sums?——Yes, both.

Has it been a growing account?——Yes.

Have you had knowledge of it since 1906?——Yes; ever since it started.

Can you tell us approximately how much money has passed through your hands during that time?——Without referring to my books it would be impossible for me to give you any estimate of the amount; but large sums have passed through.

Do you think I would be right in saying that £100,000 have passed through the account?——I should say that that would be within the amount.

I am not over-stating it?——I should say not.

I suppose you could not tell me how much money was paid into it during the first year?——Not without reference to the books but it was comparatively small.

And there has been a rapid increase?——A steady increase year by year.

Have you the accounts of other societies and organisations?——Oh, yes, a good many.

Are there any that compare with ours in progress?——I find it rather impossible to say.

Have you any accounts of a public character as large as ours?——Yes; many larger.

Would you say that this is a flourishing concern?——I should say it is conducted on extremely good business lines.

Thank you; I think the evidence you have given proves that. As regards the Meetings account, I am not the Treasurer, and I was very much impressed by what you said as to the transference of sums of money from the Meetings account to the General account. Am I right in concluding that these meetings show a profit? It is a profitable account, is it not?——Do you mean to the banker? (Laughter.)

No; to the Union? (Laughter.)——I think that is rather a matter of opinion. One can hardly know what were the expenses; the debit entries do not tell me what the payments were for.

But apparently there seems to be a balance?——Yes.

As to the General account, would you say that it is evidence of prosperity?——Decidedly.

And you would gather that this organisation is one which is increasing in popularity and in strength so far as finance can give evidence?——Undoubtedly.

Thank you.

Frank Glenister, manager of the London Pavilion, gave evidence regarding the letting of the Pavilion for the purpose of meetings of the Women's

Social and Political Union. He produced correspondence and also agreements under which the theatre was let.

Public Opinion.

Mrs. Pankhurst (cross-examining): Were those meetings well attended?——Yes; very well attended.

Large meetings?——Very large.

Orderly meetings?——Very orderly.

What sort of people attended the meetings?——The better class, I think, and many of them of the middle class.

Have you ever let the hall to other people?——Yes.

How do these meetings compare with other meetings?——I could scarcely see very much difference from the point of audience.

They were responsible people?——Quite.

You would consider they expressed public opinion?——I should think so.

They were sympathetic?——Very.

And you found the Union satisfactory tenants?——In every way.

Mr. Healy: It did not occur to you that you were letting the Pavilion as part of the machinery of a great conspiracy?——Oh, dear no.

Harry Percival Towers, business manager of the Savoy Theatre, also spoke to that theatre being let to the Women's Social and Political Union for the purpose of meetings. Payment was made by cheque . . .

Orderly and Enthusiastic.

Mrs. Pankhurst: Were you present at these meetings?——Part of them.

Were they large meetings?——The theatre was quite full.

Were there people turned away from the doors?——Well, yes, I should think so.

The meetings were orderly?——Quite.

Would you call them enthusiastic meetings?——Yes.

Very enthusiastic?——Yes, I think so.

You heard some of the speeches probably?——Yes.

Were they well received by the audience?——Oh, yes, very well received.

What kind of audiences?——Well, mostly ladies, I think.

Ladies. You would not call them ill-behaved people?——Well-behaved.

"Ladies" is rather a difficult word, is it not?——Well, women then. (Laughter.)

Women who had obviously come there for a very serious purpose, and were all in earnest about what was being done at the meeting?——I think so.

Were there interruptions?——Well, I think there were one or two slight ones.

But as a whole the audience was sympathetic and enthusiastic?——Yes.

Mr. Healy: Is it now quite safe to take lunch at the Savoy after these proceedings? (Laughter.)——Yes; I think so.

Mr. Bodkin: Is not the Savoy Restaurant quite distinct from the Theatre?——Oh, yes. (Renewed laughter.)

Inspector Charles Crocker, of Rochester Row, said he was on duty at Cannon Row Police Station on the night of November 21, and attended to the bailing out of the women who had been arrested. About 180 were brought in, and he bailed out 175. Fifty of the women gave their addresses as 4, Clement's Inn. Mr. Pethick Lawrence arrived at the police station at eleven o'clock and said he wanted the women to promise him—as he had given an undertaking on their behalf—that they would not offend again before they had been taken before the Court. Witness heard the undertaking given. Mr. Pethick Lawrence had a list of the names, and his signature appeared in the bailing out book (produced) 175 times as being surety for that number of women. Witness gave the names of some of the women who were bailed out. In further reply to Mr. Bodkin, witness said he was again on duty at Cannon Row on March 1 when ten women were charged. Mr. Pethick Lawrence did not become bail on that day for anybody. He was also on duty on March 4, when about fifty women were charged. He attended to the bailing out of forty-seven of them. Some of them gave the Clement's Inn address. At about eleven o'clock Mr. and Mrs. Pethick Lawrence came to the station. Mr. Pethick Lawrence again gave an undertaking that the women would not offend until they had been before the police court the following morning. The women gave the promise to Mr. Pethick Lawrence collectively. Witness produced the bailing out book, which showed that Mr. Pethick Lawrence bailed out twenty-three and Mrs. Pethick Lawrence twenty-four women.

On counsel, referring to some names, witness said, "I don't think they belong to me." (Laughter.)

Mr. Bodkin: Well, you don't claim the ownership of persons you have bailed, do you?

Albert Canning, a detective-constable of New Scotland Yard, examined by Mr. Bodkin, said he had looked through the file of *Votes For Women* from November 19, 1911, up to and including March 1, 1912, and produced a list of certain passages which appeared therein.

A file of *Votes For Women* was handed up to the Judge . . .

Counsel proceeded to read quotations from speeches delivered at the Savoy Theatre meeting of February 15, Mrs. Pethick Lawrence, who presided, referred, he said, to "status lymphaticus" and Dr. Forbes Winslow, and then proceeded to address the audience. Miss Christabel Pankhurst followed, and then Mrs. Pankhurst, referring to the next deputation, said:

That great as had been the need on previous occasions, the need now was greater still. If the deputation were strong enough and influential enough the battle would be ended. No matter how obscure any woman thought herself she could rise to the level of the highest. The people of China won freedom at the price of blood, but the women of England would win freedom only at the price of a few panes of glass. "I have come to the conclusion," said Mrs. Pankhurst, "that if I had broken a pane of glass with other women when younger than my daughter, women would have had the vote long ago. Since we cannot get our freedom by women's ways then I am going out to throw my stone with the rest of you."

Cross-examination.

Mr. Pethick Lawrence questioned witness regarding the paper *Votes For Women* and its contents.

Am I right in saying that in each issue of the paper there are about two pages devoted to what is called "The Campaign Throughout the Country"—in London and in the provinces?——Yes.

And, roughly speaking, there is set out in each issue a programme of meetings to be held in the forthcoming week; and roughly, fifty or sixty meetings were being held in London and the same number in the provinces each week?——Yes.

That is over a hundred meetings of the Women's Social and Political Union each week?——Yes.

Witness also stated in further answering Mr. Pethick Lawrence that there was in each issue from half to a whole column of names of contributors to what was called the £250,000 Fund.

There are special paragraphs relating to protests from time to time?——Yes.

Those play but a very small part in the paper as a whole?——Sometimes they formed the subject of a leading article.

Quite so; but they did not form a large feature of the paper?——No.

On Page 83 there is an extract from the *Times* newspaper, and these words occur in the extract:

There is dismay and wrath among the Woman Suffragists, who see a mine exploded under the so-called Conciliation Bill. That Bill they hoped to carry through the House, in which a large number of members are hampered by pledges hastily given to obviate opposition, and perhaps now viewed with regret. They are all provided now with an excellent excuse for doing nothing; for it is obvious that if a truly democratic Woman Suffrage measure is to be in the hands of the House next Session, it would be absurd to waste time in tinkering the question. On the other hand, Adult Woman Suffrage is not what many ardent Suffragists desire, and there is the further possibility that the House of Commons may recoil from a wholesale creation of feminine votes which would give women a predominant electoral power throughout the country.

Witness: Yes, that is there.

Mr. Pethick Lawrence next called attention to the article in the issue of November 10, 1911, written by himself, in which he had set out "The Record of Postponement and Evasion" by Liberal Prime Ministers regarding women's suffrage. It included quotations from speeches or letters by Mr. Gladstone, Sir Henry Campbell-Bannerman, and Mr. Asquith.

Next he read the leading article under "The Outlook," in the issue of November 24, 1911, dealing with the successful adoption of militant tactics, when—

The Judge, stopping him, said: The allegation of the prosecution is that you and the persons sitting with you entered into a conspiracy to incite certain persons to commit breaches of the law. Now, anything that has any bearing on that issue I am sure the jury and the Court will listen to at any length ("Hear, hear!" by several of the jurors), but how the misdeeds of the Government, if they be misdeeds, or the changes of policy of this or that Minister can have any bearing on the issue now being tried I for my part fail to see. If you can persuade me that what you are reading has any bearing on the issue we will all listen to it with great patience, but to deal with what Mr. Lloyd George or Mr. Asquith has said or done—unless it has some bearing on whether you did or did not incite any persons to conspiracy—is no more to the point than what the man in the street says or does.

Mr. Pethick Lawrence: I submit that the Prosecution having read considerable extracts from this file, it is open to us to read a few extracts.

The Judge: The extracts read by the Prosecution, so far as I could gather, were devoted to showing—successfully or unsuccessfully it is for the jury to say—the scheme by which was carried out the actions which they are going to prove . . . I am not stopping you, Mr. Pethick Lawrence. I am only asking you what bearing it has on the case, and the question remains unanswered.

Mr. Pethick Lawrence: I think that when we come to the defence you will see that what I propose to read has a very important bearing on the case. Of course, I could read all the extracts.

The Judge: I hope you won't. (Laughter.) . . .

Mr. Pethick Lawrence: I shall be strictly reasonable, and shall only read what it seems to me is absolutely material. Proceeding, he quoted the following from the leading article in the issue of November 24, 1911:

> Mrs. Pethick-Lawrence drew an analogy from the case of Ireland. There had been a great agitation in that country for Home Rule, in response to which the Government were proposing to introduce an Irish Home Rule Bill. What would be the temper of the Nationalist party if the Government had proposed instead to introduce a Home Rule Bill for England, another for Scotland, another for Wales, and to leave Ireland under the Imperial Government? That was what the Government were proposing to do for women, and there was no answer to it

except vigorous and determined protest. In a remarkable leading article on the following morning, the *Times* discussed the situation, and pointed out that the diagnosis of the situation by the W.S.P.U. was entirely correct.

"Except by Violence."

The next extract was from the issue of December 1, 1911, which dealt with Mr. Lloyd George's Bath speech. Mr. Pethick Lawrence read the following from that speech:

> I lay down this proposition—democracy has never been a menace to property. I will tell you what has been a menace to property—when power was withheld from the democracy, when they had no voice in the government, when they were oppressed and had no means of securing redress except by violence.
>
> And I will give you the last reason I have got. Why are they angry now? They ran the Conciliation Bill, a measure of limited suffrage which, in my judgment, would have been grossly unfair to Liberalism. Now that Bill has been torpedoed, and the way is clear for a broad and democratic amendment of the suffrage for women.

The following from the leading article of December 22 was next read by Mr. Pethick Lawrence:

> Perhaps the most important of our questions was that which enquired as to the basis of Mr. Lloyd George's professed belief that a democratic proposal for Woman Suffrage can be carried except as a Government measure. This vital point Mr. Lloyd George evaded altogether. Both he and Sir Edward Grey expressed the opinion that a democratic proposal can be carried as an amendment, but neither of them made the smallest effort to support their statements by facts and calculations. The precise terms of our question were: If you believe that your proposal can be carried as an amendment, how do you reconcile your belief with the following facts:
>
> a) That as the proposal will not appeal to Unionists, support must come from the ranks of the Coalition?
>
> b) That Anti-Suffragists belonging to the Coalition will be given freedom of action by the Government to vote against the proposal, and thus wipe out the Coalition majority, leaving the supporters of your proposal in a minority?
>
> c) That if it is not made a Government measure, there will be no adequate means of preventing Nationalists and other M.P.'s from being absentees when the Woman Suffrage question is being voted upon?
>
> Now, until they supply an answer to this question, Ministers who ask us to trust to the success of an amendment are simply insulting our intelligence.

The next quotation was from the article entitled "Do Ut Des," in the issue of January 5, 1912. It began:—

DO UT DES.
(I give that you may give.)

In a notable speech (September, 1878), the great Chancellor of the German Empire, Bismarck, pointed out to his Parliament that the basis of all political negotiation was the principle *do ut des* (I give that you may give). He proceeded to refute a statement made by Bebel concerning an alleged political understanding arrived at between himself (Bismarck) and the Socialist orator Lassalle, by saying: "He (Lassalle) had nothing which he could have given me as a Minister. . . . He was not a man with whom definite agreements upon the basis of *do ut des* could be concluded."

* * *

When the Liberal Party in 1906 found themselves in power with a majority so great that they were independent of the Irish vote in the House of Commons, they showed no disposition whatever to touch the question of Home Rule or to commit themselves in any way to the Irish Party.

The article went on, Mr. Pethick Lawrence said, to show that the vote was the only power by which the Government could be brought to compromise.

Mr. Hobhouses's Incitement.

Mr. Pethick Lawrence's final reference was from an article in the issue of February 23, by Mrs. Pethick Lawrence, entitled "Inciting to Violence," and dealing with a speech by the Right Hon. C. E. H. Hobhouse. Mr. Pethick Lawrence said he attached the greatest importance to this extract:

In the Colston Hall, in Bristol, the Rt. Hon. C. E. H. Hobhouse, at an Anti-Suffrage meeting, said (vide report in the Press) "that in the case of the suffrage demand there had not been the kind of popular sentimental uprising which accounted for Nottingham Castle in 1832 or the Hyde Park railings in 1867. There had been no great ebullition of popular feeling."

We have often said that members of the Government do not understand the language of reason or of argument, nor the appeal to justice and that the only argument that carries any weight with them is the argument of militancy. Mr. Hobhouse on Friday last bore irrefutable evidence to the truth of that statement. He altogether ignored the constitutional agitation for Woman Suffrage, which is the greatest agitation which has ever been carried out in this country for franchise reform. Twenty years ago, April 27, 1892, Mr. Balfour pointed out on the floor of the House of Commons that the agitation for Votes for Women was at least as strong at that time as had been the agitation for the enfranchisement of the agricultural labourer in 1884:—

"I think those who wish to be enfranchised (women) have used the only methods they could use in the matter, that is to say, they have expressed the desire to obtain the vote on platforms and by public meetings and by whatever other means were open to them. The hon. gentleman appears to think that there was a widespread desire on the part of the agricultural labourer to claim the franchise. I do not believe the desire existed, and I am sure it was never demonstrated.

We challenge any student of political history to furnish us with facts showing that franchise agitations in the past were carried out on a constitutional scale comparable to the Woman Suffrage agitation in this country during the past six years. We challenge them to show that larger funds were raised, more meetings held, greater demonstrations organised, more public support forth-coming of the kind given by recent municipal councils. The only way in which the woman's Suffrage agitation was outdone by the franchise movements of men in the past was in violence and destruction of property and of human life. It is this fact which the Rt. Hon. C. E. H. Hobhouse selects with which to taunt the Woman Suffrage Movement with futility and failure. It is well that women should take this lesson to heart, and that they should go back to the history of the agitation in 1832 in order to glean from it reasons for the conduct of their own campaign.

"The popular sentimental uprising," to which Mr. Hobhouse refers, burnt the Castle of the Anti-Suffrage Duke of Newcastle to the ground. Colwick Castle, the country seat of another Anti-Suffrage gentleman in the neighbourhood, was set on fire, and his wife died from illness caused by the shock. No arrests were made in connection with these crimes. The King, thoroughly alarmed at the state of the country, begged the Whig Ministry favourable to the Bill not to resign, and it was intimated to them that this was also the wish of the now terrified Peers who had thrown out the Bill.

The article went on to say:

By holding up to women the example of men in 1832 and in 1867, when the Hyde Park railings were pulled down, Mr. Hobhouse takes the very grave responsibility of inciting them to serious forms of violence, in comparison with which Mrs. Pankhurst's exhortation is mildness itself. It is undeniably true that the history of the Woman's Movement shows nothing in any way comparable with the violence and destruction wrought in Nottingham and Bristol. Neither do we believe that it will ever be necessary for women to resort to these extreme measures. Women to-day are less emotional, less hysterical, and more politically minded than were the men of the country in 1832. They are prepared to go just as far in their demonstrations of public uprising as is necessary in order to convey the fact that they are determined to win their freedom—and no further. They make up in individual self-sacrifice, and in readiness to accept the consequences of their action, what is lacking in destructive violence.

Mr. Healy (to witness): I gather that you made these extracts yourself—unaided?——I made them myself.

Unaided?——Certainly, unaided.

Your object was to pick out passages for this particular trial?——Yes.

What guided you in selecting those passages?——I selected passages which in my opinion incited to violence, and where calls were made by the leaders for volunteers.

You constituted yourself an intellectual judge of what would incite to violence and what would not?——Yes.

Therefore we may take you as an expert in this matter?——I don't wish to pose as an expert.

Just listen to this:

> The days are past for rioting, and we do not need to have recourse to bloodshed or violence to carry on our schemes of progress and reform, because we have a fairly good franchise, which is an assurance that the will of the—

Mr. Bodkin: What are you quoting from?

Sir Rufus Isaacs and Violence.

Mr. Healy: Wait and see. (Laughter.)
Continuing, Mr. Healy read:

> people, in these democratic days, must prevail. Formerly, when the great mass of the people were voteless, they had to do something violent in order to show what they felt; to-day the elector's bullet is his ballot. Let no one be deceived, therefore, because in the present struggle everything is peaceful and orderly, in contrast to the disorderliness of other great struggles in the past.

Mr. Bodkin objected to the passage unless his friend showed that it came from one of the papers published by Mr. and Mrs. Pethick Lawrence. Otherwise, it was a purely academic question.

The Judge said that in blasphemy trials quotations were allowed from other writers in order to test whether a particular writing would come under the heading of blasphemy.

Mr. Healy: Yes, my lord; that has always been allowed.

Mr. Bodkin: I would suggest to my friend that he postpones this question until the Attorney-General is present.

Mr. Healy: That I am very happy to do, because I am quoting from a speech by the Attorney-General. (Laughter.) To Witness: Do you think that speech is an incitement to violence?——I don't care to express an opinion.

Mr. Healy: I think that is the safest course. (Laughter.)

Inspector Crocker was recalled at this stage, and stated that he had been able to trace the record of the bailing out of the following prisoners: Sarah Benett, Ethel Slade, Grace Stewart, Georgina Helen Grant, Mary Richmond, Marie S. Brown, Elizabeth Thompson, Agnes Alice Wison, Mary Jones, and Doreen Allen. These, he said, had been bailed out for the most part by Mr. Pethick Lawrence, and in some cases by Mrs. Pethick Lawrence. The offences were malicious damage, and in one case throwing missiles.

Mr. Healy: A case of missing the window, I suppose. (Laughter.)

Mrs. Pankhurst: Are those all you have been able to trace?——Yes.

A very awkward and inconvenient way of recording your information?——We do not find it so.

It has proved very awkward to-day?——There is a general index to the charge-book which enables us to refer to these cases.

Mrs. Pankhurst: It is an inconvenient system, and perhaps when we get the vote we will find a better way of doing it. (Laughter and "Hear, hear!")

Mr. Bodkin: You will report that to the Chief Commissioner, Inspector . . .

Chief-Inspector McCarthy, special branch, New Scotland Yard, described the arrest of Mr. and Mrs. Pethick Lawrence at the offices of the Union in Clement's Inn on March 5. He took them to Bow Street Police Station and then returned to the offices, where other officers had been left.

"A Diligent Search."

Mr. Bodkin: Miss Christabel Pankhurst is named on the warrant?——Yes.

And have you made and caused to be made a diligent search for her since that date?——Yes.

And have not been able to find any trace?——No . . .

Mr. Pethick Lawrence, cross-examining, said that he gathered from the fact that the witness had selected the documents which had been read that he considered them as evidence of procuring people to take illegal action.

Witness: I did have something to do with the selecting of them, but, of course, the final selection was not with me.

You made some rough selection?——Yes.

Mr. Pethick Lawrence: I have an extract here:

> Parliament has never been hearty for reform or for any good measure. It hated the Reform Bill of 1831–1832. It does not like the Franchise Bill now upon the table. What should be done, and what must be done, in these circumstances? You know what your fathers did thirty-four years ago, and you know the result. Men who in every speech they made insulted the working men, describing them as a multitude given over to vice, will be the first to yield when the popular will is loudly and resolutely expressed. If Parliament Square, from Charing Cross to the venerable Abbey, were filled with men seeking the Reform Bill, these slanderers of their countrymen would learn to be civil, if they did not learn to love freedom.

If you had found such a letter at Clement's Inn, would you have taken it?——I cannot answer that unless I know the other circumstances.

You do not express any opinion upon that?——No.

Are you aware that is a letter written by Mr. John Bright?——I will take it that it was, of course.

You said one of the exhibits you put in was a series of words professed to be a code?——Yes.

So far as you know, is there any evidence that the code was actually used?——I do not know that it was ever used. I never saw the code used in any letter or telegram.

So far as you are concerned, this code may be a matter of jeu d'espirit on the part of someone in the office?——Yes; I don't know anything beyond that.

Replying to Mrs. Pankhurst, who cross-examined, the witness said that two or three copies of the code were found at Clement's Inn.

Doesn't it suggest itself to you that since the letters which have been read are very open in their character, and that there is no concealment whatever, it is very unlikely that people who have been writing such private letters and public articles should use a code of that kind?——It would have been very useful for telegraphing.

As a matter of fact you have no evidence whatever to show that the code has been used?——No.

Would you be willing to take it from me that the code really was a joke?——Possibly it was.

The Judge remarked that he noticed that in one letter the initial "A" had been used, and, according to the code, denoted Mr. Asquith's secretary.

Mr. Bodkin said he thought that in this case the "A" meant Mr. Asquith.

Mrs. Pankhurst: It is very obvious that the "H of C" which occurs means the House of Commons. It is not the code . . .

The Court adjourned at this stage till Friday morning.

13

Closing Days of the Trial
[May 17–22, 1912]

EVIDENCE OF DAMAGE AND ARRESTS WAS THEN CALLED.

P. C. Frederick Price said that while on duty in Downing Street on the evening of March 1 he saw a motor-car stop immediately in front of the Prime Minister's residence. Mrs. Pankhurst, Mrs. Tuke and Mrs. Marshall got out, and Mrs. Pankhurst threw several stones at the windows of No. 10, breaking four panes of glass. He arrested Mrs. Pankhurst, and conveyed her to Cannon Row Police Station, where she was charged with committing damage. When charged she made no reply. At the station she handed over three large flint stones. The other ladies were arrested by other officers. At the police court he heard Mrs. Pankhurst make the following statement:

> It is not the first time I have come before you in connection with this agitation. The last time I was here I laid before you certain reasons for my taking part in the agitation, with which I do not propose to trouble you this morning. At that time I hoped that what we were doing would be sufficient to make the Government realise that women who pay the taxes are entitled to the protection and the privileges of the vote on the same terms as men who pay the taxes. Since then the Government have left me and other women no possible doubt as to our position. We have not the vote because, hitherto, we have not been able to bring ourselves to use the methods which won the vote for men, and within the last fortnight a member of the Government has challenged us to do very much more serious things than we have done—we, who are charged before you this morning.
>
> In Bristol, Mr. Hobhouse said women had not proved their desire for the vote because they had done nothing like that which characterised the men's agitation that led to the burning of Nottingham Castle and the pulling up of Hyde Park railings. The Government, as a whole, has provided us during the last few days with evidence that only the most stupid people could fail to understand. Why we have failed so far is that we have not done enough to bring pressure to bear on the Government. A week ago last Monday I wrote to the Prime Minister with regard to the question of the Referendum, asking him to see a deputation of women in order that they might discuss this matter with him. The request was refused with contempt. Yet Cabinet Ministers have gone cap in hand to the Miners' Federation to persuade them to come to terms with their industrial opponents.

What we have done, Sir, is a fleabite as compared with what the miners in this country are doing to-day. They are paralysing the whole of the life of the community. They have votes, they have a constitutional means of redressing their grievance, but they are not content to rely on the constitutional means. If we had the vote we would be constitutional, but since we have not the vote we learn our lesson, a lesson that has been given to us. I hope this will be enough to show the Government that the woman's agitation is going on. If not, if you send me to prison, as soon as I come out of prison I will go further, to show that women who have to help pay the salaries of Cabinet Ministers, and who help to pay your salary, too, Sir, are going to have some voice in the making of the laws which they have to obey. I have only to fear that perhaps our self restraint has prevented us from doing as much as is necessary, but I want to make it perfectly clear that although we do not desire to go one step further than is necessary, we are prepared to take all the steps that are necessary, and to face the consequences.

You are going to send me to prison. I am quite ready to go and to pay the price, however high that price may be. Like those who went before us, we think it quite worth while. We are not fighting this battle for ourselves, but for our sex. What happens to us does not matter, but what comes of what happens to us does matter very much. The individual will disappear, but the Cause is going on.

Mrs. Pankhurst: You were present when I was arrested on a charge of throwing stones at the Prime Minister's house?——Yes.

How many panes of glass were broken?——Four.

How many panes of glass did I break? Do you know how many panes I broke?——No.

Would you be prepared to accept it if I said that I broke one pane?——Yes.

And you were in the police court when I was tried and sentenced?——Yes.

Did you hear the value of the pane of glass?——Nine shillings.

That was the total value of the four panes of glass?——Yes, the total value was nine shillings.

Then if I broke one pane of glass, the damage I did was something under 3s.?——Yes.

Mr. Healy: Two shillings and three pence.

You remember the sentence I got?——Two months.

Mr. Healy: A shilling a month.

Mr. Bodkin: You are not quite right, because there is an odd threepence.

P. C. Thomas Whitbread, examined by Mr. Graham Campbell, said that while on duty in Parliament Street on November 21 he saw Sarah Benett throw a stone at the A. B. C. windows, 35, Parliament Street. No glass was broken. He then saw her throw a stone at No. 34, the offices of the London and North Western Railway Company, breaking the window, and when he arrested her two stones were on the pavement.

Mr. Pethick Lawrence: Have you been acquainted with the outdoor meetings and demonstrations of the Women's Social and Political Union?—— Yes, sir.

For some years?——Since they started.

Did you see the demonstration that took place last June, which consisted of a procession from the Embankment to the Albert Hall?——Yes, sir.

Did you form any idea of the size of the demonstration?——It was a very large procession.

Would it be incorrect to say it was several miles in length?——It was a very long procession.

Would it be incorrect to say it took between two and three hours to pass a given point?——I should say about an hour and a half.

Was that a perfectly peaceful demonstration?——I think so, sir.

Mr. Healy: Was Sarah Benett a lady of at least sixty years of age?——I think so, sir.

You had no difficulty in taking her to the station?——None, whatever.

Did you hear her make a statement at the sessions?——Yes, sir.

What sentence did she get?——Two months in the second division.

What was the value of the pane that was broken?——About £6.

What did she say at the sessions?——She made a speech, but I don't exactly know what it was she said . . .

To P. C. Freeman, who furnished the evidence of the conviction, Mr. Healy put the following statements made by the three ladies in their defence at Newington Sessions.

Mrs. Jones said:

It was the breaking of faith by Mr. Asquith towards women in regard to the Conciliation Bill which made me feel that this breach of faith could only be responded to by another breach of faith, which took the form of the breaking of glass. I think myself that it is more important to break faith than to break windows. If that is the opinion of the Court, my sentence will depend on whether they take a different point of view from myself. I consider, also, that there was much damage done to women in November, last year, and I consider that it is better to go and break windows than to allow men to damage women as we were damaged in November last year.

Miss Atheling said:

If you men were in our position, you would not be breaking windows, you would be breaking people's heads.

Mrs. Rowe said:

I cannot give such an undertaking, and I pleaded not guilty in the sense that I am not deserving of punishment. The idea of punishment is not more acceptable to me than to the rest of this Court. It is preposterous to regard me as a person dangerous to society. I have not fallen into the ranks of the criminal class. We are out to destroy other things than windows. We are out against worn-out ideas. Men regard us partly as stupid angels and partly as silly children. They never take us seriously. We want your attention, and not only your attention but the attention of the Government. We may have to use stronger weapons. We are fighting for the women who are forced to sell their honour, for the young girls who are held by the evil of the white slave traffic, and for women who are denied full opportunity of self-development.

Mr. Healy: How much, after making these speeches, did they get?
Witness: Two months' each.
Mr. Bodkin: Did you hear the judge say this: "If you will abstain from breaking the law and give an undertaking that you will not break the law again, you will be left free to agitate in any way you please as long as you keep within the limits of the law," and did she decline to give the undertaking and was accordingly dealt with?——Yes . . .

P. C. Self, P. C. Palmer, P. C. Blackwell and P. C. Kiernan deposed to acts committed under similar circumstances by Violet Taylor, Ellen Archdale, Eileen Connor Smith and Violet Hudson Harvey in the Strand on November 21, 1911.

Mrs. Pankhurst cross-examined P. C. Blackwell as follows:

Mrs. Archdale is a dignified sort of lady, is she not?——I should describe her as a matronly lady.

Did she make any attempt to run away?——No.

Would you say she was the sort of person who would form her own convictions?——I cannot judge what is working in her mind.

Did she appear to you to be a person of self-possession and with her own ideas?——I should say her own ideas were pretty strong. (Laughter.)

Were you present at her trial?——Yes.

Did you hear it stated that she was the daughter of two pioneers of the women's movement ? She was the daughter of a pioneer woman physician and of the great newspaper man Russel, editor of the *Scotsman*?——I did not hear her say that.

Well, that is a fact. I should like to ask if she must not have had very strong feeling to have done such a thing?——I cannot judge.

You are not accustomed in your ordinary business as a policeman to deal with ladies of the type of Mrs. Archdale?——I don't know; we all have our weaknesses.

Have you had anything to do with our demonstrations?——I have witnessed four or five.

Orderly demonstrations?——There was only one demonstration which I could call orderly in connection with the Suffragists.

It was not part of your duty to be present at our meetings?——No . . .

Police Evidence Disallowed.

Thos. McNamara, an inspector in the Criminal Investigation Department and New Scotland Yard, was next called, and stated that he was present at a meeting of the Women's Social and Political Union on November 23, 1911. He took notes of the speeches in longhand on the margin of a copy of *Votes For Women* which he bought in the theatre. He made his report, based on these notes, next morning. The speakers were Miss Christabel Pankhurst (presiding), Mr. Pethick Lawrence, Mrs. Cameron Swan, and Miss Evelyn Sharp.

The Judge: What is this report made from?——From my notes with additions.

The Judge: You have filled it in from your memory?

Mr. Graham Campbell: Were the facts fresh in your memory when you made the report?——Yes, sir.

The Judge: If you are to rely on verbal evidence and the recollection of this man—

Mrs. Pankhurst: He said he took the notes on the margin of a newspaper.

Mr. Graham Campbell: He said he made his report shortly afterwards.

The Judge: Next day.

Mr. Healy asked where were the original notes.

Mr. Graham Campbell quoted from the laws of evidence in support of the admission of McNamara's evidence.

The Judge: One cannot help knowing that a man who is taking longhand notes of a speech which is rapidly delivered is not in the best position to recall what was said that he has not taken down, because his attention has been directed to what he has taken down, and therefore his memory is not so good as that of a man who takes nothing but relies on his memory alone. If you are relying upon verbal accuracy of phrasing and so forth, which I presume you are, then you know it is merely discretionary on the part of the Court to permit it or not. You are relying upon the accurate memory of a man whose attention at the moment was directed to taking down what he could and I think it is rather dangerous to rely upon accuracy of notes so taken even though his report was made next morning.

Mr. Graham Campbell: Can you remember what was said without looking at your notes?——In part.

Mr. Graham Campbell said that there was a report of the meeting in *Votes For Women* of December 1.

The Judge, reverting to the question of taking notes in longhand, said he had a constant experience of it, and he found that while writing in longhand things frequently escaped him which he would have heard had he not been writing . . .

Mr. Pethick Lawrence (cross examining) elicited from the witnesses that it was a crowded meeting, and that judging by the size of the collection, of the promises made, the audience was composed of people of position and standing. It was an enthusiastic and approving audience. It was witness's duty as an officer of the C.I.D. to attend a good many meetings with a view of ascertaining if anything was said that transcended the proper limits of public speech.

Listen to this. "Violence is always deplorable, so is bloodshed."

The Judge: What are you reading from?

Mr. Pethick Lawrence: It is not a speech by anyone of the defendants. (Proceeding with the quotation)—"Yet violence and bloodshed in Ulster would be an incomparably smaller misfortune than cowardly acquiescence in a revolution, which, if consummated, would assuredly plunge the whole country into civil war." Such a sentence as that is one that you would put down as a rather serious incitement, is it not?——Yes.

It is a considerably more serious statement than any made at that meeting?——I would put it down.

Do you know that that statement was made by an eminent lawyer—Mr. F. E. Smith?——I have heard of it.

Answering Mrs. Pankhurst, witness said that he had heard a good many speeches by her and other prominent members of the Union.

Have you heard these speakers say that if women had the constitutional means of redressing their grievances that men possess there would be no militancy—I mean no violence?——If is quite possible that they have said that. I cannot recollect it.

Have you heard me many times express concern as to the future and the hope that the Government would take this question seriously and deal with it before the women got out of the hands of their leaders?——I have heard some speakers say so.

Mr. Healy: I don't want to embarrass you, but what became of your original notes?——I destroyed them.

You threw them overboard like the log we heard of the other day. Did you destroy them at anybody's direction?——No.

You took them on the margin of a newspaper and embellished and expanded them next day?——Yes.

James McLean, clerk in the C.I.D. at Bow Street, a shorthand writer, stated that he attended the W.S.P.U. meeting in the Savoy Theatre on November 23, 1911, and took a note.

Mr. G. Campbell: Verbatim?——It was not verbatim, it was condensed.

Witness added that the shorthand note was verbatim but the report was condensed.

Did you make a synopsis of the speeches the same evening?——Yes.

Was there anything in the synopsis which was not in the original short-hand note?——No.

Mr. Healy: Is synopsis a Scotch word, my lord?

The Judge asked how the sentence by King David "I had said in my haste all men are liars" would appear in a synopsis.

Mr. Healy: King David said "All men are liars." (Laughter.)

Mr. G. Campbell submitted that although it was not a verbatim transcript the witness's synopsis was admissible as evidence.

The Judge: Has he got his shorthand note?

Mr. Healy: Or has he thrown it overboard?

Mr. G. Campbell: He has got what is equivalent. He has got a document.

The Judge: You characterise it as a synopsis. I do not know what that may mean.

Mr. G. Campbell: It is his own word. It is a document transcribed from notes taken at the meeting.

The Judge: The word synopsis implies omissions. He has culled from his notes what in his discretion he thought proper. He had a complete record, and had he copied it all out it would have been absolutely unassailable. A speech must be taken in its entirety. It is possible to cull certain expressions from a speech in such a way as to misrepresent its author. Speeches may be very unfairly used in that way.

Mr. G. Campbell: If your lordship feels there is any doubt I would rather not press this evidence, especially having regard to what is reported in the newspaper.

Mr. Healy asked what became of the original shorthand notes.

Witness: They were not kept, sir.

Mr. Healy: The log was thrown overboard. (Laughter.)

Further examined, witness said he attended a W.S.P.U. meeting held in the Savoy Theatre on February 15, 1912. He took and had retained short-hand notes of the speeches delivered at that meeting. Twelve or thirteen hundred people attended. Mrs. Pethick Lawrence was in the chair, and the speakers were Mrs. Pankhurst and Miss Christabel Pankhurst.

Counsel proceeded to read the speeches made at the meeting, the first of which related to the Ball Case.

Mrs. Pankhurst, interposing, asked counsel to emphasise the word "unless" in the following sentence of her speech: "We mean next month to make a great protest *unless* before the day we have fixed for it we get complete satisfaction."

A report of the same meeting, witness said, appeared in the issue of *Votes For Women* of February 3.

Mr. Pethick Lawrence asked if witness was at a meeting at Croydon at which the Right Hon. Sir Edward Carson said: "There is a point at which resentment becomes so acute that we are entitled to adopt any method of preventing liberty of discussion being taken away, and we tell Mr. Asquith that he had better count the cost." Were you at Croydon when Sir Edward Carson said it?——No.

You know, of course, that in Ireland they are drilling a number of men in a part of Ulster?——I do not know that as a matter of fact.

Answering Mrs. Pankhurst, witness said he had attended many meetings of the W.S.P.U. in Scotland and in the provinces.

Do you remember that I used to urge the need for self-restraint on the part of women?——I cannot recollect any particular reference bearing that out.

Have you ever heard me emphasise that women went unarmed and took no weapons in these deputations?——I cannot recollect that.

Then, speaking generally, would you say that the tone of my speeches was that of extreme violence or that of argument and explanation? Perhaps you would give us your own idea.——I don't know that I am qualified to express any idea on that. I have only come into intimate connection with your meetings since I came to London. It was in the capacity of a newspaper reporter that I attended them formerly.

Well, that would enable you to form a very good opinion of speeches. Would you characterise me as a speaker addicted to very violent language?——I would not until recently.

Then references to violence have been quite recent?——Yes; within the past few months as far as my experience goes.

Before that much more time was spent in arguing and explaining and converting?——There was a lot of time devoted to that.

Would you say that that was a characteristic of the speeches of members of the Union?——Generally; but my experience is that they were always hinting at some possibility, some force behind the movement, some hidden weapon.

You have heard speakers say it was necessary to find some way of bringing pressure to bear on these people who had power to give us the vote and refused to do it?——Yes.

And you have heard us say: "Men have constitutional means of bringing pressure to bear which women have not." Have you heard us contrast the position of women with that of men?——Yes; you said at these meetings that men had won their freedom at the price of blood, and that you wished the women would imitate them.

Have you not heard us say that we wished to win reform without going to the lengths that men had to?——I have no recollection of you saying that.

Mr. Healy: Were you dispatched by the Government to report Mr. Lloyd George's speech at Limehouse?——No, I did not fulfil that position . . . (Laughter.)

Important Cross-Examination.

Police-constable Hall deposed to attending meetings of the Women's Social and Political Union at the London Pavilion and taking shorthand notes of portions of the speeches. The transcripts were produced and read.

Mrs. Pankhurst: We are quite prepared to accept the reports in our own paper, but we question the accuracy of the speeches read. They are not our speeches.

Mr. Healy: My client also says she does not accept the accuracy of the transcripts.

Mr. Pethick Lawrence: You have given us the transcripts of your shorthand notes of these meetings?——That is so.

Did you take down the whole of the speeches or parts of them?——Parts of them, extracts.

You did not make that clear in your examination. What I understood you to say was that this was a shorthand report of the meeting. If this is a shorthand report of extracts of the speeches, I put it to you it is not really a report of the meetings at all?——It is not verbatim.

It is not a shorthand verbatim report of the meeting; it is merely a few extracts which you have selected from the speeches?——That is so.

What certificate do you hold for shorthand?——I hold a certificate for 110 words a minute.

Yes, but when you take down certain portions of a speech which you select as suitable to take down, do you take down the whole of that portion?——I use my own discretion.

It is quite possible that you omit certain sentences or words?——I take all the points leading up to the sentence in question.

You say you take only extracts. Do you also only take extracts from sentences?——Oh, no, sir; I take the whole sentence.

Do you mean that a paragraph in your transcript is a continuous piece as it appeared in the speech, or does that represent a series of little extracts joined together by you to make it into a paragraph?——No, they would be all continuous.

Let me put this to you: Here is a part of the paragraph which you have read, and which you have put down as a continuous speech. This is what your extract reads, and I ask you to verify it. It is the speech of Miss Christabel Pankhurst on January 22:

> Ladies and gentlemen,—I am not going to keep you very long as chairman today, because I know that you want to hear Mrs. Pankhurst speak. Perhaps some of you may have noticed that we have a new statement in the Press by Sir Edward Grey with regard to the position. The question has been very much debated in the newspapers of late, some are in favour of the proposition and others are

against it. All this time the Government have maintained a strict silence. Would the Government refuse to have the referendum taken on the subject of Woman Suffrage? If the House of Commons are going to put forth the referendum, that is another matter, and if that represents the view of the Government, then it is a pledge of their undertaking. The Government cannot disassociate themselves from this scheme. On the other hand, if the Government hold the view that Sir Edward Grey has described, then they are all tarred with the same brush. The Government cannot leave this to the discretion of the House of Commons, for if the House of Commons decide for a referendum then they are bound to quit office, as they are bound to treat this question as a breach of confidence.

I put it to you that, as a pronouncement by a person who is certainly expert in political affairs, is sheer and unutterable nonsense?——I am no judge of that, sir.

What Miss Pankhurst Said.

I put it to you that it has absolutely no meaning and no sense whatever. I put it to you that a person of Miss Christabel Pankhurst's intelligence, her power of holding an audience, could not have uttered a speech approximately similar to that nonsense. I will put it to you presently what she did say. I will put what she probably said, and ask you whether it does not sound much more likely to be correct. I shall put in a few words and small sentences, which will make sense of the whole paragraph:

We have a new statement in the Press of Sir Edward Grey with regard to the question of the referendum (not with regard to the "position"). This question has been very much debated in the newspapers of late. Some are in favour of the proposition and some against it. All this time the Government have maintained a strict silence.

Now we come to a sentence which I suggest you have omitted altogether.

The question we asked Sir Edward Grey was, "Would the Government refuse to have a referendum taken on the question of woman suffrage?" Sir Edward Grey's answer was that he himself was against it, but if the House of Commons were going to decide in favour of the referendum, then that was another matter.

I suggest to you that that last sentence was a quotation from Sir Edward Grey and formed no part of Miss Pankhurst's own statement. And then Miss Pankhurst goes on to say:

If that represents the view of the Government then the Government cannot dissociate themselves from this proposal for a referendum. The Government could not leave this question to the discretion of the House of Commons, for if the

House of Commons decided for a referendum, then they are bound to quit office, as they are bound to treat this question as a breach of confidence, as they are against the referendum on other questions.

I put it to you that that is probably what she said.

Witness said that he did not dispute the accuracy of Mr. Pethick Lawrence's rendering. His note, he added, was not put forward as a verbatim one.

Mr. Pethick Lawrence: Then I am correct in saying that, instead of taking down whole sentences or paragraphs, you have selected sentences out of paragraphs, and words here and there, which conveyed what you thought was the interpretation of the sentences in the paragraph?——It is according to my notes.

Mr. Pethick Lawrence: I believe that perfectly. (Laughter.)

I think you must admit that to attempt to extract bits of sentences and bits of paragraphs and piece them together in your own fashion is to make such abject nonsense of the sense that no report you can make is of the slightest value?——I am no judge, sir.

I put it to you. If you made certain statements in court consisting of sentences and words, and if I selected every second sentence out of the ones you used and out of each sentence selected two words out of three, I put it to you that I should make such nonsense of your evidence as would not be accepted in this court. What is the value of a verbatim shorthand writer if he only takes from a sentence such parts as suit his own convenience or such words as he happens to hear?

Mr. Bodkin: He said he could only write 110 words a minute.

Replying to further questions, witness admitted that a certain portion of the transcript of Mr. Mansell-Moullin's speech appeared as follows: "Now, what are you going to do, we must go forward with the fight even if we have to use violence."

Mr. Pethick Lawrence: I put it to you that that is neither grammar nor sense.

The Judge: What is the error in grammar, and what is the error in sense?

Mr. Pethick Lawrence: I ought to have said syntax. It really is two sentences. A note of interrogations ought to be there.

The Judge: It does not make it bad grammar because a note of interrogation is left out.

Mr. Pethick Lawrence: I put it to you that what Mr. Mansell-Moullin really said was this:

The question is: What are you going to do? How are you to nail such shufflers and wrigglers, how are you to nail them to their pledges? Some one in the audience says "Wait and see." It will be too late then. You want to nail them now, and the only thing is to keep straight on for your principle—the one that was laid down at the start. Keep perfectly straight for the principle. "As it is, or may be, granted to men." I know what it means, and I am afraid you all know as well as I do. I know the hundreds who have been imprisoned. I know the brutal treatment that so many of you have received at the hands of the police and of prison officials if not by the direct orders of the Home Secretary, at least with his active connivance. I know that some of you have been maimed for life. I know that some have died; died as directly of the violence they have received as if they had been put up against a wall and shot. I know all this, and so do you. But there is nothing for it but to go on. Your cause is a sacred one. It is the cause of justice and liberty and civilisation. It is the finest and the noblest cause the world has ever known, and it is one that must and will succeed.

Is that, do you think, the correct report of what Mr. Mansell-Moullin said, which you have put down into that one sentence which is not divided, as it should be, by a note of interrogation?

Witness said that he was not prepared to say that the words Mr. Pethick Lawrence read were not uttered.

Do you not think that there is a small amount of difference between saying "We must go forward with the fight, even if we have to use violence," and saying, "I know that some have died, died as directly of the violence they have received," &c?

Witness: Oh, yes, there is.

Mr. Pethick Lawrence: I do not think I will question this witness any further.

Mrs. Pankhurst elicited from the witness the admission that he did not regard himself as an expert shorthand writer.

Have you any knowledge of familiar quotations? You know that quotation, "Who would be free himself must strike the blow"?

Witness: I do not know it very well.

I do not think you do, seeing that you report Mrs. Pethick Lawrence as saying, "Who would be free herself must strike the first blow." (Laughter.) You will agree with me that you are not a very expert reporter of speeches at meetings?

Witness: The only thing I can say is that the phrase was used.

The Judge: Possibly the speaker did not verify her quotation. (Laughter.)

Replying to Mr. Bodkin, witness said that he was prepared to swear that every word that appeared in the transcript was uttered at the meeting.

Mr. Pethick Lawrence: Every word; yes. (Laughter.)

Mrs. Pankhurst: Are you prepared to swear that every word you reported me as saying in my speech, and Mrs. Pethick Lawrence and Miss Pankhurst in their speeches, were actually uttered?

Witness: Yes . . .

More Evidence of Damage.

Harry John Walker, representing Messrs. D. H. Evans, of Oxford Street, stated that the damage done to the windows of the firm on March 1 amounted to £250. Twelve windows were broken.

Mrs. Pankhurst: You have considerable knowledge of commercial life in the West End. You know that women are largely engaged in business nowadays?——Yes.

A business like yours depends very largely for its success upon women—customers, saleswomen, and women who make the goods?——To an extent.

If the women you employ serve you faithfully, that helps your business?——That is so.

Do you know many women in business for themselves?——I don't know any personally.

You know of them?——Yes; there may be some.

Someone has a vote in respect of Messrs. Evan's premises?——Possibly.

I suppose they have taken good care that someone is qualified to vote in respect of the premises?——I don't know.

There may be a shop next door, and it may be occupied by a woman?——Possibly.

That woman, unlike the occupier of your premises, is not qualified to vote?——I believe not.

Yet she has to pay the same rates and taxes as the man next door who does have a vote. Now, I put it to you, sir, if you were in that woman's position and had to pay all those charges just like a man, would you now get very indignant if you had not the same power to protect yourself as the man?——That is a suppositious question.

I do not think it is. Would you not feel indignant if, because you are not six feet high, you were not allowed to vote. (Laughter.) I think you would if you saw someone next door enjoying the vote. I would like to ask you whether the incidents which occurred that day may not have led many people to realise better than they had done before the fact that a large number of women engaged in business may feel very indignant because, when they are displeased with the Government, they have no power to express their displeasure in the way a man would.

Witness: Do you mind repeating that question. (Laughter.)

From one reason or another business is bad at present, is it not?——I should not like to say so.

The Coal Strike and other things have led many businesses to complain?——I don't know.

There are a great many bargain sales going on just now?——Not more than usual.

And I think that a good many people are saying to themselves that the Government is to blame for this?——I don't know what the people are saying at all.

Suppose you thought the Government was to blame, would you not consider whether you would vote against it at the next election?——I might consider it.

And would be very glad you had the power to do so?——I don't attach very much importance to the vote myself. (Laughter.)

No? But perhaps you are not in business for yourself. But if a woman found that instead of selling twenty hats a day she was only selling one, and she thought the Government was to blame for that, and she could not vote against that Government at an election, she would feel that her pocket was touched, and that she had no remedy?——Certainly, if she thought that the Government was responsible.

Thank you.

Mr. Bodkin: You do not know which department of the Government influences the sale of hats, do you?——I do not . . . (Laughter.)

The Union's Colours.

Francis Powell, Inspector, New Scotland Yard, deposed that in November last he was engaged in connection with meetings of the W.S.P.U. He attended at Cannon Row Police Station and Bow Street Police Court in connection with the events of November 21. He also attended the meeting of the Union held in the Pavilion on the afternoon of March 4, and spoke to the accuracy of the reports of the speeches handed in. About 900 attended the meeting, he said, at which there was considerable interruption. After the meeting witness said he went to the vicinity of the Gardenia Restaurant. He saw from 150 to 200 women entering, many of them well-known to him as having been previously charged. They went to the second floor of the restaurant.

Mr. Bodkin: Do the members of the Union wear any distinctive symbols?——Yes.

What are they?——They've had many.

What are they now?——Some wear a miniature gate as a brooch, which denotes that they have been in prison; others wear badges and colours.

What colours?——Blue, green, and white (laughter)—or perhaps it's purple.

Any yellow?——No; no yellow.

And do the members always wear these badges or symbols?——Always.

Were they worn on this occasion?——Not one.

Witness, proceeding, said he followed two of the women who came out—Myra Sadd-Brown and Mary K. Richmond. They went into a Lyons' tea-shop, and after passing some time went to the War Office at precisely 8 o'clock. They threw a missile and broke windows.

Officer's Tribute to W.S.P.U.

Mr. Pethick Lawrence questioned witness at length as to the history and character of the agitation of the W.S.P.U., constitutional and otherwise. Witness frankly admitted that there had been many peaceful demonstrations organised by the Women's Social and Political Union, one of them, the monster demonstration in Hyde Park, which for size and successful management outdistanced anything within his thirty years' experience of demonstrations in the Metropolis. The succession of Albert Hall meetings were also without parallel in his knowledge of the history of political organisations. He agreed that one of the non-peaceful demonstrations followed the refusal by Mr. Asquith of an application that he should receive a peaceful deputation to convey the resolution passed at the mammoth demonstration in Hyde Park. Witness also testified to the abnormal size and importance of the women's procession in London on the eve of the Coronation last year. He had never seen anything larger nor more orderly. All the propaganda meetings of the organisation were well attended, well conducted, and enthusiastic.

Mr. Pethick Lawrence was putting it to the witness that large demonstrations held by men were usually followed by the granting of the demand made by the demonstrators, but his lordship suggested that was rather a matter for argument by the jury.

Witness answered, further, that he knew of no men's organisation which had so considerably and consistently demonstrated constitutionally as the W.S.P.U.

In reply to Mrs. Pankhurst, witness said he had been in attendance at Caxton Hall at all the pre-demonstration meetings, but had not been inside the hall. On some occasions men were not admitted.

Mrs. Pankhurst: I think an exception was always made in the case of reporters and the police.

Witness: I never risked a refusal. (Laughter.)

Do you think the speeches generally were characterised by a considerable amount of self-restraint?——I don't think so.

Men sometimes make violent speeches?——They do.

Have you attended meetings addressed by members of the present Government?——Yes.

Would you include them among the violent speakers?

Mr. Bodkin objected to the question.

The Judge: The jury are the judges of what is violent.

Mrs. Pankhurst: I was anxious that you and the jury should hear what the Inspector has to say on the point. (To witness.) Were you the police officer who said you wished the Government would come out and do their own dirty work on the occasion of a demonstration?——No, I was not.

Did you assist in searching Clement's Inn?——I did.

Was it you who found a private letter in the office written by me?——No.

Do you know who did find it?——I don't.

You were asked a question about the colours of the Union?——I know them very well, but I can't remember them. (Laughter.)

I hope that is not typical of your evidence with regard to more vital questions.

Mr. Bodkin: Perhaps you will tell us what are the colours, Mrs. Pankhurst?

Mrs. Pankhurst: Certainly. Purple, white, and green.

Mr. Healy: You were present at the Pavilion meeting?——Yes.

Counsel proceeded to read the speech of Mrs. Pethick Lawrence at the meeting, in which reference was made to the advice of Cabinet Ministers.

The Judge (interrupting): I think the jury know every word of Mr. Hobhouse's speech by heart. (Several jurors: "Hear, hear.")

Mr. Healy replied that the defendants laid great stress on that speech, their contention being that these members of the Government quoted were the real inciters to violence.

The Judge suggested that counsel's speech was the better place for emphasising his point to the jury; but Mr. Healy persisted in reading it at this stage.

The Court had sat almost an hour beyond its usual time, when Mrs. Pankhurst mentioned that she and Mrs. Pethick Lawrence were feeling fatigued after the long sitting.

The Judge intimated that he would rise at 5 o'clock, and Mr. Bodkin filled in the time by calling witnesses to prove the damage resulting from various acts of window-breaking in the early part of March last.

The Court then adjourned until Monday morning.

Monday.

The resumed hearing on Monday opened with the calling of further evidence bearing upon the acts of window-smashing committed by members of the W.S.P.U. in March last. . . .

Detective-Sergeant Seale said he had followed two women from the Gardenia Restaurant on March 4.

Mrs. Pankhurst: After meetings you have followed women to see where they went?——Yes.

Have you had instructions to follow particular women?——Generally.

Some special women?——Yes.

Are you entirely engaged in following women?——Not entirely.

You follow other people?——Yes.

Politicians?——On some occasions.

Do you do ordinary criminal work or political work?——Political work.

Political work only?——Yes.

Have you been one of the gentlemen allotted to go into the country for the protection of Cabinet Ministers?——I don't follow.

When a Cabinet Minister has been going to speak in the provinces, has it been part of your duty to accompany him—to go in the same train?——No.

But you said that is done?——Yes, I know it is done.

Can you give me any idea from what Cabinet Ministers need protection?——No, madam, I could not.

You could not say whether they were to be protected from violence, say, on my part? (Laughter.)——I could not say.

Would it be the duty of the officer to prevent women saying, "When is the Liberal Government going to give women the vote?"——Possibly.

Detective-Sergeant Thomas Hanson, of the Criminal Investigation Department, spoke to attending a meeting under the auspices of the Actresses Franchise League, in the Criterion on December 1.

Mrs. Pankhurst: You were present and heard Miss Christabel Pankhurst speak?——Yes.

Was her speech received with approval by the meeting?——Yes.

This was not a meeting of the Women's Social and Political Union?—— No, the Actresses' Franchise League.

Was it well attended?——Well attended, yes.

Crowded?——Not exactly, there were some seats vacant.

Was it an enthusiastic meeting?——Yes. It was rather enthusiastic, but there were one or two interruptions during Miss Christabel's speech.

That was the occasion when Miss Pankhurst invoked the interrupters to go and sit in the front row?——Yes.

They were men weren't they?——Yes.

Who made very senseless interruptions? (Laughter.) I mean not pertinent interruptions—harassing interruptions, and they referred to the meeting at the City Temple where Mr. Asquith was interrupted. They were Liberals— rather rabid Liberals—partisans?——Yes.

These gentlemen attended the women's meetings to try to do the same thing?——Yes.

Miss Pankhurst restored order by inviting the gentlemen to come and sit in the front row and treated them with great good humour and successfully?——Yes.

You heard the other speeches?——Yes.

On the whole, this was a very unanimous and enthusiastic meeting?—— Yes, after the interruptions ceased.

After the interruptions were so successfully dealt with?——Yes.

And would you agree that if Cabinet Ministers showed such good humour in their meetings as that shown on this occasion, political meetings generally would go all the better? (Laughter.)——That I cannot say.

Have you attended many of the meetings organised by the Women's Social and Political Union?——I have attended five or six.

Have you always found that when there have been interruptions the speakers have been able to deal with them in the same successful way?——Yes.

Mrs. Ball's Evidence.

Lilian Ball, a dressmaker, of Tooting, was the next witness. On being called she showed signs of emotion, and on entering the witness-box, broke down completely, and a few moments elapsed before Mr. Bodkin proceeded to examine her.

She said that she was a member of the Balham branch of the W.S.P.U., and a member of a deputation that went to the House of Commons in October, 1910. In November, 1911, she received a typewritten message inviting her to go to the Woman's Press, in Charing Cross Road. She went into a room upstairs, having given up a card which had been sent to her. In the room were a number of ladies. She heard her name called, and went into a smaller room where there were two or three ladies. A lady asked her if she had a pocket in her skirt, and she said no. "The lady then gave me a bag of stones, which was tied around my waist, under my coat," witness proceeded. "I said it was too heavy, and some of the stones were taken out. We were told to try to get to the back of the House of Commons and break the windows."

Mr. Bodkin: Where did you go when you left the Woman's Press?—— With two other young ladies, similarly equipped, I went to the House of Commons.

How long did you remain there?——From eight till nine.

What did you do there?——Simply walked about.

Did you use any of the stones?——No, sir. I did not.

Did either of the other young ladies?——Not while I was there.

What did you do then?——I went home.

Taking the bag and stones?——Yes.

In March of this year, witness further answered, she went to prison.

Counsel next read the circular sent out to members of the Union prior to the window-breaking demonstration of March 4, in which sympathisers were asked to take part in the fighting policy:

"Militancy alone can bring pressure to bear upon the Cabinet," it said. It was signed "E. Pankhurst," and asked those responding to send in their names. Witness said she sent in her name. She also received a further circular dated February 20, 1912, acknowledging her letter, and telling her to see Mrs. McLeod at Clifford's Inn. Witness said she did not go.

Other documents arrived including a card of admission to the Gardenia Restaurant for the evening of March 4. There was also a piece of paper instructing her what to do when arrested. This she left at the place where she worked as a dressmaker at Clapham Common.

Witness was shown a document which she identified as the "Instructions to Volunteers" circular. It informed volunteers that after arrest they would be bailed out. They were advised to bring with them to the police court the following day such things as they would need during their imprisonment.

Yet another circular she received on March 1, also signed E. Pankhurst, in which the writer said she was taking some preliminary action, and she knew the rest of the volunteers would make a brave fight.

On March 4, witness proceeded, she went to the Gardenia, and on showing her card was admitted. There were many women in it. A lady asked her if she was prepared for a long or a short sentence. I said a short sentence— not more than seven days, because I could not remain longer away from home. I was then told to go to the United Service Museum in Whitehall.

Why was that?——She said there were small panes there and I could not possibly get more than seven days.

Were you given anything?——Yes, a hammer, on which was a motto in writing, "Better broken windows than broken promises." I was advised to put the hammer up my sleeve. I did so, and went off with two other ladies.

Was anything said about time?——We were told to do it before nine o'clock.

What did you do?——I broke a window of the United Service Museum. I was arrested and taken to Cannon Row Police Station. I was afterwards bailed out by Mr. Pethick-Lawrence.

Next morning I went to Bow Street bringing things with me. I was sentenced to two months' hard labour.

And the sentence is now expired?——Yes.

On the occasion when she went to the Women's Press in November, 1911, she, acting on written instructions, did not wear any badge or colours. She had the same instructions on March 4. None of the ladies wore them on these occasions.

Cross-examined by Mr. Pethick Lawrence, witness said she had taken part in a previous demonstration in 1910, and had had her foot injured by the mob who sprang upon the women.

Mr. Pethick Lawrence: Were you wearing a badge on that occasion?—— I was wearing a deputation badge.

Was the setting of the mob on you intentional or accidental?—— Intentional.

Did you hear it said that the reason why the women did not wear their badges was because of the injuries they had received on previous occasions when they did wear their badges?——No; I did not hear that said.

Did you not think that with the experience you had had at the hands of some of the rougher elements of the mob that it was advisable not to wear the distinctive badge of the Union under the circumstances?——Certainly.

You have heard of a man called William Ball?——Yes sir.

Are you any relation of William Ball?——None whatever.

Mrs. Pankhurst put no questions.

Mr. Healy: Are you now in favour of manhood suffrage?—

The Judge: Has that any bearing on the issue, Mr. Healy?

Mr. Healy: How was it that the police selected you to make a statement?——When I was in Holloway I petitioned the Home Secretary, and friends did the same. The police visited my home, and found the papers and stones and that is, I suppose, why they came to me in Holloway. I don't know any other reason why I was singled out.

Who was the officer?——Mr. McCarthy and Mr. Powell.

Who saw you first?——They both saw me together.

With a common instinct they both saw you together?

Mr. Bodkin: Possibly they both came together?——They did.

This closed the case for the prosecution, and Mr. Lawrence then made his opening speech to the jury.

The Real Conspiracy.

Mr. Pethick Lawrence Outlines the Defence.

After the close of the case for the prosecution, Mr. Pethick Lawrence, . . . said he proposed shortly to address the jury at this stage for the purpose of outlining the case for the defence, and later on he would deliver his final address to the jury. He said:—

May it please your lordship, Gentlemen of the jury, You have heard at considerable length the case which the prosecution has made out against myself and against my co-defendants here in the dock on a charge of conspiracy and incitement to break windows. The case that I have to put before you is that neither the conspiracy nor the incitement is ours; but that the conspiracy is a conspiracy of the Cabinet which is responsible for the government of this country; and that the incitement is the incitement of the Ministers of the Crown—of Mr. Asquith, Mr. Lloyd George, and Mr. Hobhouse, and of the other Ministers, including the Attorney-General, who has taken this case against us. And I say that if these honourable gentlemen had shown that they were prepared to listen to reason and to argument, that these events which you have so patiently listened to during these days would never have taken place.

Speaking for myself, I loathe the idea of any such thing as the deliberate breaking of shop windows. It is a thing which to me is essentially ugly and repugnant. But I know that these women who have taken that course have been driven, by the inexorable logic of facts, to do what they did. And I for one am not going to condemn them for their action.

Now, gentlemen, in order to enable you to understand how I propose to conduct my defence, I want to tell you that I intend—not at very great length—to put before you certain facts in this opening speech of mine which will enable you to understand the situation as it has occurred. I shall then call before you a number of witnesses—men and women of honour and distinction—who will give you facts relating to these affairs; and after you have heard those witnesses I shall deal shortly with the facts they have given, and I shall show you that it is not the co-defendants who are here before you, but that it is with others that the real blame lies for this state of things.

Now, gentlemen, I want you to get out of your heads all the facts about the window smashing, all the facts about the career of the Women's Social and Political Union which you have learned from the Press of the country. You must remember that you must take the facts, not as you read them in the newspapers, which are fond, shall we say, of a little embellishment here and a little omission there, in their desire to present a good picture for their readers rather than to be strictly accurate and to give everything in its full perspective and proportion.

Now, gentlemen, you have seen the two women who are here in the dock with me. You have been told in your newspapers that the women in this movement are hysterical and excited, and that they do not know what they are doing. You have seen the two women who are here with me, and I think it must have come to you, perhaps as a surprise, the calmness and deliberateness and the self-possession which those two women have shown. You have not had before you the others concerning whom we are charged with regard to this conspiracy. But you have heard some of the speeches that they made in the dock when they were before the judge at the Newington Sessions. And however much you may disagree with the political sentiments which those women are said to have uttered, I think you will acknowledge that theirs were not the speeches of people hysterical, inflamed, and excited. If you have ever listened to political speeches—and I take it that all of you have—you will know that men very often lose control of themselves in a rhetorical outburst, especially when they are taking part in a revolutionary campaign. But I think you will admit that the speeches which have been read to you, and which the witnesses have admitted were the speeches made by the women on these occasions, do not show any sign of hysterical or excited behaviour or point of view. We had in the box one witness who spoke of a particular woman—I think it was Miss Wylie—who had broken his shop window, and he said that she seemed to be a woman whom he would have thought to be the very last person to take such a course; and the only conclusion he could come to on the first consideration of her action, was that she had gone mad. But he had seen that this was a mistaken judgment. Her action certainly produced a shock on his mind, and he could find no adequate cause to explain the situation. Now what I want to put to you and to convince you of is that you are dealing here with something outside the ordinary affairs of life; you are dealing with something outside your ordinary experience. You are accustomed to deal with the ordinary affairs of men and women—of commerce—the affairs of the shop, with the affairs of the business concerns of the world. Here, we are concerned, in this agitation and in this trial, with something which is beyond and outside the ordinary affairs of life. We are dealing, and you are dealing here with people whose life is devoted to an ideal, and whether you agree with them or whether you disagree with them, you are faced with the fact that they have calmly and thoughtfully and deliberately come to a certain conclusion, that a certain course of action is right—though it may or may not commend itself to you, and may or may not commend itself to other people, but which is calmly and deliberately thought out, and which is the result of a solemn and grave determination at which they have arrived.

Who are the Defendants?

Now I want to say to you a few words about the lives of the defendants who are here in this dock.

Mrs. Pankhurst is the widow of Dr. Pankhurst, a great lawyer, who was a comrade of John Stuart Mill, and who worked with him for many years in the early days of the fight for the emancipation of women. Mrs. Pankhurst has been the mother of four children—one son and three daughters—and when she had brought them up and given them their education, she took part in public work in Manchester, where she was for some years a Guardian of the Poor.

My wife, Mrs. Pethick Lawrence, before she came into this movement, had spent many years of her life in work among women and girls of the poorer class. She worked in connection with the West London Mission, and there some of the most arduous, some of the most serious, and some of the most painful work which it is possible for a human being to have to do, fell to her lot. It was part of her work to look after those members of her sex who through misfortune or other terrible calamity had sunk into a position in which they were outcasts from society. Many of those women, with whom she came into contact, she was able to bring up from those depths into which they had fallen and to make them responsible citizens, and to give them a life that was worth living in after years. She was also instrumental in starting a large club for working girls, and she and her friend, Miss Mary Neal, started the Esperance Club—a club which some of you may have heard of, that has been the means of restoring to the people of this country the old folk songs and games which seemed to be leaving Merrie England. The members of that club, of which she and Miss Neal have been the leaders, have been all over the countryside, all through the towns, bringing back to the people the life and gaiety of the old days.

Now as to myself, as the Attorney-General has already told you, I am a member of the Bar, and he has told you that I, therefore, ought to be especially opposed to anything in the nature of illegal action. I will go further than that and say that I am by very nature and temperament a believer in law and order, that I dislike anything which is disorderly, and that I am deeply sensible of the necessity, in a great community, of the preservation of law and order, in all the ordinary conduct of life. I do not propose to say to you very much about my previous life, but I should like to say that after my work as a student at Eton and at Cambridge, I set myself to the investigation of the wages of men and women in different parts of the country, and the comparison of these wages, and it was upon that investigation that I obtained my Fellowship at Trinity College. After I left the University, I spent three years in a University Settlement at Canning Town, and it was there that I learned of the tragedy that comes to many people in this country owing to their poverty and to their inability, under the present condition of life, to free themselves from that tragedy. After that I had a controlling interest in—I was practically the proprietor of—one of the London evening newspapers, and when that paper came to an end—I say this to you with some diffidence, because I hate speaking about myself—I did not consider that my obligations were limited by the ordinary legal obligations of creditors of that paper; and the staff of that paper received from me personally a considerable sum in consideration of the debts which I felt were morally due to them, even though my legal obligations did not go so far. I say that to you because I want to explain to you my own view of the duties and responsibilities of a citizen go far beyond the mere legal obligations that the law lays down. And I want to remind you that there have been men like John Hampden, who, finding a political situation arise which seemed to them to transcend all the ordinary dealing of life, were prepared first of all to come into conflict with the law through tax resistance, and then to go further than that, as you will remember John Hampden did; and failing to establish his point in a court of law, there was nothing left for him but to take up arms. And so he won for the people of this country—it was largely through his sacrifice—the liberties which we possess at the present day.

Forty Years of Patience.

Now the Attorney-General, in opening this case, said that we could not altogether keep politics out of our discussion. That has proved to be so, because in a great many of the speeches that have been read to you, a great deal of political matter has inevitably been introduced. Therefore, although it is my desire to deal as briefly as possible with the political circumstances which have led up to the events with regard to which this trial is being conducted, I feel that I cannot pass over altogether in silence the state of affairs which the Attorney-General has put before you. I feel that it is necessary to represent correctly the facts of the case and the situation which has arisen. The Attorney-General was not entirely correct in his statement. He said he thought the Women's Social and Political Union was founded in the year 1907 or thereabouts. As a matter of fact, the Women's Social and Political Union was founded in 1903. That, of course, was many years after the struggle for the emancipation of women had begun. Dr. Pankhurst, husband, as I have told you, of Mrs. Pankhurst, and John Stuart Mill and Mrs. Wolstenholme Elmy, who is at the present time a member of the Committee of the Women's Social and Political Union—were engaged for a number of years—for forty years prior to that date, in working along the ordinary lines for Women's Suffrage. Great meetings were held, monster petitions were sent to Parliament, and the large majority of the Members of Parliament were pledged to support Women's Suffrage.

Now I want you to notice that that all failed to achieve its object because politicians behaved treacherously. The story of more recent events bears out this fact. We are plain men and women who expect honest dealing in every day life, and for the most part we get it, but when we come to politicians and members of Parliament, and when it comes to questions of politics, we find they fail. We find the way they treat political questions is by methods of trickery and chicanery. And it is because these ordinary methods of business life are not successful when it comes into the realm of politics, that we have this situation. There was a large majority in the House of Commons to carry Women's Suffrage in the days when Mr. Gladstone was Prime Minister, yet he broke his word, and induced his followers to go back on their pledges, and to be false to the promises which they had made. Following upon that, whenever the question of Women's Suffrage was mentioned in the House of Commons it was greeted by cries of "humbug," and by ribald jests by members of Parliament.

Trickery and Humbug.

Now I have told you that the Women's Social and Political Union was founded in 1903, and for two years following that date the ordinary methods of constitutional agitation were pursued. Mrs. Pankhurst and her daughter, Miss Christabel Pankhurst, who is mentioned together with us in this indictment, but who has not joined us here in the dock—these two women for two years devoted themselves to all the ordinary methods of propaganda. But they found they were not making progress, because they were up against this. They were marching on the swampy ground of trickery and humbug. And so it was that, towards the close of 1905, Miss Christabel Pankhurst and Miss Annie Kenney went to a meeting of one of the great Liberal leaders—Sir Edward Grey—at a time when the Liberal Government—this Liberal Government which is now in office—was just on the verge of coming into power. These two women went to that meeting with the intention of finding out the true facts. They knew that Liberal statesmen had been in the habit of making promises and indulging in wide generalities, and they knew that nothing had ever come of them. At the close of Sir Edward Grey's meeting they rose to put a simple question—what was the Liberal Government going to do with regard to the demand of women to be enfranchised? They put it at the proper time, at the close of the meeting, and in the proper way. But instead of receiving an answer to that question, these two women were flung out of the hall. They were thrown out with great violence, and held a demonstration in the street, and they were arrested and sent to prison. That was how what is called militancy began, and I dwell upon that for two reasons. First of all, I want to show you that it was due to the trickery and humbug of the Government that anything more than ordinary methods were adopted. I also want to draw attention to it for this reason. You have frequently heard the word militancy used. You may have thought, unless I had given you this story, that militancy meant some violent outbreak or stonethrowing. This has not always been the sort of method adopted. Militancy simply means that you take some step that is disagreeable to somebody else, and, incidentally, it will be proved in this case that it was exceedingly disagreeable to the people taking part in it themselves. During the whole course of this six or seven years, since that historic meeting in October, 1905, one of the methods of militancy has been that to which you have had frequent allusion made in the course of this trial. There have been meetings at which the speeches of Cabinet Ministers have been interrupted by interjections on the part of women. Part of the evidence you have had before you was brought, I think, in order to show the nature of the work of this Women's Social and Political Union, and reference was made to one occasion when Mr. Asquith was very largely interrupted and was unable to obtain a hearing owing to the words which were spoken at his meeting by women who came to know why he took up his present attitude on Votes for Women. Now that has been, during all these six years, one of the methods of what is called militancy. They are methods which men politicians have used for a very long time. You have had Liberals going down, and deliberately going down, in order to interrupt Conservative meetings. There is no doubt whatever about that. You have had Liberal newspapers—we have not in this country what is exactly an official Press, but we have what is tantamount to an official Press—you have had these papers glorying in what they call "the voice," which constantly interrupted and interfered with the progress of the speeches of their opponents. But when women, at infinite cost to themselves, have been present, and have suffered in many cases severe injury—a man on one occasion had his leg broken, and many other severe injuries have resulted—when women have been there, you have had a man like Mr. Lloyd George taunting these women and making a statement, which he knew to be absolutely false, that that "was a very nice way of earning a living, wasn't it?" to come there and interrupt him when he wanted to make a great speech. Now I say that that has been a very serious incitement. Supposing, gentlemen, that you had felt that you had some great public duty to perform, and, at great personal sacrifice, you had attended—supposing you had gone to the *Titanic* inquiry, where you had some important evidence to give, and supposing you had gone there at considerable personal inconvenience. If, as the result of the evidence you had given, you had been mauled about, had your clothes torn, had bruises inflicted upon you, and then, on the top of that some gentleman said to you that that was a very nice way of earning your living, wasn't it, would you not be incited by such an outrageous statement of that kind? Would it not make your blood run hot, and would it not make you angry, and would not that affect you in your feelings upon the question? I put it to you, gentlemen, that when Mr. Lloyd George after he had had the facts before him—for the facts have been sent to him, he has been shown the balance-sheet, he has been given categorical information that such statements are absolutely false—for him to make that statement to the women is an incitement which you must realise is very serious. As you know, he made it again the other night. He is a man who is in receipt of money for his professional services. I don't say there is anything wrong in that—I do not think there is; but I think that for a man who is in receipt of a large sum for his professional and political services to taunt women, who do not receive money, with their being hired for certain work when they are doing it voluntarily, and without any form of payment whatever, in order to take a course which, however unpleasant to themselves, they feel to be their duty, I say that is an incitement of a very serious kind. I want to return to that first act of militancy at Sir Edward Grey's meeting to which I have just referred. My wife and I heard shortly after that of this new society which was formed, and we determined to see who were the people responsible for it and what was the nature of the work they were doing. When we had come into contact with them we realised that they were right, that, though their methods were different from the methods which we had been accustomed to, they were the only ones that were likely to succeed where others had failed, and we determined to throw in our lot with them.

Now, gentlemen, that was a very serious step, and when I come to my speech at the close of the evidence I propose to say to you a few words as to why that very grave and very serious step was taken by us. I want to pass on. I am confining myself to the facts of the situation, and I want to tell you this: this Women's Social and Political Union of which you have heard so much, and of the militant side of whose policy you have heard so much, has carried on a political and educational side far greater than any political agitation that has been carried on, at any rate, in recent years, and I don't think that I am overstating it when I say that it has a larger political and educational side than that of any political movement in the history of this country. We had a witness in the box—Inspector Powell—who admitted that in the course of his thirty years' experience he had never known an agitation carried on so long and so widely as that of the Women's Social and Political Union. I might tell you that in the course of the six years of its existence it has held over a hundred meetings a week—you have it in evidence before you that it has held a hundred to three hundred meetings every week in different parts of the country—so that in the whole six years it has held something like 100,000 different meetings in different parts of the country. These meetings have been held in the largest halls in London, Manchester, Leeds, Liverpool, Glasgow, Bristol, and in parts of Scotland and Wales. The great Albert Hall—I think the largest hall in the country— has been filled thirteen times with women taking part in this constitutional agitation: the Queen's Hall hundreds of times, and at the London Pavilion and other places a great number of meetings have been held. In the course of the year 1911 a letter was sent to the Prime Minister, in which he was shown that during that particular year this organization alone had held more meetings—several times more meetings—than all the other political societies throughout the country, and had done several times the amount of political work. When the question came up in the House of Commons in the year 1908 or 1909, I forget which, Mr. Gladstone, now Lord Gladstone, said that it was not sufficient for women to hold meetings indoors: they ought to show by meetings held out of doors, that they could agitate in the same way as men. Largely in consequence of that statement it was arranged to hold a great demonstration in Hyde Park. I do not propose to tell you at great length about that. I propose to read to you what the *Times* said, and the *Times* has not, as you know, any great bias in favour of Woman Suffrage. The *Times* correspondent wrote:

> The organisers of the demonstration had counted on the attendance of 250,000. That expectation was certainly fulfilled. Probably it was doubled and it would be difficult to contradict anyone who asserted confidently that it was trebled. Like

the distance and numbers of the stars the facts were beyond the threshold of perception.

That was one great outdoor demonstration held by this Union to show the demand of women for the vote. What was the result of a great demonstration of that kind? After it had been held the leaders of the movement wrote to Mr. Asquith, the Prime Minister, and asked him if they had shown the great demand there was for the vote, and asked him to receive them in deputation in order to lay certain facts before him. Mr. Asquith, in his reply, not only opposed Women's Suffrage, but treated the request with contumely; he refused, absolutely and totally, to receive any deputation representing this society. And that is the kind of method—absolute contumely when it has not been trickery and chicanery—with which the constitutional and the normal and proper demand of the women has been met. The women who were engaged in that conflict were forced to compare his attitude to them to his attitude to the request which came from the men in Woolwich. The men, who were anxious about the question of Government labour at Woolwich, said they wanted Mr. Asquith to receive a deputation on a certain night. Mr. Asquith said he had another engagement—he was going out to dinner— and that he could not receive them. The men said they were coming whether he could receive them or not, and they were going to wait until he did receive them. His answer to them was that he had changed his mind, and that he would make it convenient to see them after all. When he was dealing with the women, in spite of the fact that they came as representatives of this enormous and unparalleled demonstration, he treated them with contumely. When they came out in order to see him they were arrested for obstruction and sent to prison for considerable terms. That, for many years, was one of the number of militant methods—as they were called—of the Union. The three principal methods were: an anti-Government policy at by-elections— of that I do not propose to speak to you as it does not affect this case; going to meetings of Cabinet Ministers in order to place their views before the Ministers; and these deputations, or as they were euphoniously called by the newspapers, "raids."

I want to emphasise to you that these militant methods meant nothing illegal. There was nothing illegal whatever about this policy at by-elections, and there was nothing illegal in going to meetings to put questions, or even to interject remarks to Cabinet Ministers. Yet these were always called "raids," and they came in for quite as much censure and hostility as those other methods which brought women into contact with the law. I want to show you now how women who took part in this stone-throwing in November and in March last were incited to do so not only by the speeches of Cabinet Ministers, but by the contumely, by the trickery, and by the falsity of politicians, and the falsity of leading members of the Liberal Government in dealing with their case. The demand the women had always made was that the Government, which nowadays, and under our present methods of the conduct of Parliament, is responsible for legislation—should bring in a Bill to give women the vote.

The Conciliation Bill.

They had demanded that that Bill should remove the sex barrier. They had demanded, where a woman was qualified on precisely the same lines as a man, that just because she was a woman she should not be shut out from having a vote, and they asked the Government to bring in a Bill for that purpose. It was only when the Government had failed to do so for all these years, and had failed to make any promise that they would do so, that these militant methods were adopted. In the year 1910 it was represented that the Government could not very well give way to this militant claim, even though it was backed up by these enormous peaceful demonstrations, and it was suggested that if some means could be found of saving the face of the Government probably some Bill for Women's Suffrage could be got through. I do not want to make any false impression. I cannot suggest to you that that was said by prominent members of the Liberal Government, but I do say that it was said by the women who were conducting this fight. It was suggested that if some Bill could be devised which could be introduced by a private member the Government would probably see their way to allow that Bill to become law. That was the origin of what was known as the Conciliation Bill. It was a Bill to conciliate the different sections in the House of Commons upon which Liberals and Labour men, Irish and Conservative, could all agree, and it was a Bill framed so as to give the vote to women householders, that is to say, the women who paid the rates and taxes, and it would enfranchise about a million women throughout the country. That Bill was brought into the House of Commons, and the Women's Social and Political Union, although it did not entirely agree with the terms of the Bill, said, "If this is going to conciliate the different sections, we are not going to raise any objection to the progress of that measure; but we will take that as an instalment, at any rate, towards our precise requirements, from which it does not differ very widely, and we will give our support to that." In 1910 there was little business before the House of Commons, because of the number of events taking place which cut up a great deal of the work the House of Commons had planned to do. But in spite of that fact, Mr. Lloyd George threw his whole influence against the passage of that Bill, and, although he did not succeed in preventing its being carried through one of its stages, called the Second Reading, he did bring it about that the Government refused any time for the passage of this Bill into law.

Towards the end of that Parliament, at the end of the year 1910, the women wanted to know how they stood.

"Black Friday."

Mr. Asquith made a statement in the House of Commons dealing with a great number of other subjects, but he made no reference at all to this question of Women's Suffrage, and as the result of that, the women said, "We must have another deputation; we must find out where we stand. We must go to Mr. Asquith," and they went. Some of the most distinguished women in the country went on that deputation. Mrs. Garrett Anderson, who had been chosen Mayor of her native city—one of the first women Mayors in this country—Mrs. Hertha Ayrton, one of the leading scientists in the world, went to interview the Prime Minister to find out what really were his intentions. Had a deputation of men, half as influential as this deputation of women, gone to see the Prime Minister on what to them was a vital and important question, that deputation would undoubtedly have been received. Instead of that, on this occasion the Prime Minister refused to see the deputation, and owing to his action, and owing to the action of the Home Secretary, that deputation was met by a great body of police.

Now, they had decided that if he would not see them, they would not go quietly away, because that would have been to admit failure, and that, whenever a Prime Minister chose, he could treat them with contempt. So they resolved to stand their ground; it was not stone-throwing or damaging property. The women thought they had a right to see the Prime Minister. What was the result? Several hundred of the women—I lay very great stress upon this—came into conflict with the police and crowd for the space of several hours. They were not only jostled and hustled and knocked about, as you may say is natural when women meet a crowd, but many of them were very seriously injured. They were subjected to indignities and insults which, in the opinion of several hundred of them, could not have been merely accidental; but were deliberately given. That was what was called "Black Friday." The women came out; I think that you had it actually in evidence that they had special instructions to leave umbrellas behind, lest, perchance, they might take any step which afterwards they might regret. They came out in a perfectly peaceful manner, absolutely unarmed, without stones or hammers, and as a result hundreds of these women were injured, and one woman died as the consequence of the injuries she received. Other women were for months laid up, some for twelve months as a consequence of what took place on that day. I say emphatically that that was one of the reasons why, when it came to the necessity of making some protest later, the women were determined that they would not subject themselves again to treatment of that kind, and that though they might be breaking the law, in doing damage to private property, they were not prepared to face again what they had passed through on that awful day in 1910. Now, I want to return to the political story I was just telling you. The Conciliation Bill was reintroduced in the following year, and there was not only in London, but throughout the whole of the country, great evidence of the support which that Bill had. Every Women's Suffrage society supported it, and nearly every great County Council—I think this is very important—in all parts of the provinces sent a resolution up to the Cabinet pressing them to carry this Bill. Cities like Manchester, Liverpool, Bristol, Leeds, Glasgow, Edinburgh, and many others—the County Councils in these cities sent up asking the Government to allow this Bill to be carried into law. The women organised what I believe to be the greatest political peaceful demonstration that this country has ever seen. The demonstration marched from the Embankment to the Albert Hall. The Albert Hall was taken by the Women's Social and Political Union, and on that occasion every single seat and every portion of standing room was filled, and an overflow meeting was held in another hall.

This was organised by this organisation alone. Other Suffrage organisations took other halls and filled them to overflowing. You heard witnesses for the prosecution admit that that procession took over an hour and a half to pass a given point. I think they would have been more accurate if they had said, as some of our witnesses will tell you, that it took a period of something like three hours to pass. The demonstration was such as had never been seen in this country before, and what was the result? The Prime Minister gave a certain promise. I am not going to give you details, but I am going to give it to you broadly. He said that they had no time to deal with the question in 1911, but that full facilities would be given in 1912, and that that promise would be kept in the spirit as well as in the letter. Now, I am going to give you details, but I am going to tell you how politicians regard the spirit of a promise. Before I tell you that, I want to say that the women accepted that pledge as a bona-fide pledge. They thought that these men who made them that promise would keep the promise. They stopped what were known as militant methods; the Women's Social and Political Union stopped that. They ceased their anti-Government policy at elections; they did not go to Cabinet Minister's meetings to create difficulties; they did not go up in deputation to the House of Commons.

That went on right away until November last year. Now we come to the facts that are brought before you in the course of these proceedings. Just before that demonstration took place in November to which your attention has so often been directed Mr. Asquith made a certain statement. He made it, as is well known, with the connivance, and to some extent at the instigation, of Mr. Lloyd George. The statement was that a Reform Bill would be introduced in the House of Commons. It was known as a Bill to give Manhood Suffrage; and he said that so far as women were concerned, the case might be met by an amendment including women in the Bill. Mr. Lloyd George said that that was a splendid opportunity for women, and that they ought to be satisfied with it.

The Ruin of the Bill.

Now, it is necessary for me to put to the Court very shortly why that proposal was not acceptable to the women. The women had been told on more than one occasion that they could only win the vote by combining their friends in the different parties in the House of Commons. There were some Liberals who were in favour of Women's Suffrage and some Liberals who were against it. There were some Conservatives in favour of it and some against it. The Liberal supporters of Women's Suffrage are not enough to make a majority alone. But the Liberal supporters and the Conservative supporters together are enough to form a majority in the House of Commons, with the inclusion of Labour members, who are all in favour of it, and those Irish members who are in favour of it. So, you see, the Conciliation Bill was a Bill to gather the support from all parties. But this Manhood Suffrage Bill was a Bill which was entirely opposed to the whole convictions of Conservatives, who do not want a Manhood Suffrage Bill, and therefore an amendment to such a Bill as that, which would give votes to a large number of women as well as to a large number of men, would only get support from that portion of the House which is both Liberal and in favour of Women's Suffrage. Therefore, the amendment in favour of including women would undoubtedly have been defeated. You see that this so-called opportunity of getting Women's Suffrage in the form of an amendment to the Manhood Suffrage Bill was entirely illusory, because it broke up the compromise—it broke up the principal means by which it was going to be carried by getting some support from one party and some from another, and between them making a majority sufficient to carry it. The proposal was sure of the support only of a section of the Liberal party, and was, therefore, absolutely certain of defeat. Not only was it without hope of success, but the apparent advantage of having two strings to the Women's Suffrage movement was equally illusory. It was really a case of having two birds in the bush instead of one in the hand. That the Conciliation Bill was ruined by this proposal can be demonstrably proved. The minds of politicians would be so fixed upon this large scheme of getting Manhood Suffrage that it would be impossible to carry a preliminary little Bill like the Conciliation Bill. That is the view which was taken by the *Times* newspaper, which, commenting on the situation, said:

Women's Suffrage is not a party question. It cuts across the regular party lines. But the Government propose to bring in a Reform Bill which will be an out and out party measure. If they include Women's Suffrage in that Bill it might command the whole force at the back of the Government; but they are not going to do that. They are going to let it be included as an amendment if the House chooses to have it. In order to secure its adoption as a non-party principle the amendment would require to be supported by the Opposition, which would be expecting them to treat a party measure as a non-party one. It would fall between two stools: the Conservative supporters would be alienated, and no pressure would be put upon the Ministerial side to make up for them. If, on the other hand, the matter is left, as the National Union suggested as an alternative, to be dealt with in the form of the Conciliation Bill, it will not have the smallest chance of consideration. The way will be blocked by the Reform Bill.

So that you see, in the opinion of the *Times,* the Government, which had given a promise that it said it would keep in the spirit as well as in the letter, was deliberately breaking that promise and substituting something which was purely illusory. But our view of this question does not rest absolutely upon our own words. No less a person that Mr. Lloyd George himself openly said a few days afterwards that this new measure had "torpedoed" the Conciliation Bill. When you think that these women had, for the space of four or five months, proved their absolute faith in what they thought was the integrity of the Government—they had abandoned their political attack upon the Government because they had a pledge upon which they thought they could rely—for Mr. Lloyd George and Mr. Asquith frankly to torpedo the whole base upon which the women were relying, was, I think you must admit, incitement of a very serious kind. It was not merely an incitement, it was a conspiracy to upset the understanding which had existed, and it was a conspiracy in which the leading members of the Government had taken part. In consequence of that action, the women members of the Women's Social and Political Union thought that a further protest was necessary. They determined that it was necessary to make their position perfectly clear, that could only be done by a great demonstration of hostility to the Government. You have seen what happened when they went out on a demonstration of the previous kind in the previous November. I have told you how they found themselves knocked about, injured, and insulted. Some of them said that this time "we will not do the same thing." My wife, who was one of the members of that demonstration, took part in the demonstration merely. She was arrested, coming into conflict with the police. A certain number of women who went out on that day said, "We will not be buffeted about and insulted again. Rather than that, we will break windows and be arrested and go to prison for doing so." So some of the women who went on that occasion took stones and hammers with them, and broke windows. Following upon that, there was considerable discussion as to the political situation with regard to Women's Suffrage. A suggestion was put forward in one of the leading Liberal papers—one of the quasi-official papers—and the suggestion had such prominence in the paper, that no one who knows politics could doubt that it was in fact a proposal of one of the members of the Government. The suggestion was that this question of Women's Suffrage should be dealt with by means of a referendum. The question of a referendum is, however, a large one, and I will not trouble you with that at any length except to say that, whether a referendum on a question of politics be good or bad, at least what is good on one set of questions is good on another set; what is sauce for the goose is sauce for the gander. If a referendum is to be adopted on Women's Suffrage, it ought to be adopted on Home Rule and Welsh Disestablishment. When Mr. Lloyd George went to the Albert Hall and made a great speech upon Women's Suffrage, members of the Women's Social and Political Union went there to ask him what was the attitude of the Government to this great question. Mr. Lloyd George's answer to that was that he personally "took a certain line, and that he was not speaking on behalf of the Government at all; women must find that out from Mr. Asquith." In regard to how the amendment was to be carried to the Manhood Suffrage Bill, he returned an absolutely evasive answer. What I have told you just now was proved by a process of political arithmetic, but he did not attempt to quote any figures or show any facts to refute that line of argument. He told the women that Mr. Asquith could give them an answer, so they went to Mr. Asquith to ask him to see them, as this new question had arisen. He treated them with the same contempt, with the same contumely, with which he has always treated the members of this Union. He refused to see the lady who had written. He refused to discuss the matter, and refused to see any new situation which demanded his attention. While he was taking that course, another Cabinet Minister, Mr. Hobhouse, was making that speech which you have heard, and to which such insistent reference has been made. I do not want to go through his speech again, but I want to put it to you that when you realise that the women have carried out consistently an agitation of the kind I have described, doesn't it strike you as rather extraordinary that a Cabinet Minister should dare to get up and to say that there is nothing in all these demonstrations, nothing in all this agitation and political organisation; that the only thing which really counted in winning the vote for men was when men went to Nottingham Castle and burned it to the ground. Doesn't it strike you as an extraordinary statement for a Cabinet Minister to make? "There has been no such sentimental uprising as accounted for Nottingham Castle! Women have not done what men did; they have not burnt a castle to the ground, and I see no reason for giving them the vote." Do you not think that in view of that extraordinary statement the events which took place, from the point of view of women who took part in them, showed considerable self-restraint? They had been taunted by a Cabinet Minister that they had not burnt a castle to the ground. They went out and broke windows, and did no damage that was likely to hurt anyone. Now, that is all I propose to say at this stage, and I will call witnesses who will give important evidence. Among the witnesses I propose to call are many men and women who are well known to you. They include Father Adderley, who is a leading clergyman in Birmingham, Sir Edward Busk, the Rev. Dr. Cobb, of St. Ethelburga's, Mrs. Morgan Dockrell, President of the Women Teachers' Union, Lady Lamb, Miss Eva Moore, Sir John Rolleston, M.P., Mr. D. A. Thomas, the well-known Welsh colliery owner, and a number of other men and women. [This closed Mr. Pethick-Lawrence's opening address.]

"A Discreditable Proceeding."

After the luncheon interval Inspector Powell was recalled, and was questioned by Mrs. Pankhurst.

In the course of your inquiries in preparing this case, I believe you questioned the manager of the Inns of Court Hotel, did you not?——I did.

You finally decided not to call this gentleman?——It was not for me to decide.

Would you tell me if it is true that you asked that gentleman questions which appear to me to relate entirely to my private affairs, and which had no connection with this case?——I don't think so, madam.

You asked him, I understand, who paid my accounts at the hotel?——I might have done.

Will you tell the Court why you asked that question?——To know whether the Union was paying the account or yourself, because there are other accounts there besides yours. I wanted to distinguish the accounts. Other leagues meet there, such as the Men's Political Union, and so on.

If you tell me that there are other suffrage societies meeting there, in addition to my living there as a private resident, that is news to me. I have no knowledge of them.——It is so, madam.

In order to make it quite clear that I have no connection with other meetings was it necessary to ask whether I paid my accounts by cheque or otherwise, and whether I had any accounts personally or someone else had them for me?——I wanted to know by whom the cheques were drawn. I don't think I asked any impertinent questions. I should not like to think I had. Witness added that he wanted to know whether Mrs. Pankhurst had discontinued her tenancy. She did not do so herself.

Mrs. Pankhurst: For a very good reason, because I was in Holloway.

Witness: I wanted to know whether it was a member of your own family or a member of the Union who did it.

Mrs. Pankhurst: I want to know the motive, because there may have been some reason for asking those questions. I want to know whether they could have any connection with the statement made by the Chancellor of the Exchequer in Wales on Saturday?——I don't know. I was not there.

Mrs. Pankhurst: My Lord, it seems to me it is entirely exceeding the reason and the cause of this prosecution that the private life of the defendants in this dock should be inquired into in this inquisitive way.

The Judge: He had to establish any fact that connected you with the Women's Social and Political Union.

Mrs. Pankhurst: Do you think this was material? I am anxious to be satisfied whether my private life and the way in which my personal accounts are paid is material to this prosecution.

The Judge: It might be.

Inspector Powell: I thought it was.

Mrs. Pankhurst: And the reason you did not call this gentleman was because you could not implicate me in anything dishonourable.

Witness: It does not rest with me at all.

Mrs. Pankhurst: May I ask who sent you to make inquiries?——I went on my own initiative.

Mrs. Pankhurst: I think it was a very discreditable proceeding!

Evidence for the defence was then called.

Miss Eva Moore.

Miss Eva Moore, the well-known actress, was then called. She said she was vice-president of the Actresses' Franchise League, and had been acquainted with the work of the Women's Social and Political Union for several years. She was present at the meeting in the Royal Albert Hall on November 16 of last year, and heard speeches by Mrs. Pethick Lawrence and Miss Christabel Pankhurst on that occasion. It did not seem to her that there was anything in the speeches inciting to violence.

What was the general trend of the speeches?——That work was demanded of us to further our cause. It was a very large meeting.

Was the meeting friendly or the reverse?——Absolutely enthusiastic.

The Attorney-General: You understood that what was advocated was that the militant campaign must go forward more than ever?——No.

Did you not hear this: "If we don't get what we want to-morrow the militant campaign goes forward with more vigour than ever"?——I cannot say that I heard those words.

The Attorney-General quoted from Mrs. Lawrence's speech, and asked the witness what she suggested the words he had quoted meant.

"I don't suggest anything," replied the witness amidst laughter.

Did you attend any of the meetings at which people were asked to come forward in the campaign of window breaking?——I cannot remember any special one.

You have not taken part in the window breaking?——No.

Mrs. Pankhurst: You have heard of the Church militant?——Yes.

I put it to you whether in your mind militancy does not mean being very determined to work in every possible way for something you think right?——Yes.

Sir Edward Busk, M.A., LL.B.

Sir Edward Busk, of Sussex Place, Regent's Park, said he was present on February 16 at a dinner given to the women who had recently been released from prison, and heard the speeches of Mrs. Pankhurst and of the released prisoners. So far as he recollected, Mrs. Pankhurst's was a very enthusiastic speech, and was received with very great enthusiasm. He gathered that the women who had been in prison adopted the course they had by their own deliberate intention. They did not seem weakminded people likely to be influenced by others.

Mrs. Pankhurst: You heard the speech made, and you have heard me make other speeches. Do you agree that that was perhaps the most violent speech I have ever made?——Yes.

Mrs. Pankhurst read her speech, which, under the heading of "The Argument of the Broken Pane," appeared [earlier in this volume.]

Replying to the Attorney-General, Sir Edward Busk said he realised Mrs. Pankhurst's speech was a very serious one to make.

It was a speech to induce persons to volunteer to come forward and throw more stones?——That will be for the jury to decide.

I am asking you what your view is.

The Judge: You have been asked for your opinion one side, and now you are asked for it on the other.

The Attorney-General (to witness): Will you please answer my question. I am putting it to you that this speech which you heard was violent in parts. Did not that convey to you that the object of it was that other persons should copy at the earliest opportunity the excellent example of those who had been sent to prison for throwing stones?——I think that was one of the objects.

We have heard the speech read. It would no doubt have a very considerable effect upon the ladies who were present, would it not?——It might have.

Further questioned by the Attorney-General, witness thought that the window-breaking campaign was a very small part of the movement.

The Attorney-General: I suggest it is a most important part to the persons whose windows were broken?——Oh, yes.

Did not it strike you that that was a very dangerous speech to make?——I should not have made it myself.

No. Because you would recognise that there was a number of persons there who would no doubt be influenced by Mrs. Pankhurst, and would follow her in whatever she advocated?——Yes.

Witness added that he should be very glad to be able to make such an eloquent and powerful speech as the rest (the part which was not violent) was.

The Attorney-General said he was not attempting to belittle the speech in any way. Quite the contrary. He suggested it was a very dangerous speech. It was a very dangerous form of speech, was it not?——It was.

The Attorney-General: For the reason that it endangered the public peace?——I have heard Cabinet Ministers advise stronger measures. (Laughter.)

Mr. Healy: Possibly the Attorney-General? (Renewed laughter.)

Witness: Yes, possibly the Attorney-General.

The Attorney-General: If you want a good form of them, I suggest you may take Mr. Healy's. (More laughter.)

Further questioned, the witness said he refused to judge the action of the women who broke windows.

The Attorney-General: I am not asking you to judge them. I am asking you what your general view is. Do you suggest that if you can't get what you want by constitutional means you are entitled to throw stones?——My knowledge is that all reforms have been got that way.

If I want something which I cannot get, do you think I should go to Sussex Place and break the windows?——That is not the question.

The Attorney-General: It is because they are your windows. (Laughter.)

Dr. Jessie Murray.

Dr. Jessie Murray was next called.

Mr. Pethick Lawrence read to her a list of the names of prisoners who had been convicted of window-breaking, but an objection was raised. Mr. Pethick Lawrence said he understood the prosecution regarded the actions and words of these ladies as part of the conspiracy . . .

The Judge remarked that no evidence had been given on the part of the Crown as to the statements of any of these women whose names Mr. Pethick Lawrence had introduced . . . If that lady swore on her oath that nothing you had said or done, or that any of you had said or done, had induced her in any way to commit the act that she did commit on November 21, it would be relevant. At least, unless I hear any material argument to the contrary . . .

Mr. Pethick Lawrence said that in view of his lordship's ruling he would not waste the time of the Court by calling the other ladies and gentlemen who had come prepared to give evidence. In these circumstances this closed his case.

The Judge: Are you, Mrs. Pankhurst, calling any witnesses?

Mrs. Pankhurst: I am not able to call the only witnesses I should desire to call. They are the Right Hon. Mr. Hobhouse and the last two Home Secretaries and the present Home Secretary. I am not able to call them.

Mrs. Pankhurst asked and received the permission of the court to deliver her address to the jury on Tuesday morning.

Mr. Pethick Lawrence's Defence
Tuesday

Speech to the Jury at the Old Bailey, May 21, 1912.

Addressing the jury for his defence, Mr. Pethick Lawrence said:

It will be your duty at the close of the hearing of this case to give your verdict upon what you have heard. I ask you to show by that verdict that you understand that this is a political fight, I ask you to show, by your verdict, your appreciation of the political position in which we are placed. Now, gentlemen, the prosecution in their evidence with regard to my relationship to this trial, have put forward several grounds in order to implicate me. They have shown my connection with this organisation of the Women's Social and Political Union. They have shown that I had an office in the offices of the Union; they have shown that I have spoken at meetings; and they have shown that I have taken part in the work of the Union. So far as that is concerned I cannot see that that makes me guilty, or that you will think that it makes me guilty, in any way in this case. I have shown to you that the prosecution—the Attorney-General—has admitted that this Women's Social and Political Union has carried on a great constitutional work—work of meetings and work of political propaganda, requiring great funds and requiring in connection with it the support of a great newspaper. All that is perfectly honourable, and I think they have failed to show in any way anything dishonourable or underhand connected with this organisation. In the second place, they have brought, as part of their case against me, that I went in November and again in March to bail the women who were arrested for the part they had played. It seems to me that this is the first time it has ever been claimed that anyone who goes to bail those who have been arrested is in any way implicated by that action. They would say, no doubt, that I knew beforehand that the women were likely to be arrested. I admit that, but I put it to you that not only I knew beforehand, but the police knew beforehand that the women were going to make a protest which would probably lead to arrest and imprisonment. The police knew it beforehand, and they put it to me that if anyone were arrested on that day, would I come to bail them out? It seems to me that there is nothing dishonourable about offering to perform that function, and there is nothing which implicates me in the facts which are under your notice. Then, in the third place, they have put in against me a number of speeches which I have made. Before I deal with those speeches, I want to say a word about the method in which these speeches have been reported by some of the witnesses for the prosecution.

The Police Reporters.

It is a very difficult thing to report speeches accurately. It is a very important thing, when you are dealing with the actual words which people have spoken, to get the precise words, and not some different form of words. I put it to you that the great majority of the witnesses for the prosecution have failed to give in evidence that they did report the actual words used. Many of them came to the meeting and did not take down shorthand notes, but afterwards put down what they believed or remembered. I need not go into that at any great length, because his lordship has ruled that these particular statements put down from memory were not relevant evidence in the case. But I do think it necessary to say a word to you about the witness Hall. You remember that the witness Hall came into the box and swore that he was a verbatim reporter, and put in a number of statements which he professed to have taken down in shorthand concerning some eight or ten meetings which had been addressed by myself or others of those who are in the dock; and though this man denied that he had selected sentences, and even words out of sentences, in order to make up his report, yet, in the course of his report there was a political speech made by Miss Christabel Pankhurst, which, according to his report, made absolute nonsense. I was able to show what the probable sense was, and I put it to him, having interpolated a great many words and sentences in his report, that that was probably the thing she actually said, and he admitted that that was quite likely to be what she said. A more flagrant case still was his report of a speech by Mr. Mansell-Moullin, the surgeon. This was how the witness Hall reported a part of that speech: "Now, what are you going to do? We must go forward with the fight, even if we have to use violence." I put it to the witness, you will remember what Mr. Mansell-Moullin really said, and he admitted that what Mr. Mansell-Moullin said was this:

The question is, What are you to do? How are you to nail such shufflers and wrigglers, how are you to nail them to their pledges? Someone in the audience says, Wait and see. It will be too late then. You want to nail them now, and the only thing is to keep straight on for your principle. The one that was laid down at the start. Keep perfectly straight for the principle *"as it is, or it may be granted to men."* I know what it means, and I am afraid you all know as well as I do. I know the hundreds who have been imprisoned. I know the brutal treatment that so many of you have received at the hands of the police and of prison officials, if not by the direct orders of the Home Secretary, at least with his active connivance. I know that some of you have been maimed for life. I know that some have died; died as directly of the violence they have received as if they had been put up against a wall and shot. I know all this, and so do you but there is nothing for it but to go on. Your Cause is a sacred one. It is the Cause of justice and liberty and civilisation. It is the finest and the noblest Cause the world has ever known, and it is one that must and will succeed.

Now, gentlemen, I do protest most strongly against a man being sent to report a speech and reporting it like this:

We must go forward with the fight, even if we have to use violence.

Then what I have read to you is what was actually said, and nothing of the kind that he gave was ever said. And I put it to you in the first place that every single report that this witness has given is absolutely and totally incorrect. And I think you will all agree that it is a very scandalous thing that men should profess to report meetings and should so absolutely distort the meaning of speeches in this way. I venture to lay it down that the man who undertakes reliability to report speeches should be either trained as a politician and understand the meaning of phrases that politicians use, in order that he may correctly gather what they mean, or he should be a thoroughly qualified stenographer who puts down every word that is said. Fortunately, in this case, I have a verbatim report of the speech, and I was able to put before you the correct version. But suppose we had not been able to employ our own stenographers; and suppose we had been hauled up for some statement which it was alleged we had made and we had been unable to prove that we had not made it. You will see that it is of the utmost importance that only a correct report should be given; in this case it was totally incorrect.

What is Militancy?

Now I want to say something to you on the question of militancy. I referred to it in my opening speech, but I am afraid that what I said then may not have been perfectly understood. Militancy has been used as a method of the Women's Social and Political Union long before any question of stone-throwing ever arose. Women have been arrested in the course of this agitation while going on a perfectly peaceful deputation to the House of Commons. While acting thus constitutionally, they have been arrested and sent to prison for considerable terms. Mrs. Pankhurst herself was going to the House of Commons with a petition in her hand, and for seeking admission, and for that alone, she was arrested and sent to prison for several weeks. My wife has been dealt with in the same way. Several hundreds of women, for merely going in procession to the House of Commons and asking to be admitted, sometimes in quite small numbers, have been arrested and sent to prison for long terms. The technical reason for which they were sent to prison was obstruction of the police in the performance of their duty. To use the word militancy does not mean stone-throwing by any means necessarily. That is borne out by what Mrs. Morgan Dockrell said when she explained that the letter which she received from Mrs. Pankhurst which spoke of a militant protest, did not convey to her mind any idea of stone-throwing, even though it spoke of the possibility of arrest as the result of her action. Then I want to read to you from the file the report of what one member of a demonstration—Cissy Wilcox—said at her trial, when she spoke of what happened on "Black Friday."

On November 18, 1910, when I went in a perfectly peaceful way to the House of Commons to present a petition to Mr. Asquith, I was obstructed by the police. One policeman took hold of my head and forced it back as far as it would go. Another got hold of my arms and twisted them. I was kicked until I became unconscious and had to be removed to the police-station on an ambulance. My feet and ankles were bruised, and one wound was still open, certified by a doctor who saw me six weeks afterwards. The police have generally been kind and considerate, and I have come to the conclusion that they must have had orders to maltreat us on that occasion. Mr. Churchill refused to have an inquiry afterwards, as he evidently did not wish the blame to fall upon the right shoulders. I broke these windows simply as a protest, and as one who has no constitutional defence open to her.

She is giving there the reason why she threw stones on the occasion in November, 1911. The Attorney-General put this to you that if you failed to bring in a verdict of guilty against us, if a stop was not put to this form of agitation, if we were not punished, and punished severely—I don't know that he said punished severely: I want to be quite fair to him—that there would be nothing to prevent anyone who had a grievance from thinking that the right way to deal with it was to go and break windows. Gentlemen, that is not correct. The fact is that the demand for the Franchise differs fundamentally from the ordinary grievances of daily life. Let me say a word or two by way of illustration. Supposing you had some trouble with a tradesman; supposing your butcher supplies you with some bad meat; supposing some one cheats you in a business transaction; supposing your landlord behaves improperly to you in some way—you don't go and break the windows of the person who has dealt with you improperly; you don't do anything of the kind. There is a fundamental and essential difference between such a case as that and the demand for the franchise, and the grievance of these from whom it is withheld. If your butcher sends you bad meat, you go to him and say, "I won't have it," and, if he persists in sending you bad meat, you have your remedy, you tell him that in future you will deal elsewhere. Everyone has that power over his tradesman. If a customer cheats the tradesman, he can refuse to supply him with any more goods. If your landlord does not do what in your lease he covenants to do, you can go to law against him, and at the expiry of the lease you can leave the premises and go elsewhere. But the case is entirely different when you come to a case between the citizens of the country and the Government. If people have votes they can turn out the Government. If they have not got votes, they are deprived of the ordinary means of redress which one has in ordinary everyday life of bringing pressure to bear upon those against whom they have a grievance. And that is why, as a matter of fact—whether it be right or whether it be wrong—we people are fighting for the franchise and that is why we have adopted methods which under ordinary circumstances would be absolutely unjustifiable. Mr. Lloyd George, as you have heard, on this difference, said the following:

> I lay down this proposition—democracy has never been a menace to property. I will tell you what has been a menace to property. When power was withheld from the democracy, when they had no voice in the Government, when they were oppressed, and when they had no means of securing redress except by violence— then property has many times been swept away.

That is what Mr. Lloyd George said. He perfectly-clearly distinguishes between the agitation for franchise reform and all agitations relating to ordinary everyday grievances.

Further, history teaches you that in the demand for the franchise people have gone far beyond the methods used in all the ordinary dealings of life. They have gone far beyond what the women have done on this occasion. Take the South African War. That was a fight to obtain the franchise for a comparatively small number of people in South Africa. That question involved war between two Governments, it involved the loss of the lives of thousands of innocent people on both sides, it involved the expenditure of millions of pounds of national prosperity. Take the case of the Bristol Riots. In that case a hundred thousand pounds' worth of property was destroyed in one night. Take the case of Ireland. There in many cases the actual execution of violence has been the one means by which the Home Rulers on the one hand and the Orangemen on the other have sought to make their positions strong.

Woman Suffrage and the Race.

In addition to this, there is this peculiarity in the demand for the franchise as compared with individual grievances. To these women who have broken windows, the situation in their opinion must be very grave indeed, and I think you will see that these women would never have acted so contrary to their peaceful and peace-loving ordinary attitude towards life unless they had felt the matter was of the utmost gravity indeed. Now I am not going to give you a lecture on Women's Suffrage, that is the last thing I would do here, but I do want to convince you that the women who have taken part in this struggle, and Mrs. Pankhurst, my wife, and I, do not feel that it is a mere question of academic interest only. It is a question which in our opinion is fundamental, not only for women but for the whole race. My training as a political economist has taught me that serious evils, such as the sweating of women—and you know that there are women who are earning 5s., 6s., and 7s. per week for eleven or twelve hours' work a day, and who have to keep a whole family on this pittance—that this is intimately bound up with this question of the franchise. Then there is the White Slave traffic—young girls, fourteen and fifteen years of age, of respectable families—they might even be your own daughters—trapped and taken away to some foreign country to be treated in the most abominable way in which human beings can be treated. These questions do not receive from the House of Commons as much attention as they would if women had the vote, and I would like to deal with one question by way of example at a little greater length. That is a question which I think appeals to all of you. It is the question of child life.

Now you know that in this country an enormous number of little children die in the first year of their life—as many as 110 out of every 1,000 born—roughly speaking about one million children are born every year, and over 100,000 of that number die in the first year of their life—and doctors tell us that very few are born in such a condition that they could not live if properly cared for. Doctors tell you that this appalling death rate is almost entirely due to causes which are preventible. Now we who know the importance of strengthening our population, we who know the need of rearing strong men and women, must view with very grave apprehension this preventible loss of so many of the children of our country. Not only so, but the same causes which kill off that 100,000 children weaken and impair the 900,000 who survive. That is not a question which we can treat lightly or without the fullest concern. But, you will ask, has it got anything to do with the question of women franchise? I say most emphatically yes. For if you will look at those countries where women have already won the vote—Australia, New Zealand—you will find that the infantile death rate, instead of being 110 per 1,000, is only 62 and 72 respectively, while in Canada, where women have not got the vote, it is as high as 132 per 1,000. But you will say perhaps, even so, it will be an accident. Perhaps you will say Australia is a very healthy country, and that is the reason why their infantile death rate is so low. But I will convince you that that is not the reason. For in 1893 the death rate in South Australia was one of the highest in the whole civilised world. In that year, in that state—a small state compared with ours in point of population—1,245 infants died in the first year of their life. The next year the women got the vote. They at once looked into the matter and pressed forward a great quantity of legislation. I shall not enumerate in detail the very rapid strides that were at once made. But in 1909—with a much larger population than before—the number of infants who died in the first year of their life was only 616, so that through the efforts made by the women, more than half of the children that were born, and who would presumably have died, have been saved. Instead of 1,245 dying in a year, only 616 died, and that of a larger population.

The Price of Life.

The question of infantile mortality is a thing which we men naturally feel very strongly. But you must remember this, that women feel this question much more strongly than we men do. They pay the price of life, and when you have to pay for a thing you place a far higher value upon it. If you buy a very expensive picture, or some splendid thing for your house, and pay for it out of money that you have earned, and if someone else destroys it you feel more strongly about it than you would feel if you had not paid for it. It is the women who have to pay the price of these little children. We take precautions to prevent loss of life in dangerous trades, but what trade is more dangerous than theirs? There was very severe loss of life in the South African War, both from wounds and disease; yet every year over 5,000 die in, or as a result of, childbirth—in giving birth to the new generation. Is it not natural, therefore, that they should feel more keenly than you or I can do the absolute necessity of getting a voice in the framing of the laws which will save the lives of the little children? Let me give you one or two illustrations so that you may understand their feeling to some extent. Supposing you are passing a house in which is a little child. Through the windows you hear its piteous cries. You know it is seriously ill, and you know that if you can only get at it you can save its life. You knock at the door. It is opened by some contented and portly old gentleman. He says, "What do you want? What are you knocking for? You can't get in here." You say, "There is a little child inside whose life is in danger, and I want to save it." He says, "Go away; I am too busy; you can't come in here." You say, "I must get in, it is imperative that I should get in." He won't let you in; he stands in the way. You argue with him for forty minutes, and you think you have argued long enough. The wail of the child is in your ears. You call on the neighbours to help you, and you force your way in. Suppose the neighbours are all asleep—do you think you would be doing anything very terrible if you broke one or two of their windows to waken them up? Don't you think you would be doing something quite justifiable? That is the individual case. But there is a broader case. Take the case of the *Titanic* that we have all been reading and thinking a great deal about in recent times. You know that over a thousand lives were lost in that disaster. I do not wish to anticipate the findings of the investigation that is going on into the matter, but I think we must all recognise that there was a great deal of negligence and carelessness on the part of someone, and if people could have been wakened up to the seriousness of the need for precautions beforehand, a great many of these lives could have been saved. Some people had been trying to hammer into the heads of the Government departments the necessity for saner regulations. We may not have heard of it, but it was going on. It was not dealt with in the Press because it was not of sufficient interest. Probably we would not have read it had we seen it in the papers. But supposing that some public-spirited people had said: "We are very much concerned about these regulations. If they are not attended to there will some day be a terrible accident." Supposing they went to the Board of Trade and broke a few windows to rouse the officials to the urgency of the matter. Don't you think that would have been better than doing nothing and allowing these 1,500 people to lose their lives on the *Titanic?* Let me put it in another way. There was another ship close by. She had a wireless installation but the operator was asleep. If she had received a message the lives of the people on the *Titanic* would have been saved. Supposing someone had wakened up that operator and that in doing so it had been necessary to break a few windows, don't you think it would have been worth while? I think you would. Now what you have to deal with in this case is not a single circumstance. It is not even a case of saving one thousand lives. It is a case of saving a thousand lives this week and next week and every week of every year. That is why the women are waging this fight. That is what has driven them to do illegal things. They think it is worth while to take steps which under ordinary circumstances they would never dream of taking, and they do it in order to waken people up, to draw people's attention to what is urgently necessary. Now women say that all the resources of civilisation at the present time are controlled by men, and they say that if they had power to look into these things as they have done in South Australia they could save the lives of thousands of little children, and that is why they have gone to the lengths they have already gone. They feel it is absolutely necessary to take that course.

What History Teaches.

Some of my speeches have been put before you by the prosecution, but I do not think if you look carefully at the speeches I have made, and which have been put before you that you will find a single case of incitement in any of them. I do not think any of the speeches I have made are in the form of incitement to women to take part in any violence. I do not think it is my place to incite women to do violent actions. As a man and voter, possessing the franchise, it is not my place to do violent actions, but if you say I am not to speak in approval of what women have done, that I am not to speak on a public platform, that I am not to tell them that the method they are adopting to win the vote is the method that has been adopted in history, then you are asking me either not to think at all or to speak with my tongue in my cheek and not to tell them the whole truth, because in history, when it has been a question of franchise reform, men have always resorted to methods of this kind in order to win their way. It is not what I say, it is what many of the statesmen of the past have said, and what the statesmen of to-day are saying upon this question of franchise. Read what Mr. W. E. Gladstone said, "I am persuaded," he said, "that there is nothing so demoralising to a community as a passive acquiescence in unmerited oppression."

Sir Edward Carson said the other day with regard to the position in Ireland:

"There was a point at which resentment became so acute that they were entitled to assert any method to prevent their liberty of discussion being taken away."

And he told Mr. Asquith that before he entered on a campaign of that kind in which the vital issues involved were the severance of his country and his (the speaker's) own, he had better count the cost. Mr. John Bright, in a passage I have read, said he was prepared to lead a hundred thousand people to Parliament Square in order to enforce his demand. Mr. Bright, as you know, was actually a Quaker. Mr. Ramsay MacDonald, who is the leader of the Labour Party in the House of Commons, went so far as to write in the *Daily Chronicle* of February 14 these words:

"If the State has forfeited, in the mind of labour, its reputation for impartiality, then Labour in the conflict will isolate law and order as the passive resister does."

Then some of them go even further than that. Mr. F. E. Smith[1] said he utterly declined to be bound in his resistance to the progression of those who had been guilty of those constitutional outrages within the strait waistcoat of constitutional resistance.

He also said:

"Violence is always deplorable. So is bloodshed. Yet violence and bloodshed in Ulster would be an incomparably smaller misfortune than cowardly acquiescences in a revolution which, if consummated, would assuredly plunge the whole country in civil war."

Lord Selborne, in writing in the *Oxford and Cambridge Review*, said:

"I do not think that men of our race are likely to part with their liberty or their property without fighting for them, with rifles in their hands if need be."

Now, gentlemen, in view of these speeches, which are the speeches of some of the most highly-placed men in the past and in the present, I put it to you that nothing I have said in standing by the women or taking part in this agitation can make me guilty of this crime.

The Editorship of the Paper.

Then the prosecution no doubt rely considerably for their case on the paper, *Votes For Women,* of which, until the date of my arrest on March 5, I was, with my wife, one of the editors. Now, with regard to this paper, there are just three distinct points that I want to put to you. In the first place, there are the unsigned articles in the paper. Of course, you have not had the paper before you—it would have been impossible, and I don't want to go through it in any detail—but you must have noticed that of the un-signed articles, and practically all "The Outlook," which week by week has set out the political situation, I do not think a single word has been in evidence by the prosecution. "The Outlook" comes at the beginning. This is the pronouncement of the editors on the situation, and it is the part for which the editors are, more than any other, responsible. Not a word of it has been put in by the prosecution as being any incitement on this question. Then there are the signed articles. Some of them have been put in, and the reports of speeches, and also of invitations to take part in the protests. With regard to the signed articles I maintain it is the duty of a newspaper to give to its contributors a free hand, in order to state their view of the position of affairs. With regard to the reports the business of the newspaper is to give a faithful and accurate report—many do not do so, I know, but that is their business—and we have set ourselves to give a faithful and accurate report of the meetings, and proof that we have succeeded—at any rate so far as this case is concerned—is that witness after witness has gone into the box and has sworn to being at the meetings and reading the report, which is an essentially accurate and faithful report.

Finally, with regard to the invitation to take part in the protest, I say that when I and my wife started this paper four or five years ago, we devoted it to this women's cause, and devoted it in particular to the Women's Social and Political Union, and when the Women's Social and Political Union has found it necessary to make protests in order to demonstrate their refusal to accept the political situation, so far as *Votes For Women* is concerned, I have never hesitated to open our columns to their rescue. You see, my position is this: I am a man, and I cannot take part in this women's agitation myself, because I am a man, but I intend, I have intended, and I intend, to stand by the women who are fighting in this agitation. Knowing what methods have succeeded in history, I am not going to say that these methods have been a mistake. I say that because I think in the first place it is not merely that it is a women's battle, it is not merely a battle for women—I think it is a battle for the good of the people of this country. And when I see other men standing out against this agitation, then I am more determined to stand in with it, and I feel this further, that but for some of those who have stood in with this agitation there might be a danger of this agitation becoming a sex war. I think a battle of women against men is an ugly thing—a thing to be deplored, and I say it is because of the men who have stood in the battle that a sex war has been prevented. I say that children are dying because women's points of view are not understood, and I say, "How long are women to have no say in the government of the country?" I say, "How much longer is it to go on?" You cannot say to the women, "You are not to go out to throw stones. You should have gone out and had your bodies broken, your persons assaulted, had yourselves arrested for doing nothing at all." I say to you that you and I as men who have not got to face these things have no right to say that to the women. I take my stand with one of the greatest statesmen that this country has ever had, and I do not think the Attorney-General, who is prosecuting us in this case, will deny the statement that one of the greatest men was Mr. Gladstone. I will read what Mr. Gladstone said:

Do you think, sir, that under these circumstances it is the duty of Ministers, or of anybody else, to go to the people of this country, when they have the formidable obstacles in their front that they have now, and say to them: "Love order and hate violence"? It is certainly one's duty to advise people to love order and hate violence, but am I to say nothing else? Am I to make no appeals to them? Am I never to remind them of the dignity and force that attach to the well-considered resolution of a great nation? Are we to cast aside all the natural, legitimate, and powerful weapons of our warfare? I would go all lengths to exclude violence, and on that ground I object to the speech of the Marquess of Salisbury. But while I eschew violence, I cannot, I will not, adopt that effeminate method of speech which is to hide from the people of this country the cheering fact that they may derive some encouragement from the recollections of former struggles, from the recollection of the great qualities of their forefathers, and from the consciousness that they possess that still. Sir, I am sorry to say that if no considerations had ever been addressed in political crisis to the people in this country except to remember to hate violence and love order and exercise patience, the Liberties of this country would never have been obtained.

[This ended Mr. Pethick-Lawrence's speech to the jury.]

Dr. Ethel Smyth then entered the witness-box, and in reply to Mrs. Pankhurst said she was a doctor of music, was a daughter of the late General

Smyth, and was the lady mentioned by the man who was released from acting on the jury because he had conducted some of her work, "The Wreckers." She was a member of the W.S.P.U., and was present at a meeting at the Pavilion Theatre on February 26 last.

That was the meeting when I made what may be described as the "Referendum" speech?——Yes, I was there.

Mrs. Pankhurst then read the speech in extenso.

Dr. Smyth said that the speech was delivered by Mrs. Pankhurst exactly as it had been read in court.

The report put in evidence by the prosecution was what had been called a synopsis. "Need I say any more?" added Dr. Smyth, amid laughter.

Mrs. Pankhurst: Since I am charged with having incited you and other people to take part in the demonstration—

The Attorney-General: I do not think you are charged with having incited Dr. Smyth.

Mrs. Pankhurst: Am I in order in asking her if she was incited by me in any way?

Dr. Smyth: No. I did not wish to take any part in your March agitation because I was too busy. Then came the refusal of the Home Office to permit the inquiry into the conduct of the police on Black Friday. I know what these women had been through. I then wrote straight away to Mrs. Pethick Lawrence to say that I begged to take part in the next protest. I went so far as to say that I hoped whatever the protest might be, it would not be such a protest as the one on Black Friday, because I did not think that any women should subject themselves to that sort of usage again. If that letter has disappeared I am rather glad of it, because I think that it might possibly be cited as a case of inciting my leaders to violence. (Laughter.)

I gather that you had made up your mind to take part in some form of protest before you heard that speech?——Oh, yes.

Did you take part in the protest?——Well, as a matter of fact, I was very badly bitten in a dog-fight the week before, and I was laid-up for a month, and could not take part. (Laughter.) I was very sorry it was so.

Were you asked to take part in the protest of March 4?——No; I said that I had done my "bit," that I was sorry that I had not had the opportunity of identifying myself with these splendid people, but that I must turn my face the other way and go back to my work.

I believe, as a matter of fact, that you did take part in the protest of March 4?——I did.

How came you to take part after you had not volunteered?——When I was at Cardiff in a sanatorium, Mr. Hobhouse made the celebrated speech, and then I wrote up and said that I was coming. I did not see how any self-respecting woman could stay at home after that.

There was some applause among the ladies in the gallery at this remark.

Mrs. Pankhurst: You took part in the protest and broke a window?——Yes.

You were arrested, and what was your sentence?——Two months' hard labour.

Why did you choose that particular window? Were you asked to do it?——No one asked me to do it or to do anything. What I did I did entirely on my own.

You selected the window of some private person?——Yes.

The Attorney-General: It was hardly a private person.

Dr. Smyth: I am sorry. I did not mean to mislead the Court. It was the window of a gentleman who made what, I think, was the most objectionable remark about the Women's Suffrage question that has been made. That was when he said in answer to a deputation of women that he would be very happy to give the vote to women if all women were as intelligent, as well behaved and as admirable in every way as his own wife. (Laughter.) I thought that the most impertinent thing I had ever heard, also the most fatuous because it was as if he thought he had the pick of the basket. (Loud laughter.) So I said to myself, that is the window I am going to break.

It was Mr. Harcourt's window—Mr. Lewis Harcourt?——Yes.

He is a member of the Government and represents a constituency in which the majority of the wage earners are women?——Yes, and also he represents the Colonies. He was on the "anti" platform, and when I thought of Australia having sent that resolution, of which, I dare say, you gentlemen have heard, advocating the Suffrage in England, and assuring the Prime Minister that it had been a most tremendous success in Australia—a resolution that was passed absolutely unanimously—I said that I had selected his window. (Laughter.)

You thought that you were doing it on behalf of the women of the Colonies as well as for the women at home?——Yes.

You were given the option of being bound over?——No, but I should not have accepted it if I had.

The Attorney-General (cross-examining): I suppose you read *Votes For Women?*——Yes.

Did you see the report of what you had done? You have a paragraph to yourself headed "Dr. Ethel Smyth." It says:

After the magnificent appeal to the women in the audience at the London Pavilion on Monday afternoon, it was not surprising to hear subsequently that Dr. Ethel Smyth herself made a vigorous protest against the Government. Driving up to the private house of Mr. Lewis Harcourt, which was guarded by police, Dr. Smyth inquired a direction of one of them, and while he was replying threw a stone, and broke some glass in Mr. Harcourt's house.

Dr. Smyth said that the paragraph was quite correct in its report.

Mrs. Pankhurst: Following upon that, may I ask you if it was not you yourself who made the eloquent appeal referred to?—Of course, it was. I had had the pleasure of speaking on that afternoon. I said that every self-respecting woman who was not held up by great difficulties at home ought to go, and therefore it would have been surprising if I had not gone myself, as I am an independent woman.

The Attorney-General: Your appeal was an appeal to break a window, was it?——My appeal was to do as we considered it necessary to do.

The Judge: That is to break windows?——Certainly. I did not intend to do nothing.

The Attorney-General: And you do not now intend to do nothing?

Dr. Smyth: Is not that a hypothetical case? Am I bound to answer that? (Laughter.)

The Attorney-General: I will not press that here. (Renewed laughter.)

At this juncture Mr. Healy pointed out that the words of the statute were "Aid, abet, counsel, and procure the commission of a misdemeanour." The prosecution had chosen to use the words "solicit and incite," which were words of quite a different character, and were non-statutory. He submitted, therefore, that the counts of the indictment were bad in themselves, since the statutory phraseology had not been used. Unless the prosecution could refer the Court to some evidence of a conjunct incitement on the part of the three defendants, there was no evidence to go to the jury on any of the counts in which this was charged, and these counts should be withdrawn from the jury.

Mr. Muir also pointed out that there must be either direct evidence, or some evidence which showed that the incitement alleged reached the mind of the person who was alleged to be incited. There was no evidence that the women named in the indictment were incited on November 20 to commit the misdemeanour named in the counts. There was no proof that the incitement, if there were any, reached Sarah Benett. He was not arguing as to whether there was incitement at all. He added that he wished to make it clear that the only place upon which Mr. Pethick Lawrence's name appeared was the paper, *Votes For Women*. Mr. Pethick Lawrence was not a member of the W.S.P.U., which was exclusively a women's union, and he did not take any official part in the Union's work at all.

The Attorney-General said that if the submission of Mr. Muir were right, it would get rid of ten or twelve counts, but his (the Attorney-General's) submission was that there was ample evidence to go to the jury, and he called his Lordship's attention to the facts proved. He contended that the matter did not admit of any doubt.

The Judge said the matter was one to go to the jury on all counts. In the case of Mrs. Pankhurst she was in America in November, and so far as she was concerned that part of the charge was withdrawn.

The rest of Tuesday afternoon was occupied by the speech of Mrs. Pankhurst for her defence:

Mrs. Pankhurst's Great Speech.
Address to the Jury at the Old Bailey, May 21, 1912.

Before I enter into my personal defence in this matter, I would like to say a few words to you about the matter of conspiracy. Like you, I am not a lawyer, and unlike you, I have an additional disadvantage of being a woman. It is assumed that men by their education and training are fitted to deal with these matters. Women have never been encouraged to think questions of law were the concerns of women; but in spite of that, a certain number of women have tried to study law and qualify themselves, because the law does not admit that women to-day are in a position of calling upon members of their own sex trained in law to plead for them, defend them, or to put their case. And so, when I speak of this charge of conspiracy brought against us, I can only speak to you as a lay woman to whom, presumably, the same advantages as yours are not given; but I do, having paid some attention to these matters and having been much interested in public affairs, wish to say a few words about the word conspiracy. I know the legal interpretation and legal meaning of the word conspiracy is not our meaning of the word. In the public mind the word conspiracy contains some suggestion of secrecy, suggesting intrigue.

Nothing to Conceal.

I know what we say of conspiracy: we naturally think that that means something done by people who are ashamed of what they are doing—people who think that it is essential that they should preserve secrecy and intrigue to make their conspiracy successful. I am sure that you came into that jury-box with the idea that you were going to hear of some disgraceful conspiracy, some conspiracy in which the parties did things of which they were ashamed, and things which they wished to conceal in order to succeed. That interpretation has by this time been entirely removed from your mind. If one thing more than another has been made plain in this trial it has been that we defendants at the bar have not behaved as people who are ashamed of what they are doing and who desire to conceal anything which they do, or desire to intrigue in any secret way. I venture to say, although I am not a lawyer, had it not been for the evidence which we ourselves have openly supplied there would be absolutely no case to come before you to-day. Through our newspaper, through our speeches, through our acts, we have been beyond reproach so far as any disgraceful reproach can attach to us, so far as any criminal intent is concerned, and the word criminal in the sense which a layman attaches to the word. And so, although we must defer to the legal interpretation of the word conspiracy—both you gentlemen in the jury-box and we prisoners at the bar—although we must defer to the legal interpretation of that word, and we prisoners here may have to suffer because of that legal interpretation, I submit to you and the Judge on the bench that so far as the ordinary acceptation of the word conspiracy is concerned, the general public, thinking of conspiracy as they undoubtedly do, can and will attach a different interpretation to that word from the mere legal interpretation.

Then I want to say a word as to whether this is a political case or not. I say this because the Attorney-General said to you—I hope I am correct in my interpretation—although you might hear a good deal about politics in the course of this trial, it really was not a political case which was being tried; that you must not regard it as being political or the offence as political. I hope I am not in any way distorting what the Attorney-General has said. Well, now, with regard to that point I want to say in the very clearest and most definite terms that if we defendants here, the accused people, are not accused of a political offence, than I can't see how we can be accused at all. Is it for a moment to be supposed that we three defendants, and my daughter who is not here, would have taken part in this agitation for any reason but for a political one? It is unthinkable to suggest for a moment that we people would in any way break the law for a selfish purpose, for our own interests or for our personal ends! Now, greater people than I have laid down so clearly that even the simplest of untrained women can understand it; that a political offence is one committed in breaking the law for an end which is not a personal one; that the breach of the law is made not for personal gain, not for personal advantage, but because the offender is satisfied in her or his own mind that it is necessary to break the law in order to get a political grievance remedied. I think it has been already clearly established—I think it was clearly established before my friend, Mr. Pethick Lawrence, made his speech—that, rightly or wrongly, we persons accused here to-day are persons who never would have come within the precincts of the Court or committed any breach of the law but for political purposes.

And the definition of the word criminal is very different. Authorities have laid it down, and in other countries it has been generally accepted, that a criminal is a person who breaks the law for personal advancement or personal gain. In the course of these days during which the case has occupied your attention, it has not been proved, although I have felt myself that an attempt has been made to suggest, that the accused had some personal objects to serve. If that was so intended, and it seems to me intended (not so much here, but in the preliminary examinations before the police courts), if that suggestion was intended it has absolutely failed. And I want, before going into my personal defence, to try to convince you and his Lordship that this offence with which we are charged is a political offence. I know in other countries than ours, France, for instance, there would be no need for any prisoner to stand at the bar and plead that this was a political offence. In that country—and I wish our own country had reached the same height of civilisation—political offences are recognised and political status is accorded to political offenders even when they commit breaches of the law passing in seriousness the breaches of the law of which we are accused. In fact, they have gone so far in trying political prisoners in France as to lay down that the possession of arms by the accused is not a criminal offence, but a political offence, if the person can prove that the possession of these arms is for a political purpose. That I wanted to say with regard to our status as prisoners whose guilt you are called upon to decide in the course of this trial. I would like to spend a little time in dealing with the definition of a word that has been very much used in describing this political movement for the enfranchisement of women carried on by the Women's Social and Political Union, to which I belong. There are several organisations for women's suffrage, but our organisation has been distinct from others by the use of the word "militant." I have thought, and have been proud to think, that probably we had the word "militant" attached to our organisation because we showed by our readiness even to suffer in the course of our agitation, and to pay heavy penalties in the course of the agitation, that we were more in earnest, more determined than the other organisations; that we did not content ourselves merely with discussion; that we did not merely talk about our grievances, but that we were prepared even to put ourselves in the way of having great violence done to us in order to call attention to those grievances; that we were not merely content with words because in this country everybody has a right to talk about their grievances but we felt that we were distinct as a militant class even when we were a young organisation, which had just come into existence, determined not only to talk about our grievances, but to terminate them by securing the object for which we existed. In fact, we adopted the motto, "Deeds, not words." There is a great deal of talk in politics, and there are a great many political gentlemen who make very strong speeches—even members of the Government make strong speeches. Even the gentleman who is representing the Crown here to-day makes strong speeches. (Laughter.) But we women had thought in our agitation that we would never say anything if we did not feel ourselves justified in acting also, if we thought action necessary. Now because we have taken that attitude we have been called a militant organisation. We have not been called militant in the first instance because we were violent, because we did actual deeds of violence. Had that been so I do not think the Prosecution would have limited the scope of the indictment to last November.

Some Definitions.

Fortunately, we have definitions of the meaning of every word in the English language, and I want to call your attention to some of the definitions of the word "militant." It is a word which is liable to be misunderstood, my lord, and I have felt myself, sitting in this dock in the course of this trial, that I have reason to be grateful—I think that is a curious thing to say—for the way in which this agitation has been tried; that I have been grateful even in a Court of Law like this for the opportunity of putting our case, however imperfectly, to my fellow-countrymen and fellow-countrywomen. Now, as to the meaning of the word militant. I find in Webster's dictionary militancy defined as "a state of being militant, warfare." Well, that sounds like violence, doesn't it? Then I find militant, or militant in the sense of "engaged in warfare, fighting, combatting, serving as a soldier, also combatting the powers militant." Then, on reference to Millman, I find that the "Church must become militant in its popular and its secular sense." Then, again, it is defined as meaning "a conflict, to fight." In Nuttall, I find it is "to stand, opposed to, or to act in opposition." In the Century dictionary I find a quotation from Froude which refers to a "condition of militancy against social injustice." Then it is described as "being militant, a state of warfare," and then I find "in a state of conditional militancy," and that is taken from a divine named Montagu. And so I could go on showing you that the word "militant" is not necessarily interpreted to mean only violence done by those people who are militant. I want to prove to you, in the course of my defence, that although women ever since 1903 have been described as militant suffragists, never until November of last year had there been anything done by this organisation which could be in any way described as organised violence. I say that advisedly, and no one is better qualified to say that than myself. It may be said that there were isolated occasions on which stones had been thrown, but on those isolated occasions stones had been thrown by isolated individuals who might be members of the Women's Social and Political Union or might not be. But those women on their trial—and the police have always admitted it, and even gone out of their way to confirm what the women said—have never said they were instructed by the leaders of this movement, and the leaders of this movement, while they have never, as some politicians have done, repudiated their followers, have always made it clear that they did not think the time for violence had come, and they also made it clear that they hoped that the time for violence would never come. And so we have been described as militant.

Mr. and Mrs. Pethick Lawrence.

I want to say a word or two as to my co-defendants. I want to say something about Mr. Pethick Lawrence, and I feel this very strongly because the Attorney-General in his opening thought fit to call attention to the fact that Mr. Lawrence is a member of the learned profession. Well, it is not the first time, and I am glad to think it, that members of the learned profession have helped to fight the people's battles. The Attorney-General's remarks brought

to my recollection events of which my husband used to talk to me. Out of
these events arose a trial in the Central Criminal Court, in the buildings on
the site of which this building is, I believe, erected. At that Central Criminal
Court a man—a barrister—was put upon his trial on a similar charge to
ourselves. That was Ernest Jones, the Chartist.[2] I never knew him personally,
but my husband was a personal friend of his. My husband used to feel that
Ernest Jones was his inspirer in the part he took in public affairs later on.
That man, a man who had great expectations of wealth, a man of great
learning, a man who might have risen to the highest position in his profession chose to give it all up, chose to relinquish all opportunity of advancement in his profession, because his conscience made him espouse an
unpopular cause, and he was put upon his trial in what I might term this
very Court. History has a very curious way of repeating itself, and it has
repeated itself in the case of Mr. Lawrence. When Ernest Jones was prosecuted for his political activities, the then Attorney-General—on looking over
the list of counsel engaged for the prosecution I find repeated the name of
one of the counsel engaged in this case—made just the same statement
about Ernest Jones that the Attorney-General has made about Mr. Pethick
Lawrence. He seemed to suggest that because Ernest Jones was a lawyer
and a member of the learned profession he ought not to have taken the part
he took. Well, I think that things more disgraceful to your great profession
can be done by the members of your profession than were done by Mr.
Ernest Jones or are charged against Mr. Pethick Lawrence. It seems to me
no profession is degraded by unselfish men. It seems to me no man is unworthy of his position if he even brings himself within the grasp of the law
because he has followed the dictates of his conscience, because he is generous, because he goes to the side of those he thought oppressed. And so
when judgment is passed I think it will be decided that it is much better to
find ignominy, to be imprisoned, it is better even to bear shame in your
own generation than to use your profession for personal advance, for personal gain, or for personal ends. And so, speaking as a woman who is at a
disadvantage because I am a woman, I want to say I am grateful to Mr.
Pethick Lawrence because, being a member of a great and privileged profession, he has disregarded the privileges of his profession, and is in the dock
by the side of women less fortunate than himself. And then Mrs. Pethick
Lawrence. These two people are very dear, personal friends. I met them first
at a stage of this agitation when it seemed just touch and go whether we
could carry on the agitation any longer. They came into it when some of us
who were not rich women had exhausted our means, sold our personal
property and little things like jewellery dear to us, in order that we might
carry on the agitation. At that critical stage these people came to our aid,
and so I want to say what is due to these people. I know they would have
come into the movement sooner or later, being what they are. I want to say

it is due to these people, coming as they did then into the cause, that we have been able to create a great constitutional organisation—I mean a great political organisation—an organisation which has not only done much to advance the cause in this country, but throughout the whole world. It was inevitable that Mrs. Pethick Lawrence should come, and she was the first to come into it. She is in it in the fuller sense of the word, because she is a woman. Mr. Lawrence could never be in the organisation, because one of the essential conditions of membership is that no man can be a member. It is restricted to women, and Mr. Pethick Lawrence is, therefore, I think, in a unique position in the history of politics.

He would not have the glory—if there were any glory—attaching to the movement. He could not have had the political recognition that he would undoubtedly have had if he had devoted himself to any of the great political parties. He has been content to play a part which I think no other man has ever played in politics: entirely to withdraw himself from the ordinary opportunity of advancement in politics to play a secondary part in the Women's Movement, because he felt we wanted some men to stand by us and help us in order to make our position secure.

Why She is in the Dock.

There is an old proverb which says that to know all is to understand all. It is impossible, gentlemen, to tell you all about this movement. We have not taken up very much time in the ordinary methods of defence in this trial. The prosecution has occupied many days. There has been a great deal of repetition; a great deal of unnecessary time has been spent in the opening of the case against the defendants, and I am sure, when you remember what this trial means to me and to my co-defendants, how it may possibly mean loss of liberty for a long time, when you, although you have been wearied by this case, will go away, that you will bear with me a little. I will try to be as brief as possible not to weary you too much. Well, I will try to make you understand what it is that has brought a woman no longer young into this dock. My Lord, I think I have already said that if one lives long enough one sees strange things happen, and I cannot forbear from reminding you that forty-two years ago next November, your father, who was not then the Lord Chief Justice, the great judge that he afterwards became, was at the bar pleading on behalf of women after the Reform Act of 1867. He was counsel for the women associated with my husband in the case of Chorlton v. Lings. He pleaded their cause very ably, and I want to tell the jury exactly what the case was about. After the passing of the Reform Act of 1867 women imagined—and, I think, had good reason to imagine—that that enfranchising Act would entitle women to register as Parliamentary voters. The great Reform Act of 1832, which has been referred to in this case, because it was characteristic of very great violence on the part of men, enfranchised a great many men, but, at the same time, excluded women from the franchise because the word "male" was used for the first time in history. In regard to the word "male," it made it impossible for the woman to be registered, and women maintained that while it was enfranchisement for men it was disenfranchisement for women. That is to say, that until that Act was passed women had the right to vote, and to a certain extent exercised that right to vote for Members of Parliament. A large number of women claimed to be put on the register, and in Lancashire alone four thousand women were put on the register in response to that claim. The overseers accepted them as qualifying voters. When the Revision Courts sat, the Revising Barristers considered the claims of the women. Some allowed the claims, others disallowed them.

Now that was the case to which I have referred just now. It was a case brought by a woman in Manchester named Chorlton against a revising barrister whose name was Lings, and by the result of the case women had to stand or fall. Sir Charles Coleridge was the leader in that case. My husband, who at the time was a confirmed Suffragist, and who was already making considerable sacrifices—because men have had to make great sacrifices in this cause, which was so long unpopular—my husband prepared the case.

Together those two lawyers argued the case. It was argued at considerable length. Evidence was given that prior to 1832 women had a vote; arguments were used against their having a vote. The case was finally decided, and to us laymen and laywomen, it was an extraordinary decision. In effect it was this, that where it was a question of rights and privileges a woman is not a person, but where it was a question of pains and penalties woman is a person. So, gentlemen, in this Court, Mrs. Pethick Lawrence and I are persons to be punished, but we are not persons to have any voice in making the laws which we may break; and which we may be punished for breaking. That was the decision—the final decision—that we must pay our taxes, we must obey laws; but when it comes to choosing the men who impose the taxes and make the laws, we have no legal existence; we have no right to help choose these men. That was the decision. I venture to say, my Lord, to you and to the jury, that had the judges of that time decided as a judge last year decided in Portugal, that since the women paid taxes and obeyed laws, they have the right to choose their tax-masters and their law-makers like men—had the judges of that day agreed with the argument laid before them by your lordship's father and my husband, this agitation would not have been necessary, the status of women would have been established, and sex exclusion would have disappeared. It has an intimate bearing upon this question of violence on the part of the members of the Women's Social and Political Union.

The Right of Petition.

The year before last I was convicted with other women for having gone to the House of Commons with a petition in my hand, insisting upon going to the door of the House of Commons, and insisting on my right to remain there until my petition was received. I argued that I had a constitutional right to do that; I argued that it is established in the Bill of Rights that every subject of the King has a right to present a petition in person, and that in the case of men it was not very necessary to emphasize or insist upon that right, because that right, in the case of men, had been replaced by the Parliamentary franchise, and that men could freely vote for their representatives on the floor of the House of Commons to voice their demands and claims; and I argued that, since the right of petition had not been replaced in the case of women by any other right, women still had the right to go in person to-day, not as in the old days to present their petitions to the King—the conditions have changed to-day—but to present their petitions to the King's representative, the Prime Minister. That was our case. It was very ably argued before the magistrates, and as the result of that argument a case was stated, and it was argued out before the judges in the Higher Court as to whether or not women had this right. It was decided, as in 1867, that we had not the right; we had not the right to present petitions in Parliament. That, in substance, was the decision, that we had not the right to insist upon presenting this petition. We had the right to petition and we had the right to present petitions, but if the person to whom we wished to present them would not receive them, we could not present them. So we were acting illegally in insisting upon the right to present. I want to say here, my Lord, that had these judges in 1909 decided that women had the right to petition there would have been no organised violence, there would have been no stone-throwing in this agitation. It was because the women were made to feel that they had no hope in the law—in the consciences of specious politicians—that there was no one to whom to appeal; that the women said, "Well, this is a belated agitation; it is the twentieth century, when these things were supposed to be settled, but we have got to fight out the weary fight as women and get this question settled somehow as best we can. Now, this is how it all started. I do not want to go over the ground covered by Mr. Pethick Lawrence. I do not want in any way to repeat what he has said; but I do want—as a woman who has taken part in the Suffrage Movement for something like thirty years—to try to make you understand how it is that things have come to be where they are.

Early Agitations.

When that case was argued—that case which decided that women were not persons—I was a small child. I had not grown up; but when I grew up, quite early in life, I had the great honour and privilege of joining the Suffrage Movement as it was then, under the leadership of Miss Lydia Becker, in Manchester, and under the leadership of people like Mr. Jacob Bright, people universally known as they were; and at the same time I had the great happiness of being married to the man I have mentioned, who fought the women's battle in the Law Courts with your Lordship's father. From that time on I took an active part in the Suffrage agitation. I was put upon the executive committee of the then Suffrage Society when I was about twenty-one years of age. I took part in the agitation of the eighties, right through the eighties—the late seventies and eighties—my connection with it began in the year 1879. From that time on until the passing of the next Reform Act, which enfranchised agricultural labourers, I took an active part in the agitation, and I say without hesitation that if constitutional methods alone could win women the vote, they would have become voters in 1884 when that Reform Act. was passed. We held more meetings and greater meetings than did the agricultural labourers. You have heard from Mr. Pethick Lawrence how the great towns and cities of England petitioned in support of the Conciliation Bill, which was "torpedoed" out of existence by Mr. Lloyd George, according to his own words. In those days, in the early eighties, the great towns and city councils petitioned in favour of the inclusion of women in the Reform Act of 1884. We filled all the great halls in the country with women, who enthusiastically passed resolutions in support of their enfranchisement; we got up monster petitions, we got a petition so huge that it had to be wheeled into St. Stephen's Hall on a trolley by several men. Members of Parliament came out and looked at it, and they smiled and went back to their places and forgot all about it. We found friendly Members of Parliament to move an amendment to that Reform Act, and that amendment had, I think—at least, we thought then that it had (we were less trained politically in those days)—we thought that it had an excellent chance of being passed into law; it certainly had a better chance of becoming law than the suggested amendment to the Manhood Suffrage Bill, because, as you remember, the Act of 1884 was not a measure like the Manhood Suffrage Bill; it insisted upon a certain qualification of residence. We thought we were going to win our enfranchisement. What happened? The very men who introduced the amendment were told by their Parliamentary leader to throw over their amendment, because, they were told, it "overweighted the ship." It was even threatened by their leader, Mr. Gladstone, that he would withdraw the whole measure if they persisted in the Women's Suffrage Amendment. The women had not votes to bring pressure to bear upon the Government, and women at that time did not dream of using violence or threatening violence. The result was that the agricultural labourer, who burnt some hayricks to show their impatience—the agricultural labourers, who were to be marched over a hundred thousand strong to the House of

Commons by Mr. Chamberlain—those men got their votes, and the women, who had been content to agitate by constitutional means, were left voteless. That was the beginning of a decline in the Women Suffrage agitation. Many women lost heart and hope; many of us, whilst we still continued to be Suffragists, listened to men who told us that we ought to join political parties and show what good and useful work we could do in those parties in order to win the gratitude of the parties. Others told us that it was now competent for us to go on boards of guardians and school boards, to do useful public work, and they urged us to do that to prove that women were fit and worthy for the vote. We ought to have known, gentlemen, that that was an argument that had never been used in the case of men. It was never urged upon the agricultural labourers that they should show fitness for the vote; it was never suggested to the working men that they show themselves fit for the vote. We listened to that argument—some of us; I was one of those women. I did join a political party, and worked very hard for it in the belief that the gentlemen who promised that when their party came into power they would deal with our grievance, would keep their pledges.

Social Work.

When my children were old enough not to need my constant service, I became a member of a Board of Guardians.[3] In this agitation there are always strange things happening, and yesterday, as I was stepping into the dock, a member of the Bar in the Court came up to me and recalled himself to my recollection. He was a member of the Board of Guardians, on which I served, with me, and I suppose I was recalled to his recollection because he is now a member of the Bar, and he was interested to see that a former colleague was being tried on what is called a criminal charge. I served about five years on that Board of Guardians. In speaking of myself, I am, in my own person, telling you what a great many other women have done. A very great many women have tried to do this useful public work to show that they were fit for the rights and responsibilities of citizenship—as fit as some drunken loafer who neglects his family, but who, because he is a man and has necessary qualification, is entitled to decide not only his own fate and the fate of other men, but the fate of women and children as well. All this I did, and at the end of it—since there is no distinction in sex where brains are concerned—at the end of it all I was forced to the conclusion that so far as our enfranchisement was concerned, we had been wasting time. I found that men would say that you were not unfit for the vote, and that if all women were like you they would have no objection to giving you the vote. Oh! we women, who have done the dirty work of the political parties, have never had any reason to complain that our services have not been appreciated personally. But some of us came to realise that after all this appreciation we were blacklegs[4] as the working men called it—blacklegs to our own sex, and so some of us decided that a time had come when this became a sort of reproach to us, which we could not endure any longer. Now, gentlemen, I want to tell you a few of the things that led me in 1903, when the Women's Social and Political Union was founded, to decide that the time had come when we had reached a situation, which I think I can best describe in the words of the Chancellor of the Exchequer, Mr. Lloyd George, when he was addressing an audience in Wales a little while ago. He said, "There comes a time in the life of a people suffering from an intolerable injustice when the only way to maintain one's self-respect is to revolt against that injustice." That time came for me, and I am thankful to say it very soon came for a large number of other women as well; that number of women is constantly increasing. There is always something which I may describe as the last straw on the camel's back, which leads one to make up one's mind, especially when the making up of one's mind may involve the loss of friends, loss of position, loss of money—which is the least of all things, I think—and the loss of personal liberty.

Handicaps in the Work.

I have told you that I have been a Poor Law Guardian. While I was a Poor Law Guardian I had a great deal of experience which I did not possess before of the condition of my own sex. I found that when dealing with the old people in the workhouse—and there is no work more congenial to women that the work of a Poor Law Guardian—when I found that I was dealing with the poor of my own sex, the aged poor, I found that the kind of old women who came into the workhouse were in many ways superior to the kind of old men who came into the workhouse. One could not help noticing it. They were more industrious; in fact, it was quite touching to see their industry, to see their patience, and to see the way old women over sixty or seventy years of age did most of the work of that workhouse, most of the sewing, most of the real work which kept the place clean, and which supplied the inmates with clothes. I found the old men. One could not get so much work out of them. They liked to stop in the oakum-picking room, because there they were allowed to smoke; but as to the real work, very little was done by these old men. I am not speaking in a prejudiced way; I am speaking from actual experience as a Poor Law Guardian. Any Poor Law Guardian could bear me out. I began to make inquiries about these old women. I found that the majority of them were not criminal during their lives, either as wives and mothers, or as single women earning their own living. A great many were domestic servants, or had been, who had not married, who had lost their employment, and had reached a time of life when it was impossible to get more employment. It was through no fault of their own, but simply because they had never earned enough to save, and anyone who knows anything about the wages of women knows it is impossible to earn enough to save, except in very rare instances. These women, simply because they had lived too long, were obliged to go into the workhouse. Some were married women; many of them I found were widows of skilled artisans who had pensions from their unions. But the pensions had died with them. These women, who had given up the power of working for themselves and had devoted themselves to working for husbands and children, were left penniless; there was nothing for them but to go into the workhouse. Many of them were widows of men who had served their country, women who had devoted themselves to their husbands; when the men died the pensions died, and so these women were in the workhouse. And so I found younger women—always women doing the bulk of the work. I found there were pregnant women in that workhouse, scrubbing corridors, doing the hardest kind of work almost until their babies came into the world. I found many of these women were unmarried women—very, very young, mere girls. That led me to ask myself, "How is it that these women, coming into the workhouse as they do, staying a few weeks, and going out again—how is it they occupied this position?" I found these young girls, my lord, going out of the workhouse over and over again with an infant two weeks old in their arms, without hope, without home, without money, without anywhere to go. And then, as I shall tell you later on, some awful tragedy happened—simply because of the hopeless position in which they were placed; and then there were the little children, and this is the last example I am going to give out of my experience.

Human Tragedies.

For many years we Poor Law Guardians, especially the women, tried to get an Act of Parliament dealing with little children. We wanted an amendment of the Act of Parliament which deals with little children who are boarded out—I do not mean by the Union, but by their parents, the parent almost always being the mother. It is from that class—young servant girls—which thoughtless people always say working girls ought to be; it is from that class more than any other that these cases of illegitimacy come. These poor little servant girls, who only get out perhaps in the evening, whose minds are not very cultivated, and who find all the sentiment of their lives in novelettes, fall an easy prey to those who have designs against them. These are the people by whom the babies are put out to nurse, and the mothers have to pay for their keep. I found, as other Guardians found, when we examined that Act, that it was a very imperfect one. The children were very ill-protected. We found that if some man who had ruined the girl would pay down a lump sum of £20 when that child was boarded out, the inspectors, whom the Guardians had to appoint, had no power to enter the house where the child was to see that it was being properly cared for. We found, too, that so long as a baby-farmer took one child at a time the women inspectors, whom we made a point of appointing, could not perform their object. We tried to get this law amended. For years, as the Attorney-General knows, efforts were made to amend that Act, to reach all these illegitimate children, to make it impossible for some rich scoundrel to escape from any future liability with regard to the young child if this lump sum were paid down. Over and over again we tried, but we always failed because those who cared most were women. We could go and see heads of departments, we could tell them precisely about these things, we could talk to them and get all their sympathy. In fact, in this movement on the part of the women, we have been given a surfeit of sympathy. Sympathy? Yes, they all sympathised with us, but when it came to the women asking them to do something, either to give us power to amend the law for ourselves or to get them to do it for us, it has always stopped short at sympathy. I am not going to weary you with trying to show you the inside of my mind, trying to show you what brought me to the state of mind I was in in 1903; but by 1903—I was at that time a member of the Manchester Education Committee—I had come to the conclusion that the old method of getting the vote had failed— had absolutely failed—that it was impossible to get anything done; that some new means, some new methods, must be found. Well, there is another defendant, who is not here to-day, and I want to say as a woman well on in life, that perhaps, if I had not had that daughter who is not here today, I might never have found the courage to take the decision which I took in the course of the years 1903, 1904, and 1905. We founded the Women's Social and Political Union in 1903. Our first intention was to try and influence the particular political Party, which was then coming into power, to make this question of the enfranchisement of women their own question and push it.

It took some little time to convince us—and I need not weary you with the history of all that has happened—but it took some little time to convince us that that was no use: that we could not secure things in that way. Then in 1905 we faced the hard facts. We realised that there was a Press boycott against Women's Suffrage. Our speeches at public meetings were not reported, our letters to the editors were not published, even if we implored the editors; even the things relating to Women's Suffrage in Parliament were not recorded. They said the subject was not of sufficient public interest to be reported in the Press, and they were not prepared to report it. Then with regard to the men politicians in 1905. We realised how shadowy were the fine phrases about democracy, about human equality, used by the gentlemen who were then coming into power. They meant to ignore the women— there was no doubt whatever about that. For in the official documents coming from the Liberal party on the eve of the 1905 election, there were sentences like this: "What the country wants is a simple measure of Manhood Suffrage." There was no room for the inclusion of women. We knew perfectly well that if there was to be franchise reform at all, the Liberal party which was then coming into power did not mean Votes for Women, in spite of all the pledges of members; in spite of the fact that a majority of the House of Commons, especially on the Liberal side, was pledged to it—it did not mean that they were going to put it into practice. And so we found some way of forcing their attention to this question.

The New Policy.

Now I come to the facts with regard to militancy. We realised that the plans we had in our minds would involve great sacrifice on our part, that it might cost us all we had. We were at that time a little organisation, composed in the main of working women, the wives and daughters of working men. And my daughters and I took a leading part, naturally, because we thought the thing out, and to a certain extent, because we were of better social position than most of our members, and we felt a sense of responsibility. And I hope, gentlemen, you will bear with me when I tell you of two events which led me—a little worn by the world, having children about whose interests I cared greatly—which led me to throw all else aside and go straight into this thing without regard to consequences. One evening there came to my house in Manchester a Russian lady—a lady of Polish birth, who had lived most of her life in Russia. We sat round the fire on that winter evening talking about agitations, the Suffrage, and a number of other things. And then quietly this woman said to me and to my children sitting there: "For a great number of years of my life I have never got up in the morning without feeling that before the day closed some member of my family, some relation, some friend, might be arrested and might be torn away from us altogether." And she said this calmly, so sadly and so quietly, and without any feeling, that it made a very deep impression on my mind. And when she had gone my children and I—for we were quite alone—talked about it. And of course I, being older than they, must take the greater responsibility for what we decided that night. I don't think we ever reopened the discussion. I think it was settled once and for all. We said, "What is there that we can sacrifice or risk compared with what that woman has spoken about?" and so we decided to go on. In the course of our discussion I said to my daughter—because we were then talking of transferring our work to London, and launching out on a larger scale—"What is there in our power to do? We are not rich people. We are already doing without a great many of the things which we hitherto thought necessary. Few people have hitherto helped us with money. How can we expand our work?" And she said: "Never mind, Mother, go on, and the money will come," and when I heard that from that girl—who is not in the dock to-day, not because of any lack of courage, not because of any unwillingness to share our position, but because she has a sense of public duty—because of what that girl said I felt inspired with the courage to go on.

The First Militants.

Then came the election of 1905, and the first of the acts which, my lord, can by any stretch of imagination be described as militant. What those acts were Mr. Pethick Lawrence has told you. The first act was the going to a great Liberal demonstration in the Free Trade Hall, Manchester, of two girls with a little banner, made on my dining-room table, with the inscription, "Votes for Women," and asking Sir Edward Grey, the speaker, not "Are you in favour of Woman's Suffrage?" but "Will the Liberal Government when it takes office give women the Vote?" For asking that question, just as men would have asked it, but with more respect for order than men would have shown, because they sat patiently, and waited for their opportunity, while many men had interrupted with questions about Chinese labour, and were respectfully answered—for insisting upon an answer to that question when the speech was finished, these girls were treated with violence and flung out of the meeting; and when they held a protest meeting in the street they were arrested, and were sent to prison, one for a week as a common criminal, and the other for three days. That was the so-called militancy. I ask you, gentlemen, whether if that had been done by men, the word militant would have bourne any construction but one of determination and earnestness and insistence upon having that question answered. As long as they had a chance of putting questions, even if they were thrown out after having asked them, women were content to do nothing more. Then these gentlemen developed a desire to catch trains; they rushed away from their meetings directly their speeches were finished, and the women got no opportunity of putting their questions. Now bear in mind that no politician of to-day can feel as deeply about any political question as women feel about this disfranchisement, having regard to the things we are out for—reforms for women, for old and for young women and for little children, who are dying through the absence from legislation of the effective influence of women.

Now what did they do next? I want you to realise that no step we have taken forward has been taken until after some act of repression on the part of our enemy, the Government—because it is the Government which is our enemy—it is not the Members of Parliament, it is not the men in the country; it is the Government in power alone that can give us the vote. It is the Government alone that we regard as our enemy, and the whole of our agitation is directed to bringing just as much pressure as necessary upon those people who can deal with our grievance. The next step the women took was to ask questions during the course of meetings, because as I told you these gentlemen gave them no opportunity of asking them afterwards. And then began the interjections of which we have heard, the interference with the right to hold public meetings, the interference with the right of free speech, of which we have heard, for which these women, these hooligan women, as they have been called—have been denounced. I ask you, gentlemen, to imagine the amount of courage which it needs for a woman to undertake that kind of work. When men come to interrupt women's meetings, they come in gangs, with noisy instruments, and sing and shout together, and stamp their feet. But when women have gone to Cabinet Ministers' meetings—only to interrupt Cabinet Ministers and nobody else—they have gone singly. And it has become increasingly difficult for them to get in, because as a result of the women's methods there has developed the system of admission by ticket and the exclusion of women—a thing which in my Liberal days would have been thought a very disgraceful thing at Liberal meetings. But this ticket system developed, and so the women could only get in with very great difficulty. Women have concealed themselves for thirty-six hours in dangerous positions, under the platforms, in the organs, wherever they could get a vantage point. They waited starving in the cold, sometimes on the roof exposed to a winter's night, just to get a chance of saying in the course of a Cabinet Minister's speech, "When is the Liberal Government going to put its promises into practice?" That has been the form militancy took in its further development.

What happened to those women and to the men who, I am thankful to say, when they began to understand the movement, rallied to our support? You may not have heard of it. You would not read it in the papers, because it was not reported. Two Cabinet Ministers have incited women by their insults to do more serious things. The Minister for War, for instance, on one occasion when women interrupted him, said, "Why do you content yourselves with pin-pricks? Why don't you do something serious?" Then you get Mr. Lloyd George—I refer to the speech of his where he talked about human beings who suffered an intolerable sense of injustice, revolting—and, at that very self-same meeting, after saying those eloquent words which I could not improve upon, because I agree with them entirely—directly after that, a woman got up fired by those words, and said, "Then why don't you deal with our grievance?" and he looked on smiling and remarked, "We shall have to order sacks for those ladies." And it has not been one member of the Government only. There is hardly a member of the Government who has not used those insulting words to women, and there were other insults that we have not cared to make public, because there are some things women do not like to tell about. But they have faced rough usage because they have felt it was their duty to remind the Government that there was a question which would have to be dealt with sooner or later, and I would say again, gentlemen, that I welcome this trial because we have here, what I have often wished for—we have at any rate someone in close touch with the Government present, and he perhaps will convey to the Government some of the things that we women have long desired to tell them. When we tried to present petitions in the old days at the House of Commons, the women went unarmed, with petitions only in their hands. We always held a preliminary meeting at Caxton Hall, Westminster. Yesterday, when we had a police witness in the box, I asked him about a particular meeting, because I hoped that he was present, and I wanted to elicit something from him, and I will tell you what it was.

Leeds By-Election.

In 1908 there was a great by-election at Leeds, and we had been opposing the Government candidate, not because we had anything against his opinions, but because we believed by defeating him and by getting men to work against him, we should bring pressure to bear upon the Government, and make the Government realise that if they lost that election and other by-elections, there was some serious question they had neglected, and that required attention. Well, upon that occasion we very much reduced the majority. The Press boycott had extended to our election work to a very large extent. We have never been able to get the facts of what we have done at elections in the Press. Little by little the facts of our work have filtered through, but the public have never been told the amount and the extent of our work at by-elections. Women have held bigger meetings and better meetings, more sympathetic and more orderly than the candidates. On some notable occasions, when the Government candidate has sustained defeat, the papers have attributed it to, say, an increasing feeling in favour of Tariff Reform, rather than to the real cause, which was the opposition and the part played by women in the contest. Well, I had just returned from this particular election to take part in a demonstration outside the House of Commons. I was to lead one of those deputations a small deputation of women, well within the Act of Charles II—which defined the number of persons who can take petitions to Parliament. I was to lead that deputation, and I came straight back from this election, where I had spoken at hundreds of outdoor meetings to men and women. I remember distinctly the speech I made in Caxton Hall. It was just after Mr. Herbert Gladstone had given us the advice to hold great demonstrations such as the men had in Hyde Park and elsewhere. Well, we had had in Leeds at that election a procession, a huge procession, of women, the day before the election, culminating in a great open air meeting on the moor in South Leeds. That night a great many working women came out of the factories which abound, you know, in Leeds, and where they work hard for little pay. They joined our procession. The students, who as you know are always very irresponsible and one always wonders how the responsible sex should be so very irresponsible in the days of their youth, these students tried to break up our procession, and I was alarmed at the resentment shown by the crowd. In fact, I had to use what influence I had gained in order to save the lives of some of these students by appealing to the crowd, otherwise something serious would have happened. I returned by the night train to London, and on the following afternoon addressed that meeting in the Caxton Hall, and then, as on many other occasions, I explained why I was hoping that the Prime Minister would receive us. I said there comes a time when movements may outgrow the people who start them. There comes a time when people who desire that everything shall be orderly, suddenly may fail, and I felt so seriously that day that time was rapidly coming, my lord, that I earnestly hoped, and I put it in my speech, that members of the Government, although we were only women, would see us, would hear us, and would look for themselves, and not merely look to the columns of the newspapers which excluded all references to the magnitude of this agitation.

Armed with Lilies.

What was the result? I only got a few yards from the Caxton Hall when I was arrested. I had a petition in one hand; I had a little bunch of lilies in the other hand. And the other women who were with me were no more armed than I was. We were arrested. Next day we were taken before the magistrate, and in consequence of that act I suffered my first imprisonment of six weeks in Holloway Gaol. Now on the floor of the House of Commons, in describing these so-called raids, even Home Secretaries—more than one, had talked about the women scratching and biting policemen and using hatpins. These things were said not merely by the sensational Press, nor by irresponsible members of the Liberal Party, but these gentlemen, Cabinet Ministers, have thought fit to attack women who, they knew, had very little opportunity of answering, because even the columns of the Press were closed to us—these gentlemen have thought fit to say these things about the women, although not one tittle of evidence has ever been produced to substantiate these charges which have been made. Now, I ask you, gentlemen, if you could put yourselves into the place of women so maligned, would you not feel some sense of resentment against such injustice? We say in this country that everybody at least is entitled to justice, but in the police-courts, whatever the women said was disregarded. The police evidence was beyond all contradiction. It has not been until quite recently, when we have got out of the atmosphere of the police-court—an atmosphere in which this movement ought never to have been kept so long—at least a little light has been let in upon the character of the women engaged in this agitation, because when these women whose actions have been mentioned in the course of this case came before Mr. Wallace at the Sessions, and contested the evidence against them, he said he was prepared to take the word of those women, for from his experience of them he knew that their word—whether he approved I cannot say, I am quoting roughly—that whatever they might do they were honourable people whose word was to be trusted. Well, that is something gained. If you gentlemen had as much experience of this movement as I have, you would know that is a great deal gained—to be admitted as persons of ordinary truthfulness; because every method has been taken to traduce this agitation, to misrepresent it, to pour contempt on the women engaged in it, and to crush it.

Two Months for 2s. 3d.

Now it has been stated in this court that it is not the Women's Social and Political Union that is in the court, but that it is certain defendants. The action of the Government, gentlemen, is certainly against the defendants who are before you here to-day, but it is also against the Women's Social and Political Union. The intention is to crush that organisation. And this intention apparently was arrived at after I had been sent to prison for two months for breaking a pane of glass worth, I am told, 2s. 3d., the punishment which I accepted because I was a leader of this movement, though it was an extraordinary punishment to inflict for so small an act of damage as I had committed. I expected it as the punishment for a leader of an agitation disagreeable to the Government, and while I was there this prosecution was started. They thought they would make a clean sweep of the people who they thought were the political brains of the movement. We have got many false friends in the Cabinet—people who by their words appear to be well-meaning towards the cause of Women's Suffrage. And they thought that if they could get the leaders of the Union out of the way, it would result in the indefinite postponement and settlement of the question in this country. Well, they have not succeeded in their design, and even if they had got all the so-called leaders of this movement out of their way they would not have succeeded even then. Now why have they not put the Union in the dock? We have a democratic government, so-called. This Women's Social and Political Union is not a collection of hysterical and unimportant wild women, as has been suggested to you, but it is an important organisation, which numbers amongst its membership very important people. It is composed of women of all classes of the community, women who have influence in their particular organisations as working women; women even of Royal rank are amongst the members of this organisation, and so it would not pay a democratic government to deal with this organisation as a whole.

They hoped that by taking away the people that they thought guided the political fortunes of the organisation they would break the organisation down. They thought that if they put out of the way the influential members of the organisation they, as one member of the Cabinet, I believe, said, would crush the movement and get it on the run. Well, Governments have many times been mistaken, gentlemen, and I venture to suggest to you that Governments are mistaken again. I think the answer to the Government was given at the Albert Hall meeting held immediately after our arrest. Within a few minutes, without the eloquence of Mrs. Pethick Lawrence, without the appeals of the people who have been called the leaders of this movement, in a very few minutes ten thousand pounds was subscribed for the carrying on of this movement.

Not Wild or Hysterical.

Now a movement like that, supported like that, is not a wild, hysterical movement. It is not a movement of misguided people. It is a very, very serious movement. Women, I submit, like our members, and women, I venture to say like the two women and like the man who are in the dock to-day, are not people to undertake a thing like this lightly. May I just try to make you feel what it is that has made this movement the gigantic size it is from the very small beginnings it had? It is one of the biggest movements of modern times. A movement which is not only an influence, perhaps not yet recognised, in this country, but is influencing the women's movement all over the world. Is there anything more marvellous in modern times than the kind of spontaneous outburst in every country of this woman's movement? Even in China—and I think it is somewhat of a disgrace to Englishmen—even in China women have the vote, and they have it as the outcome of a successful revolution with which, I daresay, members of His Majesty's Government sympathise—a bloody revolution. One word more on that point. When I was in prison the second time, for three months, as a common criminal—because we women have gone through all that; we have been searched, we have been stripped, dressed in prison clothes and subjected to all the restrictions of a prison system which needs amendment— when I was in prison the second time, for no greater offence than the issue of a handbill—less inflammatory in its terms than some of the speeches of members of the Government who prosecute us here—during that time, through the efforts of a Member of Parliament after I had been in prison some time, there was secured for me permission to have the daily paper in prison, which had hitherto been denied me, and the first thing I read in the daily Press was this: that the Government was at that moment feting the members of the Young Turkish Revolutionary Party, gentlemen who had invaded the privacy of the Sultan's home—we used to hear a great deal about invading the privacy of Mr. Asquith's residence when we ventured to ring his door-bell—gentlemen who had killed and slain, and had been successful in their revolution, while we women had never thrown a stone—for none of us was imprisoned for stone-throwing, but merely for taking the part we had in this organisation. There we were imprisoned while these political murderers were being feted by the very Government who imprisoned us, and being congratulated on the success of their revolution. Now, I ask you was it to be wondered at, that women said to themselves perhaps it is that we have not done enough; perhaps it is that these gentlemen do not understand women folk; perhaps they do not realise women's ways, and because we have not done the things that men have done, they may think we are not in earnest.

Incitement by Statesmen.

And then we come down to this last business of all, when we have responsible statesmen like Mr. Hobhouse saying that there had never been any sentimental uprising, no expression of feeling like that which led to the burning down of Nottingham Castle. Can you wonder then, that we decided we should have to nerve ourselves to do more, and can you understand why we cast about to find a way, as women will, that would not involve loss of human life, and the maiming of human beings, because women care more about human life than men, and I think that is quite natural that we should, for we know what life costs. We risk our lives when men are born. Now, I want to say this deliberately as a leader of this movement. We have tried to hold it back, we have tried to keep it from going beyond bounds, and I have never felt a prouder woman than I did one night when a police constable said to me, after one of these demonstrations, "Had this been a man's demonstration, there would have been bloodshed long ago." Well, my Lord, there has not been any bloodshed except on the part of the women themselves—these so-called militant women. Violence has been done to us, and I who stand before you in this dock have lost a dear sister in the course of this agitation. She died within three days of coming out of prison, a little more than a year ago. These are things which, wherever we are, we do not say very much about. We cannot keep cheery, we cannot keep cheerful, we cannot keep the right kind of spirit, which means success, if we dwell too much upon the hard part of our agitation. But I do say this, gentlemen, that whatever in future you may think of us, you will say this about us, that whatever our enemies may say, we have always put up an honourable fight, and taken no unfair means of defeating our opponents, although they have not always been people who have acted so honourably.

We have assaulted no one; we have done no hurt to anyone; and it was not until "Black Friday"—and what happened on "Black Friday" is that we had a new Home Secretary, and there appeared to be new orders given to the police, because the police on that occasion showed a kind of ferocity in dealing with the women that they had never done before, and the women came to us and said, "We cannot bear this"—that we felt that this form of repression should compel us to take another step. That is the question of "Black Friday," and I want to say here and now that every effort was made after "Black Friday" to get an open public judicial inquiry into the doings of "Black Friday," as to the instructions given to the police. A certain course was adopted. That inquiry was refused; but an informal inquiry was held by a man whose name will carry conviction as to his status and moral integrity on the one side of the great political parties and a man of equal standing on the Liberal side. These two men were Lord Robert Cecil and Mr. Ellis Griffith. They held a private inquiry, had women before them, took their evidence, examined that evidence, and after hearing that evidence they said that they believed what the women had told them was substantially true, and that they thought there was good cause for that inquiry to be held. That was embodied in a report. To show you our difficulties, Lord Robert Cecil, in a speech at the Criterion Restaurant, spoke on this question. He called upon the Government to hold this inquiry, and not one word of that speech was reported in any morning paper. That is the sort of thing we have had to face, and I welcome standing here, if only for the purpose of getting these facts out, and I challenge the Attorney-General to institute an inquiry into these proceedings—not that kind of inquiry of sending their inspectors to Holloway and accepting what they are told by the officials—but to open a public inquiry, with a jury, if he likes, to deal with our grievances with the Government and the methods of this agitation.

The Government's Conspiracy.

I say it is not the defendants who have conspired, but the Government who have conspired against us to crush this agitation; but however the matter may be decided, we are content to abide by the verdict of posterity. We are not the kind of people who like to brag a lot; we are not the kind of people who would bring ourselves into this position unless we were convinced that it was the only way. I have tried—all my life I have worked for this question—I have tried argument. I have tried persuasion. I have addressed a greater number of public meetings, perhaps, than any person in this Court, and I have never addressed one meeting where, substantially, the opinion of the meeting—not a ticket meeting, but an open meeting—I have never addressed any other kind of meeting—has not been that where women bear burdens and share the responsibilities like men they should be given the privilege men enjoy. I am convinced that public opinion is with us—that it has been stifled—wilfully stifled—so that in a public Court of

Justice one is glad of being allowed to speak on this question. Then, your Lordship—because if we are found guilty I shall not say why sentence should not be pronounced—I want to say a word in connection with our status. Twice I have been to prison as a common criminal. I know what it is—you and the gentlemen of the jury I hope do not know what it is—to lose one's liberty and be sent to prison. I want you to understand what it is. God knows it is hard enough for the ordinary criminal, living a degraded life, to face all that prison means; it is doubly hard for those who have not been accustomed to what prison life is. But I am not pleading with your Lordship because of the hardships—I am not pleading with your Lordship because of the sense of the indignity which self-respecting women feel with those indignities imposed upon them—but I am pleading with your Lordship because I want to see my country raised to the level of every other civilised country in the world. Where political fitness is concerned, I think it is a disgrace to this country that we should be so far behind. There was a time in this country when the ordinary criminal was treated with more severity than to-day. We have improved—we have become more humane since those days, and though much remains to be done with regard to the ordinary criminal, it cannot be said that their lot is as bad. But it was different with the status of the political offenders. Still, in this country when it is a foreigner we do regard by our extradition laws political offences.

If we are to be convicted, our feeling very deeply on this question of our status, I assure you, is not so much for ourselves, it is because we want to have established by you, with the great legal traditions of your position—we want it to be established that the political prisoner should not be degraded to the status of the lowest criminal; but that his or her offence was not to be characterised by criminal tendencies, and therefore ought not to be degraded and stigmatised as disgraceful. I may, as a woman, say one word more. We say in England that every man is tried by his peers. I might have been justified as a woman, if at the opening of this case I had said you are not entitled to try me for this offence. What right have you, as men, to judge women? Who gave you that right; women having no voice in deciding the legal system of this country; no voice in saying what is a crime and what is not a crime, it is not right to set yourselves up as justices? But in this Court I have not made that plea, and I have consented to be tried by this Court, and I think you will agree with me that the right of judgment of a Court depends upon consent. I have consented, and consent merely because I believe the end of this trial marks the last in this hard struggle women are making for recognition. I feel that women, who have now, as they always have had, to perform the ordinary duties of citizenship, are now going to win some power to fix the conditions of their sex and decide their duties, and I feel it all the more because this Government, which has instituted proceedings against us, is a Government dealing more with the lives of mankind than any Government which ever ruled this country. Year by year, and month by month, the fate of women is decided. How they are to live, their relationships with children, the marriage laws under which they are joined in union and pledge their affections, these great questions are being settled, and also will be settled, and so, my Lord, I feel it is a great advantage, though it is at the risk of our liberty, that we are undergoing this trouble. I may say to you, gentlemen, referring to what I said about your right to try me. I might tell you of a case—and that is my last word—of this young girl that I mentioned in the earlier part of my speech, who was put on her trial for her life before a great Irish judge not long ago. And the judge said to those who were responsible for her being there, Where was the man? There was nothing in the law to make the father of that child responsible for the murder of the child for which the girl was being tried. But the judge said: "I will not try that child till the participator of her guilt is in the dock with her," and that case was never tried by that jury at all; but was adjourned till the father of the child also stood in the dock. If we are guilty of this offence, this conspiracy, other people, some of the members of His Majesty's Government, should be in the dock by our side. But I do not ask you to say that you will not sentence us until they are by our side, though I do suggest that members of His Majesty's Government and Opposition have used language at least as inflammatory and dangerous as ourselves, and I think in justice, while these people set us such an example, the verdict of this Court in our case should be one of Not Guilty.

[Mrs. Pankhurst thus concluded her speech.]

[At this point Mr. Healy addressed the jury on Mrs. Pethick-Lawrence's behalf. He described the charge of conspiracy as a "convenient" one because "[t]he mesh is flung so wide. No man can say what act may not be an overt act in connection with conspiracy . . ." It was Mr. Healy's primary point that every act of violence against property had already been punished by the imprisonment of the perpetrators. He claimed that, "for every act committed, some woman had lain upon the plank bed, some female had eaten bread and water." If the acts of violence had already been punished, then the current trial took on a different purpose. Mr. Healy appealed to the jury, "So that when you are asked to vindicate the law and are appealed to in the interests of private property, I beg you to remember that there is not one broken pane for which there is not a broken heart suffering for it. Accordingly, I suggest that the law has been vindicated; property has been protected, and we are engaged now in what is not a trial but a political duel as between his Majesty's Government and the organisation which has been opposed to them." For the majority of his speech, Healy focused upon governmental duplicity concerning the Conciliation Bill and the comparison between the personal nature of government officials and the defendants. Healy pondered, "I question whether in the future to which we all appeal all the members of the Government who are prosecuting my client will stand upon a higher pedestal; I question whether the incense of history will be as fragrant in the nostrils when their names are mentioned as even when the humble name of Emmeline Pankhurst, or Christabel Pankhurst and Mrs. Lawrence are brought up in future times." The Attorney General followed with his speech for the prosecution and countered Mr. Healy's claims of vindictive prosecution by lauding the fairness of the criminal justice system. As Attorney General, Sir Rufus claimed responsibility, not the government in power, for instituting this prosecution in order to protect the public. Early in his speech, he pointed out that the defense had neglected to call women as witnesses to claim that the speakers had *not* incited them, and he focused on "The Argument of the Broken Pane" speech by Emmeline Pankhurst as an example of such incitement. Despite numerous interruptions and corrections by Emmeline Pankhurst and Frederick Pethick-Lawrence, the Attorney General spoke of varying public views on women's suffrage, put forward a version of the order of events in November and March, and summarized the evidence of the concerted effort and planning needed for such attacks on property. Frederick Pethick-Lawrence had put forth the special defense that, as a male, he was not a member of the WSPU, had not incited women in his speeches, and took no part in the protests. The Attorney General countered that Frederick Pethick-Lawrence was joint editor of *Votes For Women,* had rented theaters for speakers, and had appeared at the police station to bail out the arrested women. Although the Attorney General claimed to want to avoid the issues of suffrage and the position of women, he could not resist toward the close of his speech a passing reference to the *Titanic.* When he stated that "where there is grave peril . . . the order that has gone forth is 'women and children first,'" Emmeline Pankhurst interrupted him to ask "What about the women on the street?" Finally, the Attorney General urged the jury to ignore the motives of the defendants for their acts but instead to focus on the evidence presented of those acts.]

Judge's Summing Up.

[Following the speeches by Mr. Healy for Emmeline Pethick-Lawrence and the Attorney General for the prosecution], the Judge then summed up as follows:

We now come to the conclusion of a long investigation, and whatever criticism of our proceedings there may be, I do not think it will be laid to the door of this Court that the accused persons have not had an open, free, full and impartial inquiry. They are charged with certain offences against the law, and they are charged, it is true, in an indictment which has been criticised because it is voluminous. That is necessary. If the indictment had been less voluminous, it would have been open to the criticism by the accused that where the indictment did not allude to any particular act charged, they were not in peril on that charge. And, therefore, it is that the necessities of the law require a certain amount of voluminousness—it may be legal verbosity—in the indictment which is referred. And, after all, these three accused persons are of high intelligence; one of them learned in the law, and I do not think that the indictment could have caused them any trouble in understanding it. The Attorney-General proceeded to make a brief epitome of the indictment, for an abstract of which see *Votes For Women* for May 17.

And if, he continued, it has been brought home to their door that they did incite any one of the women, your verdict must be against them in regard to that particular charge, if the charge be proved. They are also charged with committing the damage themselves, and that is a legal inference to be drawn from the facts of the case, because although it is not suggested that of any particular acts charged they were the actual authors; although they were not present when the acts were committed, it is alleged that they were accessories to what was done, and that they procured and counselled the acts, or any of them, to be committed, and if they did that, they can be, by the law, indicted and tried and convicted as though they were the actual authors of the acts themselves.

What is Conspiracy?

Conspiracy is the joining together of two or more minds to effect an unlawful purpose or to do an unlawful act. It stands to reason from that definition that one person cannot conspire alone. The conspiracy exists in the agreement of two or more minds, an agreement for the common and the unlawful purpose. And if two of these persons agreed, they may be found guilty, although the other person may not have agreed, even if they be all jointly charged together. Not that I am suggesting any distinction between the cases in that regard. All who so agree are guilty of the crime of conspiracy. It is the agreement in itself that is the crime, and it matters not whether the object be carried into effect or be attained; the agreement to do the unlawful act is the conspiracy, and the conspiracy is the crime.

What is Incitement?

In the eyes of the law it is incitement to commit an unlawful act that is unlawful in itself. It matters not whether the incitement, again, be effected. The person incited, it is quite clear, may change his or her mind, but if the incitement be proved the crime has been committed.

Now, to prove the incitement in any particular case. You have heard the arguments that have been addressed to the Court. It is well I should point out to you that it must be shown that something which the accused persons said or did reached the mind of the person incited. You remember a case was quoted to the Court in which there was an incitement to murder, but the incitement never reached the person incited, because he was dead before the letter reached him. And although the moral guilt on the inciter was the same, legally, it could not be proved, because the mind of the person incited was never affected by the person inciting. And so here there must be some connection between the mind of the person who incites and the mind of the person who is incited. Of course, that may be proved directly, or it may be proved indirectly. It may be proved by the admission of the person incited or it may be proved, as has been said to be proved in this case, in all instances but one, by what is called circumstantial evidence—by the natural inference to be drawn by reasonable and thinking minds from facts of each particular case. And if the natural and reasonable inference drawn from the fact so proved before you leads you to the conclusion that it is shown the natural inference is that the incitement did reach the mind of the person incited, then the incitement is proved. So again, if any of the accused persons counselled or procured the women, or any of them, to commit the acts of malicious damage, they are in the eye of the law as guilty of committing the acts as if they committed them themselves.

But in that case also the action must be proved, and the reasoning and arguments which after all are only reasoning and arguments of common sense—they are not recondite law—the reasoning and arguments applied to the later acts as to the former.

Words and Deeds.

The proof of the allegations in this case is sought to be established in two directions. It is sought to be established by proof of speeches that have been made by the various inciting persons, and it is sought to be established by the other acts of conduct or facts as regard to themselves. Now you must be satisfied in each of these cases, whether it be incitement and counselling and procuring, or whether it be by way of conspiracy, you must be satisfied in each case in regard to each of the persons accused that the proof of the charges that it is sought to establish against them is brought home to your reasonable conviction. And if a doubt—not an unreasoning or fanciful doubt, certainly not a doubt which arises from any pre-conceived idea or prejudice of your own, should affect your mind, but if it is some reasonable doubt—the accused are entitled to say the case has not been proved beyond that reasonable doubt. And in the presence of that reasonable doubt you are entitled to say that the charge—a particular charge—has not been made out against them. That is a commonplace of our Courts, and I will not refer to it again; and whatever thing I say to you during the course of my remarks, don't forget that all that I say is qualified by what I have said in regard to the necessity of strict and necessary proof.

Now, gentlemen, to go on, let me say a word or two in regard to proof by speech. I wish to say in as public a manner as I can say it, that the bare academic expression of opinion in this country is free. Avoid blasphemy, avoid indecency, avoid defamatory matter, and you may express—and I hope juries will always bear in mind—you may express what opinions you please without fear of the law. Juries are not, and ought not to be, the custodians or the judges of the views of others. The most unpopular views often slowly, painfully, and against heated opposition, win their way to a recognition of their truth in the minds of men, and it is well that it should be so. But a speech which incites others, if it does so incite them, a speech which incites others to commit unlawful acts differs not in degree, but in kind from the bare expression of an opinion. The difference between, for instance, to give an illustration, the difference between expressing an academic opinion that history furnishes us with examples that revolution has ofttimes effected a beneficial change in the constitution, and the conspiring with others and inciting others to revolt—the difference between those two statements, when you come to reflect upon it, are as wide as the Poles asunder. The one is a free and lawful expression of opinion, the other is a crime, and must always be a crime in all civilised communities where law and order prevail, and must in the interest of all be enforced. But, in the matter of speech as contrasted with the written word, the law is charitable. It is so in the case of defamation, where you may say things of a man defamatory which you may not write, and in the words of a great authority I would say this, quoting, "Writings are permanent things. They are acts of deliberation capable of satisfactory proof, and are not ordinarily liable to misconstruction. At least, they are submitted to the judgment of the Court naked and undisguised as they came out of the author's hands. Words are transient, and as fleeting as the wind. The poison they scatter is always confined to the narrow circle of a few hearers. They are frequently the effect of a sudden transport, usually misunderstood and often misrepresented." Therefore, it is that having regard to the wise and eloquent words of that great authority, I have taken what pains I could in this case to exclude evidence imputing, in imputed speech, where I thought there was any possibility that any error had crept in. Anyone who has ever stood before an audience must know how often words, a phrase, a sentence, issues from the person, a moment's coinage of the brain, without adequate reflection, and sensible men will excuse them, will make allowance for them, and will not necessarily think that they reflected the settled purpose of the speaker, where from evidence, as from the circumstances of the moment, or from the subsequent utterances or conduct of the speaker, it appears that they have been loose words, loose words only, not illustrating any settled purpose, and not intended to have any permanent effect. Then the nature of the audience, too, has to be considered. The speaker must consider this, and be responsible accordingly. Words addressed to a Chamber of Commerce may be harmless which might be provocative of disorder if addressed to an assembly of women of all ages, under circumstances of excitement and of passion; and the speaker must remember that. But, gentlemen, where the words spoken are revised, where they are published with the authority of the speaker, it is in vain then for the speaker to escape from the natural responsibility attaching to his utterances.

Some of the strongest expressions upon which the prosecution rely on evidence of inciting language have neither been denied nor dis-avowed by any of the accused persons. The paper, *Votes For Women,* in regard to which the prosecution allege responsibility of all of the accused, has published some of these alleged incitements, thereby undermining, it may be in your view, the argument in palliation of their use, that they were loose words only, and not representing the settled purpose of the speaker.

Some History.

The history of the case appears to be this. I am not going to elaborate. I will give you credit for intelligence and memory. The Women's Social and Political Union is an organisation which was started some years ago, somewhere about 1903. It is not suggested that the Union itself was an illegal association. It formed, it is true, the most forward, and not to use an offensive expression, the most aggressive branch of the various organisations working towards the common object of the enfranchisement of women. Mrs. Pankhurst was the founder and the hon. sec. Mrs. Pethick Lawrence was hon. treasurer, Miss Christabel Pankhurst was the organising secretary. It had an account at Barclay's Bank, the main account of the Women's Social and Political Union. That account was operated on by Mr. and Mrs. Pethick Lawrence, by Mrs. Tuke, and by Miss Christabel Pankhurst. Cheques signed by any two of them were the authority to draw. One of the two had to be either Mr. or Mrs. Pethick Lawrence. Mr. and Mrs. Pethick Lawrence are here. Miss Christabel Pankhurst absconded—(laughter)—and the police are unable to trace her whereabouts. There was another account operated on in the same way, called the Meetings Account, which, obviously was drawn upon for the purpose of defraying the expenses of meetings. There was another account, the *Votes For Women* account, and that obviously represented the account connected with the paper, *Votes For Women,* which was the organ of the Union, and that account was operated upon by Mr. Pethick Lawrence alone, he being one of the two editors of that paper. And as he has said—he has acknowledged it—the inference of the law would be that he is responsible for what had appeared in the paper of which he was the editor. He has told you that he does not in any way disclaim that responsibility.

There was another account, the "Woman's Press Account," and that was operated upon solely by Mr. Pethick Lawrence, and that was obviously the account dealing with the office in Charing Cross Road which played such a prominent part in the disturbance of November 21. Mr. Pethick Lawrence also had a private account at the same bank, with which we need not deal. Large sums were transferred from time to time from one account to the other and back again. But, without going into the intricacies of the internecine finance, suffice it to say that it is a reasonable inference that from one or other of these accounts the whole expenses of the movement were defrayed—the hiring of halls, the printing of the paper, the pamphlets, the leaflets, the offices, the residential chambers, everything. The home of this organisation or industry was 3 and 4 and 5 and 6, Clement's Inn, consisting partly of rooms and offices and partly of residential chambers. The residential chambers were in all rented at £270 a year by Mr. Pethick Lawrence, and he and Mrs. Pethick Lawrence lived there. Mr. Pethick Lawrence is also the tenant of the offices of the Woman's Press, in Charing Cross Road. He rented it at a rental of £275 per annum. That is the substance of the finance of the various branches of this organisation. There was later an office taken at the Gardenia Restaurant, which played so prominent a part in the disorders of March 4, and that I will come to at a later stage.

Now about October, 1911, it is said that it was in contemplation to begin, in the event of the wishes of the members of the Union not being fulfilled,

A Campaign of Militancy.

A meeting was held at the Steinway Hall, as we have heard, at which it would seem that Mrs. Pankhurst urged militancy. Now I agree with the Attorney-General that too much importance must not necessarily be attached to an epithet of that kind. Our peaceful struggles are generally conducted under the most military phrases. We talk of soldiers, armies, battles, campaigns, officers, camps, routing the enemy, swords, weapons, victory, and all the lot of it—all in the most harmless oratorical manner. I think Mrs. Pankhurst actually alluded to "the Church militant" to show that the word was a harmless oratorical flourish. But it is for you to say whether, under the circumstances as disclosed in this case, the word militant used so often in connection with the methods of the movement was a mere harmless oratorical flourish or whether it was meant or understood to mean a deliberate policy of breaking the law.

Now the action of the Government, of which we have heard so much, the attitude of its individual members, divided as it was, and as the Opposi-

tion was, divided in personal opinion as to the subject of women's franchise—all this really, when you come to reflect upon it, has no bearing
whatever upon the issue which we are now investigating. What Mr. Asquith
said, what Mr. Lloyd George, Mr. Hobhouse, or Sir Edward Carson—these,
I think, are the four names which have been mentioned so often—I believe
that the Attorney-General on some occasions was also mentioned—all this,
has it any bearing upon the nature of the charge which you are investigating?
I understand—I gather from the evidence—that there was a Conciliation
Bill, which was thought to be a mode of compromising between the con-
tending parties—those who wished only a few women, those who wished
all women to have votes—there was some Conciliation Bill by which, by
way of compromise, it was thought larger support might be secured than
by any other form of women's franchise reform, and it was said, so I understand, to have been jeopardised in some measure by the announcement on
November 7, I think it was, of a proposal, by the Prime Minister, to advocate
manhood suffrage, coupled with a promise—so I understand it, to include
women on the same terms as men, if the House of Commons should so
decide. But apparently the chief violence and the wrath of the Association
or Union was heaped upon the head of Mr. Lloyd George, and the only
speech that has been put in in evidence of Mr. Lloyd George is the speech
of an ardent advocate of the Suffrage to women, and I say—I walk diffidently
in these matters—but it seems to me a piece of topsy-turveydom for them
to attack most strenuously the person who is most ardently in favour of
their cause. As I say, I am not gifted with the requisite intelligence to understand it, and, if so, I must be pitied rather than censured. Mrs. Pankhurst
made great play on some refusal of the Prime Minister to receive a deputation in person. I think she forgot that in the earlier stage, before the events
of November 21, it appears that an influential deputation *was* received by
the Prime Minister, and a long account of it appears in the Press—in which
they ask him all the questions they dared to ask.

Mrs. Pankhurst: No, my lord.

The Judge (continuing): And apparently from every quarter. The position
of the Government might be satisfactory or it might be unsatisfactory, but
at any rate it was perfectly clearly indicated and laid down by the Prime
Minister to them, and that before many of the explosions took place. I must
say they seemed to have treated him with more candour than civility, because
I read that Miss Pankhurst said, "Then you can go, and we will get another
head." They were apparently very straightforward in the language they addressed to him. But the argument that the Prime Minister, perhaps the
busiest man in the country, whoever he may be, is bound to be at the beck
and call of anybody, of any woman, apparently, who chooses to force herself
upon him, and that the Constitution demands this from the Prime Minis-

ter—well, all I can say is that it would require none but a very idle man to occupy that distinguished position.

I mention these facts to explain how it is that the speeches and articles, on and after November 17, seem to deal with two main subjects. Firstly, and, secondly, the advocacy of militancy, whatever that may be.

The Iniquities of the Government

Now, come to the evidence. Mrs. Pankhurst apparently left this country at the beginning of September and did not return until January 22. I think that is the first date on which any speech is delivered by her. And the prosecution say that so far as any incitement is concerned in regard to the matters of November 21, no charge is made against her in that regard. That, of course, does not mean any withdrawal concerning the accusation that she did, though she was in America, nevertheless conspire with the other two defendants to incite others to break the law. Now, on November 15, 1911, there appears to be a letter from Mrs. Pethick Lawrence addressed to "Dear Colleague in the Women's Movement," in which she asks for volunteers in a protest "Against this outrage upon the honour of women," and in which she called upon women to join in that protest, and to put aside consideration of health (how was health to be endangered by an innocent, lawful act on the part of anyone?) They were asked to put aside business and private relationship, so that they might be able to strike a blow against the enslavement of half of the nation. They were invited to come for active service, and to send in their names for tabulation in a register. Then there was a meeting at the Albert Hall on November 16 at which Mrs. Pethick Lawrence spoke. (The Judge here quoted from that speech.) That is the way, he said, in which Mrs. Pethick Lawrence urged the meeting to take action, and she called upon women to support them.

Evidence of Conspiracy.

It was at that meeting, and after he had heard that appeal, that Mr. Pethick Lawrence subscribed the handsome sum of £1000. What was that £1000 for? For pamphlets, leaflets, to help the distribution of literature, to hold peaceful public meetings? It was after the expression of those speeches, and, as he says, in consequence of them. Now, on November 17 the deputation waited upon Mr. Asquith, of which I have given you an account, and following upon that, came a leaflet, of which Mrs. Pethick Lawrence was the author dated November 17 (this was quoted by the Judge and had reference to the demonstration of the 21st—he also quoted from a leaflet issued on the 18th by Miss Christabel Pankhurst, which also related to the demonstration of the 21st. In both documents reference was made to militancy). Now, said his lordship, all that is open to the bare construction that the word militant was rhetorical flourish, but it is followed up by some instructions to members of the demonstration, and it is for you to say what is the meaning and what could be meant by this word (the Judge here read the circular of instructions to intending prisoners). This, he said, was followed by another leaflet which bore the name of Mrs. Pethick Lawrence, which gave further instructions to prisoners. What is the inference to be drawn from that, asked his lordship? Did not that show the conspiring together of the defendants to produce disorder, and, in so doing, to ensure that it should be all done at the same moment, and that the volunteers called for from time to time were the volunteers who were to take part in these militant demonstrations? Is that not a natural and reasonable inference to draw from the facts of the case? In pursuance of these arrangements, a meeting was held, as we know, at Caxton Hall, immediately preceding the disorders that took place. There was a procession, headed by Mrs. Pethick Lawrence, and that evening others went to the office of the "Woman's Press," at Charing Cross Road, where they got a bag of stones hung round their waists. Is that all news to Mr. and Mrs. Pethick Lawrence? Have they disavowed it? Have they said that they had no connection with what was done at the "Woman's Press," of which Mr. Pethick Lawrence was the tenant? They have not. Therefore, you must draw the natural and reasonable inference from these facts. What happened that evening? Almost—I do not say exactly—at the same time, but in the course of that evening 219 women were arrested, and 13 women at any rate, we know from evidence supplied to us in this case, did damage to private property to the extent of £225, and 50 of them gave as an address 4, Clement's Inn. And down came Mr. Pethick Lawrence with a list in his hand which he checked, and wherever the person arrested was on the list, Mr. Pethick Lawrence bailed them out. He bailed out 178 of the 219 women. Is it not a reasonable inference that he knew that the outrages were to take place, that he knew who were to be guilty: that they were all women whose names were on the list at the Women's Union office, and that he came for the purpose of doing what the circular said would be done? Or was it a casual visit of Mr. Pethick Lawrence unannounced, unexpected, without any forethought or conspiracy or connection with the acts of the women? Did he only appear as a saviour in the matter of bail? The next issue of *Votes For Women* for which Mr. Pethick Lawrence admits responsibility, of course, had to deal with this matter. Was there expression of regret or disavowal or remonstrance throughout the whole of the paper that appeared on November 24? Not one word, not one syllable. Indeed, the distinguishing feature of the issue was an article headed, "Why We Did It." Did what? Committed these disorders? There you have—I do not say it is conclusive—but there you have the editor, able to put in the paper what he pleases. Here was his co-adjutor, Mrs. Pethick Lawrence. Yet there is not a single word in the paper in remonstrance, but the article by Miss Christabel Pankhurst, "Why We Did It." Then there begins a series of advertisements—I can only characterise them as advertisements—which appear in the paper under the heading, "The Next Protest," which was an appeal for new volunteers for active service. Does not all this point to Mr. and Mrs. Pethick Lawrence conspiring together to cause these outrages, and to incite, by every means in their power, women to do the acts which they did? If you don't think so, of course, you will acquit them. The next event is a meeting at the Savoy Theatre, and the evidence in regard to that, I admit, is somewhat unsatisfactory, and I think it better not to place it before you. But on November 27 there was a meeting at the London Pavilion, and, according to *Votes For Women*, Miss Christabel Pankhurst made a speech, and in that speech she read a message from Mrs. Pethick Lawrence, who was in gaol, saying, "Be ready!" Ready for what? For a repetition? On December 1 there is a remarkable article, written by Miss Christabel Pankhurst, headed, "Broken Windows," in which she says it is part of the effect of militancy (here a definition is given of the word) to excite regret and consternation. It was intended by this militancy to excite regret—not regret on her part—and consternation. Then, on November 30, there was a meeting at the Caxton Hall, at which Mr. Pethick Lawrence made a speech, in which he spoke of the magnificent part played by persons in the protest, and explained the policy of the Union. There is no disavowal or regret for the disorder, but moral approval given to what had taken place. On January 22 there was a meeting at the London Pavilion, and by this time Mrs. Pankhurst had returned from her travels. She returned in a mood certainly not less militant than that she had left in. Speaking at that meeting, and calling for volunteers, she said, "I will be the first stone-thrower." There is no ambiguity of language about that. We have had a sample of Mrs. Pankhurst's eloquence, and you can quite understand the effect of words of that kind on an excited audience. On January 29, Mrs. Pankhurst was again at the London Pavilion, all these halls being hired and paid for by the Women's Social and Political Union. On this occasion she said: "The only mistake that we have made in the past is that we have not been militant enough."—(Apparently breaking windows was not sufficient.)—"We have only to be militant enough and within twenty-four hours we will be victorious."

The Judge next quoted from a speech by Miss Christabel Pankhurst delivered at the London Pavilion on February 25 as follows:

We are going to march forward in a victorious army, and they have not the prisons that will hold us, and they cannot break our spirit. Do not hold back, because everyone that stays outside makes it harder for those who go forward. We can have such a procession to Westminster, and break so many windows, that we shall be able to snap our hands at the police and members of the Government, provided there are enough of us. The date is practically arranged; our plans are practically completed; all we want now is volunteers. We will stagger humanity, and the Government, too, when the day of protest comes, for Mrs. Pankhurst herself will lead the way.

Mr. Pethick Lawrence: You will point out, my lord, that this is part of the evidence of the witness who had to admit—

The Judge: The witness said he did not report the whole speech, but he swore that the words he took down were actually used.

Mrs. Pankhurst: We have never used that bombastic language.

The Judge: If it had been said that these words were qualified by such language as would render them harmless, that would have to have been taken into consideration.

Mr. Pethick Lawrence: May I suggest, my lord, that the credibility of this witness as a reporter was, I think, very strongly shaken by my cross-examination?

The Judge: The jury has heard your cross-examination. It was not a full report of everything that took place, but it was a shorthand note of something that he heard and swore to. If anything had been said which rendered these words meaningless or harmless, no doubt we should have heard of it, but we have not heard that it was qualified, and it has not been suggested that it was qualified.

On the occasion of February 19, at the London Pavilion, Miss Christabel Pankhurst, who was in the chair, said:

If we are thousands, our punishment will be less than if we are hundreds. Send in your names and be ready. . . . It is by fighting, and by fighting alone, that women can get the vote. . . . Send in your names for the next protest.

On February 16 there was a speech which was not opened by the prosecution, but which was alluded to by Sir Edward Busk, one of the witnesses, who was called on behalf of one of the accused. He attended the meeting at which that speech was delivered at the Connaught Rooms, and, speaking to Mrs. Pankhurst, he said: "You said that you applauded the acts of the prisoners; you said you were going to continue the use of the stones; you said you were prepared to use that argument." This witness said the speech recommended others to come forward and throw stones. I understand the movement advocates throwing more stones. This witness thought persons would be influenced by that speech. "I should have decided not to make that speech," he said; "it was a very dangerous form of speech." Then, on February 17, comes a circular from Mrs. Pethick Lawrence, asking sympathisers to volunteer to take part in the militant protest of March 4. And here comes the fixing of the date. It is to be March 4. That circular reached, amongst others, Lilian Ball. Lilian Ball had already, as you will remember, on November 21, gone in response to a circular to Charing Cross Road, and had walked about with a bag of stones upon her person, and had decided not to take any part. On February 19 came a meeting at the Savoy Theatre, and at that meeting Miss Christabel Pankhurst spoke of the great protest of March 4, which was to be the most magnificent protest in which the Union had ever been engaged. On February 26 a meeting took place at the London Pavilion, and at that meeting Mrs. Pethick Lawrence spoke, appealing to the women to join in the coming protest, and stating that if they were numerous enough, and determined enough, they would, within twenty-four hours of the protest, have Cabinet Ministers asking them to confer with them. On February 2 a room had been taken at the Gardenia Restaurant by one of the secretaries of the Society on behalf of the Women's Social and Political Union. On February 20 Mrs. Pankhurst issued a circular regarding the militant protest of March 4, thanking intending demonstrators. So that Mrs. Pankhurst was inviting persons to take part in this militant protest on March 4. Cards for admission to the Gardenia Restaurant seemed to have been issued, and on February 22 and 23, these hammers were bought by the mysterious lady from Mr. Melhuish, in Fetter Lane, some of the hammers being discovered on the persons of the girls or women who broke the windows.

The Events of March.

About February 24, Mrs. Pankhurst wrote a private letter to Dr. Ethel Smyth, which was never sent. It was a private letter, and the only importance of it is that it describes a skirmish that is to take place on March 1, in order, I presume, to make the demonstration on March 4 more overwhelming and unexpected. I presume it would be thought that the Government would surmise that the Union had exhausted its efforts on March 1, and would not be prepared for a repetition on the 4th. In this letter appears this expression: "On Friday there will be an unannounced affair—a sort of skirmish in which some of the bold, bad ones will take part—an unadvertised outbreak. I shall take part in that," and so on. It shows that there was a scheme for March 1. There would be a protest on March 1 as a preliminary skirmish to the general action on the 4th. On March 1, as it has been described, took place an intelligent appreciation of coming events. Mrs. Pankhurst herself breaks windows in Downing Street, and we hear that simultaneously £1,200 worth of damage was done to unoffending private citizens—I do not say all private citizens, because some of those windows might have been those of public offices.

On February 28 Mrs. Pankhurst had issued her instructions to the volunteers who were participating in the March 4 demonstration. This circular was sent to Lilian Ball, amongst others. It stated:

When arrested and taken to Cannon Row and other police stations, you will have, after an interval, to be bailed out, and may then return to your homes or hostesses. In the morning you will surrender at the time mentioned on the charge sheet at the police court, bringing with you a bag packed with everything you are likely to need during your imprisonment.

And on March 1 further instruction was issued. Then there was the letter from Mrs. Cousins to Mrs. Pankhurst:

Thank you very much for your kind letter. We shall certainly send you some representatives —at least six. But in view of the fact that a great deal of local militant work will have to be done at the time of the National Convention, several of our members who cannot face imprisonment twice will have to be reserved for this date.

That is another set of disorders in contemplation by Mrs. Cousins, either in Ireland or here. Now, gentlemen, on March 4 came the disorders which we have had allusion to. I need not go into them, nor the amount of damage that was done, nor into the names of the persons taking part in them. Taking a broad general view, the circumstances leading up to the events of March 4, what is the impression, the conviction in your mind? Were they unconnected, wholly unconnected, with any speech, or action, or incitement on the part of the accused or any of them? Did the accused, or any of them, together conspire and agree that these events should take place?

Gentlemen, throughout this case, the difficulty has been that none of the accused have raised the one defence, the main defence, that in law is open to them. They have not denied the facts alleged and proved; they have not denied that they agreed together to incite these other women to commit the unlawful acts which they did; they have not denied the speeches, and in some instances they have not denied the phrases used in the speeches to which I have drawn your attention; they have not denied the authority of the leaflets and the pamphlets; they have not disavowed these documents which may be said, and which, it was suggested, caused the congregation of these women, caused them all to act at the same moment, at specified and indicated places, so as to produce the greatest public effect; they have not denied the acts that took place; they have not denied the incidents that took place at the Gardenia Restaurant, which I need not detail to you ; they have not denied their responsibility of the illegalities, nor their encouragement, both before and after, of those who committed these acts of malicious damage, or disavowed the acts which were done.

"Responsible Politicians."

Their plea is rather what we lawyers sometimes define as "confession and avoidance." They say: "Oh, yes. Other people—Cabinet Ministers—have also incited to such acts." If it were true, is it a defence? Is it a sound defence to a charge of committing a crime to say there are others who are equally guilty? Is it true? What responsible politician on either side of the House has been proved to have incited, urged, counselled, or procured any of these women to break the windows of peaceful citizens? The question has only to be asked, you know, to be at once answered in your minds. Again, it is said, and eloquently said, they are persons of high character who have done good and useful, and, it may be, self-sacrificing public work in many ways. Nobody is concerned to deny it; the prosecution do not deny it.

Not Motive, But Intention.

It is said that the motive is political and not for private gain. Is, then, a crime not a crime when the motives are not criminal? Gentlemen, the criminal law deals not with motives but with intention. Crimes are not the less offences against the law because their object is political. To assassinate a monarch for the purpose of establishing a republic is a political act, it is none the less a crime. That a crime is committed for political purposes may or may not affect the punishment. It cannot make the act a legal one justified by law. If I intend to rob any man, and do rob him by violence, do I the less commit robbery because I distribute the money among the deserving poor?

The man who is robbed by violence has the right in all civilised countries to appeal to the law for protection, and he may demand that the law shall be obeyed by citizens. Is it, therefore, an answer to the citizen whose property has been intentionally damaged to say that those who did so did the damage not for private gain, but for some ulterior, and it may be innocent, and it may be lawful object? Whether a violent act was done by accident or of set purpose is a question with which a jury is competent to deal, and on the evidence and upon their decision rest the issue as to whether a crime has been committed or not. But whether a violent and illegal act has been committed from this or that or the other motive, is not within the province of the jury to decide. It rests within the breasts of the actors. Love of a child is one of the noblest instances of motherhood; that does not justify the mother in murdering the father—because, he being a drunkard, she thinks it is for the moral welfare of her child that he should die. Such illustrations might be infinitely multiplied. The law relies on the strong, sober, common-sense of juries to distinguish between intentions which govern the act and make it a crime, and the motives which prompt the commission of that crime.

It is finally urged in retaliation of these charges, that they are political, that they seek to redress some grievance, and that in trying to redress them the defendants are to be excused from the law. What your views may be on the vexed question of woman suffrage I know not. It is better so. It is right that we should be mutually ignorant, but our views are equally immaterial in the decision of this case. Whatever they are they should sway neither you nor me, who are here engaged alike upon a supreme and solemn duty—the administration of the law. You are taken up by chance for the moment from the vast body of citizens. You are chosen by the State to be arbiters of fact and to decide according to the evidence laid before you, and to lay aside, in so deciding, all prejudices, all predilections, all partiality, and I am confident by the verdict which you shall pronounce that you will vindicate the trust that is reposed in you.

The Verdict.

The jury retired at twelve minutes past two, and returned to the Court at 3:25 with a verdict of "Guilty" against each of the defendants. In the case of Mrs. Pankhurst, they found that she was guilty on all counts, excluding 3 to 19, which had been withdrawn. In the case of Mr. and Mrs. Lawrence, they found them guilty generally on the indictment.

Foreman of the Jury (addressing his lordship): We unanimously desire to express the hope that, taking into consideration the undoubtedly pure motives that underlie the agitation that has led to this trouble, you will be pleased to exercise the utmost clemency and leniency in dealing with the case.

These remarks were received with applause in the Court.

Mr. Lawrence's Address to the Judge.

Mr. Pethick Lawrence: Before passing sentence, may I be permitted to say a few words? It must have been evident to your lordship, apart from the recommendation of the jury, that we have been actuated by political motives in taking the course that the jury have decided that we have taken, and that we are in fact political offenders. And, as your lordship knows, it has been decided in the Courts of this country that a political crime is different from the ordinary crime.

Mr. Pethick Lawrence then referred to a case in which a Swiss subject was tried for extradition, and it was decided by the court that even if the crime of murder were committed with a political motive it was a political crime. It was decided, he said, that the offence was political, and extradition was not granted. That had not only applied to cases of extradition, but motive had been taken into account in cases of men tried in this country. The late Mr. W. T. Stead[5] was convicted of a crime, but in view of his motive he was made a first-class prisoner, and was allowed his own furniture, his own food, and was permitted to have visits from his wife and children, conduct his correspondence and carry on his business.

In the case of Dr. Jameson[6], although the offence was of a political character, he could have been charged and convicted of an offence of a non-political kind, because twenty-one men were killed and forty-six wounded; yet when he was sent to prison he had in prison treatment similar to that granted to Mr. Stead. It seemed to him that there were certain prisoners who might be punished by simple detention, and not deprivation from having their own food and clothes, their own furniture and books, or from having newspapers and writing materials, and being able to carry on their private business, with visits from their friends and secretaries. He submitted that that intention was embodied in a statute when sedition was made an offence, and he submitted that, in their case, although they had not been charged with sedition, the offence was really similar to sedition. He ventured to submit that it was a fitting occasion for his lordship to use his discretion in giving them first-class treatment after sentence.

Mrs. Pethick Lawrence also addressed the Judge, as follows:

O Liberty, How Glorious Art Thou!
Mrs. Pethick Lawrence's Appeal to the Judge at the Old Bailey, May 22, 1912.

My lord, May I add one word to that of my husband. I endorse what he has said, but it is another point of view which I want to lay before you— the woman's point of view. My husband has mentioned cases where those connected with political agitation and those who have been actuated by pure motives have received imprisonment in the First Division. I want to call to your lordship's memory the cases of men who have been found guilty, and have been sentenced to imprisonment in the First Division. In particular, I want to call the attention of your lordship to the case of a member of the City Council of Bradford, who, on September 30, 1909, was convicted of having been guilty of a criminal assault upon his little servant girl, aged fifteen. The magistrate decided to convict, and said this kind of offence was serious—too serious to be met by a fine, and that the defendant must go to prison for fourteen days in the First Division. I also want to direct your lordship's attention to another case—the case of Colonel Valentine Baker— who was charged and found guilty of having committed a criminal assault upon a lady in a railway train. He was sentenced to one year's imprisonment in the First Division, and his treatment was described in Hansard in this way:—"He has a right to amuse himself, to receive his friends and entertain them, and leave to have what food he pleases; and is subject to no restraint whatever."

My lord, I want to use this case as an illustration of how very widely the point of view differs between men and women. If I were to tell you how women regard this particular crime you might think I was speaking with exaggeration; you might think, even if I spoke quite simply and sincerely, that I was speaking under the stress of emotion. I will only remind your lordship that there are stories in history and literature where women, rather than be the victims of this particular crime of assault, have chosen death. Now, there are in the minds of men some special considerations which enable them to be lenient with cases of this kind, and I venture to suggest that if those two men had been tried by a jury composed entirely of women—if they had been sentenced by a woman judge—then I think they would never have had a fair sentence. I do not think they would have had a fair trial.

My lord, let me put to you the situation. Supposing the daily life of every man was ordered by laws that were made by women! Supposing that when he broke one of those laws he had to come up for judgment before a jury of women and be tried by a woman judge. I think a man in those circumstances would wish to address a word to his judge, and appeal, not for leniency, not for indulgence, but for imagination and for understanding. In this case I appeal to you. I ask you, what will the women of the country think if men who have committed a crime which, from the women's point of view, is so very serious—if these men are treated with imprisonment in the First Division, and a man is to be put into the Second or Third Division who has had an almost quixotic standard of honour to men and the same standard of honour to women, a man who is not even accused directly of destroying private property, a man whose crime is that he has devoted his life, his gifts, his intellectual gifts and his genius for organisation, to the women's cause, a cause which is really primarily and fundamentally an effort to put right those terrible evils and grievances under which women suffer— what will the women of the country feel if we, who are the leaders of a great political movement, are treated as ordinary criminals in the Second or Third Division, while men who committed such outrages as I have quoted are sentenced to the First Division? Do you not think, my lord, that it will leave a permanent sense of outrage in the minds of the women of the country which will be fraught with disastrous results to the community?

Not to Escape Punishment.

We do not seek to escape punishment, though I would point out to you, my lord, that I myself have been twice arrested in regard to these very offences that have come before us in this Court. I was sentenced to two months' imprisonment in November, and on the night of March 4, this year, I was suddenly arrested in my home, was taken suddenly to Bow Street, and had to spend a night in the police station, and was then remanded in prison. And though this charge of which we are accused is misdemeanour—is not a felony—we were kept in prison between three and four weeks, we were kept in prison by a particular device, by being remanded from eight days to eight days. And twice for taking a petition to the House of Commons, for being concerned in an agitation in which no one did any violence to anybody or any destruction to any private property—twice before I have suffered imprisonment.

Mrs. Pankhurst also has suffered imprisonment for these offences with which we are now charged, and as the result of her imprisonment she is still suffering very serious ill-health. It is not prison that we mind, though that is bad enough—bad enough to be shut out from the glory of the sun and the beauty of the earth at a time of the year like this; and to be cut off from one's friends. Think of the separation between husband and wife, my lord, and the separation between parent and child; it is of the very essence of bitterness. But of that we do not complain, for this is part of the price that has to be paid for the emancipation of women. But the question of our status is another matter altogether. The question whether we are to be imprisoned in the First Division with the rights of political prisoners, or whether we are to be imprisoned in the Second or Third Division with, it may be, privileges under conditions, but no rights, that is the serious question to us. I want to explain, because it is a question which touches our honour; and not only our honour, but also the honour of this great movement of which we are representatives, and we must maintain our honour with the last breath in our body. Men and women have suffered in their attempts to maintain their honour in this particular connection. We have heard in this Court how one man has been driven to the verge of insanity; one woman is in a nursing home to-day at the very point of death, and another is very dangerously ill as the result of the treatment which she has received in prison.

Justice.

I do appeal to you, my lord, to restore to women something of our old faith in the justice of men; something of our belief in the spirit of fair play which actuates men in their dealings with women. I do ask you to allay, as far as it is in your power to do so, the bitterness of this struggle. I ask you, whatever sentence you may give us, to give us a sentence of imprisonment in the First Division. I will put it to you in a different way. This movement cannot be crushed by severity. Experience has shown that, and history has shown it. There have been over a thousand imprisonments of women already. We sometimes speak of the dogged tenacity of the men who have conquered land and sea for our country's glory. There is an undaunted spirit in the mothers of the race also, or it would not be made manifest in the land; there is a bit of the bull-dog breed in the women of our country as well as in the men. We have been bruised and battered by Government spleen; we have been pursued by the Government's prosecution. But the spirit of liberty has grown apace, and the women of the country will hold on to the idea of liberty like grim death. I use these words advisedly—Grim death! We shall win in the end; though we ourselves may be crushed, because we all know how very narrow are the limits of human vitality and human strength. One by one the women have died. One by one they have fallen out of the ranks. But the cause has gone on.

We feel liberty to be a very precious thing. "O, Liberty, how glorious art thou!" We know it has to be bought with a great price.

My lord, if you send us to prison, we shall go to prison with a firm and steadfast faith that our imprisonment, whether it be long or whether it be short, will be accepted as part of the great price that has to be exacted for the civic and legal liberty of women, which is the safeguard of the moral and spiritual liberty of the women of our country and of our race. May God defend us, as our cause is just!

[Following Mrs. Pethick-Lawrence's speech, Mrs. Pankhurst spoke:]

Mrs. Pankhurst.

Mrs. Pankhurst: My lord, I have nothing to say except to endorse what my friends have said. I have thought so little of what penalty you could impose upon us that I do not know whether you can in your judgment send us to prison for seven years or even longer. But I do say this deliberately, that I would rather stay in prison for seven years with the status of political offender, free from the taint of crime of the ordinary kind, than I would spend seven days as a prisoner in the second or third division, associated in the public mind and made to feel myself the indignity of being classed with those who break the law with criminal intention. And, my lord, I want to say as I said yesterday that I believe the honour of our country is involved in your decision, because there is no civilised country in the world which does not recognise a different status of political offenders—persons who break the law with political motives. There is no other civilised country in the world which does not recognise that, and I say we have departed from the standard that prevailed in the days when men like William Cobbett[7] were convicted for incitement and sent to prison with every consideration for the reality and sincerity of the motives that underlay the committal of the crime.

The Sentence.

The Judge, in passing sentence, said: Frederick Pethick Lawrence, Emmeline Pethick Lawrence, and Emmeline Pankhurst, you have been convicted of a crime for which the law would sanction, if I chose to impose it, a sentence of two years' imprisonment, with hard labour. There are circumstances connected with your case which the jury have very properly brought to my attention, and I have been asked by you all three to treat you as first-class misdemeanants. If in the course of this case I had observed any contrition or disavowal of the acts that you have committed, or any hope that you would avoid the repetition of them in future, I should have been very much prevailed upon by the arguments that have been addressed to me. But as you say openly you mean to continue to break the law, to make you first-class misdemeanants would only be to put into your hands further capacities for executing that purpose.

The sentence of the Court upon each of you is that you be imprisoned for nine months in the second division, and as the Crown has been placed to great expense and private citizens have been badly damaged in their property by your acts, as to Frederick Pethick Lawrence, and as to Emmeline Pankhurst, I made a further order that you pay the costs jointly and severally of the prosecution in the case.

The jury were exempted from further service for five years.

Part VII
Martyrs to the Cause

IN REFERRING TO WSPU MARTYRS TO THE SUFFRAGE CAUSE, I AM TAKING a very broad view of martyrdom. Two Union members sacrificed their fortune and their position in the WSPU for the cause of suffrage, many suffragettes sacrificed their previous conception of themselves in order to take violent action, and one woman made the ultimate sacrifice of her life.

Despite their sentencing to the second division at the close of the conspiracy trial, the Union leaders were soon moved to the first division. They went on hunger strike with the rank and file members (who were in prison for window breaking) until such time that all would be granted the privileges accorded to political prisoners. Forcible feeding of all the prisoners began on June 22, 1912. Emmeline Pethick-Lawrence was forcibly fed one time.[1] However, when the doctors and wardresses reached Emmeline Pankhurst's cell, they were met by Pankhurst who brandished an earthenware ewer, a sight that inspired a hasty retreat. Any other prisoner would have been overcome by numbers, physically restrained, and forcibly fed. It is a measure of Pankhurst's charisma and the natural respect she seemed to inspire in others that she was never forcibly fed, despite her numerous imprisonments and hunger strikes. The Pethick-Lawrences and Emmeline Pankhurst were soon released; a short time later all the suffrage prisoners were free.[2]

Christabel Pankhurst called for a strategy meeting in Boulogne with her mother and the Pethick-Lawrences. It was there that the Pankhursts outlined an expansion of reformist terrorism that would involve wholesale attacks on public and private property. Rather than conducting massive but symbolic attacks on private property (such as the window breaking of the recent past) and allowing themselves to be arrested, WSPU members would operate in the "guerrilla" fashion. They would strike secretly and avoid capture if at all possible. The Pethick-Lawrences strongly disagreed with this plan, ascertaining that it would cost the movement its expanding public support. Instead, they counseled that Christabel should return to London. If arrested, hers would be a show trial; if not, she would draw large crowds when speaking at public meetings. Thus, in what "resembled a family quarrel," the leadership came to the most important juncture in WSPU strategy.[3]

The Boulogne meeting ended amicably with an agreement to wait until later to decide the future. A great welcome for the leaders was planned for October in the Albert Hall. Because Emmeline Pankhurst wished to stay in Paris to recuperate from her stay in prison and consult with her daughter, the Pethick-Lawrences graciously accepted her promptings to visit a relative in Canada. According to the plan agreed upon by all, this delay in returning to London would allow the three leaders to return to public life together.[4] When the Pethick-Lawrences returned to London following their trip to Canada, they were met by a friend with advance warning that they were to be turned out of the Union. At first, the Pethick-Lawrences were unable to believe that Emmeline Pankhurst would take such action or that Christabel would support her in it. Meetings with both women confirmed their desire to sever all connections with the Pethick-Lawrences. Christabel made clear that the Pethick-Lawrences could continue editing *Votes For Women*, but that the WSPU would begin its own official newspaper, *The Suffragette*. The Pethick-Lawrences could appear at the Albert Hall meeting, she went on, but if they did, no Union official would join them on the platform.[5]

The response of Emmeline and Frederick Pethick-Lawrence was remarkable in its unselfishness and restraint. Not only were they being shuffled aside by a Union to which they had dedicated their lives, but they were also in the process of losing their fortune in the same cause. While in Canada, they had learned that their house had been seized to pay the costs of the Conspiracy Trial. A further £800 was owed and a suit by London shopkeepers increased the debt by £2000 more. Frederick Pethick-Lawrence refused to pay on principle. He was bankrupted to meet the debt; and, in a spectacularly tasteless move, the Reform Club expelled him as a member.[6] Yet, at this low point, the Pethick-Lawrences were primarily concerned for the health of the suffrage cause. Therefore, they signed the following statement that appeared in *Votes For Women:*

Grave Statement By the Leaders
    At the first re-union of the leaders after the enforced holiday, Mrs. Pankhurst and Miss Christabel Pankhurst outlined a new militant policy which Mr. and Mrs. Pethick-Lawrence found themselves altogether unable to approve.

    Mrs. Pankhurst and Miss Christabel Pankhurst indicated that they were not prepared to modify their intentions, and recommended that Mr. and Mrs. Pethick-Lawrence should resume control of the paper, *Votes For Women,* and should leave the Women's Social and Political Union.

    Rather than make schism in the ranks of the Union, Mr. and Mrs. Pethick-Lawrence consented to take this course.

    In these circumstances, Mr. and Mrs. Pethick-Lawrence will not be present at the meeting at the Royal Albert Hall on October 17th.
    [signed]

Emmeline Pankhurst   Christabel Pankhurst
Emmeline Pethick-Lawrence   Frederick Pethick-Lawrence[7]

Although Roger Fulford was correct when he said of the Pethick-Lawrences, "Such magnanimity is rare in the history of British political organizations,"[8] historians have tended to heap praise on the Pethick-Lawrences (and Teresa Billington-Grieg and Mrs. Despard before them) in order to further criticize the Pankhursts. The Pankhursts are portrayed as irrationally "steering a headlong course," saved from disaster only by the good sense of "those whom they hurled overboard."[9] Yet the demand for unanimity of policy in the leadership was consistent with the Union's intended function as a suffrage "army," capable of quick action and coordinated effort. Although discussing and voting on every decision in a perfect model of democracy may fit most scholars' image of the appropriate procedure for a women's reform group, it was perhaps less conducive to the type of militant action the WSPU gradually adopted. The epithet most often leveled against Emmeline and Christabel Pankhurst is that of "autocrat," but, if this was their failing, it is one shared by most reform movement leaders. Sandra Holton was much closer to the truth when she claimed that, in a movement so firmly based in morality, "compromise and consensus were simply not compatible with authenticity." A "parting of the ways," according to the Pankhursts' views, was not a personal rejection but a means of allowing "each viewpoint [to] be pursued single-mindedly."[10]

The meeting at the Albert Hall went forward on October 17 with Emmeline Pankhurst in the chair. Word was out that morning about the split in the leadership and the membership was in some disarray. In such a situation a masterful speech was necessary, and Pankhurst obliged. She continued the image of a suffrage army and used the metaphor to justify the separation from the Pethick-Lawrences. She placed culpability for damage to private property firmly in the lap of the government, because it was responsible for not righting the wrongs done to English women and children. She continued the claim that suffrage women were simply responding in kind to earlier government attacks. Pankhurst made this point with a wonderful simile, saying that antisuffrage criticism of militancy was "very like beasts of prey reproaching the gentler animals who turn in desperate resistance when at the point of death." Pankhurst here exercised her ability to tap into variations on acceptable images of women, for the mother-animal-protecting-her-young was the one traditional image that granted women a right to use violence. She urged women to match the violence against property of male Chartists of the 1830s and offered a menu of ways that Union members could participate in the new policy. Finally, Pankhurst's speech builds in excitement, capped by her ringing, "I incite this meeting to rebellion." She displayed her own personal resolve by declaring that, as long as the Ulster leaders (who had incited to violence to resist Irish nationalism) were still at large, she would not allow herself to remain in prison. Even relatives of the Pethick-Lawrences and those who disagreed with the policy of increased militancy reported feeling themselves "falling under her sway."[11]

The second speech to be presented in this section is a spiritual interpretation by Emmeline Pethick-Lawrence of the physical violence beginning to take place. Here, she pictures the suffrage workers as agents of the Divine Will, and even describes their opponents, the "men of malignant purpose," as unwitting tools through whom God would shape history. It is of particular interest that the woman who opposed increased militancy could be such an eloquent apologist for its use.

On January 24, 1913, debate spread in Parliament on the Franchise Reform Bill, the Reform Bill on Manhood Suffrage that "torpedoed" the second conciliation bill. This bill actually offered women's suffrage as one of a number of amendments to the bill. The Union leaders had called a brief truce, not because they had any faith in government action, but because they did not want any failure to be blamed on militancy. Cynicism was rife in the Union, and "how the government would manage to wriggle out of their promise was a matter of excited speculation."[12] The demise of the bill came because of a surprise ruling by the Speaker of the House of Commons that, should the woman suffrage amendment be passed, the bill would be so altered that it would have to be withdrawn.[13] The Cabinet voted to withdraw the whole bill. Asquith may have been surprised by the Speaker's action but he was certainly not displeased, writing to a friend, "The Speaker's *coup d'etat* has bowled over the Women for this session—a great relief."[14]

Now came reformist terrorism on a greatly expanded scale and an increase of the secret arson campaign. Individual acts of arson had been conducted previously by Union members. Emily Wilding Davison had set light to three pillar boxes as early as December, 1911, and Nurse Ellen Pitfield, aware that she was dying of cancer, set fire to a basket of wood shavings in a post office in March 1912. These acts were purely individual efforts and were not authorized by the Union leadership. The first serious attempts at arson by the Union had been conducted in the summer of 1912, but following the withdrawal of the Franchise Reform Bill, arson became a consistent tool of the WSPU.[15] A few of the militant acts were irritations more than anything else. Golf greens were scraped with slogans, house numbers were painted over, cushions in railroad carriages were slashed, and envelopes loaded with red pepper and snuff were sent (successfully, it was said) to Cabinet Members.[16] However, many of the terrorist acts of the Union were very serious:

> Boathouses and sports pavilions in England, Ireland, and Scotland, and a grandstand at Ayr race-course were burnt down . . . Thirteen pictures were hacked in

the Manchester Art Gallery . . . Empty houses and other unattended buildings were systematically sought out and set on fire, and many were destroyed . . . Bombs were placed near the Bank of England, at Wheatly Hall, Doncaster, at Oxted Station, and on the steps of a Dublin Insurance office.[17]

As the violent militancy campaign continued, individual events, large and small, would stand out among the ongoing events of arson and bombing of summer homes and isolated railway stations. One of the jewel cases at the Tower of London was smashed; telegraph lines were destroyed, severing the connection between London and Glasgow; windows were broken in the Kew Garden Orchid House, resulting in the destruction of orchids that had taken ten years to cultivate; and the Rokeby Venus was slashed by Mary Richardson.[18] On February 19, 1913, the militants completed one of their most famous actions by bombing Lloyd-George's unfinished house in the Surrey countryside.[19] Reportedly, the bomber was Emily Wilding Davison, who escaped while leaving suffrage literature behind her. Emmeline Pankhurst immediately claimed responsibility for the action, telling a public meeting in Cardiff, "We have blown up the Chancellor's house!"[20]

Although their actions were strictly voluntary, perhaps the greatest martyrs to the suffrage cause were the Union members who had to carry out the new militant policy. Certainly, the suffragettes had already suffered through the rigors of arrest and forcible feeding, but the psychological strain of defying convention and committing actual crimes (albeit for a good cause) must have been overwhelming. Several of the autobiographies of the suffrage militants reveal not only the excitement and "gamelike" atmosphere of surreptitious acts of violence but also the stress and despair involved.[21] Brian Harrison has addressed this element of stress, first reminding the modern reader of the greater courage (physical and moral) required for an Edwardian woman to commit acts of violent militancy:

> The fear of looking foolish, the danger of arrest, and the threat of physical assault were the least of it; far more daunting was the fear of letting down much-loved suffragette leaders and colleagues, and the torture involved in upsetting uncomprehending parents and incredulous relatives. Worst of all was the internal battle involved, steeling oneself to break with upbringing and convention for the cause.[22]

In the third speech in this section ("The Women's Insurrection"), Emmeline Pankhurst lauded the courage and restraint of the Union members who carried out the militant policy. She compared the "women's revolution" to the Mexican Revolution and Irish agitation, and made the claim that "no great reform has ever been won, or ever will be won . . . by constitutional means." Yet, even in their turn to violence, Pankhurst claimed that women were superior in their methods and had avoided the bloodshed that marked men's attempts to gain liberty. Men, according to Pankhurst, had neglected to end the moral cancer of prostitution and the White Slave Traffic, and an all-male Parliament elected by men was unlikely to do so. "Is it not," Pankhurst asked her audience, "very like asking the wolf to protect the lamb?"

The personal martyrdom of the Pethick-Lawrences or the average militant for the cause would soon be overshadowed by a memorable and still controversial event. On May 5 and 6, 1913, a private member's bill on women's suffrage had its second reading and, to no surprise of the suffrage forces, was defeated by 266 votes to 219. Conservatives had claimed the measure too broad; other prosuffrage Parliamentarians feared the dissolution of Parliament by Asquith if it passed.[23] As it turned out, this effort in May 1913 would be the last full debate on the franchise of women in the House of Commons.

A still more dramatic event in the history of the suffrage movement took place on June 4, 1913. During the Derby at Epsom Downs, as the horses rounded Tattenham corner, Emily Wilding Davison ran onto the track and grabbed for the bridle of Anmer, the King's horse. Struck by the horse's hooves, Davison somersaulted through the air. Her skull fractured, she died on June 8 without regaining consciousness. Davison had always been an initiator of new acts of militancy: she was first to firebomb a letter box and she was the reputed bomber of Lloyd-George's country house. Until recently it was generally accepted that Davison had committed suicide, a theory supported by her words earlier in the movement that only one great tragedy, one great sacrifice, would end "the intolerable torture of women."[24] However, in 1988 (the seventy-fifth anniversary of Davison's death), two books appeared that came to much the same conclusions in challenging the suicide theory. Before her journey to the race, Davison had gone to WSPU headquarters and requested two of the Union flags of purple, white, and green. When she darted onto the Derby track, she carried one flag rolled up and disguised in her hand and had one pinned inside the back of her coat. Frame by frame analysis of the newsreel of the event shows that she avoided a large group of horses and headed directly to the King's horse, reaching for his bridle. The new interpretation (and one with which I strongly concur) is that Davison wished to take her symbolic petition directly to the King by stopping the horse and possibly pinning the suffrage colors to his bridle. John Sleight considers Davison naive to think that she could stop a racehorse in full gallop; Liz Stanley and Ann Morley believe that Davison knew and accepted the risk of death or injury but was not deliberately seeking either. Evidence found on Davison at her death (her helper's card for the WSPU festival the following day, the return ticket to Victoria station) seems to point to a woman who hoped and expected to continue her life the next day.[25] Whatever the final verdict on Davison's death, her funeral was the last grand procession of the suffragettes through the streets of London. Spectators deeply lined the streets to watch women dressed in white, black, or purple—carrying laurel wreathes, purple irises, or crimson peonies respectively—as they marched with the funeral cortege.[26] Presented here is a speech in memory of Emily Wilding Davison given by the Reverend Gertrude Von Petzold on June 16, 1913. In this sermon, the Rev. Petzold equates Davison with Christ in her willingness to die for the poor and outcast and even for the "sinners" (the press, the government, or the unheeding public) against the suffrage cause.

14

Great Meeting in the Albert Hall

Mrs. Pankhurst Defies the Government.

Mrs. PANKHURST (WHO ON RISING WAS RECEIVED WITH LOUD CHEER-
ing), said:

From all over the world come messages to this great meeting. Of these
messages I have selected two representing the rest which I think of special
importance at this particular moment. The first comes from the seat of war
in the East to the seat of war in England—to this meeting. It is from our
friend, Mr. Nevinson—(applause)—and I think when he wrote it he had
not only in mind the events of which he was a witness, but he had in mind
the situation at home and the enemy with whom many have to deal in this
war of ours. He says: "My thoughts are with your meeting. Forward against
all Turks." (Laughter and applause.)

The second message to this meeting comes from Paris—from Christabel
Pankhurst, who would be here did she not feel it her duty to be where she
is. She says: "We must fight as never before, and give no quarter to the
enemy." (Applause.)

It is my duty from the chair to move the following resolution:

"That this meeting pledges itself to continue the militant agitation for
Women Suffrage, and declares relentless opposition towards the Government and its allies until they abandon their anti-Suffrage policy and introduce
a Government measure for the political enfranchisement of women."

Unity of Purpose.

Whenever I stand upon this platform in the Albert Hall I can never feel
that I am speaking to an ordinary political meeting. It seems to me rather
that I am assisting at a review, and tonight I feel more than ever that we are
reviewing our forces. We are considering and measuring our strength, we
are seeing where we stand, considering the force of the opposing army,
deciding how our campaign is to be pursued. One thing is essential to an
army, and that thing is made up of a two-fold requirement. In an army you

need unity of purpose. In an army you also need unity of policy. In the Women's Social and Political Union, from its initiation until quite recently, we have had complete unity of purpose, and we have had complete unity of policy. That unity of purpose is still the same. I can not continue my speech without referring to a statement which has been published by the agreement of all parties concerned, in two Suffrage papers to-day—in "Votes for Women," which is so well known to you all, and in the new infant of the Women's Social and Political Union, which henceforth will be its official organ, "The Suffragette." (Applause.) That statement is signed by four persons—by Mr. and Mrs. Pethick Lawrence, by my daughter and myself. When unity of policy is no longer there, then I say to-night, as I have always said, a movement is weakened—(hear, hear)—and so it is better that those who cannot agree, who cannot see eye to eye as to policy should set themselves free, should part, and should be free to continue their policy, as they see it, in their own way, unfettered by those with whom they can no longer agree. I give place to none in appreciation and gratitude to Mr. and Mrs. Pethick Lawrence—(loud applause)—for the incalculable services that they have rendered to the militant movement for Woman Suffrage, and firmly believe that the women's movement will be strengthened by their being free to work for Woman Suffrage in the future as they think best, while we of the Women's Social and Political Union shall continue the militant agitation for Woman Suffrage initiated by my daughter and myself and a handful of women more than six years ago.

Now for the resolution. In that resolution we declare that we mean to continue the militant agitation for Woman Suffrage, and that we offer uncompromising opposition to the Government and its allies. We have to deal not merely with a Government composed of members of one party, we have in this country a Coalition Government. That Government is kept in office by the coalition of three parties. You have the Liberal Party, which is nominally the governing party, but they could not live another day if it were not for their coalition with the Nationalist Party and the Labour Party. And so we say, not only to the Liberal Party, but we say also to the Nationalist Party and to the Labour Party, "So long as you keep in office an Anti-Suffrage Government you are parties to their guilt, and from henceforth we offer to you the same opposition which we give to the people who are kept in power by your support." We have summoned the Labour Party to do their duty to their own programme and to go into opposition to the Government on every question until the Government do justice to women. (Hear, hear.) They apparently are not prepared to do this. Some of them tell us other things are more important than the liberty of women—(cries of "Shame!")—than the liberty of working women. We say, "Then, gentlemen, we must teach you the value of your own principles, and until you are prepared to stand for the right of women to decide their lives and the laws under which they shall live, you, with Mr. Asquith and Co., are equally responsible for all that has happened and is happening to women in this country in their struggle for emancipation." (Loud applause.)

Property to be Attacked.

What do we mean when we say we are going to continue the militant agitation for Woman Suffrage? There is a great deal of criticism, ladies and gentlemen, of this movement. We have critics whose intentions we have every reason to suspect when they criticise us. It always seems to me, when the Anti-Suffrage members of the Government criticise militancy in women, that it is very like beasts of prey reproaching the gentler animals who turn in desperate resistance when at the point of death. It seems to me that gentlemen who do not hesitate to turn out armies to kill and slay their opponents, who do not hesitate to encourage party mobs to attack defence-less women in public meetings (loud cries of "Shame!") when we get criticism from them, their criticism scarcely rings true. But we have friendly critics. I get letters from people who tell me they are ardent Suffragists, but who say they do not like the recent developments of the militant movement, and who implore me to urge the members of our Union not to be reckless with regard to human life. (A voice, "White slavery.") Ladies and gentlemen, the only recklessness the militant Suffragists have shown about human life has been of their own lives, not of the lives of others; and I say here and now that it has never been, and it never will be the policy of the Women's Social and Political Union to recklessly endanger human life. We leave that to men in their warfare. (A Voice, "Lloyd George" and hisses) It is not the method of women. No; even from the point of view of policy, militancy affecting the security of human life would be out of place. There is something that Governments care for far more than they care for human life, and that is the security of property. Property to them is far dearer and tenderer than is human life, and so it is through property we shall strike the enemy. I have no quarrel with property, ladies and gentlemen, and it is only as an instrument of warfare in this revolution of ours that we make attacks upon property. I think there are a great many people who own property who understand it very well, but if they would only understand it a little more quickly they would do what we want them to do. We want them to go to the Government and say, "Examine the causes that lead to destruction of property. Remove the discontent (hear, hear) remove the sense of outrage; remove the outlawry; then women, who always have been law-abiding—although they have no voice in making these laws—will return to what they formerly were, the most law-abiding members of the community." (Hear, hear.) But I say, from henceforward the women who agree with me will say, "We disregard your laws, gentlemen, we set the liberty and the dignity of women and the welfare of women above all such considerations, and we shall continue that war as we have done in the past, and what sacrifice of property, what injury to property occurs will not be our fault. It will be the fault of that Government which admits the justice of our demands, but refuses to concede them without the evidence—so they have told us—without the evidence afforded to Governments of the past that those who ask for liberty were in earnest in their demands.

Why We Are Militant.

Now, why are we militant? There are women in this hall who still think it right to be patient, who still think they can afford to wait until there is time to deal with the enfranchisement of women. I tell you, women, in this hall that you who feel like that, you who allow yourselves to be tricked by the excuses of politicians, have not yet awakened to a realisation of the situation. The day after the outrages in Wales I met some of the women who had exposed themselves to the indecent assaults of that mob. ("Shame!") I say "indecent" advisedly, because in addition to the facts reported in the newspapers—facts verified by photographs—in spite of the contradictions of Mr. Lloyd George, in addition to what found its place in the newspapers, those women suffered from assaults of a kind which it was impossible to print in a decent newspapers. There was one woman whom I saw the day after, a woman with grown up children, the mother of a son twenty-five years of age. She described to me the way in which she had been assaulted. She said she did not feel she could even tell her husband or her son the nature of the assault, and then I said to her, "How could you bear it! It seems to me that is the hardest thing of all to bear." And she said, "All the time I thought of the women who day by day, and year by year, are suffering through the White Slave Traffic—("Shame!")—and I said to myself, "I will bear this, and even worse than this, to help to win power to put an end to that abominable slavery." (Loud applause) In our speeches on Woman Suffrage, we have not dwelt very much on that horrible aspect of women's lives, because some of us felt that to think of those things, to speak very much about them, was apt to cause a state of feeling which would make it impossible for us to carry on our work with cheerful hearts, and with courage and with hope; but it seems to me that recent developments—legal developments—with regard to that question have made it essential that we should use that question to rouse women to a realisation of the simple fact that until women have the Vote, the White Slave Traffic will continue all over the world. Until by law we can establish an equal moral code for men and women, women will be fair game for the vicious section of the population inside Parliament as well as outside it.

Women will be fair game for the worst section of the population, inside Parliament as well as outside. People will tell you that in order that you may live happy and protected lives it is necessary. (Cries of "Never!") That is a lie. But even were it the horrible truth, there are other things we women have to deal with. Even if we tolerated the degradation of the grown women, can we tolerate the degradation of the helpless little children? When I began this militant campaign—("Bravo!")—in the early days of the movement, I was a Poor Law Guardian, and it was my duty to go through the workhouse infirmary, and never shall I forget seeing a little girl of thirteen lying in bed, playing with a doll, and when I asked what was her illness I was told that she was on the eve of becoming a mother, and she was infected with a loathsome disease, and on the point of bringing, no doubt, a diseased child into the world. Wasn't that enough? (Cries of "Yes!") A little later, in a by-election campaign against the Government candidate in Leeds I had occasion to visit a Salvation Army hotel in that city, and in the matron's room there was a little child eleven years of age. She didn't look older than eight, and I said: "How was it she was there? Why wasn't she playing with other children?" And they said to me: "We dare not let her play with other children. She has been on the streets for more than a year." These, women in this meeting, are facts. These are not sensational stories taken from books written to attract the attention of those who like to think about matters that we have been accustomed to believe ought not to be spoken about. These I vouch for from my own experience, and they are but specimens and examples of a horrible state of things which flourishes in every so-called civilised centre of Europe and of the whole world.

A Great Mission.

Now, I say to the men in this meeting, can you put an end to this horrible degradation of the race without our help? It is you who are responsible for the present state of things. You have inherited it. It is not the men of to-day who are directly responsible, but you are responsible so long as you refuse to women the right to help you to deal with evils which you are admittedly unable to cope with by yourselves. We women Suffragists have a great mission, the greatest mission the world has ever known. It is to free half the human race, and through that freedom to save the race. You, women in this meeting, will you help us to do it? ("Yes!") Well, then, if you will, put aside all craven fear. Go and buy your hammer; be militant. Be militant in your own way. Those of you who can express your militancy by going to the House of Commons and refusing to leave without satisfaction, as we did in the early days—do so. Those of you who can express their militancy by facing party mobs at Cabinet Ministers' meetings, and remind them of their unfaithfulness to principle—do so. Those of you who can express your militancy by joining us in anti-Government by-election policy—do so. Those of you who can break windows—(great applause)—those of you who can still further attack the sacred idol of property so as to make the Government realise that property is as greatly endangered by women as it was by the Chartists of old days—do so.

And my last word is to the Government. I incite this meeting to rebellion. (Tremendous applause and great enthusiasm.) You have not dared to take the leaders of Ulster for their incitement. Take me if you dare! ("Bravo!") But if you dare, I tell you this, that so long as those who incite to armed rebellion and the destruction of human life in Ulster are at liberty you will not keep me in prison. (Great applause.) You will not keep militant Suffragists in prison any more than you kept Mrs. Leigh and Miss Evans. As long as men rebels and voters are at liberty we will not remain in prison, first division or no first division!

Women in this meeting! Although the vote is not yet won, we who are militant are free; our souls are free, and you who have free souls forget all about the body. Remember only the freedom of the spirit, and join in this magnificent rebellion of women in the twentieth century.

15

The Rune of Birth and Renewal.
By Mrs. Pethick Lawrence

(A speech delivered in the Wharncliffe Rooms, December 17, 1912.)

WE WHO ARE GATHERED HERE DO NOT MEET AS HUMAN ATOMS BLOWN together by a little wind of chance. Neither do we meet merely as personal friends.

A life force has taken hold of us and has welded us with all our different individualities into one, just as the tones and overtones in a musical scale are welded into one in some chord, or as words are welded in a line or a verse of a song.

We and many others who are present in our thoughts and whom we represent—we individually and collectively have been caught in the meshes of a Will that we may be used in the accomplishment of its purpose. By the decree of this Will, the time has come for a new birth of humanity, the hour has struck for the redemption of Woman from her age-long servitude, into the liberty of full human equality with Man, that she may fulfil with him the joint sacrifice and service that they owe to the human race.

In common we have seen this Vision that has changed our entire outlook upon the world. In common we have been subjugated by this Idea that has altered the trend and habit of our life. In common we have felt the compulsion of this Law that has brought us into association together and has made us part of a living pattern, woven by destiny in the loom of Time, to a rhythm and rune which is making the world's story. Moreover, we share a common wealth of deep experience. Most of us have, as a result of bearing witness to the faith that is in us, been through the ordeal of isolation or ridicule. We have been made to feel at one time or another, aliens in the world of everyday human life. Most of us have endured physical insult and violence. We have suffered assault and ignominy. Some of us have thrown aside position and place in the world and have sacrificed livelihood or career. Many amongst us are wearing, as I am, the prison badge with its broken chain. We are those who have been arrested; and in prison have taken our place at the very bottom of the human scale, side by side with the shamed and the outcast. We have tested our conviction in the living sepulchre of the prison cell. In order to keep the sword of our faith we have hungered to the point of exhaustion and have endured the final attempt to break down the will by the infliction of forcible feeding.

Yes, we have tasted, each in our own measure and degree, the bitter cup, and have found it sweet. In weakness we have discovered our strength, in loss we have found gain, in isolation we have realised our inviolate union with all sentient life, and in extremity we have seen the face of death trans-figured for evermore. And this is our common revelation and our common inheritance.

We then, who saw in this Woman's Movement the promise of awakening and regeneration for the world, have, in giving ourselves up to become the channels of it, become ourselves awakened to a new fulness of life, have become ourselves regenerated.

Thus in the little circle of our own experience we have seen how the law that guides this Movement operates, we have seen how the bitterest foes have been used as the unconscious agents of deliverance, and how men of malignant purpose have been turned into blind tools for the shaping of history. In overcoming the obstacles that have been placed by enemies in its path, the Idea for which we stand has dominated the human consciousness of the world.

As it is in the small circle of our own experience so it is and must be in the ever extending spheres of the operation of this Movement. In all coun-tries men and women will become its willing agents or its blind tools. It will meet with hatred, opposition, and betrayal. But in the eternal rune that is the story of the world it is by the very enemy and the betrayer that the law is accomplished and destiny fulfilled. One thing is absolutely certain. And that is the triumph of the Idea and its established victory in the evolution of the human life.

The word has gone forth. The rune of the awakening of the Soul of Womanhood has begun and will not end until in the visible world the strong-holds of ignorance and materialism have been shaken to their foundations and overthrown, to give place to the new kingdom of the spirit which is to be established upon the earth.

We must look for destruction. The smashing of glass in West London last March was a symbol of deep significance. It was the breaking through of reality into a dream. It was the rending of the tomb by the bursting forth of the living spirit that had been imprisoned there. Our thoughts were of the resurrection, but the world saw only evidence of violence in the barriers broken down and the grave clothes tossed away. For the world does not see the risen spirit, yet is in mortal terror at the thought of it. It wants no new birth. It cares supremely for the stability of its old institutions which are menaced by new life. The world is right from its own self-interested point of view. Its fears are well grounded.

We must be prepared for the breaking up of the material substance of life before the spiritual force that is in this Movement. When the rune of destiny is being chanted the walls of palaces totter and the stones of the temples fall. We who have given ourselves up as willing agents of the Will that is behind the rune have to smash and be smashed. We must be ready both to break up and destroy material substance of things and also to acquiesce in the breaking up of the material substance of our own lives and even of our own bodies.

To play the game, while conscious that the game is being played through us! That is the essence of our militancy. We live by faith, we serve by action. Militancy itself has become a living and a quickening force. None of us will ever know the countless multitude of men and women who have become alive to their own nobility through the glorious spirit that has been liberated in the world during the seven years of this Militant Movement for the Emancipation of Woman.

What this militant spirit means to humanity, and especially at this crisis to womanhood, was told in a wonderful parable a few days ago in *Votes For Women*. Nothing as beautiful or so true has been said of our Movement, as is said in that parable and the introductory comment upon it. The story tells how the transforming Spirit of Illumination has visited the ardent expectant soul, has been made one with it, leaving behind as his gift the transfiguring sword. And the soul awed and exultant sings:

"From now there shall be no fear left for me in this world and thou shalt be victorious in all my strife. Thou hast left death for my companion and I shall crown him with my life. The sword is with me to cut asunder my bonds, and there shall be no fear left for me in the world."

16

The Women's Insurrection.

Verbatim Report of Mrs. Pankhurst's Last Speech before her Arrest.
Given at the Town Hall, Chelsea, on Friday, February 21.

I AM VERY GLAD TO HAVE THIS ONE MORE OPPORTUNITY OF EXPLAINING to an audience in London the meaning of the women's revolution, because it is as much a revolution which is going on in Great Britain as is that series of events taking place in Mexico—a revolution. We here in Chelsea are too far away from Mexico to be able to judge of the merits of the case over there, but one thing we do know, and it is this: that rightly or wrongly a large proportion of the population of Mexico have come to the conclusion that life under the form of government there was intolerable for them, and therefore they have done what men in all the history of the world have thought themselves justified in doing; they have revolted against their government, and they have adopted the usual methods employed by men. They have taken to methods of insurrection.

Now when the treatment of the Franchise Bill and the Woman Suffrage amendments were under discussion in the House of Commons, Lord Robert Cecil said that had men in this country been treated as women had been in that matter, there would have been insurrection. There was no doubt about it. Well, I think we have convinced the British public that when women are treated in that way they also take to insurrection. Now if you get the right point of view about what we have been doing, you will realise that our insurrection is characterised by very much greater self-restraint than the men's insurrections. I read that in Mexico thousands of non-combatants have not merely had their letters destroyed, but they have had their lives taken, and so terrible were the circumstances there that these human bodies had paraffin poured over them and were set alight and burned, in order to put a stop to the danger of pestilence. That is how men conduct civil wars.

Well, you know perfectly well that in spite of the alarmist accounts that you see in the Press, so far in our agitation no human being has suffered except the women who are fighting for the liberty of women. As far as we can secure it, even at tremendous risk to ourselves, that self-restraint on the

286

part of women, and that safeguarding of human life will be maintained until we have won, but short of that we mean to do everything and all things that become necessary in order to settle this question of the status of women in this country once and for all.

"I Am a Law-Abiding Woman."

Now when people take to methods of insurrection, when they proclaim a civil war, they take upon themselves a very serious responsibility. No one recognises that more than the women who are fighting in this women's civil war. I am by nature (and so are all our women) a law-abiding woman. Nothing but extreme provocation leads women to break the law. Nothing but extreme provocation would lead women to interfere with the ordinary life of any other human being, but I maintain, without fear of contradiction, that never in any civil war in this country, or any other country, have men had greater provocation, greater grievances than have women at the present time. I accept any challenge to prove that the condition of women, that the dangers to which women are exposed, the grievances of women, are as great—no, are greater—than have been the grievances of any section of any population in any country when civil war has been thought justifiable.

I have with me here to-night a report of women, and men too, who are engaged in dealing with these most unfortunate members of the community who are not safeguarded by law, or the administration of the law, as they ought to be, and who never will be until women possess political power and have a better control over the law. I say to women in this meeting: listen to what I am going to read to you in a few words, and then tell me if you are not satisfied that this sort of thing can only be stopped by a revolution such as ours. I ask you whether we are not justified in everything that we have done in our attempt to wake up the public conscience of this country, and force the Government of the day to do something to remove these griev-ances. It is from a report presented at the last annual conference of that highly respectable and constitutional body, the National Union of Women Workers. These facts are given by a woman who read the paper. Early this year a girl of fourteen and a-half years, expecting confinement, appeared at the Central Criminal Court against a man of forty-five years old. He pleaded guilty. The judge heard no evidence, gave the police no opportunity of showing there was much against the man besides. The sentence was six months' hard labour, and only this morning women who from the highest motives have broken the law because they have been driven to it by the insult to them, these women were sentenced to the same term of imprisonment as this man. But this is worse: At the September Sessions this year, a girl of thirteen and a-half, and expecting confinement, appeared against a middle-aged man who was proved guilty and the sentence pronounced was three months in prison. That is only a month more that I got on the last occasion when I was sentenced for breaking a window valued at 3s. At every assizes and at every sessions there are cases like this, and even worse.

In addition to those facts, reference was made at that conference on the need that existed for rescue homes, not for women of full age, but for little children under twelve years of age. Facts were given there, and that was at a meeting where only women were present, because it was considered that these facts were not fit for discussion in ordinary public meetings. They are fit, ladies and gentlemen, so long as these things are permitted to go on. When we read of babies of two and a-half years being brought into these private Lock Hospitals suffering from unnamable diseases because of the awful conditions of our so-called civilisation in great cities, I say, Are women not justified in trying to get some political power to put a stop to them?

"Fight the right way," says someone. Well. I was speaking the other night in a hall which is named after a great man who fought in this country against absolute monarchy. Cromwell and his army fought against the divine right of kings. Charles I. believed sincerely—and many agreed with him—that kings, because they were kings, had a divine right to rule; they had a divine right to tax the people of this country and spend their money as they pleased without being responsible in any way. Well, you have abolished the divine right of kings, but you have got the divine right of the man voter substituted for it, and we women to-day are fighting against that divine right. You admire the courage of men like Cromwell. Well, so do we; but it takes a great deal more courage, ladies and gentlemen, to fight against eight million divine rulers that it did to fight against one.

Rulers by Divine Right.

I know perfectly well that these rulers by divine right of ours are not against women really. I know perfectly well that the average man is fair-minded and reasonable, and I know, speaking of the average voter, he is quite ready to admit that if a woman qualifies for a vote like a man, if she pays her own rent and her rates and taxes like a man, she has as much right to a vote as he has. All the public opinion worth having is on the side of justice and fair-play to women, but unfortunately the average man, the average voter, wants to be allowed to go on with his business. He does not put himself very much out of the way about any grievances except the grievances that come right home to himself. Well, we have been trying to rouse him by argument; we have been trying to rouse him by persuasion. You do rouse him sufficiently at a meeting to vote for the resolution for Woman Suffrage, but he goes home after he has heard a good speech, and goes to sleep after saying what a good meeting it was, and then forgets all about it until he is roused up again. Well, now you are all moved about it. You are all excited about it. You are all interested in it.

Many of you condemn us, especially if you play golf, or if you sent a very important business letter which did not reach its destination, or if you are a shopkeeper and your windows have been broken. I expect the Chancellor of the Exchequer is coming home post haste to see what has happened to his building. You are all roused and you are all stirred up. Well, you say, "What do you hope to get by that? What is the use of making people angry?" Life-long supporters come to me and say, "You are completely alienating my sympathy." I reply to them: "What did your sympathy do for us, my good friend, when we had it? What use has your sympathy or your life-long support or sympathy been to us? It is better to have you angry than to have you pleased, because sooner or later you will come to the conclusion that this intolerable nuisance must be put an end to."

Some of you are writing letters to the papers suggesting all sorts of punishments. That won't stop us. You see, in the way of punishment you cannot go beyond a certain point without reversing the whole progress of civilisation for the last hundred years. You know they thought that when they adopted forcible feeding, which is really a torture worthy of the Middle Ages, that that would put down the agitation, but it has not done so, because you see when you take to torture as punishment you can go as far as life will let you, but your victim will escape you into another life, and then your power over that human being ends, and women in this movement have so made up their minds that there is no other way but the way we have adopted, that we shall go on, and if one falls down by the way a hundred will arise to take her place.

I want to show you that we have become not only convinced that ours is the right way to get this question of the political status of women settled, but we feel that there is no time to be lost; that we cannot wait any longer; that while we are waiting these things are going on that we want to have power to put an end to. (A voice: "I want to give you advice.") I prefer to take the political advice of great statesmen who have had the necessary experience. Let me tell you what Lord Derby said in an article in *The Nineteenth Century Review* on the Irish Land Acts. "Why have we altered the Irish Land Law? To put an end to Irish agitation. Why have we cared to put an end to Irish agitation? Because it was not only discreditable to England as a ruling power, but a practical obstruction to the transaction of English business." He said it had been the direct result of two causes: Irish outrage and Parliamentary obstruction. Now we ask for Parliamentary obstruction for Woman Suffrage, but we have no men in Parliament to obstruct for us, so we are obliged to take to other methods, similar to those which, added to Parliamentary obstruction, led to the passing of the Irish Land Acts. The answer to all the objections which may be made by people who do not like our methods is this: How else than by giving votes to women are you going to govern the women of England! You cannot govern us if we refuse to be governed. If we withdraw our consent from government no power on earth can govern us. Your police force, your police magistrates, your judges, your army, the navy if you like, all the forces of civilisation, cannot govern one woman if she refuses to be governed. Government rests upon force, you say. Not at all: it rests upon consent, ladies and gentlemen, and women are withdrawing their consent. Well, now that is a very serious situation; it is a very paralysing situation, and I would like our friends who think that they can govern us by punishment and by restriction, to ask themselves seriously how it is to be done. You see two women walking along the street. How are you to know which of those women is a Suffragette? How are you to know which of them has destroyed letters in pillar-boxes, or broken windows, or fired the orchid houses, or blown up Mr. Lloyd George's home? If you read your papers they say, "Clues to the perpetrators of the outrage to Mr. Lloyd George's home!" A galosh! Two hàtpins without heads! Two hairpins! and they are still searching, and I who have accepted responsibility several times, why have they not taken me? I suppose they know their own business best. I suppose they think it would be more difficult to manage things with me in Holloway than with me outside of Holloway. I do not deceive myself into thinking that it is out of any consideration for me. It is very wrong that other women should be sent to prison and punished, as they have been to-day, while I who have incited them should be at liberty.

This situation will have to be ended, and how are sensible men going to end it? You can only end it in one way, and that is by seeing that political justice is done to women. This Government will have to give Woman Suffrage or this Government will have to go. My advice to you men who have got votes—and you know one voter means more in the minds of politicians than any number of voteless people—make them do it when the session opens, or make them resign office and clear out and make way for people who will. That is what we have set ourselves to do. We have set ourselves to force this Government out of office, and I know that business men in this country will help us. Your stockbroker, whose communication with Glasgow was cut off for several hours during very important business hours, does not want that to be a weekly occurrence. Your business man who reads important communications through the post does not want his communications to be interfered with as a regular and permanent institution. He can put up with it once, but if it is going on and on and on, he will want it to be put a stop to. Your business man, whose customers mostly are women, does not like the idea that in the interval of buying hats, his customers may be breaking his shop windows; and your insurance companies won't like to have the drain upon their resources and their profits cut down by having to make good these insurance policies. It is an impossible situation.

"This Fight Is Going On."

Well, ladies and gentlemen, what I want to get into the minds of the people in this meeting is that this fight is going on until women have won the vote. Every right-minded person admits that it is bare justice we are fighting for: justice that for generations we thought we should get by argument, by persuasion, and by constitutional means; but we know perfectly well, and everybody knows, that in this country, whatever it may be in other countries, no great reform has ever been won, or ever will be won, perhaps, until women get the vote, by constitutional means. There is not a man in this meeting to-night who would have a vote if it had not been that in the past men waged civil war to get that vote for men, and yet men can blame women to-day! Have ever men had reasons greater than ours to win their enfranchisement? Look at the industrial position of women in this country. Is it not appalling and fearful? Socialists are telling us that the White Slave Traffic is entirely due to the economic position of women. No, it is largely due to it, but not entirely. It is very largely because of our unequal moral standard. This idea that in the pursuit of vicious pleasures women are fair game. It permeates all ranks of society; not only the upper classes. It comes down and down, and the poor woman who is called "fallen," though her partner is not regarded as fallen, goes from serving the vicious pleasure of the upper classes by degrees down to serving those of the lowest. So we have this moral cancer which is destroying the race, which is eating at the heart of the race itself. I want to say to men that from a Parliament elected by men we shall not get laws reforming it. I want to say to you—Is it not very like asking the wolf to protect the lamb? Because even a Government which is responsible for carrying through such legislation has not clean hands in this matter. What about the state of poor women in India or wherever our troops are stationed? What about those women who are looked upon as necessary victims for the British Army and Navy? These are the things that women are fighting. They are only beginning to learn about them for they have been kept from us. We have been told that it was something we must not even think about, but the women of the past generation fought for the right to enter the profession of medicine, and we have women doctors now, and we know that this moral cancer has set up a physical cancer, and that the race itself is being destroyed and undermined by these horrible diseases that come of unbridled viciousness in our social life.

And so women, while they are quite ready to fight for this thing simply for liberty's sake, so that they may say, "We are free citizens of a free country like the men," are also fighting for power to help the best of men to do what men have found themselves unable to do, because they are appalled at the social problems they have to face. Well, women have the courage to come to their aid; and we say we are determined to help men, and stand side by side as equal citizens with the best of men, so that together we may save the race and may bring about a better and a nobler humanity.

17

"She Laid Down Her Life for Her Friends."

**A Speech Delivered by the Rev. Gertrude Von Petzold,
Minister of Waverly Road Church, Small Heath,
at the London Pavilion, June 16.**

As a non-militant woman, a minister of religion, who, unlike
the lawyer, has to look beyond the mere result of action to the *motive* prompting it, I have come here to bear testimony to the high character, the heroic
nature of one who gave her life for the faith that was in her. "Greater love
has no man than this, that a man lay down his life for his friends." Ancient,
memorable words these; true both in the spirit and the letter yesterday, to-
day, and for ever! Emily Wilding Davison had worked hard for her convictions, had suffered imprisonment and the hellish tortures of forcible feeding—and now as a last desperate yet symbolical act of protest, she hurled
herself amidst the wild racers on Epsom Downs.

Here was the aristocracy of England, headed by Royalty, the wealth of
England, young sports from all over the world, women in glittering toilets,
matrons high in society, and young girls with the first bloom of youth on
their cheeks, all breathless with excitement, aglow with the mere joy of
living; and all on a sudden a solemn hush falls on that gorgeous assembly—
something has happened, something untoward—the professional better is
seized with fear for his confidently expected gains, the women stare wide-
eyed towards the edge of the course. What *has* happened? The King's horse
is rolling on the ground—a beautiful, sleek creature—furiously kicking at a
woman who lies huddled up there, unconscious; the jockey also lies there
more or less stunned, but not seriously hurt—but the woman, why does
she not move? Why does she not at least withdraw herself from the range
of the horse's hoofs? Stewards are seen hurrying to the place, a doctor is
fetched—a man doctor, a woman doctor also is there—the woman is placed
in a car and driven to a hospital, where she dies a merciful, painless death,
a last pale flush on the waxen features telling of victory gained, battle accomplished—race finished! And that other race on Epsom Downs goes on with
a renewed zest, the only difference being that there are more police, a larger

staff of detectives. The party papers proclaim the woman's deed mad, wise-acres paint gruesome pictures of what might have happened. But nothing *has* happened but that a woman has laid down her life for her friends. . . . has done so of her own free will, has done so in the midst of overwhelming difficulties, in order to remind her country with the whole power of her being of the injustice, the cruelty, the wrongs, the sufferings of women. . . .

Hers was not a common life, hers was not a shattered career; she had brilliant gifts, a great intellect, a greater heart. Because there was such a deep ache in her heart, a gaping wound that cried out for healing, she did this thing, the "pathetic futility," as one paper has called it, this "mad act of folly," as another, and note *how* she did it; without telling anyone, neither her aged mother, neither her natural protector, her brother, none of the numerous friends she met with on the day preceding—no one was impli-cated, no one should suffer but she alone.

She laid down her life for her friends.

Who were these friends? The very same that are always with us: the poor, the oppressed, the heavy-laden; women sweated in factories, women driven by the grim spectre of poverty on to the streets of our large cities, children outraged by brutes of men, innocent girls decoyed by wealth and lust, wives betrayed by husbands without adequate legal redress under an unequal di-vorce law, professional women underpaid, women debarred from important professions, kept out of all higher places in the Civil Service, women paying taxes without a voice in the expenditure of them, women driven to despera-tion, women protesting clapt into prison, women tortured—all these—all these were the friends for whom Emily Wilding Davison died. Posterity will give her that meed of honour which she so richly deserved.

"Greater love hath no man. . . ." but there is another verse following on this. "For," says the Apostle, "for the good someone would even dare to die, but Jesus Christ died for sinners."

Emily Wilding Davison also died for sinners.

What sinners? Ah, we know well. First, the indifferent, misguided multi-tude of the very type and stuff which nineteen centuries ago uttered those hideous cries: "Crucify Him! Crucify Him!"

Second, the newspaper proprietors who wilfully misrepresent a great movement, wilfully suppress a thousand little details which are absolutely essential to the establishment of truth.

Third, those politicians who are quick to make promises and equally quick to break them in the interest of party or self.

Fourth, all those who oppose the political emancipation of womanhood from a mere lazy, self-indulgent prejudice.

Fifth, those who believe in it, yet do little or nothing to make it come. To them applies the ancient saying: "To him that knoweth to do the good and doeth it not, it is sin."

Sixth, those who are merely ignorant, merely misinformed, and take no steps to inform themselves.

Seventh and last, those refined hypocrites who are always ready to see the mote in others' eyes without being aware of the beam in their own.

It is for these—all these—that Emily Wilding Davison laid down her life. It is to these that her mangled body has made its piteous appeal; it is for the redemption of these that she surrendered her beautiful, glorious life.

Will they heed her voice, or has this supreme sacrifice of hers been made in vain?

Never—never! As sure as there is a God in the heavens—as sure as Jesus Christ died on Calvary for the sins of the world, so sure will the spirit of this woman call forth the best that lies dormant in the hearts of this present generation. She will whisper her message into the ears of the judge, the Cabinet Minister, the Member of Parliament; she will call on the man in the street, the harlot in the public house, her country will awake at last, and the sun of freedom will rise on us all with healing in his wings.

Part VIII
The Cat and Mouse Act

IN THE SPRING OF 1913, WITH MANY OF THE UNION MEMBERS IN PRISON, outrage over the government policy of forcible feeding was building. On March 18, 1913, George Bernard Shaw delivered the speech "We Are Members One of Another." Shaw had long been disgusted by the government's practice of forcibly feeding the suffragettes and had written a short witty play on the subject in 1909;[1] but this was, as he explained in the speech, his first public meeting on the suffrage issue. Shaw equated the act of forcible feeding with medieval torture. He sarcastically offered Home Secretary McKenna the opportunity to be forcibly fed himself (with his favorite food, no less) and thus prove that the process was "rather pleasant than not." Perhaps the most appealing aspect of the speech is Shaw's clear view that a woman "is very much the same sort of person as I am myself," an opinion that was certainly not current in 1913. At this same meeting, Dr. Mansell-Moullin (who would later operate on Emily Wilding Davison) spoke on the same subject. His speech ("Artificial vs 'Forcible' Feeding") attempted to clear up public confusion about the difference between forcible feeding and the type of feeding conducted in hospitals and asylums. He was very graphic about the physical and psychological discomfort inherent in the act and the injuries that had already resulted to suffrage prisoners.

With opposition to forcible feeding on the increase, the government needed a tool to prevent the death of the prisoners from starvation without resorting to forcible feeding (yet, also without granting them status as political prisoners by putting them in the first division). In April 1913, there passed into law the Prisoner's Temporary Discharge for Ill-Health Act. This act made it possible to release a prisoner for ill-health—usually due to a hunger strike—then rearrest and send her directly back to prison when her health had recovered sufficiently. Lord Robert Cecil called it the "Cat and Mouse" Act, a name that stuck with the movement and the press.[2]

The act instituted a system of virtual house arrest. The special police "Cats" would keep watch over a location where a formerly incarcerated "Mouse" was recuperating from her hunger strike. Theoretically, the prisoner was to voluntarily return to prison when her days of temporary release expired. None of them did, of course, nor were many of them recovered in the usual week to two weeks they were granted. The "Cats" would pounce as soon as the suffragette ventured from the house or nursing home in which she was hiding. At least some of the public backing that the WSPU lost in its move to guerrilla militancy reappeared as the Cat and Mouse Act was enforced.

Emmeline Pankhurst was to suffer greatly under the new act. She was sentenced to three years penal servitude in April, 1913, for having "counselled and procured certain persons" to blow up a building at Walton Heath. Upon entering Holloway Prison, Pankhurst entered immediately on a hunger strike. After nine days without food, she was released on April 12 on a fifteen-day license. She spent her recovery time in, first, a nursing home and then the country home of Dr. Ethel Smyth. When Pankhurst left Dr. Smyth's home to attend a meeting at the London Pavilion on May 26, she was arrested and returned to Holloway. This time her hunger strike lasted five days and she was released on a seven day license. During this time of Pankhurst's license, Emily Wilding Davison died but, when Pankhurst attempted to attend the funeral on June 14, she was rearrested. This time she made a hunger and thirst strike and was released after three days. Pankhurst was free for nearly a month before rearrest was attempted.[3]

From reading accounts at the time, it appears that few expected Emmeline Pankhurst to survive the continuous rigors of repeated bouts of starvation. She was not a hardy woman and was now well into middle-age. As her death was anticipated, the Union members and sympathizers became more desperate to save her. In August 1913, during the prayers for prisoners and captives at St. Paul's Cathedral, forty women began to chant:

Save Emmeline Pankhurst
Spare her! Spare her!
Give her light and set her free
Save her! Save her!
Hear us while we pray to thee.

Mary Richardson, guilty of slashing the Rokeby Venus as it hung in the National Gallery, made as her written statement: "I have tried to destroy the picture of the most beautiful woman in mythological history because the Government are destroying Mrs. Pankhurst—the most beautiful character in modern history."[4]

On July 14, 1913, Emmeline Pankhurst made a speech at the London Pavilion ("Kill Me or Give Me My Freedom"), as did Annie Kenney ("Our Spirits Are Eternal"). In her speech, Pankhurst once again equated the suffragettes with the Protestant Ulster rebels led by Sir Edward Carson. Ulster opposition to the Home Rule Bill, introduced by Asquith in 1912 and necessitated by the Liberal's alliance with Irish Nationalists, had reinvigorated the 1886 opposition slogan, "Ulster will fight and Ulster will be right."[5] The lengths to which Ulster would go to oppose Irish nationalism became apparent when Carson's followers began signing "The Covenant," a document that pledged the signator to exercise "all means which may be found necessary to defeat the setting up of a Home Rule Parliament in Ireland."[6] Despite inflammatory speeches, reports of gun smuggling, open drilling in preparation for war, and the "Curragh mutiny," when a number of Conservative army officers resigned in 1914 rather than move north to counter possible Ulster violence, the Ulster protesters under Carson were granted the political and free speech rights that the suffragettes were invariably denied.[7]

In this speech, Pankhurst also continued reference to what has become known as the purity campaign. This campaign was initiated by Christabel Pankhurst's writing on venereal disease in her book, *The Great Scourge and How to Cure It*, published also in articles in *The Suffragette* in 1913. The cure, as proposed by Christabel Pankhurst, was summed up in the slogan, "Votes for women and chastity for men."[8] The Union believed that women's ability to influence the laws concerning prostitution was vital to ending the problem, as was a higher standard of self-control among men. Although the common statistics cited by medical doctors, as well as by the suffragettes, of the incidence of venereal disease were grossly inflated, the damage wrought by prostitution on the health of society was a concern of many in Edwardian England. In this speech Emmeline Pankhurst spoke mainly of White Slavery, an issue encompassing the seduction of young girls into prostitution, women forced into prostitution by economic necessity, and government tendencies to punish prostitutes harshly while excusing with nominal sentences male procurers, customers, and child abusers. In her speech, Annie Kenney focused upon this same issue, and brought up the suppression of customers' names (where upper-class and government men were suspected) in the July 10, 1913, Piccadilly Flat prostitution case.

Following this speech, Annie Kenney, also on prison release, served as a distraction for Mrs. Pankhurst's escape to the home of Hertha Ayrton. Mrs. Pankhurst's whereabouts were traced by the police and the house was surrounded. Through a clever ruse using a decoy, she escaped the house but was rearrested July 21 when she entered the London Pavilion to try to speak. By this time her health was so poor that she was released on July 24. In late August, still under release through the Cat and Mouse Act, Emmeline Pankhurst went to Paris to visit Christabel. In October, 1913, she sailed for America on the French liner *La Provence* for a third visit to America. Her trip was well publicized, and there was speculation over what kind of official reception she would have as a British prisoner on special release. When the ship anchored in New York harbor on October 26, Pankhurst was ordered to Ellis Island and placed before a Board of Special Inquiry. Files had been sent from England, possibly by Scotland Yard, and on their basis Pankhurst was found to be of questionable character. She was detained at Ellis Island for two and a half days. During this time, the case was brought by the Commissioner of Immigration before Woodrow Wilson, who ordered Pankhurst's release.[9] All of this publicity ensured great success for the American speaking tour and the equivalent of £4500 was raised.[10]

Presented here is Emmeline Pankhurst's speech in Hartford, Connecticut, delivered during her 1913 American tour. This is a lesser known speech even among scholars of the suffrage movement, yet it is one of Pankhurst's strongest speeches. Because America's past involved a revolution against the British government, Pankhurst used this fact as a point of commonality in describing the current revolution of women. Pankhurst attempted to persuade her audience to extend to women the same right of revolt against "intolerable injustice" that they historically granted to men. In making this appeal, Pankhurst gave her clearest rationale for the use of violence against the property of the general public. Of particular interest is Pankhurst's story of the breaking of the Guard Club windows and her tale of the threat to golf greens. Through such stories, Pankhurst made the claim that the new policy of guerrilla militancy was effective and justifiable.

When Pankhurst returned from America on December 4, 1913, she was immediately rearrested and again was caught up in the rigors of the Cat and Mouse Act. Following a hunger strike, she was released December 7. Rearrest followed on December 13; another hunger strike brought release on December 17. The year 1914 began with another split in the suffrage ranks, this time within the Pankhurst family itself. Sylvia Pankhurst had spent her efforts for the Union successfully organizing the working women of the slums of East London. The East London campaign slowly took on a life of its own. The East London Federation of the WSPU had a democratic constitution, allowed male members in its "People's Army," and leaned toward a Socialist view. None of these traits were consistent with the organization of the rest of the Union, and Emmeline and Christabel Pankhurst insisted to Sylvia Pankhurst that the East London Federation must now exist as a separate organization. As with earlier splits, concern for the Cause made the ousted membership smooth things over publicly, although lingering, very personal resentment forms a clear undertone of Sylvia Pankhurst's later writing on the movement. Over the protests of Emmeline Pankhurst, the East End campaigners insisted on taking as their name the East London Federation of Suffragettes and on maintaining the colors of purple, white, and green, with the addition of red for liberty.[11]

After a rest from hunger striking and after sorting out the East London issue, Emmeline Pankhurst, still at liberty, began a series of speeches that directly challenged the government to rearrest her. The speech presented here ("Victory is Assured") took place on the day Parliament reassembled, with Pankhurst addressing the crowd at Campden Hill Square. Pankhurst knew the publicity value of her image as a martyr, and despite the personal cost, she was willing to risk serving as a symbol of the injustice of the Cat and Mouse Act. In this speech and the one that followed a week later in Glebe Place, Chelsea, she twitted the government with her public presence. She pushed the government to rearrest her, hold her in prison, and forcibly feed her as they did lesser-known members of the Union. This is a strongly worded and cleverly argued speech. With Pankhurst's skillful playing off of hecklers in the audience, it is easy to see why she was one of the most original minds and premier speakers of the suffrage cause.

Arrest, hunger strike, release, and rearrest would continue as a cycle for Pankhurst. Response to her rearrests came in the form of militant acts. For example, following Pankhurst's rearrest on March 9, 1914, a timberyard in Bristol was burned, as was a house in Scotland.[12] While continuing their acts of reformist terrorism, the Union also decided this year to go directly to the King with their cause. Accordingly, during February and March, Pankhurst sent a series of letters to the King requesting that he receive the deputation. On May 21, 1914, a large deputation marched to Buckingham Palace to petition the King. There exists an amazing series of photographs of Emmeline Pankhurst lifted a foot off the ground and carted away from the King's Gate by Inspector Rolfe, a man of considerable size. Although the King thus managed to avoid the Union deputation, he had difficulty hiding from the suffragette assault. He was loudly addressed at the Opera and the theatre by beautifully attired women who chained themselves to seats in the stalls or barricaded themselves in the boxes.[13] On June 4, when receiving the debutantes at Court, he was startled by Lady Blomfield's daughter, in the midst of her deep curtsy, calling out, "Your Majesty, for God's sake, stop the forcible feeding of women!"[14] It has been reported that the King included this incident in his diary with the comment, "I don't know what we are coming to."[15]

18

"We Are Members One of Another."

By George Bernard Shaw.
Verbatim Report of a Speech delivered at Kingsway Hall, Tuesday, March 18, 1913.

IN THE RESOLUTION THAT WE ARE MOVING TO-NIGHT WE PROTEST against forcible feeding; that is to say, not alone the forcible feeding of women, because men are being forcibly fed in this way. And it is for that reason that I have come here to-night to protest against this present practice. I have not come to speak on behalf of the women. My reason for never having done this since, in order that I might clear my own conscience, I first declared myself on Woman Suffrage, is that after a very careful study of public meetings held on the subject, I came to the conclusion that the women were exceedingly well able to take care of themselves.

Now, I say this because I want you to understand that if this were merely a Suffragist meeting I should not be here. I did speak at a meeting on this subject some time ago, and I remember that I addressed some reproach to the Suffragists on that occasion. I said they had not appreciated some previous efforts of mine sufficiently. The consequence was that the next morning the first letter that I opened on my breakfast-table began, "Poor injured darling!" I don't resent that sort of treatment, because I really do think that we men in our relations with women mostly are poor injured darlings. I do not come forward to-night in the sense of the chivalrous man coming to the rescue of a weaker sex.

The Stronger Sex.

Quite seriously, I think the only consolatory thing about this forcible feeding is that those who are suffering from it at present are for the most part the stronger sex. I most seriously believe that women are hardier than men. There are physiological reasons why. Woman has to go through experiences in the quite ordinary course of her life—her motherhood—that I would like to see any man go through. Please, ladies and gentlemen, don't

301

think that I am in any way to-night appealing to the Government for any special consideration for women. I don't believe that women want to have that shown; in fact, I believe that the women who are most enthusiastic in this cause are infuriated more by any affectation of protection or magnanimity from my sex towards them than by anything else in the world.

I have the rather original view about a woman that she is very much the same sort of person as I am myself, but unfortunately that view is one which does not seem to be very general in official circles. For instance, most men recognise that their own insides are rather complicated machines, but when they have to deal with a woman, they apparently believe that what they have to deal with is a sort of sack; that the mouth of this sack is a narrow orifice which they call the throat, and that they can poke something into that orifice and squirt food through it. Having done that, they seem to think they have done all that possibly could be expected from them in the way of feeding that person properly. If you want to keep a human being alive by introducing food, the first thing to do is to induce that person to open her mouth. That is not such an easy thing as you would imagine. If a person has got a perfect set of teeth, it is an extremely difficult thing to open those teeth against the will of the person if he or she wants to keep them shut, and taking the case of somebody determinedly keeping her teeth shut, what uneducated and rough people will do is simply to take an instrument like a chisel and to attempt to prise the teeth open, and that is an impossible thing to do because you cannot get a chisel through unless you break the teeth, or unless there is a breach made in the teeth already. Now, I want to impress upon you that for anybody to prise the mouth open in that way is to perform an act of extreme violence; in fact, it may be impossible unless you actually break the teeth, and that apparently is the way the thing is done.

Mediaeval Torture.

Then, when you have got the mouth open in that way, comes the idea that you have only got to deal with an empty sack. Now, ladies and gentlemen, I can assure you, although I am not a professional medical man, that it is not so simple as that. There are two ways of getting into the inside of human beings. One of them is by the larynx, by the trachea, by the tube which leads to the lungs, and has at the top of it a very remarkable musical-box, by the aid of which I am addressing you this evening. And beside this tube there is another tube which goes down to your stomach. Now, if you want thoroughly to appreciate how very important it is that you should take the right tube when you are getting the food in, I have only to remind you that a very short time ago all Europe was greatly shocked by the death of a very eminent German politician who while in a restaurant very unfortunately dropped a false tooth into the lung tube. The consequence was that that gentleman died. Now, there you have got before the eyes of Europe a striking illustration of the fact that a slight mistake in the way the food goes down may result in the death of a person in regard to whom the mistake is made. More, those mistakes have been made in connection with forcible feeding. Perhaps it is not to be complained of that our wardresses are not educated in anatomy: I have only to say that if they are not educated in anatomy they ought not to be set to perform an anatomical operation. But pray, what are we to say of the medical gentlemen who superintend the operation! It seems to me that either they have not been properly educated, or else they are in such a temper that they really forget their scientific education. At any rate, there appears to be no doubt whatever about the fact that attempts have been made with considerable injury to the person upon whom they have been made, to feed a person through the wrong tube.

Mr. Forbes Robertson said that we could not conceive the condition of mind in the Middle Ages with regard to torture. I agree with him there. Yet I do not believe that we are superior to the Middle Ages in this matter; on the contrary, I believe that we have almost entirely lost the repugnance which leads men to turn away from the idea of torture. The people of the Middle Ages had many defects, but there was one very remarkable thing about them—they had a religion, and they believed in it. And accordingly, though there were certain things that they did which shock us, they did not in the Middle Ages refer any question to their own dark and savage passions and irritations. They did not write letters to *The Daily Telegraph* half full of lies and half full of suggestions that women should be deliberately tortured in prison, and with a signature at the end that was not the signature of the man who wrote the letter. The people of the Middle Ages really always did things, particularly if they were public and legal things, with some conviction that it was the sort of thing that God would have done, so that even when they did things which shock us, it was because they conceived that God, in His hatred of sin, might have done the same thing. I entirely absolve Mr. McKenna and the present Government from having any such idea.

The horror of the present situation is that our statesmen have never at any moment dreamed of considering this question in the serious way that it deserves. You hear of nothing in the papers but of their irritation, of their little vanity. They are face to face with the heroic temper which produces martyrs, and yet they act from a fear of having their windows broken, or something of that kind. They take no large view of the matter at all.

Forcible Feeding Illegal.

There is, however, a point which I think they might understand, and I mean to put it. I contend that this forcible feeding is illegal. I contend that when you are tried in a public court and sentenced to imprisonment, you

are sentenced to imprisonment, and you are not sentenced to torture—
except in so far as imprisonment itself may be torture. Now, supposing I
am sent to gaol for a month, and supposing I refuse to eat, what is the
proper thing to do with me? I presume that what the governor of the gaol
has got to say is: "We have got a prisoner here who refuses to eat. I place
his food before him. The prisoner still refuses his food, and it seems to me
that he may possibly die of starvation." He would then, I presume, charge
me with attempted suicide, and for that I should be sentenced to a further
term of imprisonment. The governor of the gaol, having got me back on
those terms, might then find that I still refused to eat, and then I presume
he would have again to report to the Home Secretary and say: "The prisoner
still refuses to eat, and the prisoner is dying. I have carried out my duty in
imprisoning him. I provided him with food, and my duty is so far done."
People would say, "Well, let him die if he prefers it. There is no obligation
whatever upon any individual to keep the prisoner alive under those circumstances." But supposing the Home Secretary decided to try and make the
man eat, and supposing the governor of the gaol suggested: "Well, we might
for instance keep touching him up with a red-hot poker." The Home Secretary would reply: "Yes, but unfortunately we have not any law empowering
us to burn people with red-hot pokers. Therefore I must first induce the
Government to bring in a Bill legalising the use of red-hot pokers."

I contend that it is the business of Mr. McKenna, if he wants to break
people's teeth, and force their mouths open, if he wants to wound their
lungs, if he wants to run the risk of killing them, if he wants to inflict what
is unquestionably torture upon them, it is his business first to bring in a Bill
legalising those operations. There is no reason why he should hesitate. If he
is not ashamed to do these things without the law, why should he be ashamed
to do them with it? If the Government are not prepared to legalise the
torture that they are inflicting, it proves that not only does their own conscience revolt from this torture, but they don't believe that public opinion
would be on their side. They are not prepared to face the electorate with
such a measure as that on their consciences.

It seems to me that the Government really have discovered—that the
women have beaten them. It is not merely a question of the women inflicting
humiliation on them and getting the better of them. What the women have
also proved is that the conscience of the community is on their side. What
they have proved is something more than that—that the conscience of the
very men who are doing this is on their side. See the continual suppression
that is going on; see the uneasiness, and the shame. See the miserable excuses
that are made about this matter—excuses that would not impose upon an
intelligent frog.

When I last spoke on this platform Mrs. Leigh was in Mountjoy Prison
under a sentence of several years' imprisonment for a very serious offence.

Well, on that occasion I challenged the Government to let Mrs. Leigh starve. I said that they had no right whatever to forcibly feed her, that the practice was illegal, and I said: "Let Mrs. Leigh leave her food; let her starve; let her die. It is not your business to compel her to eat; it is your business to imprison her. When you have done that you have settled your score." I am glad to say that on that occasion the entire Press of the country—the Anti-Suffragists in particular—jumped at my speech. What was the result? Did the Government accept the challenge? No; they let Mrs. Leigh out straight away.

What is the use of going on with this miserable, wanton savagery, when you dare not go through with it to the end?

Well, ladies and gentlemen, that is the case that I want to put before you to-night. When a Government has come to a pass that it cannot any longer carry out its own laws, it is time to take the course that it would take with any person who had the conscience of the community against them. If you take, for instance, the case of Dr. Crippen. Supposing Dr. Crippen had been sentenced to penal servitude for life, and if he had refused his food, do you suppose that anybody in the community would not have said, "Very well; let him starve." The conscience of the community was against Dr. Crippen; the conscience of the community would have been with the Government if they had left him to starve. The whole thing has now become a propaganda of spite, of rancour, and of brutality that is degrading our national character. I endorse everything that has been said about the damage to the character of the doctors and to the wardresses, but I don't believe that those people's characters are as much degraded as the characters of the people who write certain articles in the papers. It is degrading the whole tone of our life to read the miserable speeches in which Ministers endeavour to defend the sort of thing that is going on.

A Challenge to Mr. McKenna.

Let me offer a simple challenge to Mr. McKenna. Mr. McKenna still occasionally tries to make out that forcible feeding is rather pleasant than not. If it is, then I ask him, Will he allow us to forcibly feed him? We will do it with his favourite food. He need not resist. We will get the most skilful surgeon to administer the nourishment; we will make it as nice for him as possible. We will do everything that is not done for these women in prison. I want to find out whether, under those favourable conditions, Mr. McKenna will face it. I do not believe it. It is within his power to give us this little proof as to whether forcible feeding is such a nice thing as he says it is. I venture to say that he will not accept this challenge.

I hope he will get rid of this horrible question, and get rid of it in the logical way, because remember, if forcible feeding is done away with, still the difficulty remains, and when people ask themselves what the meaning of the whole thing is, when they ask themselves why it is that human beings should be treated as they are in prison, they can only come to one conclusion on the general Suffrage question.

I am not altogether what is called an orthodox man, but I have always in a sort of way believed in the old and simple statement that we are "members one of another." Probably the gentlemen at Westminster believe that "we are members one with another" refers to Members of Parliament only. I don't think they can see the full sense of it. There is an old sentence which runs, "Inasmuch as ye have done it unto the least of My brethren, ye have done it unto Me." I do not think they can understand that "brethren" includes sisters as well.

We are all of us very fond of talking about what people call altruism, and about our duty to others. I have always understood that altruism is the final identification of the least of these with me. If you take a woman and torture her, you torture me. If you take Mrs. Pankhurst's daughter and torture her, you are torturing my daughter. If you take Miss Pankhurst's mother and torture her, you will be torturing my mother. I go further than that. If you torture my mother, you are torturing me.

These denials of fundamental rights are really a violation of the soul. They are an attack on that sacred part of life that is common to all of us, that part which has no individuality, that part which is real, the thing of which you speak when you talk of the life everlasting. I say with an absolute sense not of saying anything hysterical to you, but of saying to you something that is most ordinary common sense—I say that the denial of these fundamental rights to ourselves in the persons of women is practically a denial of the life everlasting.

19

Artificial v. "Forcible" Feeding.

by C. W. Mansell-Moullin, M.D., F.R.C.S.,
Vice-President of the Royal College of Surgeons.
Verbatim Report of a Speech delivered at Kingsway Hall,
Tuesday, March 18, 1913.

LAST SUMMER THERE WERE 102 SUFFRAGETTES IN PRISON; 90 OF THOSE were being forcibly fed. All sorts of reports were being spread about what was being done to them. We got up a petition to the Home Secretary, we wrote him letters, we interviewed him so far as we could. We got absolutely no information of any kind that was satisfactory; nothing but evasion. So three of us formed ourselves into a committee—Sir Victor Horsley, Dr. Agnes Savill, and myself, and we determined that we would investigate these cases as thoroughly as we could. I don't want to be conceited, but we had the idea that we had sufficient experience in public and hospital practice and in private practice to be able to examine those persons, to take their evidence, to weigh it fully, and to consider it. And we drew up a report, and that report was published in *The Lancet* and in the *"British Medical,"* at the end of August last year.

We stand by that report. There is not a single thing in that report that we wish to withdraw. There are some few things that we might put more strongly now than we did then. Everything that has happened since has merely strengthened what we said, and has confirmed what we predicted would happen.

Forcible Feeding in Asylums.

Now, the first thing I wish you to dismiss from your minds completely is that there is any possible comparison between what is called in lunatic asylums artificial feeding and forcible feeding as practised in His Majesty's prisons. They are as far apart from each other as the two poles. Whenever forcible feeding is mentioned in any of the newspapers, you always see printed in large print—the largest print the papers can command—some

307

anonymous correspondent for whose good faith the editor always vouches, who is always a superintendent of some exceedingly well-known asylum, and who always declares that he has fed in that way some two thousand lunatics without the slightest trouble or the slightest accident.

I have not the least doubt of it. I only wish he would sign his name, or give us a clue to the place; but whether he does so or not is a matter of absolute indifference; the conditions have no resemblance whatsoever. The mental state of a lunatic who refuses his food is that of complete torpor, almost apathy. He is under a great cloud, hardly capable of receiving a fresh impression. The Suffragists who have been forcibly fed have all (with the exception of some half-dozen men) been women, so I shall speak of them as if they were women, though I don't deny the heroism of the men. The Suffragettes are women, many of them are graduates of the Universities, and have obtained high distinction. They are women of very high ideals. They have been driven to desperation by the way in which their cause, the cause in which they believe, has been treated; and they are ready and willing to lay down their lives as the martyrs did in times of old. There is absolutely no resemblance, no comparison possible between them and the lunatics who are fed in the lunatic asylums.

And not only are the men and women upon whom this is practised different in every possible way, but the objects with which the feeding is carried out are different. The object in a lunatic asylum is to get that patient to take his food with the least possible inconvenience to himself and everybody else. The pretext in His Majesty's prisons may be to get the prisoner to take food, but the real object is to break down that prisoner's determination. The real object is to bend or break that prisoner, to break her in the way that the Inquisitors of old used to break prisoners on the rack. That is the object—to make them give way—and the results—if you want any idea as to the comparison between the two methods—would show it at once.

"Neither Dangerous nor Painful."

I am perfectly willing to accept our anonymous asylum superintendent's figures that he has fed two thousand persons without the slightest hitch. So much the better for my argument. Of those ninety who were forcibly fed in H.M.'s prisons, forty-six—more than half—had to be discharged long before their sentences had expired, many of them after they had been fed once in this particular way, because it was dangerous to keep them in longer— because if they had been kept in they would have been killed by the treatment which, so it was said, was intended to save their lives. Can you imagine anything more significant than a comparison between two such methods?

Now Mr. McKenna has said time after time that forcible feeding, as carried out in His Majesty's prisons, is neither dangerous nor painful. Only the other day he said, in answer to an obviously inspired question as to the possibility of a lady suffering injury from the treatment she received in prison, "I must wait until a case arises in which any person has suffered any injury from her treatment in prison." I got those words from *The Times* — of course, they may not be correctly reported. Well, of course, Mr. McKenna has no personal knowledge. Mr. McKenna has never, as far as I know, made any enquiry for himself, not do I think if he did it would have had any effect one way or the other. He relies entirely upon reports that are made to him— reports that must come from the prison officials, and go through the Home Office to him, and his statements are entirely founded upon those reports. I have no hesitation in saying that these reports, if they justify the statements that Mr. McKenna has made, are absolutely untrue. They not only deceive the public, but from the persistence with which they are got up in the same sense, they must be intended to deceive the public.

Statements Absolutely Untrue.

I don't wish to exonerate Mr. McKenna in the least. He has had abundant opportunity—in fact, it has been forced upon his notice—of ascertaining the falsehood of these statements, and if he goes on repeating them after having been told time after time by all sorts of people that they are not correct, he makes himself responsible for them whether they are true or not. And in his own statements in the House of Commons he has given sufficient evidence of his frame of mind with regard to this subject. Time after time has he told the Members of the House that there was no pain or injury, and almost in the same breath—certainly in the same evening—he has told how one of these prisoners has had to be turned out at a moment's notice, carried away in some vehicle or other, and attended by a prison doctor, to save her life. One or other of these statements must be absolutely untrue.

Now I come to the question of pain. Mr. McKenna says there is none. You all of you know that different people suffer different degrees of pain. Not only that, but the same person will suffer different degrees of pain after the same injury, according to the state of his or her nervous system. That is one reason why before any surgical operation patients require a certain amount of preparation in order that their nervous systems may be in such a state that they can stand the unavoidable pain as well as possible. They go through a certain amount of preparation in His Majesty's prison. Let me read you an account of how they manage. Of course, the prison cells are ranged down either side of a corridor. All the doors are opened when this business is going to begin so that nothing may be lost. "From 4:30 until 8:30 I heard the most dreadful screams and yells coming from the cells." This is the statement of a prisoner whom I know and who I know does not exaggerate: "I had never heard human beings being tortured before, and I was never courageous. I sat on my chair with my fingers in my ears for the greater part of that endless four hours. My heart was thumping against my ribs, as I sat listening to the procession of the doctors and wardresses as they came to and fro, and passed from cell to cell, and the groans and cries of those who were being fed, until at last the procession paused at my door. My turn had come."

The Screams of a Person in Agony.

That is a statement. I hope none of you have ever been so unfortunate as to be compelled to listen to the screams of a person when you are yourself in perfect health—the screams of a person in agony, screams gradually getting worse and worse, and then, at last, when the person's strength is becoming exhausted, dying down and ending in a groan. That is bad enough when you are strong and well, but if you come to think that these prisoners hear those screams in prison, that they are the screams of their friends, that they are helpless, that they know those screams are being caused by pain inflicted without the slightest necessity—I am not exaggerating in the least, I am giving you a plain statement of what goes on in His Majesty's prisons at the present time—then it becomes a matter upon which it is exceedingly difficult to speak temperately.

You all know that a person's nose is one of the most sensitive parts of the body. It is exceedingly well supplied with nerves, because it has to guard against anything injurious that may be inhaled. And you may know that the nostrils on either side are never the same size in an adult; they are always a bit distorted, sometimes one is larger, sometimes the other, and they are rarely straight. Can you imagine—well you may know this, too—the pain that is caused by stretching them? It is one of the most painful tortures, as the Inquisitors knew of old—stretching, or a "spread," as it was called. Can you imagine the pain of a rubber tube being forced up a prisoner's nose after the prisoner has told the operator that she knows that side of her nose is blocked, that she has never been able to breathe down it? They forced the tube up that side of the prisoner's nose three or four times until the operator was compelled by the blood that poured out to desist.

And can you imagine at the present day a tube being forced up a nostril in that way, and when it had at last passed through, being withdrawn, and the operator telling the prisoner that he would do it again until she took her food in the natural way? That has been done.

I have brought forward the instance because of another thing. Mr. Ellis Griffith, who is qualifying exceedingly well as an assistant to Mr. McKenna said: "If she suffered any pain (this is from Hansard) it was due entirely to the violent resistance she offered to what was necessary medical treatment." Now, these cases I have mentioned did not offer any resistance at all. They were absolutely passive; one was a cripple who could not resist; the others did not. So you can imagine that Mr. Ellis Griffith's statement is nearly as valuable as are those of Mr. McKenna. Resistance may be involuntary. You cannot always help it.

Here is another statement—Is this too medical? "The passage of the tube caused me at first but little inconvenience, but its further passage caused me to retch violently and to choke to such an extent that in my struggle for air I rose to my feet and stood upright, in spite of three or four wardresses holding me down, and then sank back into the chair exhausted." She did not struggle; her resistance was absolutely involuntary. "The passage of the tube caused me excruciating pain . . . After the operation, two wardresses took me back to my cell . . . I vomited milk, which eventually became tinged with blood."

I don't want to go on with this. I could go on; we have got a record of all these cases. What I could tell you would be only a repetition, sometimes rather worse, of what I have told you already, and I don't think that there is any object in my doing it. I think that what I have already told you is sufficient to disprove absolutely Mr. McKenna's statement that this is unattended by pain, and Mr. Ellis Griffith's statement that the pain caused is due to the patient's resistance. As regards the other statements they have made that there is no injury, we can show the House of Commons cases of that kind.

Nor can there be the least doubt as to the very serious injuries that are inflicted. In nearly every instance there is some local injury to the nose or mouth, and this is followed very frequently by inflammatory or septic irritation, because the proper precautions that are necessary in cases of this kind are not observed in prison. Still more often the injuries that follow are constitutional. Passing a tube through a prisoner's nose not infrequently causes such collapse that even in prison she has to be surrounded with hot-water bottles and blankets; and when this occurs day after day it has a most serious effect upon the prisoner's heart. One man was driven mad, and had to be taken to a pauper lunatic asylum; and there have been several instances in which the nervous system has been so seriously affected that it is doubtful whether it will ever recover.

Food Driven into Lungs.

Then they say there is no danger. In one instance—that of an unresisting prisoner in Winston Gaol, Birmingham—there is no question but that the food was driven down into the lungs. The operation was stopped by severe choking and persistent coughing. All night the prisoner could not sleep or lie down on account of great pain in her chest. She was hastily released next day, so ill that the authorities when discharging her obliged her to sign a statement that she left the prison at her own risk. On reaching home she was found to be suffering from pneumonia and pleurisy, caused from fluid being poured into her lungs. The same thing happened only the other day in the case of Miss Lenton. Fortunately, she is steadily recovering, and the Home Secretary may congratulate himself that these two cases—there have been others—are recovering, and that there will not have to be an inquest.

Mr. Mansell-Moullin then mentioned the cases of two men who had been forcibly fed in asylums, and who had in consequence contracted pneumonia, and who had died. These two women, he said, were young and strong, and were able to get over it.

Then with regard to Miss Lenton. The Home Secretary wrote that she was reported by the medical officer of Holloway Prison to be in a state of collapse, and in imminent danger of death consequent upon her refusal to take food. This statement is not true. "Three courses were open—to leave her to die; to attempt to feed her forcibly, which the medical officer advised would probably entail death; and to release her on her undertaking to sur-render herself at the further hearing of her case." That implied that she was not forcibly fed. She had been, but that fact was suppressed—suppressed by the Home Secretary in the statement that he published in the newspapers, suppressed because the cause of her illness was the forcible feeding. That has been proved absolutely.

Well, my time is nearly up, and I do not think that anything I can say will strengthen what I have said already. I have said enough to convince you of the horrors of forcible feeding, which I don't believe the public have ever realised, of the torture for the sole purpose of breaking down these women's determination, of breaking down their will, not for the purpose of keeping them alive.

As regards the moral and mental deterioration, that has been already alluded to by Mr. Forbes Robertson[1] and Mr. Bernard Shaw, I will only say this one thing. It shows itself everywhere where forcible feeding is practised. It shows itself in the prisons, where the medical officers, I am sorry to say, have on more that one occasion, laughed and made stupid jokes about "stuffing turkeys at Christmas." It shows itself in the prison officials, in the reports they have drawn up. It shows itself in the Home Secretary in the untrue statements that he has published and the evasions that he has made; and it shows itself, too, in the ribald laughter and obscene jokes with which the so-called gentlemen of the House of Commons received the accounts of these tortures.

20

"Kill Me, Or Give Me My Freedom!"

A Speech Delivered by Mrs. Pankhurst at the London Pavilion, July 14, 1913.

It is a little over three months since I last stood on this platform, on the eve of an Old Bailey trial. The outcome of that trial was that I was sent to three years' penal servitude, and in a little over three months I stand here again. At that last meeting I tried to make my audience understand the reason why women are rebels. We are rebels, and with greater justification than my fellow-rebel—Sir Edward Carson. Sir Edward Carson is a rebel as I am. He told us so in Ireland on Saturday. He is at liberty while I am a felon, and yet I and all other women have justification for rebellion which neither Sir Edward Carson nor any other man in the so-called United Kingdom has. They have a constitutional means of obtaining redress for their grievances, women have no such means. I say we are rebels because there is no other way open to us of obtaining redress for the grievances, the grave grievances which women have.

"A Defiant Deed."

Now I wondered as I came along to this meeting if I should find the physical strength to speak to you, because during those three months I, with other women, have experienced the tender mercies of a Liberal Government, in its efforts to coerce women and break their spirits; and as I wondered if I could speak when I came before you, coming as I have off a sick bed which I have kept intermittently during those three months, I thought to myself, "At any rate, I must say one thing—that a defiant deed has greater value than innumerable thousands of words"—and I determined that even if I were arrested and taken back to Holloway from the door of the Pavilion, I would do my defiant deed. There is a spirit in this movement which gives even the weakest of women power to speak her mind when the occasion arises; and I want to say just a few of the thoughts that I have had in my mind during these three months.

One word first of all—to say how proud I am of the splendid movement; how magnificent I think it is that you all went on as if nothing had happened after that raid at Lincoln's Inn House, which was intended to break down the movement, to scatter the members, to break their spirit, to make them afraid of their own personal position, to make them fear poverty, to make them fear disgrace, and which tried to weaken their determination to win the cause of their sex. All this failed. I think the enemy is realising that there is a spirit in women which is unbreakable. I say here that if they take me back and take Miss Kenney back, and take all the women whose names are prominent in the movement, and break their bodies, although they cannot break their spirits, this movement will go on.

"I Would rather be a Rebel than a Slave."

You know there is something worse than apparent failure, and that is to allow yourself to desist from doing something which you are convinced in your conscience is right, and I know that women, once convinced that they are doing what is right, that their rebellion is just, will go on, no matter what the difficulties, no matter what the dangers, so long as there is a woman alive to hold up the flag of rebellion. I would rather be a rebel than a slave. I would rather die than submit; and that is the spirit that animates this movement. Well, we are not going to die, at any rate the movement is not going to die, and that is all that matters.

Now I want to say a word about our paper. You know when they raided Lincoln's Inn House they thought that at the same time they would put an end to the *Suffragette*. Why were they so anxious to put an end to the *Suffragette*? (A Voice: Because it tells the truth.) Yes, it tells the truth about many things besides the militant movement. It was not because the *Suffragette* advocated militancy that they seized it. *The Suffragette* was seized, or rather they attempted to seize it, for the attempt did not succeed, because there were certain articles exposing the wrong doing of the Government. You remember that at this time they put through the House of Commons an Act which pretended to deal with that infamy of modern times—the White Slave Traffic, that ordered that all procurers were to be flogged. Well, in the *Suffragette* it was pointed out that that kind of legislation is futile. That if you want legislation, that legislation has got first of all to deal with customers, and the first people to whom you want to apply the White Slave Traffic Act is the Government. That is what the *Suffragette* made clear. That is why they attempted to stop that voice of the Woman's Movement—the *Suffragette*. Well, one of the things I made up my mind I would do if I lived to come out of prison and stand on this platform again, was to repeat in the most public possible manner that charge against the Government. Why, it is verified by almost everything they do affecting women.

"The Policy of Hush Up."

There was a prosecution the other day. Just opposite this Pavilion is a flat in which infamies were carried on, degrading young women. The poor wretched creature, the intermediary and servant of others, was arrested and taken before the magistrate. She was let out on bail. What happened in the interval? The result was seen at the trial. She pleaded guilty, and the judge said by pleading guilty she had spared young women from being put into the box. No, my friends, what it had done was to help them to hush up the thing. In Miss Kenney's trial private letters were read and names mentioned in those private letters. Those letters had nothing to do with the charge, no connection with it. There were letters in that case too, but it was not thought advisable to read them, because in this hypocritical country of ours, the policy of "hush-up" is the policy which is pursued everywhere. We want to protest against that kind of thing, and the people who are most against us in the House of Commons are the men who want things hushed up. And the Government wants things to be hushed up because there are too many tarred with the same brush.

"Purveying for the White Slave Traffic."

Another illustration out of last week. The War Office has been attempting to reduce the wages of women in the Army and Navy clothing factory. Is not that purveying for the White Slave Traffic? Is not the sweating of women in the Civil Service—is not the sweating among Government employed women purveying for the White Slave Traffic? But there are things worse than that. We have heard a little about India. We do not hear very much about our other possessions. A little light has been thrown upon India, and that is quite enough to make us want to know more about what goes on in other places. Well, we know enough, ladies and gentlemen, to find absolute justification to say, as I say here deliberately, that of all the white slavers in the country, or in the Empire, the British Government is the biggest white slavery and I hope the Government reporters present are taking it down. Whether they take it down or not, you here, when our voices are silent, as probably they will be for a short time when we leave this hall, you can, while the Press takes part in the conspiracy, you can each be a missionary to carry out of this hall the spirit that brought us into it. We are going on with our protest against the infamous coercion of women naturally law abiding, who have taken to the weapons of rebellion.

"Anarchy is There!"

There are people who told me even yesterday, that men who know better—because, believe me, my friends, however women may misunderstand the militant movement, every man who has any intelligence understands it quite well—there are men who are deluding women, men who know better, men who prove that they love freedom, and can sympathise with Russians or people of any other nation, men who are agitating for bomb throwing for freedom, these people are saying to women that now they are not going to sign a petition against the "Cat-and-Mouse Act" because they so disapprove of anarchy, and that women are creating anarchy. No, it is not we who create anarchy. Anarchy is there. There is anarchy in a country which professes to be under constitutional and representative government, and denies the benefits of the constitution to more than half its people.

The anarchy is there, and we are trying to end it, and these men know perfectly well that it is not true when they say that when we have got the vote we shall break laws in order to get our own way. They know perfectly well that we are breaking the laws because we have had no voice in making them; because, whether just or unjust, we have to submit to them; because we are taxed without being represented. We also know perfectly well that when we have won the same constitutional rights that they have, we shall continue to set them an example of law abidingness as women have always done, and what we have to do, and what we are doing by this protest, this terrible protest which involves our lives, what we are teaching them is this— that they will have to give votes to women or kill women.

I mean to be a voter in the land that gave me birth or that they shall kill me, and my challenge to the Government is: Kill me or give me my freedom: I shall force you to make that choice.

21

"Our Spirits Are Eternal."

A Speech Delivered by Miss Annie Kenney
at the London Pavilion,
July 14, 1913.

FIRST OF ALL, I WANT TO GIVE A HINT TO ANY SCOTLAND YARD MEN WHO
may be present—any who belong to us, you know, for they had to create a
special department in Scotland Yard to deal with the Suffragettes—I want
to tell any such who may be here that they need not worry. I am not going
to run away. They will be able to get me later on if they want to. Now, I
want to explain to this audience that I have no intention whatever of serving
the sentence imposed upon me. Why have I no intention of serving my
sentence? Because I do not think it is right that any woman Suffragist should
be thrust into prison while Sir Edward Carson and all the rest of the Unionist
leaders are allowed to go to Belfast and rouse up rebellion among the men
and the women of Belfast. What did Judge Phillimore say to us? He told us
when we were in the dock that it was not the mere making of militant
speeches that counted; it was because militancy followed these militant
speeches. What about Sir Edward Carson? He made a militant speech the
other day, and what happened yesterday? People were shot; riots were numerous in Belfast. We want to know is the Government going to be so
cowardly that they dare not attack Sir Edward Carson and Mr. F. E. Smith,
while they are trying to hunt our women up hill and down dale. I want to
tell this audience that I, as one of the "conspirators," have no intention of
serving my sentence any more than Sir Edward Carson.

What the Government Thought.

Nor do I intend keeping out of the movement. I will tell you why. They
have said the "Cat-and-Mouse Act" is a success. I say more disgrace to the
Government if the "Cat-and-Mouse Act" were a success—which it is not. If
it were a success then I say more shame to the Government, and more shame
to the electors of this country. Why do I say that I am not going to serve

my sentence, and that I intend to continue my work in the movement? Because the Government thought that if they took a few of us away they would stop the splendid constitutional work, for many of those in the dock with me were constitutional workers in this movement. If it was not for our Union there would not have been any constitutional society at all.

Now, what does the Government want to do? They want to send us to prison and keep us there as long as ever they dare. They send doctors in daily to see whether our pulse is just normal; to see how we are in health; to see whether they ought to turn us out, or whether they can wait a few more hours before turning us out; and when we are released they expect that we are going to stay in bed for the rest of the week, to be taken away again. Well, I am not going to do it. I am here against my doctor's orders this afternoon, but I say this: If I am well enough to be sent to prison to be tortured by the Home Secretary I am well enough to come to the Pavilion. Now, what does the Home Secretary want to do—for you know if you murder in your mind it is just as bad and just as evil as doing the deed right out. You have heard how people poison a person so slowly that no one can detect it. That is what the Home Secretary wants to do. He wants it to be so slow—in prison, out of prison—that the men electors will say that they could really not detect any real intent to murder on the part of the Home Secretary. He means to murder us sooner or later. I say for myself, it has got to be sooner and not later. At every opportunity when I come out of prison, after a few days have elapsed, and I can just stand on my feet, I am going to take part in this movement; and what I said in the dock I repeat here to-day more solemnly—they have either got to kill me or give me my freedom.

I Am Not Going to Run Away.

Now, the third point is this: I am not going to run away. The Home Secretary wants me to go away, but I am going to stay, because I shall embarrass him more by staying than I should if I ran away. We read in the one of the leading articles the other day that the "Cat-and-Mouse Act" had succeeded. How has it succeeded, according to that article? First of all, they said we were laid up and out of the work; but I have come here to show them that it is not so. I have come here in sheer defiance, to show the Liberal Government that I do not intend to be put out of the way so quickly. Then they try to make you believe that money is not coming in. That is just in the hope that it won't come in; but we know that the spirit of this movement is so strong, and we build on such a firm foundation, that whatever they do funds will pour into our coffers. I say to the Home Secretary that I am not going away because he wants me to go. If he did not want me to go I should go.

I have not seen you since the famous conspiracy trial. I ask you, Were we not right in what we said? Nothing ever looked so ridiculous as that trial called the "Conspiracy Trial." What the Government wanted to do was to stop the constitutional part, because we know that our society is practically the only society, not only of Suffrage societies, but of other political societies, that makes their position uncomfortable and intolerable when they go to the electors. They therefore hoped that they would diminish our constitutional work. They failed to do that, just as they have failed to do everything else.

A Nice Christian Judge.

The judge said, in sentencing us, that if Mr. McKenna asked his advice, as was the customary practice, he would tell the Home Secretary that he should not let us out whatever happened. There is a nice Christian judge for you? He dared to talk to us about Christianity! I daresay our souls shine with a purer flame than his! He told us that we shall have to reckon with our own conscience! I think every Suffragette has reckoned with her conscience long ago. This judge sentenced me to 16 or 18 months—I do not know which, for of course I am not going to serve it—I believe it was 16 months in the third division though he knew perfectly well that we should not do any work when in prison. He knew we should be too ill within two or three days to do any work if we wanted to. How silly it is! What humbug it is for these judges to sentence women to 16 or 18 months in the third division, when they know that we shall never serve these sentences.

As it has been put so clearly, they dare not allow us to die in prison, because they know that if they did there would be another conspiracy trial, and the electors would be the jury, we should be the prosecution, and the Government would be the defendants, and we know that the case would go against them—that is why they have not the pluck or courage to let any of us die in prison. You know that Mr. McKenna said he would not allow any of us to die in prison. Mr. McKenna is not almighty. He may think he is; but even Mr. McKenna has not the power over life and death. Some day a terrible tragedy will happen in Holloway. Then what will the Home Secretary do, having allowed a woman to die instead of bringing in a measure to give women the vote? Instead of discussing a "Cat-and-Mouse Act" the Government ought to have given equality of voting rights to men and women.

Let Them Face Facts.

The "Cat-and-Mouse Act" will have to be broken down, just as forcible feeding has been broken down. We have got to break down the "Cat-and-

Mouse Act." Now, what will happen if that measure is broken down, as it will be—then what will the Government have to do? They will have to bring in another measure of coercion stronger than the other, or the alternative will have to be Votes for Women. Therefore we say instead of a Liberal Government thinking what coercive measure they can bring against the British women of this country, let them face facts as they are; let them admit that this is the living question of the day. Let them face facts, and say: "We, as a Liberal Government, can no longer bring these coercive measures against women. Instead, we will bring in a measure and give women equality of voting rights with their men folk." Would not that be more in keeping with the great principles of Bright and Cobden? The time has come when coercion ought to bring in a Bill to give equality of voting rights to men and women.

Now we come to the heavy sentences that are being passed on our women. Think of Miss Kitty Marion and Miss Giveen! Kitty Marion is an example of what Suffragettes are. Little does she care whether she is to be sent back to prison every day of the week. She is determined to get this question settled.

Why Were Names Suppressed?

A very special case was brought up in the courts the other day. You all know what I am referring to—the case of the woman arrested for keeping a brothel in some part of London.[1] What sentence did that woman get? Three months in the second division, while Kitty Marion got three years' penal servitude! I know what some people will say. The Anti-Suffragists will say: "Oh, you see, when it came to a woman who tried to get young girls to lead an immoral life, they did not give the woman the cat, as they give it to men." No, my friends. Why? The reason is not to be found in what was brought up in court, but in what was left unsaid. Why were the names of the customers suppressed? Why were the names of the men who buy these girls suppressed? Suppose the authorities found one flaw in our movement, would they suppress any names—would they have tried to keep it away from the public? You know perfectly well that at the "Conspiracy Trial" most insignificant letters were read out in the hopes of getting one little bit of something that might make the members of this Union wonder whether everything was run on straight lines or not. Every little thing was brought up, all the accounts were gone into. They did not try to suppress anything at our trial; but when it comes to a case like this the Press are asked not to make it public. Does it not show the bad state of affairs that we are living under? Does it not show you the dreadful and miserable state that we have arrived at?

Why, they are afraid of women getting the vote! That is why they had the "Conspiracy Trial." Two articles written by Miss Pankhurst first of all gave them the idea that they had got to suppress the constitutional work of this organisation. Miss Pankhurst asked them two or three questions which they have not dared to answer in the House of Commons—that is at the bottom of a lot of the opposition. As we always say, we have got the clean men on our side, and the best men on our side.

The Spirit Lives On.

It is going to be a fight to the finish, for even Mr. McKenna has had to admit that we have had no more fear of death than the savages in the Soudan. He wanted to make us feel uncomfortable when he called us savages; he knows perfectly well that we are not. He knows that we have no fear of death, because there is nothing to be afraid of. We can never find any place worse than that which we have to live in at the present time.

Then, again, I think that most of us believe that though the body goes there is something within that lives on eternally. The spirit lives on eternally, and we are just as much part of the great Universe when we have gone over to another life as we are at the present time. And if it comes about that anything happens to any of the women in our midst there will be no fear. We shall be perfectly calm and serene, because we shall know that we have done our duty, and our little bit for the great reform that we are all struggling for at the present time. Therefore I say we can go on quite calmly; we can go on serene in mind and peaceful in spirit, for our spirits are eternal, and will be ever part of the great Universe. Then let us follow out what our conscience tells us is right, and we shall be prepared to face our conscience and to face the great Maker of all of us.

22

Address at Hartford

Introduction by Mrs. Hepburn

LADIES AND GENTLEMEN:[1] WE HAVE COME HERE TONIGHT TO HEAR FROM its leader the story of one of the great revolutionary movements, the women's revolution in England. It is to me the greatest honor that I have been asked to preside at this meeting and to introduce to you such a woman at Mrs. Pankhurst. As you all know, who have gone through your histories at all, the history of the progress of civilization is filled with cruelty. Each step forward into the future is paid for by the sufferings of some individual human beings. It seems to be willed that the freedom of the many is to be paid for by the sacrifice of the few who understand; and these few in each generation stand out among us so that you can almost name them as different from the rest of the people, the few people who understand where the race is going and why progress has to be helped by individual human beings.

All of the great human rights we have now—freedom of conscience, political liberty that men have, all of the great human rights that we have— have been fought for and won by some of these individual human beings in the past. To the people of their generation they have seemed like fanatics, and they have not been understood. History alone has shown them in their true light. Now, that is true of religious freedom, the freedom of conscience; it is true, as I said, of political liberty; and in each case the few that have stood out have been people that have been willing to suffer personally for the benefit of the many that came after them, people who were willing to suffer physical torture if need be, or anything else that need be, so long as the particular injustice that they saw in their midst was cured by the time their life went out.

Now, the woman's revolution in England has in it women who have been willing to suffer in this conscious, definite, purposeful way, women who have given their lives to the suffrage movement. When Mrs. Pankhurst and her daughters first began working in England the question of "Votes for Women" was an academic one, discussed only in academic circles. Since that time the question of votes for women has become a practical political issue,

322

and it is due to the militant women in England that the question has come out of the academic sphere into the forefront of practical politics. For the past ten years, in spite of misunderstanding, in spite of ridicule, in spite of imprisonment, in spite of the torture of forcible feeding, this band of women has pushed on. They have defied a ministry that could not understand, a ministry of stubborn Englishmen, and they have defied an intolerant and uncomprehending public opinion, until now, after ten years of their work, one of the strongest governments in the whole world has practically acknowledged itself unable to defeat them; and they have accomplished another great purpose and that is this: that a torpid womanhood, a sort of womanhood that was willing to sit back and wait until the things that they ought to work for were handed to them—a torpid womanhood all over the world has been aroused into action, aroused to the real doing for the human race of what the mothers of the human race ought to do.

In the future Connecticut women will look back upon this time and they will read with pride that the great leader of this women's revolution visited their State during her struggle for the political emancipation of their sex, and I think that those of us who are here tonight must feel that it is a rare privilege to be personally able to do her honor and to understand her in our generation—Mrs. Pankhurst.

(Applause.)

Address by Mrs. Pankhurst

Mrs. Hepburn, Ladies and Gentlemen: Many people come to Hartford to address meetings as advocates of some reform. Tonight it is not to advocate a reform that I address a meeting in Hartford. I do not come here as an advocate, because whatever position the suffrage movement may occupy in the United States of America, in England it has passed beyond the realm of advocacy and it has entered into the sphere of practical politics. It has become the subject of revolution and civil war, and so tonight I am not here to advocate woman suffrage. American suffragists can do that very well for themselves. I am here as a soldier who has temporarily left the field of battle in order to explain—it seems strange it should have to be explained—what civil war is like when civil war is waged by women. I am not only here as a soldier temporarily absent from the field of battle; I am here—and that I think is the strangest part of my coming—I am here as a person who, according to the law courts of my country, it has been decided, is of no value to the community at all; and I am adjudged because of my life to be a dangerous person, under sentence of penal servitude in a convict prison. So you see there is some special interest in hearing so unusual a person address you. I dare say, in the minds of many of you—you will perhaps forgive me this personal touch—that I do not look either very like a soldier or very like a convict, and yet I am both.

Now, first of all I want to make you understand the inevitableness of revolution and civil war, even on the part of women, when you reach a certain stage in the development of a community's life. It is not at all difficult if revolutionaries come to you from Russia, if they come to you from China, or from any other part of the world, if they are men, to make you understand revolution in five minutes, every man and every woman to understand revolutionary methods when they are adopted by men. Many of you have expressed sympathy, probably even practical sympathy, with revolutionaries in Russia. I dare say you have followed with considerable interest the story of how the Chinese revolutionary, Sun Yat Sen, conducted the Chinese revolution from England. And yet I find in American newspapers there is a great deal of misunderstanding of the fact that one of the chief minds engaged in conducting the women's revolution is, for purposes of convenience, located in Paris. It is quite easy for you to understand—it would not be necessary for men to enter into explanations at all—the desirability of revolution if I were a man, in any of these countries, even in a part of the British Empire known to you as Ireland. If an Irish revolutionary had addressed this meeting, and many have addressed meetings all over the United States during the last twenty or thirty years, it would not be necessary for that revolutionary to explain the need of revolution beyond saying that the people of his country were denied—and by people, meaning men—were denied the right of self-government. That would explain the whole situation. If I were a man and I said to you: "I come from a country which professes to have representative institutions and yet denies me, a taxpayer, an inhabitant of the country, representative rights," you would at once understand that that human being, being a man, was justified in the adoption of revolutionary methods to get representative institutions. But since I am a woman it is necessary in the twentieth century to explain why women have adopted revolutionary methods in order to win the rights of citizenship.

You see, in spite of a good deal that we hear about revolutionary methods not being necessary for American women because American women are so well off, most of the men of the United States quite calmly acquiesce in the fact that half of the community are deprived absolutely of citizen rights, and we women, in trying to make our case clear, always have to make as part of our argument, and urge upon men in our audience the fact—a very simple fact—that women are human beings. It is quite evident you do not all realize we are human beings or it would not be necessary to argue with you that women may, suffering from intolerable injustice, be driven to adopt revolutionary methods. We have, first of all to convince you we are human beings, and I hope to be able to do that in the course of the evening before I sit down, but before doing that, I want to put a few political arguments before you—not arguments for the suffrage, because I said when I opened, I didn't mean to do that—but arguments for the adoption of militant methods in order to win political rights.

A great many of you have been led to believe, from the somewhat meagre accounts you get in the newspapers, that in England there is a strange manifestation taking place, a new form of hysteria being swept across part of the feminist population of those Isles, and this manifestation takes the shape of irresponsible breaking of windows, burning of letters, general inconvenience to respectable, honest business people who want to attend to their business. It is very irrational you say: even if these women had sufficient intelligence to understand what they were doing, and really did want the vote, they have adopted very irrational means for getting the vote. "How are they going to persuade people that they ought to have the vote by breaking their windows?" you say. Now, if you say that, it shows you do not understand the meaning of our revolution at all, and I want to show you that when damage is done to property it is not done in order to convert people to woman suffrage at all. It is a practical political means, the only means we consider open to voteless persons to bring about a political situation, which can only be solved by giving women the vote.

Suppose the men of Hartford had a grievance, and they laid that grievance before their legislature, and the legislature obstinately refused to listen to them, or to remove their grievance, what would be the proper and the constitutional and the practical way of getting their grievance removed? Well, it is perfectly obvious at the next general election, when the legislature is elected, the men of Hartford in sufficient numbers would turn out that legislature and elect a new one; entirely change the personnel of an obstinate legislature which would not remove their grievance. It is perfectly simple and perfectly easy for voting communities to get their grievances removed if they act in combination and make an example of the legislature by changing the composition of the legislature and sending better people to take the place of those who have failed to do justice. But let the men of Hartford imagine that they were not in the position of being voters at all, that they were governed without their consent being obtained, that the legislature turned an absolutely deaf ear to their demands, what would the men of Hartford do then? They couldn't vote the legislature out. They would have to choose: they would have to make a choice of two evils; they would either have to submit indefinitely to an unjust state of affairs, or they would have to rise up and adopt some of the antiquated means by which men in the past got their grievances remedied. We know what happened when your forefathers decided that they must have representation for taxation, many, many years ago. When they felt they couldn't wait any longer, when they laid all the arguments before an obstinate British government that they could think of, and when their arguments were absolutely disregarded, when every other means had failed, they began by the Tea Party at Boston, and they went on until they had won the independence of the United States of America. That is what happened in the old days.

It is perfectly evident to any logical mind that when you have got the vote, by the proper use of the vote in sufficient numbers, by combination, you can get out of any legislature whatever you want, or, if you cannot get it, you can send them about their business and choose other people who will be more attentive to your demands. But, it is clear to the meanest intelligence that if you have not got the vote, you must either submit to laws just or unjust, administration just or unjust or the time inevitably comes when you will revolt against that injustice and use violent means to put an end to it. That is so logically correct that we hear politicians today talk about the inherent right of revolution and rebellion on the part of human beings suffering from an intolerable injustice, and in England today we are having a situation brought about by men which exactly illustrates the case. We have got in Ireland today a very serious situation. I refer to the fact that for generations Irish agitators, Irish lawbreakers, Irish extremists, who have been sentenced to long terms of imprisonment in English convict prisons, have come over to America and have asked the people of the United States to give them money, to send them help in various forms to fight the Irish rebellion. The Irish rebellion has at last, during the past few years come into practical politics, and it has found shape in a measure which has now passed through the House of Commons and through the House of Lords, giving what the Irishmen so long wanted, Home Rule to Ireland. That is to say, next June, a Parliament is going to be set up in Dublin, an Irish Parliament, for the management of Irish affairs quite distinct from the government in London. The majority of men in Ireland desired it; presumably the majority of women acquiesced in their desire, but they were not asked whether they wished it or not. It is certain in the course of the Irish rebellion women have taken a very prominent part; and it is rather a notable point to which I should like to call your attention, that when the imprisonments of Irishmen took place in the course of their political rebellion they were put almost invariably, after a certain amount of struggle, in the first division, and were treated as political offenders; but when women, helping the men, got into the coils of the law, all those women in Ireland who were helping the men to get Home Rule, were invariably treated as ordinary criminals and got ordinary criminals' treatment. You see, ladies, even in a rebellion, there is an advantage in being a voter, and if you are not a voter you are liable to get very much worse treatment than the voters, even the law-breaking voters get. Now, the situation today then is, that Home Rule for Ireland is to take effect early next year or in the course of next year. But there is a part of Ireland which does not want home rule. There is a part of Ireland which prefers to be governed from London. That is the North of Ireland, in the

County of Ulster. For racial reasons, for religious reasons, for economic reasons, the majority of the people there do not want Home Rule at all. They call themselves Loyalists, Unionists, and they want to maintain the union with Great Britain in its present form. Directly the Home Rule bill passed, directly it was perfectly clear that Home Rule was to be granted, these people began to revolt. They had a leader, a man who formed a part of the last Conservative administration, Sir Edward Carson, a distinguished lawyer, a distinguished statesman; he is an Irishman. Sir Edward Carson came to be the leader of the Ulster rebellion. He has advocated civil war; he has not only advocated civil war, he has urged the men of Ulster to drill and prepare to fight if civil war comes to pass. Their first stage in this rebellion was the signing of a great declaration on behalf of the Union. It is rather notable that not only men signed that declaration, but women signed it also; the women of Ulster were invited to sign the declaration along with the men. And to those people who say that the province of woman is quite apart from politics, and that women by nature take no interest in politics, I would like to say that more women signed that declaration than did men, considerably more. Well, the last stage of this struggle, and the struggle is coming to a head, is this: that Sir Edward Carson has been making speeches in which he has gloried in having broken the law, he has challenged the British Government to arrest him, arms have been shipped to Ireland; and there is not a club, a young men's club, a working-man's club, or the middle class or the upper class men's club, where they are not drilling and preparing for civil war. The law has always been broken, because there has been considerable riot in the streets of Belfast, and lives even have been lost, and I want to say to you in the meeting how much have you heard of all this in the American newspapers? Have you heard loud condemnation from English newspapers echoed in your own papers? No; the newspapers and you have accepted quite calmly the fact that revolution is preparing in Ireland, and not one of you, whether you are a newspaper editor writing leading articles in your sanctum, or whether you are a business man or a professional man, not one of you has questioned the right of those men in Ulster, although they are voters and have a constitutional means for getting redress for their grievances, the right of those men to resort to revolution if everything else fails.

Well, there is another picture, another contrast I want to draw. We have Sir Edward Carson preaching revolution and justifying bloodshed in defense of what he calls the rights of the manhood of Ulster, the right of having themselves governed in the way they prefer. He has not hesitated to advocate the shedding of blood because he says it is quite worth while to shed blood, of your own and other people's in defense of your citizen rights, in the defense of your having the right to choose the form of government you wish. Sir Edward Carson has not been arrested; Sir Edward Carson has not been charged with conspiracy; Sir Edward Carson has not been sent to jail. He has been making precisely the same kind of speeches that I made up to the month of March last, with this difference: that while he has justified the shedding human blood in a revolution, I have always said that nothing would bring me to the point of claiming that we should destroy human life in the course of our woman's agitation. That is the only distinction between his speeches and mine, that he has advocated and justified the taking of life where I have always stopped short in my justification, at property, at inanimate objects. I have always said human life is sacred, and in a woman's revolution we respect human life, and we stop short of injury to human life.

Now, to those people who say that women are better treated than men when they break the laws, to those people who say that there is no need for women to take to methods of revolution, I want to draw this contrast; here is Sir Edward Carson, a man who presumably by his education and training, ought to be more respectful of the law than persons who are not either fit to understand the laws or to vote for those who make them. You have Sir Edward Carson, a chartered libertine, going to and fro in England and in Ireland, making these speeches; whereas you have me, a woman arrested and charged and sentenced to a long term of penal servitude for doing precisely what he has done, although he has not had the justification that I have, because, again I want to call your attention to the point, that Sir Edward Carson and his friends have the vote, and therefore have the legitimate and proper way of getting redress for their grievances, whereas neither I nor any of the women have any constitutional means whatever and no legitimate, recognized methods of getting redress for our grievances except the methods of revolution and violence.

Well now, I want to argue with you as to whether our way is the right one; I want to explain all these things that you have not understood; I want to make you understand exactly what our plan of campaign has been because I have always felt that if you could only make people understand most people's hearts are in the right place and most people's understandings are sound and most people are more or less logical—if you could only make them understand.

Now, I want to come back to the point where I said, if the men of Hartford had a grievance and had no vote to get their redress, if they felt that grievance sufficiently, they would be forced to adopt other methods. That brings me to an explanation of these methods that you have not been able to understand. I am going to talk later on about the grievances, but I want to first of all make you understand that this civil war carried on by women is not the hysterical manifestation which you thought it was, but was carefully and logically thought out, and I think when I have finished you will say, admitted the grievance, admitted the strength of the cause, that we could not do anything else, that there was no other way, that we had either to submit to intolerable injustice and let the woman's movement go back and remain in a worse position than it was before we began, or we had to go on with these methods until victory was secured, and I want also to convince you that these methods are going to work because when you adopt the methods of revolution there are two justifications which I feel are necessary or to be desired. The first is that you have good cause for adopting your methods in the beginning, and secondly that you have adopted methods which when pursued with sufficient courage and determination are bound, in the long run, to win.

Now, it would take too long to trace the course of militant methods as adopted by women, because it is about eight years since the word militant was first used to describe what we were doing, it is about eight years since the first militant action was taken by women. It was not militant at all, except that it provoked militancy on the part of those who were opposed to it. When women asked questions in political meetings and failed to get answers, they were not doing anything militant. To ask questions at political meetings is an acknowledged right of all people who attend public meetings; certainly in my country, men have always done it, and I hope they do it in America, because it seems to me that if you allow people to enter your legislatures without asking them any questions as to what they are going to do when they get there you are not exercising your citizen rights and your citizen duties as you ought. At any rate in Great Britain it is a custom, a time-honored one, to ask questions of candidates for parliament and ask questions of members of the government. No man was ever put out of a public meeting for asking a question until Votes for Women came onto the political horizon. The first people who were put out of a political meeting for asking questions were women; they were brutally ill-used; they found themselves in jail before twenty-four hours had expired. But instead of the newspapers, which are largely inspired by the politicians, putting militancy and the reproach of militancy, if reproach there is, on the people who had assaulted the women, they actually said it was the women who were militant and very much to blame. How different the reasoning is that men adopt when they are discussing the cases of men and those of women. Had they been men who asked the questions, and had those men been brutally ill-used, you would have heard a chorus of reprobation on the part of the people toward those who refused to answer those questions. But as they were women who asked the questions, it was not the speakers on the platform who would not answer them, who were to blame, or the ushers at the meeting, it was the poor women who had had their bruises and their knocks and scratches, and who were put into prison for doing precisely nothing but holding a protest meeting in the street after it was all over. However, we were called militant for doing that, and we were quite willing to accept the name, because militancy for us is time-honoured; you have the church militant, and in the sense of spiritual militancy we were very militant indeed. We were determined to press this question of the enfranchisement of women to the point where we were no longer to be ignored by the politicians as had been the case for about fifty years, during which time women had patiently used every means open to them to win their political enfranchisement. We found that all the fine phrases about freedom and liberty were entirely for male consumption, and that they did not in any way apply to women. When it was said taxation without representation is tyranny, when it was "Taxation of men without representation is tyranny," everybody quite calmly accepted the fact that women had to pay taxes and even were sent to prison if they failed to pay them—quite right. We found that "Government of the people, by the people and for the people," which is also a time-honored Liberal principle, was again only for male consumption; half of the people were entirely ignored; it was the duty of women to pay their taxes and obey the laws and look as pleasant as they could under the circumstances: in fact, every principle of liberty enunciated in any civilized country on earth with very few exceptions, was intended entirely for men; and when women tried to force the putting into practice of these principles, for women, then they discovered they had come into a very, very unpleasant situation indeed.

Now, I am going to pass rapidly over all the incidents that happened after the two first women went to prison for asking questions of Cabinet Ministers, and come right up to the time when our militancy became real militancy, when we organized ourselves on an army basis, when we determined, if necessary, to fight for our rights just as our forefathers had fought for their rights. Then people began to say that while they believed they had no criticism of militancy, as militancy, while they thought it was quite justifiable for people to revolt against intolerable injustice, it was absurd and ridiculous for women to attempt it because women could not succeed. After all the most practical criticism of our militancy coming from men has been the argument that it could not succeed. They would say, "We would be with you if you could succeed but it is absurd for women who are the weaker sex, for women who have not got the control of any large interests, for women who have got very little money, who have peculiar duties as women, which handicaps them extremely—for example, the duty of caring for children—it is absurd for women to think they can ever win their rights by fighting; you had far better give it up and submit because there it is, you have always been subject and you always will be." Well now, that really became the testing time. Then we women determined to show the world, that women, handicapped as women are, can still fight and can still win, and now I want to show you how this plan of ours was carefully thought out, even our attacks on private property, which has been so much misunderstood. I have managed in London to make audiences of business men who came into the meetings very, very angry with us indeed, some of whom had their telephonic communication cut off for several hours and had not been able to even get telegrams from their stock-brokers in cities far distant, who naturally came to our meetings in a very angry frame of mind, understand the situation; and if it has been possible to make them understand, if some of them even get fairly enthusiastic about our methods, it ought to be possible, Mrs. Hepburn, for me to explain the situation to an audience in Hartford, who, after all, are far enough off to be able to see, unlike men in our own country who are not able to see wood for trees.

I would like to suggest that if later on, while I am explaining these matters to you, there comes into the mind of any man or woman in the audience some better plan for getting what we want out of an obstinate government, I would be thankful and grateful if that person, man or woman, would tell me of some better plan than ours for dealing with the situation.

Here we have a political system where no reforms can get onto the statute book of the Old Country unless it is initiated by the government of the country, by the Cabinet, by the handful of people who really govern the country. It doesn't matter whether you have practically every member of parliament on your side, you cannot get what you want unless the Cabinet initiate legislation, a situation by which the private member has become almost of no account at all, the ordinary private member of parliament. He may introduce bills, but he knows himself that he is only registering a pious opinion of a certain number of electors in his constituency; it may be his own; but that pious opinion will never find its way onto the statute book of his country until the government in power, the Prime Minister and his colleagues, introduces a government measure to carry that reform. Well then, the whole problem of people who want reform is, to bring enough political pressure to bear upon the government to lead them to initiate, to draft a bill, and introduce it in the first instance, into the House of Commons, force it through the House of Commons, press it through the House of Lords, and finally land it safely, having passed through the shoals and rapids of the parliamentary river, safely on the statute book as an Act of Parliament. Well, combinations of voters have tried for generations, even with the power of the vote, to get their reforms registered in legislation, and have failed. You have to get your cause made a first class measure; you have to make the situation in the country so urgent and so pressing that it has become politically dangerous for the government to neglect that question any longer, so politically expedient for them to do it that they realize they cannot present themselves to the country at the next general election unless it has been done. Well, that was the problem we had to face, and we faced it a mere handful of women. Well, whether you like our methods or not, we have succeeded in making Woman Suffrage one of the questions which even Cabinet Ministers now admit cannot indefinitely be neglected. It must be dealt with within a very short period of time. No other methods than ours would have brought about that result. You may have sentimental articles in magazines by the Chancellor of the Exchequer who seems to be able to spare time from his ordinary avocations to write magazine articles telling you that militancy is a drag on the movement for Woman Suffrage. But our answer to that is, methinks our gentlemen doth protest too much, because until militancy became to be known neither Mr. Lloyd George nor any statesman, no, nor any member of parliament, ever thought it was necessary to mention the subject of Woman Suffrage at all. Now they mention it constantly, to tell us what damage we have done to our cause. They are all urging us to consider the serious position into which we have brought the cause of Woman Suffrage.

Well now, let me come to the situation as we find it. We felt we had to rouse the public to such a point that they would say to the government, you must give women the vote. We had to get the electors, we had to get the business interests, we had to get the professional interests, we had to get the men of leisure all unitedly saying to the government, relieve the strain of this situation and give women the vote; and that is a problem that I think the most astute politician in this meeting would find very difficult. We have done it; we are doing it every day; and I think when you take that fact into consideration you will realize why we have been attacking private property, why we have been attacking the property of men so absorbed in their business that they generally forget to vote in ordinary elections, why we have attacked the pleasures of men whose whole life is spent in a round of pleasure, and who think politics so dull and so beneath their distinguished ossification that they hardly know which party is in power. All these people have had to be moved in order to bring enough pressure to bear upon the government to compel them to deal with the question of Woman Suffrage. And now that in itself is an explanation. There is a homely English proverb which may help to clear the situation which is this: "You cannot rouse the Britisher unless you touch his pocket." That is literally true. Perhaps you now can understand why we women thought we must attack the thing that was of most value in modern life in order to make these people wake up and realize that women wanted the vote, and that things were going to be very uncomfortable until women got the vote, because it is not by making people comfortable you get things in practical life, it is by making them uncomfortable. That is a homely truth that all of us have to learn.

I don't know, Mrs. Hepburn, whether I have used the domestic illustration in Hartford, but it is a very good one; it is quite worth using again. You have two babies very hungry and wanting to be fed. One baby is a patient baby, and waits indefinitely until its mother is ready to feed it. The other baby is an impatient baby and cries lustily, screams and kicks and makes everybody unpleasant until it is fed. Well, we know perfectly well which baby is attended to first. That is the whole history of politics. Putting sentiment aside, people who really want reforms learn that lesson very quickly. It is only the people who are quite content to go on advocating them indefinitely who play the part of the patient baby in politics. You have to make more noise than anybody else, you have to make yourself more obtrusive than anybody else, you have to fill all the papers more than anybody else, in fact you have to be there all the time and see that they do not snow you under, if you are really going to get your reform realized. That is what we women have been doing, and in the course of our desperate struggle we have had to make a great many people very uncomfortable. Now, one woman was arrested on an occasion when a great many windows were broken in London, as a protest against a piece of trickery on the part of the government, which will be incredible in fifty years, when the history of the movement is read. Women broke some windows as a protest; they broke a good many shop-keepers' windows; they broke the windows of shop-keepers where they spent most of their money when they bought their hats and their clothing; they also broke the windows of many of the Clubs, the smart Clubs in Piccadilly. One of the Clubs was the Guard Club. Well, the ordinary army man is not much in politics, but he very often, because of his aristocratic and social connections, has considerable influence if he would use it. One woman broke the windows of the Guard Club, and when she broke those windows she stood there quietly until the Guard hall porter came out and seized her and held her until the policemen came to take her to prison. A number of the guards came out to see the kind of woman it was who had broken their windows, and they saw there a quiet little woman. She happened to be an actress, a woman who had come into our militant movement because she knew of the difficulties and dangers and temptations of the actress's life, of how badly paid she is, what her private sorrows are and her difficulties, and so she had come into the militant movement to get votes for actresses as quickly as possible, so that through the vote they could secure better conditions. Some of the guards—I think men who had never known what it was to earn a living, who knew nothing of the difficulties of a man's life, let alone the difficulties of a woman's life—came out, and they said: "Why did you break our windows? We have done nothing." She said: "It is because you have done nothing I have broken your windows." And perhaps out of that woman's breaking of windows has come this new movement of men of my country, where we find distinguished men who fought through the Boer war are drilling now like Sir Edward Carson, in Belfast, drilling men in order to form a bodyguard to protect the militant women. Probably that broken window of the Guard Club did a good deal to rouse men to the defense of women and to the injustice of their situation.

Well, then the shop-keepers who could not understand why we should break the shop-keepers windows. Why should we alienate the sympathy of the shop-keepers? Well, there is the other side of the question, gentlemen—

why should the shopkeepers alienate the sympathy of their customers by refusing to help them to get political power, some power to make the condition of the woman who helps to earn the shop-keeper's money by serving in his shop, easier than it is at the present time. Those women broke shop-keepers' windows, and what was the situation? Just at the beginning of the winter season when all the new winter hats and coats were being shown, the shop-keepers had to barricade all their windows with wood and nobody could see the new winter fashions. Well, there again is an impossible situation. The shop-keeper cannot afford to quarrel with his customers, and we have today far more practical sympathy amongst the shop-keepers of London than we ever had when we were quiet, gentle, lady-like suffragists asking nicely for a vote.

Well then, there were the men of pleasure, or the business men who were so busy earning money during the week that all they could think of when the week came to an end was recreation, and the great recreation in England today is playing golf. Everywhere on Saturday you see men streaming away into the country for the week-end to play golf. They so monopolize the golf links that they have made a rule that although the ladies may play golf all the week, the golf links are entirely reserved for men on Saturday and Sunday; and you have this spectacle of the exodus of men from London into the country to fill up the week-end with playing golf. They are not, ladies, putting their heads together thinking how best they can govern the country for you, what good laws they can make for you and for the world; they are there, all of them, getting their health, and I do not blame them for it, at the week-end. Well, we attacked the golf links; we wanted to make them think; and if you had been in London and taken a Sunday paper you would have read, especially if you played golf, with consternation, that all the beautiful greens that had taken years to make, had been cut up or destroyed with an acid or made almost impossible to play upon on the Friday night, and in many cases there going to be important matches on the Saturday afternoon and Sunday.

Just to give you an illustration of the effectiveness of these methods in waking the Britisher up, in conveying to him that women want the vote and are going to get it even if we do not adopt quite the men's methods in order to do so, I was staying at a little house in the country on a golf links, a house that had been loaned to me to use whenever I could get away from my work, and several times in the course of that Sunday morning I got telephone calls from gentlemen who were prominent members of golf clubs in that vicinity. It so happened that the golf links where I was spending the week-end, had not been touched. Those links had been respected because some of the prominent women suffragettes happened to be members of the club, and those women who destroyed the greens—I don't know who they were, but it was no doubt done by women—spared the links where these women whom they admired and respected, played. Well, then that morning I was rung up over and over again by excited gentlemen who begged that those golf links should be spared, saying: "I don't know whether your followers know that we are all suffragists, on our committee, we are entirely in favor of woman suffrage." And I said, "Well, don't you think you had better tell Mr. Asquith so, because if you are suffragists and do nothing, naturally you will only add to the indignation of the women. If you really want your golf links spared you had better intimate to Mr. Asquith that you think it is high time he put his principles into practice and gave the women the vote." There was another gentleman who rang up and said: "The members of our committee, who are all suffragists, are seriously considering turning all the women members out of the club if this sort of thing goes on." "Well," I said, "don't you think your greater safety is to keep the women in the club as a sort of insurance policy against anything happening to your links?"

But this experience will show you that if you really want to get anything done, it is not so much a matter of whether you alienate sympathy; sympathy is a very unsatisfactory thing if it is not practical sympathy. It does not matter to the practical suffragist whether she alienates sympathy that was never of any use to her. What she wants is to get something practical done, and whether it is done out of sympathy or whether it is done out of fear, or whether it is done because you want to be comfortable again and not be worried in this way, doesn't particularly matter so long as you get it. We had enough of sympathy for fifty years; it never has brought us anything; and we would rather have an angry man going to the government and saying, my business is interfered with and I won't submit to its being interfered with any longer because you won't give women the vote, than to have a gentleman come onto our platforms year in and year out and talk about his ardent sympathy with woman suffrage.

Now then, let me come to the more serious matters and to some of the more recent happenings. You know when you have war, many things happen that all of us deplore. We fought a great war not very long ago, in South Africa. Women were expected to face with equanimity the loss of those dearest to them in warfare; they were expected to submit to being impoverished: they were expected to pay the war tax exactly like the men for a war about which the women were never consulted at all. When you think of the object of that war it really makes some of us feel very indignant at the hypocrisy of some of our critics. That war was fought ostensibly to get equal rights for all whites in South Africa. The whole country went wild. We had a disease which was called Mafeka, because when the victory of Mafeking was declared everybody in the country, except a few people who tried to keep their heads steady, went absolutely mad with gratification at the sacrifice of thousands of human beings in the carrying on of that war. That war was fought to get votes for white men in South Africa, a few years sooner than they would have had them under existing conditions, and it was justified on those grounds, to get a voice in the government of South Africa for men who would have had that voice in five or six years if they had waited. That was considered ample justification for one of the most costly and bloody wars of modern times. Very well, then when you have warfare things happen; people suffer; the noncombatants suffer as well as the combatants. And so it happens in civil war. When your forefathers threw the tea into Boston Harbor, a good many women had to go without their tea. It has always seemed to me an extraordinary thing that you did not follow it up by throwing the whiskey overboard; you sacrificed the women; and there is a good deal of warfare for which men take a great deal of glorification which has involved more practical sacrifice on women than it has on any man. It always has been so. The grievances of those who have got power, the influence of those who have got power commands a great deal of attention; but the wrongs and the grievances of those people who have no power at all are apt to be absolutely ignored. That is the history of humanity right from the beginning. Well, in our civil war people have suffered, but you cannot make omelettes without breaking eggs; you cannot have civil war without damage to something. The great thing is to see that no more damage is done than is absolutely necessary, that you do just as much as will arouse enough feeling to bring about peace, to bring about an honorable peace for the combatants; and that is what we have been doing. Within the last few days you have read—I don't know how accurate the news cables are to America, I always take them with a grain of salt—but you have read within the last few days that some more empty houses have been burned, that a cactus house has been destroyed and some valuable plants have suffered in that house, that some pavilion at a pleasure ground has also been burned. Well, it is quite possible that it has happened. I knew before I came here that for one whole day telegraphic and telephonic communication between Glasgow and London was entirely suspended. We do more in England in our civil war without the sacrifice of a single life than they did in the war of the Balkan States when they had the siege of Adrianople, because during the whole of that siege, in the course of which thousands of people were killed and houses were shelled and destroyed, telegraphic communication was continuous the whole time. If there had been a stock broker in Adrianople who wanted to communicate with a customer in London, he could have done it; there might have been a little delay, but he was able to do it; but we, without the loss of a single life in our war, in this effort to rouse business men to compel the government to give us the vote, because they are the people who can do it in the last resort, we entirely prevented stock brokers in London from telegraphing to stock brokers in Glasgow, and vice versa; for one whole day telegraphic and telephonic communication was entirely stopped. I am not going to tell you how it was done. I am not going to tell you how the women got to the mains and cut the wires; but it was done. It was done, and it was proved to the authorities that weak women, suffrage women, as we are supposed to be, had enough ingenuity to create a situation of that kind.

Now, I ask you, if women can do that, is there any limit to what we can do except the limit we put upon ourselves? If you are dealing with an industrial revolution, if you get the men and women of one class to rising up against the men and women of another class, you can locate the difficulty; if there is a great industrial strike, you know exactly where the violence is, and every man knows exactly how the warfare is going to be waged; but in our war against the government you can't locate it. You can take Mrs. Hepburn and myself on this platform, and now, without being told, how could you tell that Mrs. Hepburn is a non-militant and that I am a militant? Absolutely impossible. If any gentleman who is the father of daughters in this meeting went into his home and looked around at his wife and daughters, if he lived in England and was an Englishman, he couldn't tell whether some of his daughters were militants or non-militants. When his daughters went out to post a letter, he couldn't tell if they went harmlessly out to make a tennis engagement at that pillar-box by posting a letter, or whether they went to put some corrosive matter in that would burn all the letters up inside of that box. We wear no mark; we belong to every class; we permeate every class of the community from the highest to the lowest; and so you see in the woman's civil war the dear men of my country are discovering it is absolutely impossible to deal with it; you cannot locate it, and you cannot stop it. "Put them in prison" they said, "that will stop it." But it didn't stop it. They put women in prison for long terms of imprisonment, for making a nuisance of themselves—that was the expression when they took petitions in their hands to the door of the House of Commons; and they thought that by sending them to prison, giving them a day's imprisonment, would cause them to all settle down again and there would be no further trouble. But it didn't happen so at all; instead of the women giving it up, more women did it, and more and more and more women did it until there were three hundred women at a time, who had not broken a single law, only "made a nuisance of themselves" as the politicians say. Well then they thought they must go a little farther, and so then they began imposing punishments of a very serious kind. The Judge who sentenced me last May to three years penal servitude for certain speeches in which I had accepted responsibility for acts of violence done by other women, said that if I would say I was sorry, if I would promise not to do it again, that he would revise the sentence and shorten it, because he admitted that it was a very heavy sentence, especially as the jury had recommended me to mercy because of the purity of my motives; and he said he was giving a determinate sentence, a sentence that would convince me that I would have to give up my "evil ways" and would also deter other women from imitating me. But it hadn't that effect at all so far. So far from it having that effect more and more women have been doing these things that I had incited them to do, and were more determined in doing them; so that the long determinate sentence had no effect in crushing the agitation.

Well then they felt they must do something else, and they began to legislate. I want to tell men in this meeting that the British government, which is not remarkable for having very mild laws to administer, has passed more stringent laws to deal with this agitation than it ever found it necessary during all the history of political agitation in my country. They were able to deal with the revolutionaries of the Chartists' time; they were able to deal with the Trades Union agitation; they were able to deal with the revolutionaries later on when the Reform Acts of 1867 and 1884 were passed; but the ordinary law has not sufficed to curb insurgent women. They have had to pass special legislation, and now they are on the point of admitting that that special legislation has absolutely failed. They had to dip back into the middle ages to find a means of repressing the women in revolt, and the whole history shows how futile it is for men who have been considered able statesmen to deal with dissatisfied women who are determined to win their citizenship and who will not submit to government until their consent is obtained. That is the whole point of our agitation. The whole argument with the anti-suffragists, or even the critical suffragist man, is this: that you can govern human beings without their consent. They have said to us, government rests upon force, the women haven't force, so they must submit. Well, we are showing them that government does not rest upon force at all; it rests upon consent. As long as women consent to be unjustly governed, they can be; but directly women say: "We with-hold our consent, we will not be governed any longer so long as that government is unjust," not by the forces of civil war can you govern the very weakest woman. You can kill that woman, but she escapes you then; you cannot govern her. And that is, I think, a most valuable demonstration we have been making to the world. We have been proving in our own person that government does not rest upon force; it rests upon consent; as long as people consent to government, it is perfectly easy to govern, but directly they refuse then no power on earth can govern a human being, however feeble, who withholds his or her consent; and all of the strange happenings that you have read about over here, have been manifestations of a refusal to consent on the part of the women. When they put us in prison at first, simply for taking petitions, we submitted; we allowed them to dress us in prison clothes; we allowed them to put us in solitary confinement; we allowed them to treat us as ordinary criminals, and put us amongst the most degraded of criminals; and we were very glad of the experience, because out of that experience we learned of the fearful mistakes that men of all nations have made when it is a question of dealing with human beings; we learned of some of the appalling evils of our so-called civilization that we could not have learned in any other way except by going through the police courts of our country, in the prison vans that take you up to prison; and right through that prison experience. It was valuable experience, and we were glad to get it. But there came a time when we said: "It is unjust to send political agitators to prison in this way for merely asking for justice, and we will not submit any longer." And I am always glad to remind American audiences that two of the first women that came to the conclusion that they would not submit to unjust imprisonment any longer, were two American girls, who are doing some of the most splendid suffrage work in America today up in Washington. I think they are making things extremely lively for the politicians up there, and I don't know whether every American woman knows what those two women, working in conjunction with others, are doing for the enfranchisement of American women at this moment. I am always proud to think that Miss Lucy Burns and Miss Alice Paul served their suffrage apprenticeship in the militant ranks in England, and they were not slow about it either, because one of them came, I believe it was, from Heidelberg, travelling all night, to take part in one of those little processions to Parliament with a petition. She was arrested and thrown into prison with about twenty others, and that group of twenty women were the first women who decided they would not submit themselves to the degradation of wearing prison clothes; and they refused, and they were almost the first to adopt the "Hunger strike" as a protest against the criminal treatment. They forced their way out of prison. Well, then it was that women began to withhold their consent. I have been in audiences where I have seen men smile when they heard the words "Hunger strike" and yet I think there are very few men today who would be prepared to adopt a "Hunger strike" for any cause. It is only people who feel an intolerable sense of oppression who would adopt a means of that kind. I know of no people who did it before us except revolutionaries in Russia—who adopted the hunger strike against intolerable prison conditions. Well, our women decided to terminate those unjust sentences at the earliest possible moment by the terrible means of the hunger strike. It means you refuse food until you are at death's door, and then the authorities have to choose between letting you die, and letting you go; and then they let the women go.

Now, that went on so long that the government felt they had lost their power, and that they were unable to cope with the situation. Then it was that, to the shame of the British government, they set the example to authorities all over the world of feeding sane, resisting human beings by force. There may be doctors in this meeting; if so, they know it is one thing to treat an insane person, to feed by force an insane person, or a patient who has some form of illness which makes it necessary; but it is quite another thing to feed a sane, resisting human being who resists with every nerve and with every fibre of her body the indignity and the outrage of forcible feeling. Now, that was done in England, and the government thought they had crushed us. But they found that it did not quell the agitation, that more and more women came in and even passed that terrible ordeal, and that they were not able with all their forcible feeding to make women serve out their unjust sentences. They were obliged to let them go.

Then came the legislation to which I have referred, the legislation which is known in England as the Cat and Mouse Act. It got through the British House of Commons because the Home Secretary assured the House of Commons that he wanted the bill passed in the interests of humanity; he said he was a humane man and he did not like having to resort to forcible feeding; he wanted the House of Commons to give him some way of disposing of them, and this was his way: he said, "Give me the power to let these women go when they are at death's door, and leave them at liberty under license until they have recovered their health again and then bring them back; leave it to me to fix the time of their licenses; leave it in my hands altogether to deal with this intolerable situation, because the laws must be obeyed and people who are sentenced for breaking the law must be compelled to serve their sentences." Well, the House of Commons passed the law. They said: "As soon as the women get a taste of this they will give it up." In fact, it was passed to repress the agitation, to make the women yield—because that is what it has really come to, ladies and gentlemen. It has come to a battle between the women and the government as to who shall yield first, whether they will yield and give us the vote, or whether we will give up our agitation. Well, they little know what women are. Women are very slow to rouse, but once they are aroused, once they are determined, nothing on earth and nothing in heaven will make women give way; it is impossible. And so this Cat and Mouse Act which is being used against women today has failed; and the Home Secretary has taken advantage of the fact that Parliament is not sitting, to revive and use alongside of it the forcible feeding. At the present time there are women lying at death's door, recovering enough strength to undergo operations, who have had both systems applied to them, and have not given in and won't give in, and who will be prepared, as soon as they get up from their sick-beds, to go on as before. There are women who are being carried from their sick-beds on stretchers into meetings. They are too weak to speak, but they go amongst their fellow-workers just to show that their spirits are unquenched, and that their spirit is alive, and they mean to go on as long as life lasts.

Now, I want to say to you who think women cannot succeed, we have brought the government of England to this position, that it has to face this alternative: either women are to be killed or women are to have the vote. I ask American men in this meeting, what would you say if in your State you were faced with that alternative, that you must either kill them or give them their citizenship—women, many of whom you respect, women whom you know have lived useful lives, women whom you know even if you do not know them personally, are animated with the highest motives, women who are in pursuit of liberty and the power to do useful public service? Well, there is only one answer to that alternative; there is only one way out of it, unless you are prepared to put back civilization two or three generations; you must give those women the vote. Now that is the outcome of our civil war.

You won your freedom in America when you had the revolution, by bloodshed, by sacrificing human life. You won the civil war by the sacrifice of human life when you decided to emancipate the negro. You have left it to women in your land, the men of all civilized countries have left it to women, to work out their own salvation. That is the way in which we women of England are doing. Human life for us is sacred, but we say if any life is to be sacrificed it shall be ours; we won't do it ourselves, but we will put the enemy in the position where they will have to choose between giving us freedom or giving us death.

Now whether you approve of us or whether you do not, you must see that we have brought the question of women's suffrage into a position where it is of first rate importance, where it can be ignored no longer. Even the most hardened politician will hesitate to take upon himself directly the responsibility of sacrificing the lives of women of undoubted honor, of undoubted earnestness of purpose. That is the political situation as I lay it before you today.

Now then, let me say something about what has brought it about, because you must realize that only the very strongest of motives would lead women to do what we have done. Life is sweet to all of us. Every human being loves life and loves to enjoy the good things and the happiness that life gives; and yet we have a state of things in England that has made not two or three women but thousands of women quite prepared to face these terrible situations that I have been trying without any kind of passion or exaggeration to lay before you.

Well, I might spend two or three nights dealing with the industrial situation as it affects women, with the legal position of women, with the social position of women. I want very briefly to say a few words about all. First of all there is the condition of the working woman. One of the things which gives strength to our agitation is that the women who are taking an active part in it are not the poorest women, are not the overworked women; they are the women who are held to be fortunate, the women who have no special personal grievance of their own. Those women have taken up this fight for their own sake, it is true, because they wish to be free, but chiefly for the sake of the women less fortunate than themselves. The industrial workers of Great Britain have an average wage, mind you, not a minimum wage, an average wage, of less than two dollars a week. Think what would happen in any country if the men in industry of that country had to subsist on a wage like that. Thousands upon thousands of these women—because there are over five million wage earners in my country—thousands of these women have dependents; they are women with children dependent upon them, deserted wives with children dependent on them, or wives with sick husbands; they are unmarried mothers, or they are unmarried women who have old parents or younger brothers and sisters, or sick relatives dependent upon them. Their average income, taking the highly skilled woman teacher and averaging her wage with the unskilled home worker, the average income is less than two dollars a week. There you have in itself an explanation of an uprising of a very determined kind to secure better conditions; and when you know that the government is the largest employer of all the employers and sets a horribly bad example to the private employer in the wages that it pays to women, there you have another explanation. Constant economies are being effected in government departments by the substitution of women's labor for men's, and there is always a reduction in wages whenever women are employed. That is the industrial situation. To speak of the sweated home-worker would take too long, but there are women, women even with dependents, only able to earn three or four shillings a week, thousands of them, and having to pay with the increased cost of living, exorbitant rents in our great cities for single rooms, so that you get several families in one room; they cannot afford even to have a room for themselves. So much for the industrial situation.

Then there is the legal situation. The marriage laws of our country are bringing hundreds and hundreds of women into the militant ranks because we cannot get reform, the kind of reform that women want, of our marriage laws. First of all, a girl is held marriageable by English law, at the age of twelve years. When I was on trial they produced a little girl as a witness, a little girl who had found something in the neighborhood of the house of the Chancellor of the Exchequer, which was destroyed by some women, and this little girl was produced as a witness. It was said that it was a terrible thing to bring a little girl of twelve years of age and put her in the witness box in a court of law. I agreed, but I pointed out to the judge and the jury that one of the reasons why women were in revolt was because that little girl, whose head just appeared over the top of the witness box, was considered old enough by the laws of her country to take upon herself the terrible responsibilities of wifehood and motherhood, and women could not get it altered, no politicians would listen to us, when we asked to have the marriage law altered in that particular.

Then, the position of the wife. It is very frequently said that every woman who wants a vote, wants a vote because she has been disappointed, because she has not been chosen to be a wife. Well, I can assure you that if most women made a study of the laws before they decided to get married, a great many women would seriously consider whether it was worthwhile, whether the price was not too heavy, because, according to English law, a woman may toil all her life for her husband and her family, she may work in her husband's business, she may help him to build up the family income, and if he chooses at the end of a long life to take every penny of the money that woman has helped to earn away from her and her children, he can do it, and she has no redress. She may at the end of a long, hard life find herself and her children absolutely penniless because her husband has chosen to will the money away from her. So that you see when you look at it from the legal point of view, it is not such a very, very great gain to become a wife in my country. There are a great many risks that go along with it.

Then take her as a mother. If the child of two parents has any property inherited from relatives, and that child dies before it is of age to make a will, or without making a will, the only person who inherits the property of that child is the child's father; the mother does not exist as her child's heir at all; and during the father's lifetime she not only cannot inherit from her child but she has no voice whatever in deceiding [*sic*] the life of her child. Her husband can give the child away to be educated somewhere else or he can bring whomever he pleases into the house to educate the child. He decides absolutely the conditions in which that child is to live; he decides how it is to be educated; he can even decide what religion it is to profess, and the mother's consent is not obtained to any of these decisions. Women are trying to alter it, have tried for generations, but they cannot because the legislatures have no time to listen to the opinions and the desires of people who have no votes.

Well then, when it comes to the question of how people are to get out of marriage, if they are unhappy, under the laws of divorce, the English law of divorce is the most scandalous divorce law in the civilized world. There may be a few states in America, and I believe in Canada, where the same law obtains, but the English divorce law is in itself such a stigma upon women, such a degradation to women, such an invitation to immorality on the part of the married man, that I think that divorce law in itself would justify a rebellion on the part of the women. You get registered in law unequal standards of morals in marriage, and a married man is encouraged by law to think that he can make as many lapses as he thinks fit in marital fidelity; whereas, if one act of infidelity is proved against her the husband can get rid of her by divorce, can take her children away from her and make her an outcast. Women who have been clamoring for an equal divorce law for generations cannot get any attention. Well now, we have had a Royal Commission on divorce and we have had a report, but there is no security for women that they are to have justice under a new law so long as men are chosen by men to legislate and those men are likely to register the moral opinions of men, not the moral opinions of women, in legislation. We have to look facts in the face. Part of the militant movement for woman suffrage has had that effect, that women have learned to look facts in the face; they have got rid of sentimentalities; they are looking at actual facts; and when anti-suffragists talk about chivalry, and when they talk about putting women on pedestals and guarding them from all the difficulties and dangers of life, we look to the facts in life as we see them and we say: "Women have every reason to distrust that kind of thing, every reason to be dissatisfied; we want to know the truth however bad it is, and we face that truth because it is only through knowing the truth that you ever will get to anything better." We are determined to have these things faced and cleared up, and it is absolutely ridiculous to say to women that they can safely trust their interests in the hands of men who have already registered in the legislation of their country a standard of morals so unequal for both sexes as we find on the statute books of England today.

When the divorce commission sat, evidence was given by all kinds of people, and women had the experience of reading in the newspapers the evidence of the man who had been chosen by other men to preside over the divorce court, the judge whose duty it was to decide what was legal cruelty and decide whether women were to continue to be bound to their husbands or not. What did he say? I am glad to think that he is not in a position to give effect to his ideas any more; he now adorns the House of Lords; but he was still judge of the divorce court when he said, that in his opinion the wise wife was the woman who closed her eyes to the moral failings of her husband; and that was the man, women in this meeting, who had for years decided what was legal cruelty and what women were to endure or what they were not to endure in that relationship of husband and wife.

Well, can you wonder that all these things make us more militant? It seems to me that once you look at things from the woman's point of view, once you cease to listen to politicians once you cease to allow yourself to look at the facts of life through men's spectacles but look at them through your own, every day that passes you are having fresh illustrations of the need there is for women to refuse to wait any longer for their enfranchisement.

Then, the latest manifestation, the latest cause of militancy has been the breaking of the great conspiracy of silence with regard to moral questions and the question of social disease that we have had during the last few years. I want to offer my testimony of gratitude to women like the lady who presides over us today and to the many of the medical men of the United States in making a lead in that direction. Before some of the suffragists had the courage even to study the question, these people spoke out; the medical profession in America has led the way, and through Dr. Prince Morrow, and other men whose names we honor, we are at last beginning to know the real facts of the situation. We know this, that whatever women's wishes might be, it is their duty for the sake of the race, itself, to save the race, to insist upon having this question of the moral health of the nation approached from the women's point of view and settled by women in cooperation with men. It is our business to show the close relationship there is between the appalling state of social health and the political degradation of women. The two things go hand in hand. I have been reading a great many articles by very profound thinkers lately, and I see that somehow or other when you get men writing about them, even the best of men, they do evade the real issue, and that is the status of women. We women see so clearly the fact that the only way to deal with this thing is to raise the status of women; first the political status, then the industrial and the social status of women. You must make women count as much as men; you must have an equal standard of morals; and the only way to enforce that is through giving women political power so that you can get that equal moral standard registered in the laws of the country. It is the only way. I don't know whether men sufficiently realize it, but we women do realize it; we more and more realize it, and so women have nerved themselves to speak out on this question. First of all, we feel that what is most important is that women should know it. Ten years ago it would have been impossible for any woman or any man to speak openly upon that question on any platform, because women had been taught that they must keep their eyes closed to all these things; women had been taught that they must ignore the fact even that a large section of their sex were living lives of degradation and outlawry. If they knew of it at all, they were told in vague terms that it was in order to make the lives of the rest of the women safe; they were told it was a necessary evil; they were told it was something that the good woman does not understand and must not know anything about. All that is now at an end. Women are refusing, men in this meeting, even if that were true, to have their lives made safe at the expense of their sisters. The women are determined. A good deal of the opposition to woman suffrage is coming from the very worst element in the population, who realize that once you get woman suffrage, a great many places that are tolerated today will have to disappear. It is perhaps a hard saying for many men that there will have to be self-control and an equal standard of morals, but the best men now, the scientists of every country, are supporting the woman's point of view. It was thirty years ago in England that a splendid woman named Josephine Butler fought to establish an equal moral code for both sexes. She fought all of her life; she was stoned; she was hooted; her meetings were broken up; her life was made absolutely dangerous; and yet that woman persisted and she secured the repeal of certain laws relating to prostitution which disgraced the statute books of our country. In those days the doctors were against her; practically everybody was against her. Men were told that it was necessary for their health that we should have an unequal moral code. Now that is all done away with. The foremost medical men and the foremost scientists are agreeing with the women; they are agreeing with the women that it is quite possible, and it is necessary for the sake of the race itself, that this equal moral code shall be established. Well, it is probably difficult; it is perhaps going to be difficult for generations; but it is to come, and it is out of the woman's movement that it is coming, because women today who have had the benefits of education, who have had the benefit of medical training and who have had the benefit of legal training, are informing their sex upon this question, and there is a good deal of opposition coming to it from strange directions; even people who have self-appointed themselves as the custodians of public morals are opposing the facts being told.

One of the strangest things that I have experienced for years is the fact that in New York, quite recently, copies of our paper, *The Suffragette*, in which were articles written by my daughter, quoting the opinions of medical men all over the world on this question, and relying on those quotations as a statement of fact, were offered for sale, and an attempt, a successful attempt temporarily, was made to prevent that paper being sold because it contained these articles telling the truth; and a book containing the articles in collected form prefaced with an article telling why this book was written, has also had an attack made upon it by that self-constituted guardian of public morals, Mr. Comstock, supported by certain sections of the American press. Well, that book is here tonight; that book is here on sale. That book was written, not for people of my age, not for people who if there are dangers to be faced have either escaped or suffered from them; that book was written for young people; that book was written so that women should know. What is the use of locking the stable after the horse is stolen? Prevention is better than cure. This book was written to convince everybody of the danger, to point out the plain facts of the situation, and to convince thoughtful people that only through the emancipation of women, only through the uplifting of women, can you ever effectively deal with the situation. We have tried, we women, for generations to undo some of this evil; we have had our rescue societies; we have made all kinds of efforts; we have taken the poor unfortunate children who have been the outcome of this unequal code of morals between men and women, and what has happened? Matters have become sadly worse; we have scratched on the surface instead of cutting out the root of the evil. All that is changed. Today women are working in my country, are sacrificing and suffering to win the political enfranchisement of their sex, so that we may get better laws and better administration of the laws.

I could go on tonight pointing out to you how in my country small crimes against property, small thefts, small injuries to property are punished more severely than are any crimes committed against the physical and the moral integrity of members of my sex. I think I have said enough at least to make you understand that this uprising on the part of the British women has as much justification and as much provocation as any uprising on the part of men in their desire for political liberty in the past. We are not working to get the vote, we are not going to prison to get the vote, merely to say we have the vote. We are going through all this to get the vote so that by means of the vote we can bring about better conditions not only for ourselves but for the community as a whole.

Men have done splendid things in this world; they have made great achievements in engineering; they have done splendid organization work; but they have failed, they have miserably failed, when it has come to dealing with the lives of human beings. They stand self-confessed failures, because the problems that perplex civilization are absolutely appalling today. Well, that is the function of women in life; it is our business to care for human beings, and we are determined that we must come without delay to the saving of the race. The race must be saved, and it can only be saved through the emancipation of women.

Well, ladies and gentlemen, I want to say that I am very thankful to you for listening to me here tonight; I am glad if I have been able even to a small extent to explain to you something of the English situation. I want to say that I am not here to apologize. I do not care very much even whether you really understand, because when you are in a fighting movement, a movement which every fiber of your being has forced you to enter, it is not the approval of other human beings that you want; you are so concentrated on your object that you mean to achieve that object even if the whole world was up in arms against you. So I am not here tonight to apologize or to win very much your approbation. People have said: "Why does Mrs. Pankhurst come to America; has she come to America to rouse American women to be militant? No, I have not come to America to arouse American women to be militant. I believe that American women, as their earnestness increases, as they realize the need for the enfranchisement of their sex, will find out for themselves the best way to secure that object. Each nation must work out its own salavation [*sic*], and so the American women will find their own way and use their own methods capably.

Other people have said: "What right has Mrs. Pankhurst to come to America and ask for American dollars?" Well, I think I have the right that all oppressed people have to ask for practical sympathy of others freer than themselves. Your right to send to France and ask for help was never questioned. You did it, and you got that help. Men of all nationalities have come to America, and they have not gone away empty-handed, because American sympathy has been extended to struggling peoples all over the world.

In England, if you could understand it, there is the most pathetic and the most courageous fight going on, because you find the people whom you have been accustomed to look upon as weak and reliant, the people you have always thought leaned upon other people for protection, have stood up and are fighting for themselves. Women have found a new kind of self-respect, a new kind of energy, a new kind of strength; and I think that of all oppressed peoples who might claim your sympathy and support, women who are fighting this fight unknown in the history of humanity before, fighting this fight in the twentieth century for greater powers of self-development, self-expression and self-government, might very well attract the sympathy and the practical help of American people.

There hasn't been a victory the women of America have won that we have not rejoiced in. I think as we have read month by month of the new States that have been added to the list of fully enfranchised States, perhaps we who know how hard the fight is, have rejoiced even more than American women themselves. I have heard cheers ring out in a meeting in London when the news of some new State being added to the list was given, cheers louder and more enthusiastic than I have ever heard for any victory in an American meeting. It is very true that those who are fighting a hard battle, those who are sacrificing greatly in order to win a victory, appreciate victories and are more enthusiastic when victories are won. We have rejoiced wholeheartedly in your victories. We feel that those victories have been easier perhaps because of the hard times that we were having, because out of our militant movement in the storm centre of the suffrage movement have gone waves that have helped to rouse women all over the world. You could only explain the strange phenomena in that way. Ten years ago there was hardly any woman suffrage movement at all. Now even in China and Japan, in India, in Turkey, everywhere, women are rising up and asking for these larger opportunities which modern conditions demand that women should have; and we women think that we have helped. Well, if we have helped at all, if, as has been said from the Chair tonight, we have even helped to rouse suffrage enthusiasm in Connecticut, can you blame me very much if I come and tell you of the desperate struggle we are having, of how the government is trying to break us down in every possible way, even by involving us in lawsuits, and trying to frighten our subscribers by threatening to prosecute even people who help us by subscribing money? Can you wonder I come over to America? Have you read about American dollars that have been given the Irish law-breakers? So here am I. I come in the intervals of prison appearance; I come after having been four times imprisoned under the Cat and Mouse Act, probably going back to be rearrested as soon as I set my foot on British soil. I come to ask you to help to win this fight. If we win it, this hardest of all fights, then, to be sure, in the future it is going to be made easier for women all over the world to win their fight when their time comes. So I make no apologies for coming, and I make no apologies, Mrs. Hepburn, for asking this audience, if any of them feel inclined, to help me to take back some money from America and put it with the money that I know our women are raising by desperate personal sacrifice at home, so that when we begin our next year's campaign, facing a general election, as probably we shall face next year, our anxieties on the money side will not be so heavy as they would have been if I had not found strength and health enough to come and carry out this somewhat arduous tour in the United States of America.

23

Victory Is Assured.

A Verbatim Report of Mrs. Pankhurst's Speech at Campden Hill Square, February 10, 1914.

LADIES AND GENTLEMEN: THIS IS AN APPROPRIATE NIGHT FOR A MEETing like this. To-day Parliament has reassembled after months of Parliamentary neglect, during which the fortunes of this country have been left in the hands of an irresponsible oligarchy. During those months, while the welfare of the country has been imperilled, those men have been paid by the men and women of this country to manage their affairs—the men, I presume, have paid willingly, the women have had no choice in the matter; they have had to pay these men who misrepresent them.

Well, to-night I am here to say the mock battle of Parliament has begun again. The sham armies are in the field. But there is a real army in the field, and that is the women's army. (A Voice: That is the W.S.P.U.) That is the W.S.P.U., my friends. (Applause.) We hear of rebellion in Ireland. Some believe it is real; others do not; but there can be no doubt in anybody's mind about the women's rebellion. (Applause.) And I believe it is because the Government has no doubt about the reality of our war, that they are fighting us, while they let the others go scot free. (A voice saying something about law-abiding women.) My friend who talks about law-abiding women is quite right. The fault we women have had in the past, is that we have neglected so long to break the laws. Had we done what the men did so long ago, we should not be where we are. But now women are fighting, and the Government recognise that in women they have far more dangerous enemies than in Sir Edward Carson and his army, in the Labour Party and their army, or in any of them; because women, who are slow to move, once moved are never quelled.

The Government's Last Game.

I want to ask the men in this crowd: Had they ever to pass a "Cat and Mouse Act" to keep your forefathers in order? They have passed legislation to put down women that was never necessary in the case of the men of the past, when I believe men had more courage than have the men to-day. I am glad that we are having this fight, because it enables women to show to the manhood of the world the kind of stuff they are made of. Is there one man in this crowd who believes that they will ever crush us? (One voice: Yes.) Well, my friend, you are in a very small minority. At any rate, the men you have placed in power know we shall never be crushed.

And I will tell you women in this meeting, women members of the W.S.P.U., that they are playing their last game against us. What are they trying to do? They know they cannot crush us with imprisonment; they know they cannot crush us with forcible feeding; they know they cannot crush us with the "Cat-and-Mouse Act"; and so they are trying to sow dissension in our ranks. They are trying to break down your trust; they are trying to make you turn traitors—(A Voice: Never!)—to the women who are risking their lives for your sake. They will never succeed. (Applause.) What would you be if you had turned traitor to women like Annie Kenney; to women like Mary Richardson; to women like Rachel Peace; to women like Kitty Marion; to women like Phyllis Brady, who are being tortured in prison to-day?

Well, my friends, we do not lack for good advice. Bishops are advising us now. To-day there appears in the papers a letter from the Bishop of London. The Bishop of London has been to Holloway Gaol. Women asked him to go and see the loathsome forcible feeding for himself, but he told us, he who is the bishop of a great diocese, that by the regulations of the Home Office he was not allowed to witness forcible feeding. I would like to say to the Bishop of London that his great Master would have broken their regulations and would have insisted on seeing that torture performed. But the Bishop of London tells women that they must not break the laws; they must not do evil, says he, that good may come. I ask the Bishop of London why does he not give that advice to Sir Edward Carson? How is it that he reserves his advice for women?

How Can He Condemn Women?

I wish to answer him when he says we do evil that good may come. I want to say to the Bishop of London, and to all those who talk as he does, that we do no evil. He says that to do violence is evil, and yet he supports the State where we maintain armies to kill human beings; he blesses warlike banners; he prays in cathedrals for the success of our armies. How, then, can he condemn women who are fighting for that which is most sacred— for human liberty? Our armies fight for possessions and property; women are fighting for human rights.

But I want to go further, and I challenge those who denounce our violence, and I say to them that if our violence is wrong then the violence of Christ was wrong, for did He not turn the money-changers out of the Temple; did He not drive the Swine into the sea? (A Voice: He did not break windows.) We break windows, my friend, to get the power to save broken lives. When your forefathers fought for their liberty they took lives. (A Voice: You are only a woman.) "Only a woman," says a man. That is what we are fighting, my friends. We women are fighting not as women, but as human beings, for human rights, and we shall win those human rights, and every one of you knows it quite well. We are going to win, and I will tell you why we are going to win: because we have courage—because nothing on earth can put down this movement. They may kill us, but they cannot crush this movement.

The Government, which is tottering to its fall, has before it this choice: it must give votes to women or death to women. And I say to you men in the meeting, I say it solemnly to-night: Are you going to share in the blood-guiltiness when women die? We are ready to die. Are you ready to have us killed? I say that the women in this movement are going on with this fight for human liberty even if every man in the world was against us. We say to you: Who gave you the right to say whether women should be voters or not? Who gave you that right? Are you rulers by divine right? No. Very well, then, you took the right, or your forefathers did, and we in our turn, as women, since you have not shared your political power with us, mean to take that right for ourselves, and let him who has the courage to prevent us try to do it.

A Challenge to the Government.

Now, my friends, I want to challenge the Government. I want to challenge this cowardly Government which makes war on defenceless and voteless women. I have returned to England in spite of them. When I came from America they sent battleships to meet me. I want you men, you taxpayers, to ask what it costs to deprive women of the vote, to ask what they pay for their armies of Continental police in plain clothes; ask what they pay for fire insurance; ask what it costs to protect Cabinet Ministers, these guardians of the public liberties. Well, if you like to pay, you men who call yourselves practical business men, go on paying. You will come to the conclusion at last that it is cheaper to give women the vote because I tell you that this fight is going on until we win the vote. Already it has cost millions. It will go on, and sooner or later the Britisher, whom we are told can only be touched through his pocket, will wake up and become a sensible man, and send these men who misgovern this country to the right-about, and give women the vote, to which they have as much right as the rest of you.

Now for my challenge. I have reached London in spite of the armies of police. I am here to-night, and not a man is going to protect me, because this is a woman's fight, and we shall protect ourselves. I am coming out amongst you in a few minutes and I challenge the Government to rearrest me. Let us see if they will dare do to me what they do not do to Labour leaders in my position, under the "Cat-and-Mouse act." (A voice said women were privileged.) You say that women are privileged. Yes, my friends, they are privileged to endure. (A Voice: You ought to be deported as a mover of sedition.) I should come back again, my friend! Here is a man whose forefathers were seditious in the past, talking about sedition on the part of women, who are taxed but have no constitutional rights. Yes, my friends, I am seditious, and I shall go on being seditious until I am brought, with other women, within the constitution of my country.

I Shall Come Out Alive or Dead.

Somebody says I must suffer the law. There is a principle in this country that those who obey the law have a right to help to make the laws. When I have a right to help to make the laws then I will obey them, but until I have that right I shall do what all self-respecting people do—reserve to myself the right to break them. When my consent is obtained, then I will obey them. "Put up with the consequences," says a man over there. I will not! I am supposed to be in penal servitude for three years. (A Voice: You will be soon.) Never, my friends, because they cannot keep me. Seven times I have come to the edge of the grave, and they have had to let me go, and I ask: Is there a life long enough to serve three years' imprisonment on those terms?

Now I want to challenge the Government still further. I challenge them to rearrest me, and I challenge them again, when they have rearrested me, to apply to me what they are applying to Rachel Pearce and her companions. If it is right that those three women should be forcibly fed, then it is right that I should be forcibly fed. I say to the Government that those women acted on my incitement, and how cowardly it is to punish in that way women less known than I am, while they dare not forcibly feed me. Very well, then, if they get me to-night, let them take me back to Holloway and forcibly feed me. I challenge them to dare to do it. I tell you this, my friends: that just as I have come out of that prison before, I shall come out of it again. I shall come out of it alive, or I shall come out of it dead, but never, never, will they make me serve three years' penal servitude.

And what is Life?

Now, one word to my own women, because my last word is to you. I say to every woman, ask yourself now whether we have not reached that supreme moment in our struggle: is it not time to put aside all other considerations and fight? Can you keep your self-respect any longer? You know that some of us who are in the van have given all things, even life itself, in this cause. And what is life? At the best it is very short. Would it not be well, when we leave this life, as leave it we must, to leave it having struck a blow for what is truer life: having struck a blow for the freedom of our sex; having struck a blow against the subjection of our sex; having struck a blow against the vicious conditions into which the majority of our sex are born; having struck one blow against the disease and degradation of the masses of our country.

Let us show the men of the twentieth century that there are things to-day worth fighting for. You all know it. Every man in this crowd knows that things are not what they ought to be. Every man knows now (if he did not know it before my daughter's book has told him) that millions—think of it, friends—millions of helpless little children are born into this world, suffering for the sins of their fathers in the shape of a loathsome disease. Oh, men in this meeting, how can women believe you when you talk of love—when you talk of care for the home and the family? How can women believe you when they know, as they are knowing to-day, that when you enter into the most sacred relationship of life thousands upon thousands of you, yes, there are men doctors who say that even 80 percent of you are not fit to undertake the solemn responsibility of fatherhood.

Well, if that is true, and we believe it is, then we say in that fact alone is justification for our civil war and rebellion. And fight we shall. And I say to you women: put aside all fear; fight with the courage that you have had through generations of suffering. Let that courage animate you to fight against evil conditions, and believe me that while you and I may die in the struggle, victory is assured, and out of our struggle, even by the laying down of our lives, will come a time so wonderful for humanity that we can only dimly see that beautiful future.

Good night.

Part IX
The War and the Vote

THERE HAS BEEN AN ONGOING ARGUMENT AS TO WHETHER 1914 WAS A period of heightened activity and potential progress for the Union, or whether militancy had lost its value as a goad to government action. The declaration of war, on August 4, 1914, completely altered the suffrage movement and made the efficacy of militancy an unprovable point of conjecture for scholars. When war was declared, there were still eleven suffragettes in prison and numerous others out on license under the Cat and Mouse Act. They were offered amnesty on August 10, 1914. On August 13, Emmeline Pankhurst called an immediate truce on militant action and temporarily suspended publication of *The Suffragette*.[1]

For the suffrage workers there was as much diversity in response to the war as there had been in determining suffrage strategy. The WSPU leadership—Emmeline Pankhurst, Flora Drummond, Annie Kenney, and Grace Roe—entered into political war work and put aside the suffrage cause until victory could be won. Christabel Pankhurst returned in triumph from Paris in September and joined in the campaign to encourage women to work in munitions factories and essential services.[2] On October 15, 1915, *The Suffragette* was renamed *Britannia* and given the new dedication, "For King, for Country, for Freedom."[3] The WSPU spoke for universal obligatory service and pressured men to enlist. One aspect of this pressure was the white feather campaign, where women handed a white feather to young men out of uniform as an accusation of cowardice.[4]

When Emmeline Pankhurst first called a halt to militant activity, she sent around a circular in which she encouraged the Union members to rally around the country at war and to take advantage of the opportunity to "recuperate after the tremendous strain and suffering of the past two years."[5] Although the active militants may have welcomed a break from the rigors of the campaign, not all the original militant suffragettes shared the Pankhursts' view of the war. A number of the former "young hot-bloods," the so-called radical rump of the WSPU, resented what they considered as the hijacking of their organization and wanted to continue with an antiwar, suffrage activism. Meetings were held in Caxton Hall in 1915 by this group of dissenters. Resolutions were passed concerning the leaders' appropriation of the WSPU name and an accounting of Union funds was demanded.[6]

Sylvia Pankhurst also took a different view of the war from her mother and sister. She spent the war years organizing services to alleviate the suffering the war brought to the poor. War prices had skyrocketed, and many nonmilitary factories had closed, causing unemployment. Unlike the WSPU, which was a major force in enlisting women for munition factory work, the East London Federation called attention to the fortunes being made by factory owners, the atrocious pay given to female (as compared to male) workers, and the unsafe conditions in the factories. Sylvia Pankhurst and the East London Federation maintained their stance that equal pay for equal work and an equal vote with men were reasonable demands for such hazardous work.[7]

The Pethick-Lawrences were highly supportive of Sylvia. Emmeline Pethick-Lawrence spoke in Europe and America for peace and was a prime mover in the Women's Peace Conference in the Hague, April 1915. Emmeline Pankhurst clearly stated her strong opposition to the Peace Conference in a speech ("What Is Our Duty?") delivered in Liverpool that same April. In fact, the Pethick-Lawrences and the Pankhursts were polar opposites in their response to the war. As Midge MacKenzie phrased it, "Political power, poverty, and peace were the three major issues that now divided the original leadership of the Women's Social and Political Union."[8]

Emmeline and Christabel Pankhurst made a long series of speeches on war issues during the next four years. Christabel, in particular, spoke almost weekly at the Aeolian Hall during the summer and fall of 1917. These speeches were minutely concerned with the conduct of the war and reflected a strong peace-only-after-victory stance. The position of women in the conduct of the war was an issue that continued to interest Emmeline Pankhurst in her wartime rhetoric. Largely on the strength of Pankhursts' pro-Government speeches, Lloyd-George, then at the Ministry of Munitions, gave the WSPU a £2,000 grant to stage a right to serve parade for women. On July 17, 1915, a parade of thirty thousand women took place, reminding some of the great processions of the suffrage movement. The government used this parade to pressure the trade unions to accept lower-paid women workers. The trade unions feared that low-paid women workers could undermine the wages and working conditions of men.[9]

With the WSPU brand of militancy stilled, the milder militant societies and the non-militants kept the women's suffrage issue alive during the war. The opportunity to seriously raise the franchise issue came because of Liberal and Unionist demands to guarantee a vote to every soldier at the front. Because of the requirement that men be householders and occupants of "a dwelling for at least one year prior to the fifteenth day of the July preceding an election,"[10] Soldiers overseas and the war workers transferred to needed areas lost their vote. A Conference on Electoral Reform recommended a variety of franchise reforms. Included was the suggestion of votes for women over the age of thirty or thirty-five, the age restriction suggested to prevent a female majority.[11]

Lloyd-George, who replaced Asquith as Prime Minister in December 1916, called together the suffrage groups at 10 Downing Street in April 1917. Included here is Emmeline Pankhurst's presentation at this deputation. This speech and her later Queen's Hall speech ("Woman Suffrage, A Necessary War Measure") are remarkable to anyone familiar with her earlier speeches. Here, she is extremely conciliatory, seemingly unwilling to expend energy in discussing the fine points of the bill.

On May 15, 1917, the Reform Bill was introduced in the House of Commons and the debate on woman suffrage took place on June 19, with the bill passing the committee by a vote of 385 to 55.[12] With only the House of Lords needing to vote on the Electoral Reform Bill, WSPU leaders formed The Women's Party. The Women's Party platform favored war until victory, harsh peace terms, and better coordination of the Allied forces. The Women's Party also supported traditional women's issues such as equality in marriage laws and work conditions, and a raising of the "age of consent" for girls.[13]

An amendment to omit the clause giving women the vote was defeated in the House of Lords on January 10 by a vote of 134 to 71, and the Reform Bill received the royal assent (the final stage in the making of a law) on February 6, 1918.[14] And so, fifty years after John Stuart Mill introduced a woman suffrage bill to Parliament, women over the age of thirty quietly obtained the vote. The age requirement intended to prevent a female majority was not altered until 1928. In light of the continuing war, the celebration was restrained. Emmeline Pankhurst addressed former members of the suffrage army in a speech at the Royal Albert Hall on March 16, 1918 ("To Women Citizens"). She did not dwell for long on the past, on suffrage pioneers or the suffrage struggle, but moved quickly to the war and Women's Party issues.

In November 1918, a bill was rushed through the Parliament to allow women to stand as candidates in the House of Commons. Christabel stood as the candidate for Smethwick in the December elections. A number of prominent suffrage women ran in this election, including Mrs. Despard and Emmeline Pethick-Lawrence, both under the Labour party. Only one woman was successful (a Sinn Fein candidate who refused, as did the other Sinn Feiners, to take her seat). Christabel Pankhurst made the best showing of the other women candidates by garnering 8,614 votes.[15] Emmeline Pankhurst would also stand for Parliament as a Conservative during the interwar period, although her health failed before the election. However, neither Christabel nor Emmeline Pankhurst were active in British feminism during the period between the two World Wars.[16] Christabel's primary interest turned from politics to religion, and she devoted considerable time from 1921 to 1940 serving as a traveling evangelist preaching the Second Advent of Christ. In 1936, she was made a Dame Commander of the British Empire in recognition of her suffrage and war work. Christabel Pankhurst spent her final years in Los Angeles and died on February 13, 1958.[17]

In 1928, the franchise was granted to all women over twenty-one years of age. That same year, Emmeline Pankhurst died on June 14 at the age of 69. Today, the statue of Emmeline Pankhurst, unveiled in 1930, symbolically stands beside the Houses of Parliament in the Victoria Tower Gardens.[18] It is fitting to end this volume on some of the final words of Emmeline Pankhurst's speech "To Women Citizens": "My last word to you this afternoon is, let us unite, we women; let us put aside all class feeling; let us get rid of everything except the real thing, and we shall do well, and we shall deserve well of those who come after us."

24

What Is Our Duty?

Mrs. Pankhurst's Speech delivered in the Sun Hall, Liverpool.

I THINK THAT THROUGHOUT OUR AGITATION FOR THE FRANCHISE FOR political emancipation, on platforms and other places—even in prisons we have talked about rights and fought for rights; at the same time we have always coupled with the claim for rights clear statements as to duty. We have never lost sight of the fact that to possess rights puts upon human beings grave responsibilities and serious duties. We have fought for rights because, in order to perform your duty and fulfil your responsibilities properly, in time of peace, you must have certain citizen rights. When the state is in danger, when the very liberties in your possession are imperilled, is above all the time to think of duty. And so, when the war broke out, some of us who, convalescing after our fights, decided that one of the duties of the Women's Social and Political Union in war time was to talk to men about their duty to the nation—the duty of fighting to preserve the independence of our country, to preserve what our forefathers had won for us, and to protect the nation from foreign invasion.

Women's right to tell men to fight.

There are people who say, "What right have women to talk to men about fighting for their country, since women are not, according the custom of civilisation, called upon to fight?" That used to be said to us in times of peace.

Certainly women have the right to say to men, "Are you going to fight to defend your country and redeem your promise to women?"

Men have said to women, not only that they fight to defend their country, but that they protect women from all the dangers and difficulties of life, and they are proud to be in the position to do it. Why, then, we say to those men, "You are indeed now put to the test. The men of Belgium, the men of France, the men of Serbia, however willing they were to protect women from the things that are most horrible—and more horrible to women than death—have not been able to do it."

Our honour as a nation at stake.

It is only by an accident, or a series of accidents, for which no man here has the right to take credit that British women on British soil are not now enduring the horrors endured by the women of France, the women of Belgium, and the women of Serbia. The least that men can do is that every man of fighting age should prepare himself to redeem his word to women, and to make ready to do his best, to save the mothers, the wives, and the daughters of Great Britain from outrage too horrible even to think of.

We have the right to say to the men, "Fight for your country, defend the shores of this land of ours. Fight for your homes, for the women and for the children." We have the right if that was the only reason, but in these days, when women are taking larger views of their duty to the State, we go further than that: we claim the right to hold recruiting meetings and ask men to fight for bigger reasons than are advanced ordinarily. We say to men, "In this war there are issues at stake bigger even than the safety of your homes and your own country. Your honour as a nation is at stake."

Our duties in this war.

We have our duties in this war. First of all, this duty begins at home—this duty to our home, because I always feel that if we are not ready to do our duty to those nearest to us we are not fit to do our duty far away. And so the first duty is to ourselves and to our homes. Then there is the duty to protect those who, having made a gallant fight for self-defence—and by that I mean the country of Belgium—what we owe to Belgium we can never repay, because now the whole German plan of campaign is perfectly plain to all those who are not prejudiced, and who are not affected by pan-Germanism; and, unfortunately, in their methods of warfare—and their methods of warfare are many—they not only fight physically, but they fight mentally and morally as well, and in this country and in France, and in every country in Europe, long before the war broke out; in fact, ever since the year 1870, they have been preparing by subtle means to take possession of Europe, and I believe their ambitions are not limited by that, they want to rule the whole world. The whole thing is clear to any unprejudiced observer.

First France—then Britain.

It is very difficult for your attacking bully to imagine that a small State—I mean small numerically, and weak physically—will ever have the courage to stand up and resist the bully when he prepares to attack. The Germans did not expect Belgium to keep them at bay while the other countries involved prepared, but there is absolutely no doubt that the plan was to press through

Belgium, to take possession of Paris, and then, having humiliated and crippled France, to cross the Channel and defeat us. There is no doubt that was the plan; it is perfectly clear. And that being so, we owe—civilisation owes—to Belgium a debt which it can never repay.

France and her ideals.

Then we have our duty to our Ally, France. How much democracy owes to France! France is the Mother of European Democracy. There is no doubt about her claim to that. If there had been nothing else worth fighting for in this war, in my opinion that alone would have been worth fighting for, to preserve that spirit and that democracy which France has given to the world, and which would perish if France were destroyed. The people of France are a people who never have been, and I believe never will be, corrupted in the sense of thinking that material things are of more value than spiritual things. The people of France have always been ready to sacrifice themselves for ideals. They have been ready to sacrifice life, they have been ready to sacrifice money, they have been ready to sacrifice everything for an ideal.

You know the old saying, that men should work and women should weep? That is not true, for it is for all of us to work and for all of us to weep when there is occasion to do so. Therefore, it is because in the French nation you have splendid qualities combined in both sexes, because the history of the French nation is so magnificent, because the French nation has contributed so much to civilisation, and so much in Art, beauty, and in great qualities, it is our duty to stand by France, and to prevent her being crushed by the over-sexed, that is to say over-masculine, country of Germany.

The duty of Women.

It is our duty as women to do what we can to help our country in this war, because if the unthinkable thing happened, and Germany were to win, the women's movement, as we know it in Europe, would be put back fifty years at least; there is no doubt about it. Whether it ever could rise again is to my mind extremely doubtful. The ideal of women in Germany is the lowest in Europe. Infantile mortality is very high, immorality is widespread, and, in consequence, venereal disease is rampant. Notice too the miserable and niggardly pittance that is being paid to the wives and families of German soldiers, while nothing whatever is being paid to unmarried wives and their children. True security for women and children is for women to have control over their own destiny. And so it is a duty, a supreme duty, of women, first of all as human beings and as lovers of their country, to co-operate with men in this terrible crisis in which we find ourselves.

Women should be trained.

If all were trained to contribute something to the community, both in time of peace and in time of war, how much better it would be.

What bitterness there was in the hearts of many women when they saw work and business going on as usual, carried on by men who ought to be in the fighting line. There were thousands upon thousands of women willing, even if they were not trained, to do that work and release men, and we have urged the authorities to take into account the great reserve force of the nation, the women who are or might be quite capable to step into the shoes of the men when they were called up to fight.

The Board of Trade issued its appeal to women just before Easter to register their names as willing to do national service in any capacity during the course of the war. I want to tell you to-night that I am very proud of the women of the country. When the first recruiting appeals were made to men, the hoardings were covered with placards and appeals, and they were making efforts by recruiting bands, in places of pleasure—everywhere in the columns of the newspapers there were recruiting appeals to men. Then the time came when the Board of Trade wished to know to what extent it could depend upon the services of the women of the country, and what was done in the case of women? There were no posters for us; there were no recruiting meetings for us; there were no appeals from great names for us; no attractive pictures, "Your King and Country want you"—nothing of that kind. And yet, in spite of that, in one week 34,000 women sent in their names as volunteers for a national service. (Loud applause.)

The talk of Peace.

And now, something about this talk of peace and the terms of peace. Well, I consider it very sinister and very dangerous. Very dangerous indeed, because nothing heartens the Kaiser and his advisers so much as weakness in any of the Allied nations. It is no use expecting Germany to understand that the people who are talking about peace are animated by a genuine love for peace. I go further as regards peace movements. I think that in this country, and in America, and in all the neutral countries, there are a great many very well-meaning people who are genuine lovers of peace. What woman does not dread the effects of war? Germans are encouraging the call for peace. The Kaiser knows he is going to be beaten, and he wants to get out of it on as easy terms as possible, and so it is worth while for German Americans to run a peace movement in America. They want America, which is a great neutral country, to intervene to try to force peace, and to let the Germans down easily without having to pay for all that they have done in Belgium and in France. Similar tactics are being pursued in this country.

Playing the German game.

Only those who have been in close touch with people who know what goes on and what has gone on, since the year 1870, after the Franco-German War, can realise how insidious this German influence is, and so I say to you who love peace (and who does not love peace?) if you take part in any of these peace movements, you are playing the German game and helping Germany. (Loud applause.) They talk of peace, but consider the position of our Allies. The Germans in possession of the North of France, devastating the country, even to-day driving thousands of innocent, helpless people at the point of the bayonet, outraging women, and burning homes! And people in this country—an allied nation—allowing themselves to talk about terms of peace.

It is for Germany to talk of peace, not for us. (Loud applause.) It is for us to show a strong and determined front, because if we do anything else we are misunderstood, and advantage is taken of the situation. Since some women have responded to an invitation to take part in a Peace Conference at The Hague, I feel bound to say that they do not represent the mass of English women. (Loud applause.) The mass of English women are whole-hearted in our support of our own Government in this matter, and in the support of our Allies—(loud applause)—and we are prepared to face all the necessary sacrifices to bring this war to a successful issue from our point of view, because we know, because we feel, that this terrible business, forced upon us, has to be properly finished to save us from the danger of another war perhaps in ten years' time. (Applause.)

To talk of Peace a weakness.

We have clear consciences on this matter. We did not want this war. France did not want this war. Belgium did not want this war. I do not believe that Russia wanted this war. It has been forced upon us, and since Germany took up the sword, the sword must be held in the hands of the Allies until Germany has had enough of war and does not want any more of it. (Loud applause.) For us to talk about peace now, for us to weaken our side now, is to make the condition of those men who are laying down their lives for us in France more terrible than it already is. We have to support them, and to stand loyally by them, and to make our sacrifices and show our patriotism to them.

The nation's duty on the drink question.

And, speaking of sacrifices, let us consider this drink question. What is our duty in that matter? Well, I think our duty is this, that, if the Government of this country seriously think it is necessary for our success in this war to stop drink altogether until the war is ended, it is our duty loyally to support and accept that decision. (Loud applause.)

At any rate, in time of war, we should be ready to say, "Let us sacrifice a personal pleasure in order to get a great national good." Would not that be a something to lift up a nation and make it a wonderful and a great nation?

The Allies fighting for things undying.

I believe that in this war we are fighting for things undying and great; we are fighting for liberty; we are fighting for honour; we are fighting to preserve the great inheritance won for us by our forefathers, and it is worth while to fight for those things and it is worth while to die for them—to die a glorious death in defence of all that makes life worth having is better than to live unending years of inglorious life. And so, out of this great trial that has come upon us, I believe a wonderful transformation will come to the people of this country and we shall emerge from it stronger and better and nobler and more worthy of our great tradition than ever we should perhaps have been without it. (Loud and continued applause.)

25

Woman Suffragist Deputation.

Mrs. Pankhurst's Speech

Mr. lloyd george, i represent here this afternoon the women's Social and Political Union. You will remember that at the outbreak of war our organisation abandoned all suffrage work, and the members devoted themselves to national service of every kind.

I think, Sir, we ought first to thank you for having made it possible for this question of women's suffrage to be dealt with in a practical way, and I would like as strongly as possible to support what Mrs. Fawcett has said about the need we feel that this matter should be secured from all contention by being dealt with in a responsible way by the Government itself. When we read in the newspapers this morning the various interpretations that were put upon your words, I felt that my chief duty in coming here this afternoon was to implore you, with all the energy I possess, to take charge of this matter yourself as Prime Minister, and in that way make it a matter which can be settled with as little dispute and as little contention as possible.

I want to say for members of my organisation, and I think for patriotic women generally, that we recognise that in war-time we cannot ask for perfection in any legislation; and although in times of peace we should want to debate every item of a Bill—we should want to discuss every part of it— in war-time we want to see this thing done as quickly as possible, and with as little dispute and as little difference of opinion as possible. And so we ask you, Mr. Lloyd George, to give such a Government measure to the House of Commons to vote upon as you feel to be just and practicable in the war circumstances; and I want to assure you that whatever you think can be passed, and can be passed without discussion and debate, or with as little discussion and debate as possible, we are ready to accept. (Hear, hear) We know your democratic feeling, and we leave the matter in your hands. We only ask you to make yourself, as Prime Minister, responsible for it, and to give your great influence and great energy to carrying it through as quickly as possible.

The two questions I have to put to you this afternoon are these. Is it to be a Government measure? Are women to be included in the Reform Bill

365

and are we to have it without loss of time? In this room, where so many women have come, one cannot help feeling that there might possibly be amongst us the spirits of those women who have died without seeing the result of their labours and their sacrifices. It will be a wonderful thing if in war-time—just as in Canada—just as it will come in Russia—and it should come to women at the heart of the British Empire—and I want to tell you that if it comes, I have no doubt whatever that women will work with greater energy, greater enthusiasm, greater patriotism, for the security of their native land. (Applause).

26

Woman Suffrage
A Necessary War Measure.

Mrs. PANKHURST SPEAKING AT THE QUEENS HALL SAID:

If the suffrage is given to women now as a war measure it will make for greater national strength in the prosecution of the war. It will encourage those women, who are already putting out great efforts in our munition works and in every department of national life. (Applause) It will sustain and support them in their efforts and it will deepen and strengthen that sense of responsibility towards their country that women have shown since war broke out.

We have to make sure that before the Bill passes through the House of Commons to the House of Lords the Women's Suffrage clause shall be an integral part of the Bill, and that the Government shall make it clearly understood that the whole measure stands or falls by the acceptance of every clause in the measure.

What we want to proclaim in this meeting is that we want the Bill, the whole Bill, and nothing but the Bill. (Applause) We are prepared, as we told the Prime Minister, when a deputation waited upon him a little while ago, to take the measure of enfranchisement which the Government in its wisdom thinks will be acceptable to the majority of Parliament and can be passed without friction or delay.

We are prepared to take it with all its limitations. It will be 50 years on the 17th of May since John Stuart Mill introduced the first Women's Suffrage Bill into the House of Commons. Is it not a remarkable thing that exactly fifty years after the introduction of the first Women's Suffrage Bill we should be on the eve of seeing this question settled? And would it not be a splendid thing if the Electoral Reform Bill should receive the Royal Assent on the 17th of May this year. Fifty years is a long time, and it seems to me that fifty years of agitation that has seen men and women going from the cradle to the grave, hoping and longing to see this thing pass, is altogether too long a time even in a conservative country like England. There must be no slip "twixt cup and lip" this time, and the women of these Isles must not be humiliated by another refusal of those rights which have been extended to women in Russia, in America and in our own Dominions.

Men have said kind and gracious things about the part women have played in this war. But women think of what we have done as simply doing our duty, and our regret is that it has taken so long for opportunities to be given to us, and that even now in the third year of the war, the organisation of women for essential war work is far from complete. What we feel about the giving of the vote is that it will deepen our sense of responsibility, that it will strengthen our work in the war, and that it will put us in a position to safeguard those domestic and human interests which always have, and which always will be the essential part of women's work in the world. We want the vote so that we may serve our country better. We want the vote so that we shall be more faithful and more true to our Allies. We want the vote so that we may help to maintain the cause of Christian civilisation for which we entered on this war. We want the vote so that in future such wars if possible may be averted. We recognise as women that this war has to be fought out to the bitter end, that the spirit which led to it, has to be crushed, that German ambitions of world conquest have to come to an end. If we get the vote all women who love the country will work side by side with men in order to bring about all that we long for and all that we hope for our Country and our Cause. (Applause).

27

To Women Citizens.

Verbatim Report of Mrs. Pankhurst's Speech at the Royal Albert Hall, March 16, 1918.

MRS. PANKHURST: BEFORE WE BEGIN THE BUSINESS OF THE MEETING, I will ask this great audience to unite with us in singing the hymn which is printed on the programme, "Oh, God, our help in ages past." The orchestra will play the tune of the hymn before you join in the singing. (The audience joined in the singing of the hymn.)

The Chairman: Fellow citizens, men and women—(cheers)—in meeting here this afternoon we have a two-fold object. First, we meet to rejoice that the long struggle is over and that women have won their political emancipation. (Cheers.) In the second place, we meet to dedicate ourselves anew to the service of our country and our country's cause. (Cheers.) For us who took part in it, it is a difficult thing to speak of the struggle that is over. I know you will feel with me that we cannot rejoice without thinking of those who are not here to rejoice with us, those pioneers who in the dark and early days undertook the work for the vote without any hope of seeing victory themselves. That little band of women, supported by a still smaller band of chivalrous men, men who never advocated Woman Suffrage because they hoped thereby to push their political fortunes, but knew that probably it would cost them their political success. Well, those pioneers have gone, those men and women are dead, but to-day their spirit is with us— (Cheers)—and they would be the first to say to us, "We are glad that you remember us, but this is not the time to spend many words on talking of us."

We want this afternoon to make you feel as we do, that a Women's Party is necessary to achieve the salvation of the cause to which women have devoted themselves, along with patriotic men, since the beginning of the war. The Women's Party calls upon women of all classes to forget their class and unite in common service of the nation. The Women's Party puts first and foremost on its programme the safeguarding of the Empire's existence, the upholding of national honour, and the defeat of the pretensions and claims of the enemy to force their conception of life and of civilisation upon

369

other nations besides their own. (Cheers.) Already our programme has met with great acceptance, not only from women but also from men. We have, I venture to say this afternoon, not only the best and the clearest programme, but the programme that finds widest acceptance, and we urge women to join us and to work with us. We offer them a programme which they can accept, and we offer them a comradeship in service in which they can find great happiness and great usefulness. There is room in the Women's Party for all women who love their country and love humanity. There is room for the woman of high rank and there is room and warm welcome for the working woman—(Cheers)—and that woman needs a Women's Party most of all. (Renewed cheers.) On all hands there are bids being made for the women electors of the country, especially for the working women. We say to working women: "What have the Parties done for you in the past that you should go into their ranks now that you have something which they are very eager to get? We have the best right to ask you to join us and work with us, because we, from first to last, have been faithful and loyal to women, have worked for them and suffered for them. (Cheers.) Now that women have the political power to realise those aspirations which we put into your hearts in the old days of stress and of struggle, we claim you, as we have the right to claim you. (Cheers.) We claim you, not for selfish ends, not for the interest of this section or the other, not even for the interests of women alone as a sex, but we claim you because we believe that working with us you can save your country. (Cheers.)

And now, indeed, the time has come when one may say it is women to the rescue. Do not let us forget that in the last 3 1/2 years many of the best men have died, and of those who live the best are in the fighting line. Of those who remain some are past active service, some are maimed and weakened in the struggle, and, unfortunately, there remains a remnant, those who have been unwilling to serve, though they cling to any emoluments that war gives them, and are using their industrial and their political power to the injury of their country. We women are a mighty force, if only because our force is intact and unimpaired. Young women, with their fresh young vigorous lives, are all here, and that is why they must go to the rescue of the country on the home front.

I have no doubt that women will be equal to the duty which comes upon us in this critical hour of our country's life. We are needed, and we have new power to serve, through our political power. But in order to serve we must combine and unite, and that is why we have a Women's Party.

I have been thinking in these last days very deeply of the great women of the past, whose life and example and inspiration should move us in this crisis, and the two women that I feel most inspiring of all that noble band are a Frenchwoman and an Englishwoman—Joan of Arc and Queen Elizabeth—one of them a great warrior and a great spiritual leader and guide,

Joan of Arc, the other, the greatest statesman that our country has ever seen. (Cheers.) They both freed their countries from the enemy at the darkest hour in the life of their country. In France, when the wise men and the warriors lost heart, Joan of Arc inspired her fellow countrymen and led them to victory. Queen Elizabeth saved this country from a foreign foe. We all know, we all have learned, of how she acted at the time of the Spanish Armada, but how many people realise that Queen Elizabeth, in her day and generation, saved us from the Germans? (Cheers.) We have often thought: Would she were alive now! But that is not fair or right. Those women played their part in their time. It is for you and me to play our part to-day and repeat in the twentieth century what they did in those far-off days. All we ask from you is unselfish devotion to the cause of national security which is the first cause that must be served to-day, and when we have defeated the Germans then our programme of Social Reform is one which all women who love their country should help us to carry out. Work with us, join the party, save this country, and let us make it better than it could be without our service and work. (Cheers.)

We have an enormous task to perform if we are to organise the women voters in readiness for the next election, which may take place within a few months. What a task it is! What a task it is to educate these six million new voters whose political education while they were voteless was neglected except by women. We are encouraged to believe that the political education of women will take very much less time and be more complete than our men friends tell us their education is after many years of political experience. We have a great and a terrible responsibility. I pray that the long training in sacrifice of self, that long devotion to the service of others, which women have learnt, partly by nature and partly by experience, will stand us in good stead in this time of trial. If we think of others and not of ourselves, if we think of our country and not of selfish interests, then we shall use our votes wisely and well.

My last word to you this afternoon is, let us unite, we women; let us put aside all class feeling; let us get rid of everything except the real thing, and we shall do well, and we shall deserve well of those who come after us.

I close the meeting, and I ask you to unite in singing that which to-day represents all that we have in our hearts, but find so difficult to express love of country, love of justice and of freedom. Let us sing together the National Anthem.

The audience, led by the orchestra, dispersed, after singing "God Save the King."

Notes

Part I: Introduction

1. Christabel Pankhurst, "History Repeating Itself," *The Suffragette*, 14 March 1913, 348.

2. Brian Harrison, "The Act of Militancy: Violence and the Suffragettes, 1904–1914," in *Peaceable Kingdom: Stability and Change in Modern Britain* (Oxford: Clarendon Press, 1982), 60.

3. The most infamous of the "humorous" takes on the WSPU is found in George Dangerfield, *The Strange Death of Liberal England* (New York: Capricorn Books, 1961).

4. For example, David Mitchell, *The Fighting Pankhursts: A Study in Tenacity* (New York: Macmillan, 1967) or David Mitchell, *Queen Christabel* (London: Mac-Donald & Jane's, 1977).

5. Autobiographies by Emmeline Pankhurst (*My Own Story*), Emmeline Pethick-Lawrence (*My Life in a Changing World*), Frederick Pethick-Lawrence (*Fate Has Been Kind*); combined movement histories and autobiographies by Christabel Pankhurst (*Unshackled*) and E. Sylvia Pankhurst (*The Suffragette Movement*); and Sylvia Pankhurst's biography of her mother (*The Life of Emmeline Pankhurst*) provide first-hand insight into the philosophy and strategy of the WSPU. However, Mary Richardson (*Laugh a Defiance*), Annie Kenney (*Memories of a Militant*), and Constance Lytton (*Prisons and Prisoners*) capture more of the danger, excitement, and physical duress of the active militant. For discussions of the construction of suffragette militancy in biographies and autobiographies, see Mary Jean Corbett, *Representing Femininity: Middle-Class Subjectivity in Victorian and Edwardian Women's Autobiographies* (Oxford: Oxford University Press, 1992); Hilda Kean, "Searching for the Past in Present Defeat: The Construction of Historical and Political Identity in British Feminism in the 1920s and 1930s," *Women's History Review* 3, no. 1 (1994): 57–80; and Laura E. Nym Mayhall, "Creating the 'Suffragette Spirit': British Feminism and the Historical Imagination," *Women's History Review* 4, no. 3 (1995): 319–44.

6. See, in particular, Roger Fulford, *Votes for Women: The Story of a Struggle* (London: Faber & Faber, 1957); Andrew Rosen, *Rise Up Women: The Militant Campaign of the Women's Social and Political Union, 1903–1914* (London: Routledge & Kegan Paul, 1974), Constance Rover, *Women's Suffrage and Party Politics in Britain, 1866–1914* (London: Routledge & Kegan Paul, 1967); and, in a study of the antisuffragist side, Brian Harrison, *Separate Spheres* (London: Croom Helm, 1978).

7. See, for example, Brian Harrison, "The Act of Militancy: Violence and the Suffragettes, 1904–1914," in his *Peaceable Kingdom: Stability and Change in Modern Britain* (Oxford: Clarendon Press, 1982); Sandra Stanley Holton, "In Sorrowful Wrath: Suffrage Militancy and the Romantic Feminism of Emmeline Pankhurst," In *British Feminism of the Twentieth Century,* ed. Harold L. Smith (Amherst: University of Massachusetts Press, 1990); Elizabeth Sarah, "Christabel Pankhurst: Reclaiming Her Power," in *Feminist Theorists: Three Centuries of Women's Intellectual Traditions,* ed. Dale Spender (London: Women's Press, 1983), 256–84; Janet Lyon, "Militant

Discourse, Strange Bedfellows: Suffragettes and Vorticists before the War," *Differ-ences: A Journal of Feminist Cultural Studies* (1992): 100–33; and the editor's *The Transfiguring Sword: The Just War of the Women's Social and Political Union* (Tusca-loosa: University of Alabama Press, 1997). For the roots of suffrage militancy, see Sandra Stanley Holton, "From Anti-Slavery to Suffrage Militancy: The Bright Circle, Elizabeth Cady Stanton and the British Women's Movement," in *Suffrage and Be-yond: International Feminist Perspectives*, eds. Caroline Daley and Melanie Nolan (New York: New York University Press, 1994), 213–33.

8. Sandra Stanley Holton, "In Sorrowful Wrath: Suffrage Militancy and the Romantic Feminism of Emmeline Pankhurst," in *British Feminism in the Twentieth Century*, ed. Harold L. Smith (Amherst: University of Massachusetts Press, 1990), 10.

9. Emmeline Pankhurst, "Mrs. Pankhurst's Address to the Jury," *Votes for Women*, 24 May 1912, 232.

Part II: Breaking Silence

1. Emmeline Pethick-Lawrence, *My Part in a Changing World* (London: Victor Gollancz, Ltd., 1938), 233.

2. Sandra Stanley Holton, "In Sorrowful Wrath: Suffrage Militancy and the Romantic Feminism of Emmeline Pankhurst," in *British Feminism in the Twentieth Century*, ed. Harold L. Smith (Amherst: University of Massachusetts Press, 1990), 10.

3. Susan Kingsley Kent, *Sex and Suffrage in Britain, 1860–1914* (Princeton: University Press, 1987), 184.

4. Emmeline Pankhurst, *My Own Story* (New York: Hearst's International Li-brary Co., 1914), 38.

5. Midge Mackenzie, *Shoulder to Shoulder* (New York: Alfred A. Knopf, 1975), 21.

6. Roger Fulford, *Votes for Women: The Story of a Struggle* (London: Faber and Faber, 1957), 122.

7. Emmeline Pankhurst, *My Own Story*, 42–43.

8. Fulford, *Votes for Women*, 122–123.

9. Mackenzie, *Shoulder to Shoulder* 28. For more on Elizabeth Wolstonholme-Elmy, see Sandra Stanley Holton, "'To Educate Women into Rebellion': Elizabeth Cady Stanton and the Creation of a Transatlantic Network of Radical Suffragists," *American Historical Review* (October, 1994): 1112–36; Sandra Stanley Holton, "Free Love and Victorian Feminism: The Divers Matrimonials of Elizabeth Wolstonholme and Ben Elmy," *Victorian Studies*, (winter, 1994): 199–222; and Sandra Stanley Holton, *Suffrage Days: Stories From the Women's Suffrage Movement* (London: Routledge, 1996).

10. Jane Marcus, ed., *Suffrage and the Pankhursts* (London: Routledge & Kegan Paul, 1987), 9.

11. Fulford, *Votes for Women*, 129–30; 137–138.

12. Ibid., 139.

13. Ibid., 130.

14. Ibid., 140.

15. Mackenzie, *Shoulder to Shoulder*, 42.

16. Ibid., 58–60.

17. Pethick-Lawrence, *Changing World*, 175–76.

18. Ibid., 174–77.

19. Fulford, *Votes for Women*, 168. Details of the later challenge to Mrs. Despard's leadership in the WFL may be found by reading internal league letters and memos currently available in the Suffragette Fellowship Collection at the Museum of London.

20. Mackenzie, *Shoulder to Shoulder*, 59.

21. Fulford, *Votes for Women*, 178.

22. Donald Bryant, Carroll C. Arnold, Frederick W. Haberman, Richard Murphy, and Karl Wallace, *An Historical Anthology of Select British Speeches* (New York: The Ronald Press Company, 1967), 444. A copy of this speech is found in Bryant, et al. collection (now out of print), and copies of the original pamphlet are located in the Suffragette Fellowship Collection in the Museum of London.

23. Duncan Crow, *The Edwardian Woman* (London: George Allen & Unwin, 1978), 96–99.

24. Crow, *Edwardian Woman*, 99–100.

25. Cheryl R. Jorgensen-Earp, "The Lady, The Whore, and The Spinster: The Rhetorical Use of Victorian Images of Women," *Western Journal of Speech Communication* 54 (winter, 1990): 82–98.

26. Fulford, *Votes for Women*, 183.

27. Emmeline Pethick-Lawrence, *Changing World*, 194–95.

28. Fulford, *Votes for Women*, 186.

29. Pethick-Lawrence, *Changing World*, 195–96.

30. Ibid., 197–98.

31. Fulford, *Votes for Women*, 187.

32. Mackenzie, *Shoulder to Shoulder*, 88.

33. Don M. Cregier, *Bounder From Wales: Lloyd George's Career Before the First World War* (Columbia: The University of Missouri Press, 1976), 30–31.

34. E. Sylvia Pankhurst, *The Life of Emmeline Pankhurst: The Suffragette Struggle for Women's Citizenship* (London: T. Werner Laurie, Ltd., 1935), 85.

35. Fulford, *Votes for Women*, 179.

36. Brian Harrison, "The Act of Militancy: Violence and the Suffragettes, 1904–1914," in *Peaceable Kingdom: Stability and Change in Modern Britain* (Oxford: Clarendon Press, 1982), 37.

37. Fulford, *Votes for Women*, 190.

38. Ian Christopher Fletcher, "'A Star Chamber of the Twentieth Century': Suffragettes, Liberals, and the 1908 'Rush the Commons' Case," *Journal of British Studies*, 35 (October, 1996): 504–30. This article provides a detailed account of the trial and the government maneuvering outside of the courtroom.

39. Emmeline Pankhurst, *My Own Story*, 134.

40. George Dangerfield, *The Strange Death of Liberal England, 1910–1914* (New York: Capricorn Books, 1961), 14–15.

41. Dangerfield, *Strange Death*, 19.

42. Donald Read, *Edwardian England* (London: The Historical Association, 1972), 22.

43. Dangerfield, *Strange Death*, 24.

44. Read, *Edwardian England*, 25.

45. F. J. C. Hearnshaw, *Edwardian England, A.D. 1901–1910* (New York: Books For Libraries Press, 1968), 105.

46. Dangerfield, *Strange Death*, 25.

47. Read, *Edwardian England*, 26.

48. Ibid., 25.
49. Ibid.

Chapter 1. The Importance of the Vote

1. A by-election is an election held in the constituency concerned to fill a vacancy in a Parliamentary seat (whether caused by death, resignation, or appointment to another office).

2. The reference is to John Elliot Burns (1858–1943), who entered the British cabinet in 1905, the first person of working class origin to do so. He served in Campbell-Bannerman's cabinet as the President of the Local Government Board. He left Parliament in 1918.

3. The Married Women's Property Act, passed into law in 1870, allowed women to keep possession of what they earned for themselves. All other property (whether acquired before or after marriage) continued to belong to the husband. More complete versions of this law passed in 1881 in Scotland and 1882 in England and Wales. (See Ray Strachey, *The Cause* (London: Virago, 1979), 273–76.)

4. Lewis ("Lulu") Harcourt was a member of Parliament from 1904 to 1917.

Chapter 2. The Prisoners at Bow Street

1. John Bright (1811–1889) was the son of a cotton mill owner and a member of Parliament almost continuously from 1843–1889. With Richard Cobden, he helped defeat the Corn Laws.

2. Joseph Chamberlain led Liberal Unionists to modify Gladstone's Home Rule Bill.

3. Hansard refers to the official published reports of debates and proceedings in the English Parliament.

4. Lord Randolph Churchill (1849–1895), father of Winston Churchill, was a Conservative leader who opposed Gladstone's Home Rule Bill. He was famous for coining the phrase "Ulster will fight, and Ulster will be right" that was revived in the Edwardian period in response to Irish agitation.

5. The form of the summons was designed to keep the case in the Police Courts. According to the WSPU, this course of action was pursued by the government because the Police Court handled cases of prostitution and drunk and disorderly conduct.

6. John Burns was tried for sedition in 1886.

7. The Star Chamber was a court that had civil and criminal jurisdiction and dealt mainly with such offenses against the Crown as conspiracy. It was abolished in 1641 but has remained as a term referring to a court that is secretive, overly severe, and arbitrary in its rulings.

8. The reference is to the wild celebrations that took place in England when, during the Boer War, the besieged force of Col. Baden-Powell at Mafeking was relieved by a British column.

9. She is referring to the marriage of Winston Churchill at St. Margaret's the month before the trial.

10. Queen Victoria's Golden Jubilee, celebrating 50 years of her reign, took place in 1887, and her Diamond Jubilee took place ten years later.

11. Richard Burdon Haldane was a Cabinet Minister from 1885–1911 and Secretary of State for War from 1905 to 1912.

12. Lord Morley was Secretary to India from 1905 to 1910.

13. Mr. Augustine Birrell was a Liberal member of the House of Commons and Chief Secretary for Ireland, 1907–1916.

Part III: Hunger Strike

1. Midge Mackenzie, *Shoulder to Shoulder* (New York: Alfred A. Knopf, 1975), 83.

2. Constance Rover, *Women's Suffrage and Party Politics in Britain, 1866–1914* (Routledge & Kegan Paul, 1967), 81.

3. Quoted in Caroline Morrell, *"Black Friday": Violence Against Women in the Suffragette Movement* (London: Women's Research and Resources Centre Publications, 1981), 21.

4. Emmeline Pankhurst, *My Own Story* (New York: Hearst's International Library Co., 1914), 137.

5. Ibid., 138.

6. Mackenzie, *Shoulder to Shoulder,* 110.

7. Morrell, *Black Friday,* 20.

8. L. E. Snellgrove, *Suffragettes and Votes for Women,* 2d ed. (Harlow: Longman, 1984), 33.

9. Emmeline Pethick-Lawrence, *My Part in a Changing World* (London: Victor Gollancz Ltd., 1938), 235.

10. Roger Fulford, *Votes for Women: The Story of a Struggle* (London: Faber and Faber, Ltd., 1957), 206.

11. Morrell, *Black Friday,* 21.

12. June Purvis, "'Deeds Not Words': The Daily Lives of Militant Suffragettes in Edwardian Britain," *Women's Studies International Forum* 18 (1995): 91–01. See also, the speech "Artificial vs. Forcible Feeding," by Dr. Mansell-Moullin later in this volume.

13. Sandra Stanley Holton, "In Sorrowful Wrath: Suffrage Militancy and the Romantic Feminism of Emmeline Pankhurst," in *British Feminism in the Twentieth Century,* ed. Harold L. Smith (Amherst: University of Massachusetts Press, 1990), 17.

14. See in particular, Jane Marcus, *Suffrage and the Pankhursts* (London: Routledge & Kegan Paul), 1987, Sandra Stanley Holton ("In Sorrowful Wrath"), Lisa Tickner (*The Spectacle of Women*), Caroline Morrell (*Black Friday*), June Purvis ("Deeds Not Words" and "The Prison Experiences") and Martha Vicinus (*Independent Women*).

15. Lisa Tickner, *The Spectacle of Women: Imagery of the Suffrage Campaign, 1907–14* (Chicago: University of Chicago Press, 1988), 107.

16. June Purvis, "The Prison Experiences of the Suffragettes in Edwardian Britain," *Women's History Review* 4, no. 1 (1995): 123.

17. Tickner, *The Spectacle of Women,* 105.

18. Fulford, *Votes for Women,* 201–02.

19. Mackenzie, *Shoulder to Shoulder,* 96–97.

20. Ibid., 98–104.

21. Ibid., 133.

22. Ibid., 136.

23. Ibid., 148.

24. Fulford, *Votes for Women*, 213.

25. Mackenzie, *Shoulder to Shoulder*, 155. For a discussion of forcible feeding and the Lytton case, see Mary Jean Corbett, *Representing Femininity: Middle-Class Subjectivity in Victorian and Edwardian Women's Autobiographies* (Oxford: Oxford University Press, 1992), Martha Vicinus, *Independent Women: Work and Community for Single Women 1850–1920* (Chicago: University of Chicago Press, 1985), June Purvis, "The Prison Experiences of the Suffragettes in Edwardian Britain," *Women's History Review* 4, no. 1 (1995): 103–33, and Laura E. Nym Mayhall, "Creating the 'Suffragette Spirit': British Feminism and the Historical Imagination," *Women's History Review* 4, no. 3 (1995): 319–44.

26. Michael Osborne, "Archetypal Metaphor in Rhetoric: The Light-Dark Family" *The Quarterly Journal of Speech* LIII (April, 1967): 115–26.

Part IV: Black Friday

1. E. Sylvia Pankhurst, *The Life of Emmeline Pankhurst: The Suffragette Struggle for Women's Citizenship* (London: T. Werner Laurie, Ltd, 1935), 94.

2. Roger Fulford, *Votes for Women: The Story of a Struggle* (London: Faber and Faber, Ltd., 1957), 218–19.

3. E. Sylvia Pankhurst, *Emmeline Pankhurst*, 95.

4. Fulford, *Votes for Women*, 221.

5. Ibid., 222.

6. Emmeline Pankhurst, *My Own Story* (New York: Hearst's International Library Co., 1914), 169–70.

7. Fulford, *Votes for Women*, 224.

8. Ibid., 226–27.

9. Ibid., 228.

10. Emmeline Pankhurst, *My Own Story*, 175.

11. E. Sylvia Pankhurst, *Emmeline Pankhurst*, 96.

12. Fulford, *Votes for Women*, 227–228.

13. Caroline Morrell, *"Black Friday": Violence Against Women in the Suffragette Movement* (London: Women's Research and Resources Centre Publications, 1981), 67.

14. Fulford, *Votes for Women*, 230.

15. Morrell, *Black Friday*, 32–33.

16. Emmeline Pankhurst, *My Own Story*, 180.

17. Emmeline Pethick-Lawrence, *My Part in a Changing World* (London: Victor Gollancz, Ltd., 1938) 249.

18. Pankhurst, *My Own Story*, 180.

19. L. E. Snellgrove, *Suffragettes and Votes for Women* 2d. ed. (Harlow: Longman, 1984), 55.

20. Morrell, *Black Friday*, 34.

21. Pethick-Lawrence, *Changing World*, 249–50.

22. Morrell, *Black Friday*, 34–35.

23. Ibid., 39.

24. Midge Mackenzie, *Shoulder to Shoulder* (New York: Alfred A. Knopf, 1978), 170.

25. Morrell, *Black Friday*, 35.

26. Ibid., 35–36.

27. For more on Black Friday and the experiences of the suffragettes during legal deputations, see Alison Young, "'Wild Women': The Censure of the Suffragette Movement," *International Journal of the Sociology of Law* 16 (1988): 279–93, and Martha Vicinus, "Male Space and Women's Bodies: The Suffragette Movement," in *Independent Women: Work and Community for Single Women, 1850–1920* (Chicago: University of Chicago, 1985), 247–80.

28. Emmeline Pankhurst, *My Own Story,* 183–84.

29. Sandra Stanley Holton, "In Sorrowful Wrath: Suffrage Militancy and the Romantic Feminism of Emmeline Pankhurst," in *British Feminism in the Twentieth Century,* ed. Harold L. Smith (Amherst: University of Massachusetts, 1990), 20.

Part V: The Argument of the Broken Pane

1. Emmeline Pankhurst, *My Own Story* (New York: Hearst's International Library Co., 1914), 188.

2. Emmeline Pankhurst, *My Own Story,* 193.

3. E. Sylvia Pankhurst, *The Life of Emmeline Pankhurst: The Suffragette Struggle for Women's Citizenship* (London: T. Werner Laurie Ltd., 1935), 99.

4. Midge Mackenzie, *Shoulder to Shoulder* (New York: Alfred A. Knopf, 1975), 174. The best analysis of the symbolic importance of the processions and banners of the WSPU may be found in Lisa Tickner's *The Spectacle of Women: Imagery of the Suffrage Campaign, 1907–14* (Chicago: University of Chicago Press, 1988).

5. Emmeline Pethick-Lawrence, *My Part in a Changing World* (London: Victor Gollancz Ltd., 1938), 256.

6. Ibid., 257.

7. Andrew Rosen, *Rise Up Women! The Militant Campaign of the Women's Social and Political Union, 1903–1914* (London: Routledge & Kegan Paul, 1974), 154.

8. Antonia Raeburn, *The Suffragette View* (New York: St. Martin's Press, 1976), 57.

9. For a complete discussion of the just-war basis of WSPU justifications for reformist terrorism, see the editor's *"The Transfiguring Sword": The Just War of the Women's Social and Political Union* (Tuscaloosa: University of Alabama Press, 1997).

Part VI: The 1912 Conspiracy Trial

1. Emmeline Pankhurst, *My Own Story* (New York: Hearst's International Library Inc., 1914), 216–17.

2. Ibid., 214.

3. Lisa Tickner, *The Spectacle of Women: Imagery of the Suffrage Campaign, 1907–14* (Chicago: University of Chicago Press, 1988), 134.

4. Emmeline Pankhurst, *My Own Story,* 218.

5. Ibid., 227.

6. Ibid., 221–22.

7. Ibid., 228.

8. *Votes for Women,* 17 May 1912, 516.

9. Pankhurst, *My Own Story,* 221.

10. E. Sylvia Pankhurst, *The Life of Emmeline Pankhurst: The Suffragette Struggle for Women's Citizenship* (London: T. Werner Laurie, Ltd., 1935), 107.

11. Frederick Pethick-Lawrence, *Fate Has Been Kind* (London: Hutchinson and Co., 1943), 93.

Chapter 11. Opening Day of the Trial

1. *Votes for Women,* 17 May 1912, 516–17.

Chapter 13. Closing Days of the Trial

1. Frederick Edwin Smith was a conservative member of Parliament (1906–1918).

2. Ernest Jones, the Chartist and Poet lived from 1819–1869. For his part in Chartist proceedings at Manchester in 1848, he was given two years' solitary confinement.

3. Members of this board were responsible for administering the Poor Laws.

4. A term meaning a strikebreaker, a scab.

5. William Thomas Stead was a journalist and reformer. He was imprisoned for three months for writing *The Maiden Tribute of Modern Babylon,* exposing "white slavery" and other legally permitted abuses against young girls and women. He drowned in the sinking of the *Titanic* shortly before the Conspiracy Trial.

6. Leander Starr Jameson (1853–1917) had a successful medical practice in South Africa. He led a raid on Johannesburg in 1895 to try to relieve the Uitlanders there.

7. William Cobbett (1763–1835) was a popular journalist and reformer who wrote under the pseudonym of Peter Porcupine. He took up the cause of rural laborers, was imprisoned in Newgate (1810–1812), and fined £1000 after denouncing the flogging of militiamen who had complained about unfair wage deductions. He was a member of Parliament from 1832 until his death.

Part VII: Martyrs to the Cause

1. E. Sylvia Pankhurst, *The Life of Emmeline Pankhurst: The Suffragette Struggle for Women's Citizenship* (London: T. Werner Laurie Ltd., 1935), 109.

2. Emmeline Pethick-Lawrence, *My Part in a Changing World* (London: Victor Gollancz Ltd., 1938), 276.

3. Pethick-Lawrence, *Changing World,* 277–78.

4. Ibid., 279.

5. Ibid., 280–81.

6. E. Sylvia Pankhurst, *Emmeline Pankhurst,* 117.

7. Midge Mackenzie, *Shoulder to Shoulder* (New York: Alfred A. Knopf, 1975), 213.

8. Roger Fulford, *Votes for Women: The Story of a Struggle* (London: Faber and Faber Ltd., 1957), 257.

9. Ibid., 257.

10. Sandra Stanley Holton, "In Sorrowful Wrath: Suffrage Militancy and the Romantic Feminism of Emmeline Pankhurst," in *British Feminism in the Twentieth Century,* ed. Harold L. Smith (Amherst: University of Massachusetts, 1990), 17.

11. Pethick-Lawrence, *Changing World,* 283.

12. Emmeline Pankhurst, *My Own Story* (New York: Hearst's International Library Co., 1914), 272.

13. Fulford, *Votes for Women,* 277.

14. Lisa Tickner, *The Spectacle of Women: Imagery of the Suffrage Campaign, 1907–14* (Chicago: University of Chicago Press, 1988), 135.

15. Caroline Morrell, *"Black Friday": Violence Against Women in the Suffragette Movement* (London: Women's Research and Resources Centre Publications, 1981), 51–52.

16. Mackenzie, *Shoulder to Shoulder,* 216–18.

17. Mackenzie, *Shoulder to Shoulder,* 218.

18. Antonia Raeburn, *The Militant Suffragettes* (London: Joseph, 1973), 189–91. See also, Rowena Fowler, "Why Did Suffragettes Attack Works of Art?" *Journal of Women's History* 2 (winter, 1991): 109–25.

19. Fulford, *Votes for Women,* 282.

20. E. Sylvia Pankhurst, *Emmeline Pankhurst,* 125.

21. See in particular Mary Richardson's *Laugh a Defiance* (London: George Weidenfeld & Nicholson, 1953) and Annie Kenney's *Memories of a Militant* (London: Edward Arnold & Co., 1924).

22. Brian Harrison, "The Act of Militancy: Violence and the Suffragettes, 1904–1914," in *Peaceable Kingdom: Stability and Change in Modern Britain* (Oxford: Clarendon Press, 1982), 70–71.

23. E. Sylvia Pankhurst, *Emmeline Pankhurst,* 131–132.

24. Mackenzie, *Shoulder to Shoulder,* 242.

25. See John Sleight, *One-way Ticket to Epsom* (Morpeth: Bridge Studios, 1988), 9–15 and Liz Stanley and Ann Morley, *The Life and Death of Emily Wilding Davison: A Biographical Detective Story* (London: The Women's Press, 1988), 163–66. Better yet, readers interested in Emily Wilding Davison's death may want to contact the gift shop at the Museum of London for their "Votes for Women" video and do their own frame by frame analysis of the newsreel of Davison's death.

26. Mackenzie, *Shoulder to Shoulder,* 242.

Part VIII: The Cat and Mouse Act

1. Midge Mackenzie, *Shoulder to Shoulder* (New York: Alfred A. Knopf, 1975), 116–19.

2. Roger Fulford, *Votes for Women: The Story of a Struggle* (London: Faber and Faber Ltd., 1957), 284.

3. Emmeline Pankhurst, *My Own Story* (New York: Hearst's International Library Co., 1914), 303–16.

4. Fulford, 294–95. For more on this act and other attacks on artwork, see Rowena Fowler, "Why Did Suffragettes Attack Works of Art?" *Journal of Women's History* 2 (winter, 1991): 109–25.

5. Donald Read, *Edwardian England* (London: The Historical Association, 1972), 39.

6. Ibid., 40–41.

7. Ibid., 41.

8. Susan Kingsley Kent, *Sex and Suffrage in Britain, 1860–1914* (Princeton: University Press, 1987), 5–6.

9. Pankhurst, *My Own Story,* 324–26.

10. Ibid., 328.

11. Mackenzie, *Shoulder to Shoulder,* 270–71.

12. Ibid., 257.

13. Ibid., 262–64.

14. Emmeline Pethick-Lawrence, *My Part in a Changing World* (London: Victor Gollancz, 1938), 304.

15. Fulford, *Votes for Women,* 297.

Chapter 19. Artificial vs. "Forcible" Feeding

1. Johnston Forbes-Robertson was a popular actor who starred in such major plays as George Bernard Shaw's *Caesar and Cleopatra.* Mrs. Patrick Campbell and Henry Irving were among the great actors with whom he was associated. He was knighted upon his retirement from the stage in 1913.

Chapter 21. "Our Spirits Are Eternal"

1. She is referring to the Piccadilly Flat Case. During the summer of 1913, police raided an upscale brothel run by Queenie Gerald. However, Parliament quashed investigation of the clientele, reportedly because prominent men in politics and society were customers. Queenie Gerald got three months for living on the immoral earnings of others. (See Susan Kingsley Kent, *Sex and Suffrage in Britain, 1860–1914* (Princeton: University Press, 1987, 155.)

Chapter 22. Address at Hartford

1. The reproduction of the Verbatim report of Mrs. Pankhurst's speech, delivered Nov. 13, 1913, at Parson's Theatre, Hartford, Connecticut (Hartford: Connecticut Woman Suffrage Association, 1913) appears here with the permision of the General Research Division, The New York Public Library, Astor, Lenox and Tilden Foundations.

Part IX: The War and the Vote

1. Lisa Tickner, *The Spectacle of Women: Imagery of the Suffrage Campaign, 1907–14* (Chicago: University of Chicago Press, 1988), 229–30.

2. Midge Mackenzie, *Shoulder to Shoulder* (New York: Alfred A. Knopf, 1975), 286.

3. Ibid., 283.

4. Ibid., 288. See, also, Nicoletta F. Gullace, "White Feathers and Wounded Men: Female Patriotism and the Memory of the Great War," *Journal of British Studies* 36 (April, 1997): 178–206

5. Caroline Morrell, *"Black Friday": Violence Against Women in the Suffragette Movement* (London: Women's Research and Resources Centre Publication, 1981), 62–63.

6. Liz Stanley and Ann Morley, *The Life and Death of Emily Wilding Davison: A Biographical Detective Story* (London: The Woman's Press, 1988), 127–28, 153, 204.

7. Mackenzie, *Shoulder to Shoulder*, 310–11.

8. Ibid., 283. There are numerous studies of the impact of World War I on the suffrage movement and on British women in general. For example, see Jo Vellacott (Newberry), "Anti-War Suffragists," *History* 62 (October, 1977): 411–25; Joan Montgomery Byles, "Women's Experience of World War One: Suffragists, Pacifists and Poets," *Women's Studies International Forum* 8 (1985): 473–87; Jean Bethke Elshtain, *Women and War* (New York: Basic Books, 1987); Jo Vellacott, "Feminist Consciousness and the First World War," *History Workshop Journal* 23 (spring, 1987): 81–101; Susan Kingsley Kent, "The Politics of Sexual Difference: World War I and the Demise of British Feminism," *Journal of British Studies* 27 (July 1988): 232–53; Claire M. Tylee, *The Great War and Women's Consciousness: Images of Militarism and Womanhood in Women's Writings, 1914–64* (Iowa City: University of Iowa Press, 1990); Angela Woollacott, "'Khaki Fever' and Its Control: Gender, Class, Age, and Sexual Morality on the British Homefront in the First World War," *Journal of Contemporary History* 29 (April 1994): 325–47; Jacqueline de Vries, "Gendering Patriotism: Emmeline and Christabel Pankhurst and World War One," in *This Working-Day World: Women's Lives and Culture(s) in Britain, 1914–1945,* ed. Sybil Oldfield (London: Taylor & Francis, 1994), 75–88. For materials on WSPU leaders during and after the war, see Martin Pugh, *Women and the Women's Movement in Britain, 1914–1959* (London: MacMillan, 1992). For a specific focus on women munitions workers, see Angela Woollacott, *On Her Their Lives Depend: Munitions Workers in the Great War* (Berkeley: University of California Press, 1994).

9. Mackenzie, *Shoulder to Shoulder*, 294.

10. Ibid., 318.

11. Ibid., 325.

12. Ibid., 328.

13. Ibid., 316.

14. Andrew Rosen, *Rise Up, Women! The Militant Campaign of the Women's Social and Political Union, 1905–1914* (London: Routledge & Kegan Paul, 1974), 266.

15. Roger Fulford, *Votes for Women: The Story of a Struggle* (London: Faber and Faber, Ltd., 1957), 305.

16. Tickner, *Spectacle*, 237.

17. Rosen, *Rise Up,* 270–71.

18. Rosen, 270–71.

Select Bibliography

Atkinson, Diane. *The Suffragettes in Pictures*. London: Museum of London, 1996.

———.*Votes for Women*. Cambridge: Cambridge University Press, 1988.

A Sylvia Pankhurst Reader. Edited by Kathryn Dodd. Manchester: Manchester University Press, 1993.

Banks, Olive. *Becoming a Feminist: The Social Origins of "First Wave" Feminism*. Athens: University of Georgia Press, 1986.

———. *Faces of Feminism: A Study of Feminism as a Social Movement*. Oxford: Martin Robertson, 1981.

———. *The Biographical Dictionary of British Feminists, Vol. One, 1800–1930*. New York: New York University Press, 1985.

———. *The Biographical Dictionary of British Feminists, Vol. Two, 1900–1945*. New York: New York University Press, 1990.

Bolt, Christine. *Feminist Ferment: "The Woman Question" in the USA and England, 1870–1940*. London: UCL Press, 1995.

Bryant, Donald, Carroll C. Arnold, Frederick W. Haberman, Richard Murphy, and Karl Wallace. *An Historical Anthology of Select British Speeches*. New York: The Ronald Press Company, 1967.

Bullock, I. and Richard Pankhurst, eds. *Sylvia Pankhurst: From Artist to Anti-Fascist*. London: MacMillan, 1992.

Byles, Joan Montgomery. "Women's Experience of World War One: Suffragists, Pacifists and Poets." *Women's Studies International Forum* 8 (1985): 473–87.

Caine, Barbara. "Vida Goldstein and the English Militant Campaign." *Women's History Review* 2, no. 3 (1993): 363–76.

Carson, Roberta Kay. "From Teacups To Terror: The Rhetorical Strategies of the Women's Social and Political Union, 1903–1918." Ph.D. diss., University of Iowa, 1975.

Castle, Barbara. *Sylvia and Christabel Pankhurst*. Harmondsworth: Penguin, 1987.

Chambers Biographical Dictionary. Edited by J. O. Thorne. New York: St Martin's Press, 1969.

Corbett, Mary Jean. *Representing Femininity: Middle-Class Subjectivity in Victorian and Edwardian Women's Autobiographies*. Oxford: Oxford University Press, 1992.

Cregier, Don M. *Bounder From Wales: Lloyd George's Career Before the First World War*. Columbia: The University of Missouri Press, 1976.

Crow, Duncan. *The Edwardian Woman*. London: George Allen & Unwin, 1978.

Dangerfield, George. *The Strange Death of Liberal England 1910–1914*. New York: Capricorn Books., 1961.

De Vries, Jacqueline. "Gendering Patriotism: Emmeline and Christabel Pankhurst and World War One." In *This Working-Day World: Women's Lives and Culture(s) in Britain, 1914–1945.* Edited by Sybil Oldfield. London: Taylor & Francis, 1994.

Dodd, Kathryn. "Cultural Politics and Women's Historical Writing: The Case of Ray Strachey's *The Cause." Women's Studies International Forum* 13 (1990): 127–37.

Doughan, David. "The End of Women's History? A View From the Fawcett Library." *Women's History Review* 1, no. 1 (1992): 131–39.

Elshtain, Jean Bethke. *Women and War.* New York: Basic Books, 1987.

Fletcher, Ian Christopher. "'A Star Chamber of the Twentieth Century': Suffragettes, Liberals, and the 1908 'Rush the Commons' Case." *Journal of British Studies* 35 (October, 1996): 504–30.

Fowler, Rowena. "Why Did Suffragettes Attack Works of Art?" *Journal of Women's History* 2 (winter, 1991): 109–25.

Fulford, Roger. *Votes for Women: The Story of a Struggle.* London: Faber and Faber, Ltd. 1957.

Garner, Les. *Stepping Stones to Women's Liberty: Feminist Ideas in the Women's Suffrage Movement, 1900–1918.* London: Hutchinson, 1984.

Gawthorpe, Mary. *Up Hill to Holloway.* Penobscot: Traversity Press, 1962.

Gullace, Nicoletta F. "White Feathers and Wounded Men: Female Patriotism and the Memory of the Great War." *Journal of British Studies* 36 (April 1997): 178–206.

Harrison, Brian. *Separate Spheres: The Opposition to Women's Suffrage in Britain.* London: Croom Helm, 1978.

———. "The Act of Militancy: Violence and the Suffragettes, 1904–1914." In *Peaceable Kingdom: Stability and Change in Modern Britain.* Oxford: Clarendon Press, 1982.

———. "Two Models of Feminist Leadership: Millicent Fawcett and Emmeline Pankhurst." In *Prudent Revolutionaries: Portraits of British Feminists Between the Wars.* Oxford: Clarendon Press, 1987.

Hearnshaw, F. J. C. *Edwardian England, A.D. 1901–1910.* New York: Books For Libraries Press, 1968.

Hirshfield, Claire. "Fractured Faith: Liberal Party Women and the Suffrage Issue in Britain, 1892–1914." *Gender & History* 2 (summer, 1990): 173–97.

Holton, Sandra Stanley. *Feminism and Democracy: Women's Suffrage and Reform Politics in Britain.* Cambridge: Cambridge University Press, 1986.

———. "Free Love and Victorian Feminism: The Divers Matrimonials of Elizabeth Wolstonholme and Ben Elmy." *Victorian Studies* 37 (winter, 1994): 199–222.

———. "From Anti-Slavery to Suffrage Militancy: The Bright Circle, Elizabeth Cady Stanton and the British Women's Movement." In *Suffrage and Beyond: International Feminist Perspectives.* Edited by Caroline Daley and Melanie Nolan. New York: New York University Press, 1994.

———. "In Sorrowful Wrath: Suffrage Militancy and the Romantic Feminism of Emmeline Pankhurst." In *British Feminism in the Twentieth Century.* Edited by Harold L. Smith. Amherst: University of Massachusetts, 1990.

———. *Suffrage Days: Stories From the Women's Suffrage Movement.* London: Routledge, 1996.

———. "The Suffragist and the 'Average Woman.'" *Women's History Review* 1, no. 1 (1992): 7–24.

————. "'To Educate Women into Rebellion': Elizabeth Cady Stanton and the Creation of a Transatlantic Network of Radical Suffragists." *American Historical Review.* (October, 1994): 1112–36.

————. "Women and the Vote." In *Women's History Britain, 1850–1945, An Introduction.* Edited by June Purvis. New York: St. Martin's Press, 1995.

Hynes, Samuel. *The Edwardian Turn of Mind.* New Jersey: Princeton University Press, 1968.

Jeffreys, Sheila. *The Spinster and Her Enemies: Feminism and Sexuality, 1880–1930.* London: Routledge and Kegan Paul, 1985.

John, Angela V. and Claire Eustance, eds. *The Men's Share? Masculinities, Male Support and Women's Suffrage in Britain, 1890–1920.* London: Routledge, 1997.

Jorgensen-Earp, Cheryl R. "Incitement to Rebellion: Subversion of Victorian Images in Pankhurst's Albert Hall Address." *Women's Studies in Communication* 14 (fall, 1991): 73–96.

————. "The Lady, The Whore, and The Spinster: The Rhetorical Use of Victorian Images of Women." *Western Journal of Speech Communication.* 54 (winter, 1990): 82–98.

————. *The Transfiguring Sword: The Just War of the Women's Social and Political Union.* Tuscaloosa: University of Alabama Press, 1997.

Kamm, Josephine. *Rapiers and Battleaxes: The Women's Movement and Its Aftermath.* London: Allen & Unwin, 1966.

Kaplan, Joel H. and Sheila Stowell. *Theatre and Fashion: Oscar Wilde to the Suffragettes.* Cambridge: Cambridge University Press, 1994.

Kean, Hilda. *Deeds Not Words: The Lives of Suffragette Teachers.* London: Pluto Press, 1990.

————. "Searching for the Past in Present Defeat: The Construction of Historical and Political Identity in British Feminism in the 1920s and 1930s." *Women's History Review* 3, no. 1 (1994): 57–80.

Kenney, Annie. *Memories of a Militant.* London: Edward Arnold & Co., 1924.

Kent, Susan Kingsley. *Sex and Suffrage in Britain, 1860–1914.* Princeton: University Press, 1987.

————. "The Politics of Sexual Difference: World War I and The Demise of British Feminism." *Journal of British Studies.* 27 (July 1988): 232–53.

Kraditor, Alison. *The Ideas of the Woman Suffrage Movement, 1890–1920.* New York: Columbia University Press, 1965.

Leneman, Leah. *A Guid Cause: The Women's Suffrage Movement in Scotland.* Aberdeen: Aberdeen University Press, 1990.

————. "The Awakened Instinct: Vegetarianism and the Women's Suffrage Movement in Britain." *Women's History Review* 6, no. 2 (1997): 271–287.

Letters of Constance Lytton. Edited by Betty Balfour. London: William Heinemann, 1925.

Liddington, Jill, and Jill Norris. *One Hand Tied Behind Us.* London: Virago, 1978.

Lyon, Janet. "Militant Discourse, Strange Bedfellows: Suffragettes and Vorticists Before the War." *Differences: A Journal of Feminist Cultural Studies* 4 (summer, 1992): 100–33.

Lytton, Lady Constance. *Prisons and Prisoners: Some Personal Experiences by Constance Lytton and Jane Warton, Spinster.* London: William Heinemann, 1914.

Mackenzie, Midge. *Shoulder to Shoulder*. New York: Alfred A. Knopf, 1975.

Marcus, Jane, ed. *Suffrage and the Pankhursts*. London: Routledge & Kegan Paul, 1987.

———. "Transatlantic Sisterhood." *Signs* 3 (1978): 744–55.

Mayhall, Laura E. Nym. "Creating the 'Suffragette Spirit': British Feminism and the Historical Imagination." *Women's History Review* 4, no. 3 (1995): 319–44.

Mitchell, David. *Queen Christabel*. London: MacDonald and Janes', 1977.

———. *The Fighting Pankhursts: A Study in Tenacity*. New York: The MacMillan Company, 1967.

Morgan, David. *Suffragists and Liberals: The Politics of Woman Suffrage in England*. Oxford: Basil Blackwell, 1975.

Morrell, Caroline. *"Black Friday": Violence Against Women in the Suffragette Movement*. London: Women's Research and Resources Centre Publications, 1981.

Mulford, Wendy. "Socialist-Feminist Criticism: A Case Study, Women's Suffrage and Literature, 1906–14." In *Re-Reading English*, edited by Peter Widowson. London: Methuen, 1982.

Murphy, Cliona. *The Women's Suffrage and Irish Society in the Early Twentieth Century*. Philadelphia: Temple University Press, 1989.

New Encyclopedia Britannica, 15th Edition. Chicago: Encyclopedia Britannica, 1994.

Osborne, Michael. "Archetypal Metaphor in Rhetoric: The Light-Dark Family." *The Quarterly Journal of Speech* 53 (April 1967): 115–26.

Owens, Rosemary Cullen. *Smashing Times: A History of the Irish Women's Suffrage Movement, 1889–1992*. Dublin: Attic Press, 1984.

Pankhurst, Christabel. *Unshackled—The Story of How We Won the Vote*. London: Hutchinson, 1959.

Pankhurst, Emmeline. Verbatim report of Mrs. Pankhurst's speech, delivered Nov. 13, 1913 at Parson's Theatre, Harftord, Conn. Hartford: The Connecticut Woman Suffrage Association, 1913. General Research Division, The New York Public Library, Astor, Lenox, and Tilden Foundation. (SNS p. v. 14).

———. *My Own Story*. New York: Hearst's International Library Co., 1914.

Pankhurst, Estelle Sylvia. *The Life of Emmeline Pankhurst: The Suffragette Struggle for Women's Citizenship*. London: T. Werner Laurie Ltd., 1935.

———. *The Suffragette Movement: An Intimate Account of Persons and Ideals*. London: Virago, 1931.

Pankhurst, Richard. *Sylvia Pankhurst, Artist and Crusader: An Intimate Portrait*. New York: Paddington Press, 1979.

Pateman, Carole. "Three Questions About Womanhood Suffrage." In *Suffrage and Beyond: International Feminist Perspectives*. Edited by Caroline Daley and Melanie Nolan. New York: New York University Press, 1994.

Peterson, Owen. "Boggart Hole Clough: A Nineteenth Century 'Speak-In'" *Southern Speech Journal* 35 (summer, 1970): 287–94.

Pethick-Lawrence, Emmeline. *My Part in a Changing World*. London: Victor Gollancz, Ltd., 1938.

Pethick-Lawrence, Frederick. *Fate Has Been Kind*. London: Hutchinson and Co., 1943.

———. *Women's Fight For the Vote*. London: The Woman's Press, 1910.

Pugh, Martin. *Electoral Reform in War and Peace, 1906–1918*. London: Routledge & Kegan Paul, 1978.

———. *Women and the Women's Movement in Britain, 1914–1959*. London: MacMillan, 1992.

Purvis, June. "A Lost Dimension? The Political Education of Women in the Suffragette Movement in Edwardian Britain." *Gender and Education* 6 (1994): 319–27.

———. "A 'Pair of . . . Infernal Queens'? A Reassessment of the Dominant Representations of Emmeline and Christabel Pankhurst, First Wave Feminists in Edwardian Britain." *Women's History Review* 5, no. 2 (1996): 259–280.

———. "'Deeds Not Words': The Daily Lives of Militant Suffragettes in Edwardian Britain." *Women's Studies International Forum* 18 (1995): 91–101.

———. "Reassessing Representations of Emmeline and Christabel Pankhurst, Militant Feminists in Edwardian Britain: On the Importance of a Knowledge of our Feminist Past." In *New Frontiers in Women's Studies: Knowledge, Identity and Nationalism*. Edited by Mary Maynard and June Purvis. London: Taylor and Francis, 1996.

———. "The Prison Experiences of the Suffragettes in Edwardian Britain." *Women's History Review* 4, no. 1 (1995): 103–32.

———. "Using Primary Sources When Researching Women's History from a Feminist Perspective," no. 2 *Women's History Review* 1 (1992): 273–306.

Raeburn, Antonia. *The Militant Suffragettes*. London: Joseph, 1973.

———. *The Suffragette View*. New York: St. Martin's Press, 1976.

Read, Donald. *Edwardian England*. London: The Historical Association, 1972.

Richardson, Mary R. *Laugh a Defiance*. London: George Weidenfeld & Nicolson, 1953.

Robins, Elizabeth. *Way Stations*. New York: Dodd, Mead and Company, 1913.

Romero, Patricia W. *E. Sylvia Pankhurst: Portrait of a Radical*. New Haven: Yale University Press, 1987.

Rosen, Andrew. *Rise Up, Women! The Militant Campaign of the Women's Social and Political Union, 1903–1914*. London: Routledge & Kegan Paul, 1974.

Rover, Constance. *Women's Suffrage and Party Politics in Britain, 1866–1914*. London: Routledge & Kegan Paul, 1967.

Sarah, Elizabeth. "Christabel Pankhurst: Reclaiming Her Power." In *Feminist Theorists: Three Centuries of Women's Intellectual Traditions*. Edited by Dale Spender. London: Women's Press, 1983.

Sleight, John. *One-way Ticket to Epsom*. Morpeth: Bridge Studios, 1988.

Smyth, Ethel. *Female Pipings in Eden*. 2d ed. Edinburgh: Peter Davies, 1934.

Snellgrove, L. E. *Suffragettes and Votes for Women*. 2d ed. Harlow: Longman, 1984.

Spender, Dale. *Women of Ideas and What Men Have Done to Them: From Aphra Behn to Adrienne Rich*. London: ARK Paperbacks, 1983.

Stanley, Liz and Ann Morley. *The Life and Death of Emily Wilding Davison: A Biographical Detective Story*. London: The Women's Press, 1988.

Stowell, Sheila. *A Stage of Their Own: Feminist Playwrights of the Suffrage Era*. Ann Arbor: University of Michigan Press, 1992.

Strachey, Ray. *The Cause: A Short History of the Women's Movement in Great Britain*. 1928. Reprint, New York: Kennikat Press, 1969.

Taylor, Rosemary. *In Letters of Gold: The Story of Sylvia Pankhurt and the East London Federation of the Suffragettes in Bow.* London: Stepney, 1993.

The Suffragette, Britannia 18 October 1912–20 December 1918.

Tickner, Lisa. *The Spectacle of Women: Imagery of the Suffrage Campaign, 1907–14.* Chicago: University of Chicago Press, 1988.

Tylee, Claire, M. *The Great War and Women's Consciousness: Images of Militarism and Womanhood in Women's Writings, 1914–64.* Iowa City: University of Iowa Press, 1990.

Vellacott (Newberry), Jo. "Anti-War Suffragists." *History* 62 (October, 1977): 411–25.

Vellacott, Jo. "Feminist Consciousness and the First World War." *History Workshop Journal* 23 (spring 1987): 81–101.

Vicinus, Martha. *Independent Women: Work and Community for Single Women, 1850–1920.* Chicago: University of Chicago Press, 1985.

Votes For Women, 29 October 1908–20 December 1912.

Ward, Margaret. "Conflicting Interests: The British and Irish Suffrage Movements." *Feminist Review* 50 (summer, 1995): 127–47.

Webster's Biographical Dictionary. Springfield: G & C Merriam Co., 1980.

Winslow, Barbara. *Sylvia Pankhurst: Sexual Politics and Political Activism.* New York: St. Martin's Press, 1996.

Woollacott, Angela. "'Khaki Fever' and Its Control: Gender, Class, Age and Sexual Morality on the British Homefront in the First World War." *Journal of Contemporary History* 29 (April 1994): 325–47.

———. *On Her Their Lives Depend: Munitions Workers in the Great War.* Berkeley: University of California Press, 1994.

Young, Alison. "'Wild Women': The Censure of the Suffragette Movement." *International Journal of the Sociology of Law* 16 (1988): 279–93.

Zacharis, John C. "Emmeline Pankhurst: An English Suffragette Influences America." *Communication Monographs* 38 (1971): 198–206.

Sources of Speeches

Evidence and Cross-Examination on Damages and Arrests in *Votes For Women,* May 24, 1912

The Real Conspiracy Mr. Pethick-Lawrence Outline of Defense in *Votes For Women,* May 24, 1912

Evidence for the Defense in *Votes For Women,* May 24, 1912

Mr. Pethick-Lawrence for the Defence in *Votes For Women,* May 31, 1912

Mrs. Pankhurst's Address to the Jury in *Votes For Women,* May 24, 1912

Summation of the Judge in *Votes For Women,* May 31, 1912

O Liberty, How Glorious Art Thou! Mrs. Pethick-Lawrence's Appeal to the Judge in *Votes For Women,* May 31, 1912

VII. Martyrs to the Cause

Emmeline Pankhurst at the Albert Hall, in *The Suffragette,* October 25, 1912

The Rune of Birth and Renewal Emmeline Pethick-Lawrence, in *Votes For Women,* December 20, 1912

The Women's Insurrection Emmeline Pankhurst, in *The Suffragette,* February 28, 1913

"She Laid Down Her Life For Her Friends" The Rev. Gertrude Von Petzold, in *The Suffragette,* June 20, 1913

VIII. The Cat and Mouse Act

"We Are Members One of Another"
George Bernard Shaw, in *The Suffragette,* March 28, 1913

Artificial vs. "Forcible" Feeding C. W. Mansell-Moullin, M.D., in *The Suffragette,* April 4, 1913

"Kill Me, Or Give Me My Freedom!" Emmeline Pankhurst, in *The Suffragette,* July 18, 1913

"Our Spirits Are Eternal" Miss Annie Kenney, in *The Suffragette,* July 18, 1913

Address at Hartford, (Pamphlet) Verbatim Report of Mrs. Pankhurst's speech, delivered November 13, 1913 at Parson's Theatre, Hartford, Conn. Hartford: The Connecticut Woman Suffrage Association, 1913. General Research Division, The New York Public Library, Astor, Lenox and Tilden Foundations

Victory Is Assured Emmeline Pankhurst, in *The Suffragette,* February 13, 1914

IX. The War and The Vote

What Is Our Duty? Emmeline Pankhurst at Sun Hall, Liverpool, in *The Suffragette,* April 23, 1915

Woman Suffragist Deputation, in *Britannia,* April 9, 1917

Woman Suffrage: A Necessary War Measure, Emmeline Pankhurst in *Britannia,* April 23, 1917

To Women Citizens Emmeline Pankhurst at the Royal Albert Hall in *Britannia,* March 22, 1918

Index